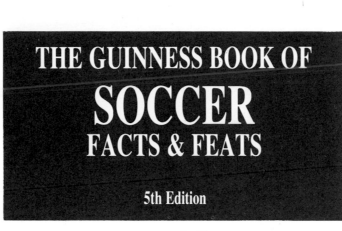

THE GUINNESS BOOK OF
SOCCER
FACTS & FEATS

5th Edition

By Jack Rollin

GUINNESS SUPERLATIVES LIMITED
2 CECIL COURT, LONDON ROAD, ENFIELD, MIDDLESEX

Acknowledgements

The author wishes to acknowledge the following sources: Maurice Golesworthy, *The Encyclopaedia of Association Football*; C R Williamson; *FIFA News*; *World Soccer*; The Association of Football Statisticians; Hamlyn's *A-Z of British Football Records*.

First published in 1978
Second edition 1979
Third edition 1980
Fourth edition 1981
Fifth edition 1983

© **Jack Rollin and Guinness Superlatives Ltd**
1978, 1979, 1980, 1981, 1983

Editor: Beatrice Frei

Design and layout: David Roberts

Artwork: Eddie Botchway, Don Roberts, Mick Hooker and David Roberts

Picture research: Beverley Waites, Karin Ilsen

Published in Great Britain by
Guinness Superlatives Ltd
2 Cecil Court, London Road, Enfield, Middlesex

British Library Cataloguing in Publication Data

Rollin, Jack
   Guinness book of soccer facts and feats.—
   5th ed.
   1. Soccer
   I. Title
   796.334   GV943

ISBN 0–85112–240–X

Colour separation by
DOT Reproductions, High Wycombe, Bucks.

Photoset, printed and bound in Great Britain by
Redwood Burn Ltd, Trowbridge, Wiltshire

CONTENTS

INTRODUCTION

The fifth edition of the *Guinness Book of Soccer Facts and Feats* has the advantage of being able to present an additional two years of the statistics presented in the fourth edition.

Once again there is the formula of new material, fresh ideas for popular features and tidying up any loose ends which have occurred since the last book.

Thanks to the vigilance of the Association of Football Statisticians and its members, long-standing discrepancies which have not been brought to light in previous records are now included.

Our review of local derby matches takes in the Dundee clubs and the Bristol teams while for those who have collected the first four editions, we have updated the local derbies which appeared in these books.

There are many of the items which have proved of interest to readers during the last few years, including new stories for the Football League and Scottish League clubs, cartoons, European Survey (which has two years on this occasion) and tales from around the world.

The pictorial section includes a photographic reminder of the 1982 World Cup finals in Spain and there is a special feature on soccer in show business. For light relief the imaginary four-page programme from a bygone age is entirely fictional except for the players named, all of whom made Football League appearances over the last 40 years.

The author (dark jersey) in 1954–55.

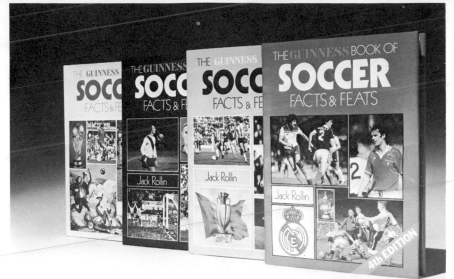

Special Features Editions 1–4

First Edition:

Directory of countries affiliated to FIFA with details of colours, season and national stadium statistics.

List of the world's oldest clubs and their date of formation.

Highlights of FA Cup winning teams.

Analysis of all Football League championship winning teams since 1888.

Everton v Liverpool derby matches.

A week in the life of a football club.

Chart of Football League attendances 1946–1978.

Complete record of clubs in European Cup 1956–1978.

International Centurians: Franz Beckenbauer, Jozsef Bozsik, Bobby Moore and Pele.

Complete record of clubs in the South American Cup 1960 to 1978.

Colour teams groups of all 1978 World Cup finalists.

Second Edition:

Football League Cup analysis 1960–79.

FA Cup finals analysed year by year.

Manchester City v United and Celtic v Rangers derby matches.

International Centurians: Billy Wright, Gylmar and Bobby Charlton.

Gerd Muller's goalscoring records.

Chart of FIFA countries with their location, number of affiliated clubs, teams, professionals and referees. The growth of FIFA's membership from 1904 to 1978. World Cup final results of all competing countries 1930 to 1978.

European Cup attendance figures in chart form 1956–1978 and leading goalscorers over the same period.

Third Edition:

Football League leading goalscorers in Division One from 1888 to 1980.

Arsenal v Tottenham Hotspur and Sheffield United v Wednesday derby matches.

The record attendances of the 92 Football League clubs in chart form.

Complete record of all European Championship matches 1958–1980.

Full colour badges of the eleven different winners of the European Cup.

Colour team groups of the the eight finalists in the 1980 European Championship.

International centurians: Bjorn Nordqvist and Thorbjorn Svenssen.

Complete record of the South American Championships from 1916 to 1979.

Fourth Edition:

Comparison of attendances and goalscoring in the Football League since the war.

Newcastle United v Sunderland and Heart of Midlothian v Hibernian local derby matches.

FA Cup giant-killers.

Scottish League attendances since Premier Division was formed.

Hints on Association Football; pre-war coloured cigarette card series.

Comparison of average First Division attendances in England, West Germany, Holland and Italy during the last decade.

Foreign imports in the Football League.

MILESTONES

1848 The first rules drawn up at Cambridge University.

1855★ Sheffield, the oldest soccer club still in existence, founded.

1862 Notts County, the oldest Football League club, founded.

1863 Football Association formed in London on 26 October.

1865 Tape to be stretched across the goals 8 ft (2·4 m) from the ground.

1866 Offside rule altered to allow a player to be onside when three of opposing team are nearer their own goal-line. Fair catch rule omitted.

1867 Queen's Park, the oldest Scottish club, founded.

1869 Kick-out rule altered and goal-kicks introduced.

1871 Start of the FA Cup. Goalkeepers first mentioned in laws.

1872 First official international, between Scotland and England at Glasgow.
The Wanderers win the FA Cup final.
Corner kick introduced.

★ The date of Sheffield's foundation was given as 1855 in the Sheffield City Almanack (1902). And in the issue of the *Sheffield Telegraph* dated 29 September 1954 an article quoted H B Willey, a previous Secretary of the club, as follows: 'I used to have the Minute Book for 1855 but it was borrowed and never returned.'

1873 Scottish FA formed and the start of the Scottish Cup.

1874 Umpires first mentioned in laws.
Shinguards introduced.

1875 The cross-bar replaces tape on the goalposts.

1876 FA of Wales formed.
The first international between Scotland and Wales.

1877 The London Association and the Sheffield Association agree to use the same rules.
A player may be charged by an opponent if he is facing his own goal.

1878 Referees use a whistle for the first time.

1879 First international between England and Wales.
Cliftonville, the oldest Irish club, founded.

1880 Irish FA formed and the start of the Irish Cup.

1882 Ireland's first internationals with Wales and England.
International Football Association Board set up.
Two-handed throw-in introduced.

1883 First international between Scotland and Ireland.

The first British International Championship.

1885 Professionalism legalised in England.
Arbroath beat Bon Accord 36–0 in Scottish Cup; still a record score for an official first-class match.

1886 International caps first awarded.

1888 Football League formed.

1889 Preston North End achieve the League and FA Cup 'double'.

1890 Irish League formed.
First hat-trick in the FA Cup Final, by Blackburn's William Townley.
Goal nets invented.
Scottish League formed.

1891 Referees and linesmen replace umpires.
Introduction of the penalty kick.

1892 Penalty taker must not play the ball twice.
Extra time allowed for taking a penalty.
Goal nets used in FA Cup Final for the first time.
Division Two of the Football League formed.

1893 Scotland adopts professionalism.

1894 First FA Amateur Cup Final.
Division Two of Scottish League formed.
Referee given complete control of the game.
Unnecessary for players in future to appeal to him for a decision.
Goalkeeper can only be charged when playing the ball or obstructing an opponent.

£10 REWARD.

STOLEN!

From the Shop Window of W. Shillcock, Football Outfitter, Newtown Row, Birmingham, between the hour of 9-30 p.m. on Wednesday, the 11th September, and 7-30 a.m., on Thursday, the 12th inst., the

ENGLISH CUP,

the property of Aston Villa F.C. The premises were broken into between the hours named, and the Cup, together with cash in drawer, stolen.

The above Reward will be paid for the recovery of the Cup, or for information as may lead to the conviction of the thieves.

Information to be given to the Chief of Police, or to Mr. W. Shillcock, 73, Newtown Row.

The FA Cup

1895 FA Cup stolen from a Birmingham shop window. It was never recovered.
Goalposts and cross-bars must not exceed 5 in (127 mm) in width.
Player taking throw-in must stand on touch-line.

1897 Aston Villa win both the League and the FA Cup.
The Corinthians tour South America.
The word 'intentional' introduced into the law on handling.

1898 Players' Union first formed.

1899 Promotion and relegation first used in the Football League, replacing Test Matches.

1901 Tottenham Hotspur win the FA Cup while members of the Southern League.

1902 Terracing collapses during the Scotland–England match at Ibrox Park, killing 25.

1904 FIFA formed in Paris, on 21 May.

1905 First £1000 transfer. Alf Common moves from Sunderland to Middlesbrough.
First international in South America, between Argentina and Uruguay.
England joins FIFA.

1907 Amateur FA formed.
Players' Union (now Professional Footballers' Association (PFA)) re-formed.

1908 England play in Vienna, their first international against a foreign side.
The first Olympic soccer tournament in London, won by the United Kingdom.

1910 Scotland, Wales and Ireland join FIFA.

1912 Goalkeeper not permitted to handle ball outside his own penalty area.

1913 Defending players not to approach within ten yards of the ball at a free-kick.

1914 Defending players not to approach within ten yards of ball at corner kick.

1916 The South American Championship first held.

1920 Division Three (Southern Section) of the Football League formed.
Players cannot be offside at a throw-in.

1921 Division Three (Northern Section) formed.

1922 Promotion and relegation introduced in the Scottish League.

1923 First FA Cup final at Wembley: Bolton beat West Ham before a record crowd.

1924 A goal may be scored direct from a corner kick.

1925 Offside law changed to require two instead of three defenders between attacker and goal.
Player taking throw-in must have both feet on touch-line.

1926 Huddersfield Town achieve the first hat-trick of League Championships.

1927 Cardiff City take the FA Cup out of England for the first time.
Mitropa Cup begins.
J C Clegg, President of the FA, knighted.

1928 British associations leave FIFA over broken-time payments to amateurs.
First £10 000 transfer: David Jack goes from Bolton to Arsenal.
Dixie Dean scores 60 goals for Everton in Division One, a Football League record.

1929 England lose 4–3 to Spain in Madrid, their first defeat on the continent.
Goalkeeper compelled to stand still on his goal-line at penalty-kick.

Sir Charles Clegg

1930 Uruguay win the first World Cup, in Montevideo, Uruguay.
F J Wall, secretary of the FA, knighted.

1931 Goalkeeper permitted to carry ball four steps instead of two.
Instead of free-kick after a foul throw-in it reverts to opposing side.
Scotland lose 5–0 to Austria in Vienna, their first defeat on the continent.

1933 Numbers worn for the first time in the FA Cup Final.

1934 Italy win the second World Cup, in Rome, Italy.

1935 Arsenal equal Huddersfield's hat-trick of League Championships.
Arsenal centre-forward Ted Drake scores seven goals against Aston Villa at Villa Park, a Division One record.

1936 Defending players not permitted to tap the ball into goalkeeper's hands from a goal-kick.
Luton centre-forward Joe Payne scores ten goals against Bristol Rovers, a Football league record.
Dixie Dean overhauls Steve Bloomer's 352 goals in the Football League.

1937 A record crowd of 149 547 watch the Scotland v England match at Hampden Park.
Defending players not permitted to tap the ball into goalkeeper's hands from free-kick inside penalty area.
Weight of ball increased from 13–15 oz (368–425 g) to 14–16 oz (397–454 g).
Arc of circle 10 yd (9 m) radius from penalty spot to be drawn outside penalty area.

1938 Italy retain the World Cup, in Paris, France.
Laws of the game rewritten.

Sir Frederick Wall

Scotland's Jimmy McGrory retires, having scored 550 goals in first-class football, a British record.

1946 British associations rejoin FIFA.
The Burnden Park tragedy: 33 killed and over 400 injured during an FA Cup tie between Bolton and Stoke.

1949 Aircraft carrying Italian champions Torino crashes at Superga near Turin, killing all on board.
England are beaten 2–0 by Republic of Ireland at Goodison Park, so losing their unbeaten home record against sides outside the home countries.
Rangers win the first 'treble' —Scottish League, Scottish Cup and League Cup.
S F Rous, secretary of the FA, knighted.

1950 Uruguay win the fourth World Cup, in Rio de Janeiro, Brazil.
England, entering for the first time, lose 1–0 to USA.

USA 1 England 0 (1950)

Scotland's unbeaten home record against foreign opposition ends in a 1–0 defeat by Austria at Hampden Park.

1951 Obstruction included as an offence punishable by indirect free-kick.

Studs must project $\frac{3}{4}$ in (19 mm) instead of $\frac{1}{2}$ in (13 mm).

1952 Billy Wright overhauls Bob Crompton's record of 42 caps.

Newcastle United retain the FA Cup, the first club to do so in the 20th century.

England lose their unbeaten home record against continental opposition, going down 6–3 to Hungary at Wembley.

1954 West Germany win the fifth World Cup in Berne, Switzerland.

England suffer their heaviest international defeat, beaten 7–1 by Hungary at Budapest.

The Union of European Football Associations (UEFA) formed.

Ball not to be changed during the game unless authorised by the referee.

1955 European Cup of the Champions and Inter-Cities Fairs Cup started.

1956 Real Madrid win the European Cup.

First floodlit match in the Football League: Portsmouth v Newcastle United on 22 February.

1957 George Young retires with a record 53 Scottish caps. John Charles of Leeds United becomes the first British player to be transferred to a foreign club (Juventus, Italy) for a substantial fee.

1958 Manchester United lose eight players in the Munich air disaster on 6 February.

Brazil win the sixth World Cup, in Stockholm, Sweden.

Sunderland, continuously in Division One, relegated.

Football League reorganisation: Division Three and Division Four started.

1959 Billy Wright plays his 100th game for England, against Scotland, and retires at the end of the season with a world record 105 appearances.

1960 USSR win the first European Nations Cup, in Paris, France.

Real Madrid win the European Cup for fifth consecutive time.

1961 Sir Stanley Rous becomes President of FIFA.

Tottenham Hotspur win the League and Cup, the first 'double' of the 20th century.

The Professional Football Association (PFA) succeed in achieving the abolition of the maximum wage.

Fiorentina win the first European Cup-Winners Cup.

1962 Brazil retain the seventh World Cup in Santiago, Chile.

Denis Law is transferred from Torino to Manchester United, the first transfer over £100 000 paid by a British club.

1963 The centenary of the FA. England beat the Rest of the World 2–1, at Wembley.

The Football League's 'retain and transfer' system declared illegal.

Billy Wright

Tottenham Hotspur win the European Cup-Winners Cup, the first British success in Europe.

1964 Spain win the European Nations' Cup, in Madrid, Spain.

More than 300 killed and 500 injured in rioting during an Olympic qualifying game between Peru and Argentina at Lima, Peru.

Jimmy Dickinson (Portsmouth) becomes the first player to make 700 Football League appearances.

1965 Stanley Matthews becomes the first footballer to be knighted.

Arthur Rowley retires having scored a record 434 Football League goals.

The Football League agree to substitutes for one injured player.

1966 England win the eighth World Cup, at Wembley.

The Football League allow substitutes for any reason.

1967 Alf Ramsey, England's team manager, knighted.

Celtic become the first Scottish club to win the European Cup.

1968 Italy win the European Football Championship, in Rome, Italy.

A world record transfer: Pietro Anastasi moves from Varese to Juventus for £440 000.

Manchester United win the European Cup: Matt Busby knighted.

Leeds United become the first British club to win the Fairs Cup.

1969 Leeds win the Football League Championship with a record 67 points.

1970 Brazil win the ninth World Cup, in Mexico City and win the Jules Rimet Trophy outright.

Bobby Charlton wins his 106th England cap in the quarter-finals to overhaul Billy Wright's record.

The first £200 000 transfer in Britain: Martin Peters moves from West Ham to Tottenham Hotspur.

1971 Britain's worst-ever crowd disaster: 66 killed at a match between Rangers and Celtic at Ibrox Park.

Arsenal achieve the League and Cup 'double'.

Barcelona win the Fairs Cup outright (to be replaced by the UEFA Cup) after beating the holders Leeds United 2–1.

1972 Tottenham Hotspur defeat Wolverhampton Wanderers in the first all-British European final, the UEFA Cup.

West Germany win the European Football Championship, in Brussels, Belgium.

1973 Ajax win the European Cup for the third consecutive time.

Bobby Moore makes his 108th appearance for England, a new record.

Johan Cruyff becomes the first £1 million transfer, moving from Ajax to Barcelona for £922 300.

1974 Joao Havelange of Brazil replaces Sir Stanley Rous as President of FIFA.

West Germany win the tenth World Cup in Munich, West Germany.

Denis Law makes his 55th appearance for Scotland, a new record.

1975 Leeds United banned from competing in Europe for any of two seasons in the next four, after their fans rioted at the European Cup final in Paris. Terry Paine overhauls Jimmy Dickinson's record of 764 League games.

1976 Bayern Munich win the European Cup for the third consecutive time.

Czechoslovakia win the European Football Championship in Belgrade, Yugoslavia, beating West Germany.

Pat Jennings makes his 60th appearance for Northern Ireland, a new record.

The Football League abandon 'goal average', introducing 'goal difference'.

Liverpool win their ninth League title, overhauling Arsenal's record.

1977 Liverpool win their 10th League title as well as the European Cup.

Kevin Keegan transferred from Liverpool to SV Hamburg for £500 000, the highest fee involving a British club.

Kenny Dalglish transferred from Celtic to Liverpool for £440 000, a record fee between British clubs.

First World Youth Cup, held in Tunisia and won by USSR.

1978 Liverpool retain the European Cup.

Nottingham Forest the only Football League club not a limited company win their first-Championship title. Forest also win the League Cup.

Ipswich Town become the 40th different team to win the FA Cup.

Kenny Dalglish makes his 56th appearance for Scotland to overhaul Denis Law's record.

Argentina win the eleventh World Cup in Buenos Aires, Argentina.

1979 David Mills transferred from Middlesbrough to West Bromwich Albion for £516 000, a record fee between British clubs.

Trevor Francis, transferred from Birmingham City to Nottingham Forest for £1 million, breaks the record for a single transfer involving British clubs. Laurie Cunningham, the

Paolo Rossi *ASP*

West Bromwich Albion and England winger, signs for Real Madrid in a £900 000 move.
Liverpool win their eleventh League title.
Nottingham Forest become the third English club to win the European Cup.
Andy Gray, transferred from Aston Villa to Wolverhampton Wanderers, breaks the record for a single transfer involving British clubs at £1 469 000.
Argentina win the Second World Youth Cup in Japan.

1980 Liverpool retain the championship for their 12th League honour.
Nottingham Forest retain the European Cup.
Steve Archibald joins Tottenham Hotspur from Aberdeen in an £800 000 deal which makes him the most expensive transfer from a Scottish club.
West Germany regain their European championship title, beating Belgium in Rome, Italy.
John Trollope overhauls Jimmy Dickinson's record of 764 League appearances for one club, reaching a total of 770.

1981 Uruguay win the Gold Cup in Montevideo, Uruguay.
Liverpool win the League Cup after a replay.
Aston Villa become League champions for the first time since 1910.
Tottenham Hotspur win the 100th FA Cup after a replay, the first to be staged at Wembley.
Ipswich Town win the UEFA Cup and their midfield player, John Wark, equals a European record with his 14th goal in the competition.
Frans Thijssen, the Dutch midfield player from Ipswich Town, is voted Footballer of the Year by the Football Writers Association.
The honours in Scotland go chiefly to the auld firm of Celtic, League champions, and Rangers, Scottish Cup winners, though Dundee United retain the League Cup.
The Football League points system changes to three for a win starting 1981–82 season.
West Germany win the Third World Youth Cup in Australia.
Bryan Robson, transferred from West Bromwich Albion to Manchester United for British record of £1.5 million.

1982 Liverpool become the first winners of the Milk Cup (formerly League Cup) and also achieve their 13th League honour.
Tottenham retain the FA Cup again after a replay.
Celtic retain the Scottish League title, Rangers win the League Cup and Aberdeen win the Scottish Cup.
Aston Villa win the European Cup.
Italy win the 12th World Cup in Madrid, Spain.

1983 Liverpool retain the Milk Cup and win their 14th League title. Manager Bob Paisley retires after winning 20 trophies with them.
Manchester United win the FA Cup after a replay.
Aberdeen achieve European Cup-Winner's Cup and Scottish Cup honours.
Dundee United win their first Scottish League title. Celtic win the League Cup.

BRITISH SOCCER

A–Z

Aberdeen were the first and last winners of the Drybrough Cup. Their initial success came when they defeated Celtic 2–1 in 1971–72 and the second in 1980–81 by the same scoreline against St Mirren.

In the 1981–82 season **Airdrieonians,** after beating Partick Thistle 3–1 at home on 27

The Drybrough Cup

February 1982, failed to win any one of their remaining 15 Premier Division matches. They collected only two points from drawn games and scored three goals in these encounters.

Albion Rovers scored only nine more goals than they conceded when they finished runners-up in the Scottish League Division Two in 1947–48. They were eleven points behind East Fife, the champions, and two in front of Hamilton Academical but lost all four games against these two teams including their only two home defeats.

Before **Aldershot** entered the Football League they had beaten Kingstonian 11–1 in an FA Cup fourth qualifying round tie at the Recreation Ground on 16 November 1929. Pools of water were lying on the pitch and a stream of icy water was flowing along the centre of it, while snow alternated with rain and sleet. Aldershot led 4–0 at half-time and in the second half Kingstonian played a man short after one of their forwards was taken ill at the interval.

Did Wellington give his name to the first waterproof boot?

Willie Garner stretching at dawn's early light?
Robertson, Alloa

Alloa player-manager during 1982–83 was Willie Garner who began the season on loan to the club from Celtic. During this time he trained full-time with the Parkhead side and on a part-time basis for Alloa. In October 1982 he went on a month's loan to Rochdale before returning to Alloa and accepting an appointment as player-manager.

Although **Arbroath** conceded only 42 goals in 34 Division Two matches in 1934–35 and kept a clean sheet in 15 games, they lost 6–0 at Sten-housemuir, 5–2 at Third Lanark the champions and 5–2 at home to St Bernard's. They were promoted as runners-up.

Arsenal probably staged the first match for which any parts were shown either live or in recorded form for television. It was a practice game at Highbury on Thursday 16 September 1937. At the time the BBC studios and transmitter were at nearby Alexandra Palace.

Aston Villa were the first Football League club to play in as many as 100 League Cup matches. They achieved this milestone in the 1980–81 season. During their first successful attempt in 1960–61 they had played in ten games including four replays.

Ayr United finished as runners-up, then twice as champions of Division Two in three consecutive seasons after their formation in 1910, before automatic promotion was applied to the Scottish League. They had been formed by the amalgamation of the Ayr Parkhouse and Ayr clubs which had previously operated separately in the Ayrshire county town. The Parkhouse club had played at Beresford and Ayr at Somerset. United used Somerset as their headquarters.

In 1910–11 Ayr United were second to Dumbarton four points behind them, champions the following term five points in front of Aberdeen and in 1912–13 they finished one point ahead of Dunfermline and were rewarded with a place in an enlarged Scottish Division One.

Hands up all those who watch the BBC . . .c. 1937
BBC Hulton Picture Library

Left to right: Mickey Lawson, Paul McGlinchey, Murray McDermott, Hugh McCann, Lindsay Muir, Davie Moyes, Willie McCulloch, Craig Lumsdaine—the Edinburgh connection of Berwick *Scotsman Publications Ltd*

Barnsley met Brighton and Hove Albion in the third round of the FA Cup on 10 January 1953 three days after the death of manager Angus Seed. After half an hour's play Brighton led 3–0. At the interval the side was rearranged and after 62 minutes Arthur Kaye scored for Barnsley and Tommy Taylor added a second two minutes later. With 15 minutes remaining Eddie McMorran equalised and Taylor scored the winner with barely three minutes left.

In the 1981–82 season **Berwick Rangers** claimed to have more Edinburgh based players on their staff than either Hibernian or Heart of Midlothian. With 26 coming from the capital, the club organised a coach to take them to Shielfield Park for training two nights a week.

Birmingham City were the first English club side to play in a European competition. On 15 May 1956 they drew 0–0 away to Internazionale of Milan in a Group D, Fairs Cup match in the 1955–58 series.

Johnny McIntyre scored four goals in five minutes for **Blackburn Rovers** against Everton in a Division One match on 16 September 1922. Rovers won 5–1 but scored only 47 League goals that season.

In the closing stages of 1903–04 **Blackpool** were involved in a tussle to avoid re-election. Having lost their League status in 1899 for one season and seen their finishing position slip from 12th to 14th in three terms prior to 1903–04 they were anxious to avoid a further application.

Leicester Fosse were firmly at the foot of the table but there was a three-cornered fight between Glossop, Stockport County and Blackpool to escape the other two re-election places. Blackpool had to win at middle of the table Bradford City, Glossop lose at home and Burnley to achieve at least a point at Stockport to prevent Blackpool facing this application. In the event Blackpool won 2–0, Glossop lost 2–0 to Gainsborough Trinity and Burnley drew 2–2 at Stockport. Blackpool escaped on goal average above Stockport.

Bolton Wanderers are the only club to have won the FA Cup at least four times without conceding a goal in any of their final victories. They have also been involved in the highest scoring Wembley final losing 4–3 to Blackpool in 1953 despite leading 3–1 ten minutes after half-time. They were handicapped by a first half injury to Eric Bell and goalkeeper Stan Hanson and left-back Ralph Banks who had the onerous task of

Ralph Banks (above) the full-back who made 107 post-war League appearances for Bolton Wanderers and often partnered his brother Tommy. Stan Hanson (below) the goalkeeper who joined the Bolton club after a trial with Liverpool, turning professional in August 1935.

marking Stanley Matthews were under severe pressure in the latter stages.

AFC Bournemouth lost only one match in the second half of their Division Four programme in the 1981–82 season. Of the 23 games they lost one and drew ten. They finished fourth and won promotion to Division Three.

Bradford City won the championship of Division Two in 1907–08 finishing two points ahead of Leicester City who inflicted City's heaviest defeat winning 5–1 at Valley Parade on 7 March 1908.

Brechin City trainer Jack Sunter, who completed 34 years in the position by 1982, considered the most memorable goal scored by the club during his service had been in the 1953–54 season. Albert Juliussen's goal away to Celtic Reserves on 30 January 1954 clinched the 'C' Division championship for the club.

Brentford were drawn away to Oldham Athletic in their 3rd round of the F.A. Cup in 1926–27. Fog shrouded the ground and after 70 minutes with Oldham leading 2–1 the referee took the players off the field. Fearing this might be only a temporary halt Brentford manager, Harry Curtis, ordered his players into the bath. The referee duly tried to call them back but abandoned the game when Curtis told him how dangerous it would be for their health. Only then did the Brentford manager realise that in their haste many of his team still had their socks and boots on.

In the re-arranged match two days later, Brentford won 4–2 with Jack Allen who had not played in the original game scoring a hat-trick for them.

When **Brighton and Hove Albion** beat Liverpool 2–1 at Anfield on 20 February 1983 in an FA Cup fifth round tie they were bottom of Division One while their opponents were top 37 points ahead of them. Brighton's caretaker manager Jimmy Melia was a former Liverpool midfield player and their winning goal was scored by another ex-Anfield player Jimmy Case. Liverpool's previous home defeat had occurred on 6 March 1982 in a Division One match when Brighton beat them 1–0.

Bristol City appointed Sam Hollis as their first manager after they turned professional in 1897 and when they were still known as Bristol South End. He was given £30 to buy players but asked for a further £10 and then managed to sign eight professionals.

In 1952–53 **Bristol Rovers** won the championship of Division Three (Southern) with two club records: 64 points and 92 goals. They finished two points ahead of Millwall who beat Rovers 3–0 on 13 September, their last defeat for 27 consecutive League games which ended with a 2–0 defeat at Reading on 21 March 1953.

Rovers used 18 players, Harry Bamford, Geoff Fox, Jackie Pitt, Ray Warren, Peter Sampson and Vic Lambden being ever present. Top scorer Geoff Bradford missed only one match and registered 33 goals. Goalkeeper Bert Hoyle was seriously injured in a motor accident in February and was advised to retire and in the later stages of the season Rovers obtained only seven points from ten games.

On 19 January 1983 **Burnley** beat Tottenham Hotspur 4–1 at White Hart Lane in the fifth round of the Milk Cup. At the time Burnley were second from the bottom of Division Two, Spurs tenth in Division One.

Bury won promotion from Division Three in 1960–61 finishing six points clear of their nearest rivals and establishing two club records: 60 points and 108 goals. Five players scored 99 goals between them: Allan Jackson (24), Don Watson (23), Billy Calder (20), Johnny Hubbard (17) and Bill Holden (15). Bury won 7–1 at Tranmere on 1 October 1960 but were beaten 1–0 by Rovers at the same venue in an FA Cup tie on 5 November.

Cambridge United were involved in the first FA Cup match to be played on a Sunday. On 6 January 1974 they drew 2–2 with Oldham Athletic in a third round tie which kicked off in the morning before a crowd of 8479.

The record aggregate of individual goals for **Cardiff City** was achieved by Len Davies from 1919 to 1937 when he scored 127 in 306 League appearances.

A product of Cardiff Schools he played for Radnor Road and Gladstone Road Schools and represented Wales v England boys at Penydarren Park, Merthyr in 1914. Later he served in the Navy before joining Cardiff. He began as an outside-right and then switched to inside-forward. He made his initial first team appearances in the club's Southern League days in 1919–20 when he turned professional.

Despite a frail look about him he once scored with a 40-yard shot in the sixth round replay of the FA Cup against Chelsea in March 1927, the referee apparently consulting a policeman before awarding a goal. Cardiff won 3–2 after a 0–0 draw.

Davies played on 23 occasions for Wales but his greatest disappointment came in a Division One match during the 1923–24 season when he missed a penalty at Birmingham which cost Cardiff the championship on goal average.

Carlisle United achieved four wins in their last five Division Two matches in 1973–74 to climb into third place after their last success, a 2–0 win over Aston Villa. Six days later Orient needed to beat Villa themselves to overhaul Carlisle but only managed to draw 1–1. Carlisle were promoted.

The 200th goal scored by **Celtic** in European matches was achieved by Murdo MacLeod in the club's 2–1 win against Real Sociedad on 3 November 1982, in a European Cup, second round second leg game. MacLeod's first goal was the milestone but the Spanish club won 3–2 on aggregate.

In 1907–08 **Charlton Athletic** were playing in

Have goalposts, will travel

Crewe Alexandra players appear happy enough with the offer of a car . . . providing that . . . *Staffordshire Evening Sentinel*

two local competitions, Division Two of the Lewisham League and Division Two of the Woolwich League. They had to use a pitch on Woolwich Common for home matches and were required to carry the goalposts a mile to and from the ground before and after every game, but they won both divisions.

Chelsea were in second place in Division Two after drawing 0–0 at home to Swansea City on 6 December 1980 in their 21st League game of the season. They won only three more matches and these were the only games in which they scored (eight goals in total) until the end of the season when they had slumped to 12th place.

After **Chester** won 5–3 away to Chesterfield on 9 March 1982 they failed to win any more of their remaining 17 Division Three matches, taking only two points from drawn games and scoring only four goals. They finished bottom and were relegated.

Chesterfield established a record for a team outside the top two divisions of the Football League by completing 65 matches in the 1980–81 season. They comprised: 46 Division Three games, four League Cup, six FA cup, and nine in the Anglo-Scottish Cup which they won. In addition their reserve team won the North Midlands League and the North Midlands League Cup.

On 31 October 1959 **Clyde** defeated Aberdeen 7–2 in a Division One match and each one of their goals was scored by a different player.

A quarter of an hour before their match with Hamilton Academical on 25 October 1981 **Clydebank** had only six players reporting for duty. Because of a fault at Old Kilpatrick on the Glasgow to Clydebank railway line several other players were delayed. Two arrived with five minutes to spare, another sprinted one mile from the station as the teams were ready to change but two others arrived fifteen minutes late and missed the game. Clydebank completed their side with a player who had gone along as a spectator and they recovered from being a goal down to win 2–1.

When **Colchester United** played Mansfield Town in a Division Four match on 5 November 1982 right-back Micky Cook was making his 550th League appearance for them. He was sent off the field for handling the ball, but goalkeeper Mike Walker playing in his 300th consecutive match for the club saved the resultant penalty kick.

Coventry City staged the first closed-circuit televised soccer on 6 October 1965 when a crowd of more than 10 000 watched on four large screens the club's 2–1 win at Cardiff 120 miles away in a Division Two game.

Cowdenbeath were one of the first Scottish clubs to play in Europe. In 1925 they played three matches in Gibraltar and then beat Cadiz 2–0 in Spain to win a cup. Three years later they toured Germany.

A local garage group offered a car worth £3500 to any **Crewe Alexandra** player who scored 30 League goals in the 1982–83 season. Crewe's entire output in Division Four during 1981–82 had been 29.

Crystal Palace can claim to bear the oldest title among London's present day Football League clubs. They were represented at the FA's inaugural meeting in October 1863 and they had in David Allport one of seven men at the FA Cup's first meeting. Later disbanded, another club of that name was founded in 1905 after an effort by the Crystal Palace Company to form club had been resisted by the FA who did not like the idea of the company that owned the Cup Final ground entering a team of their own. In the first season of the FA Cup the old Crystal Palace side had drawn 0–0 with Hitchin, beaten Maidenhead 3–0 and drawn with Wanderers before losing in the semi-final 3–0 to the Royal Engineers.

Above: Rovers and Reading players were involved at Doncaster in a feast of Third Division scoring. *Doncaster Newspapers Ltd.* Left: Kevin Hector of Derby County who equalled Ron Webster's 535 senior appearances for the club in December 1980

On 7 May 1927, just two weeks after beating South Shields 8–2, **Darlington** met Chelsea fourth from the top of Division Two. They were level on points with Clapton Orient but Darlington had a better goal average and were at home while Orient were away to Reading. Darlington led 2–1 until a minute from the end when Jacky Crawford equalised for Chelsea and Orient won 1–0 from a penalty kick to relegate Darlington.

The **Derby County** record of League appearances is held by Kevin Hector who in 1982 overtook Steve Bloomer (474) and Geoff Barrowcliffe (475) in two weeks and finally Jack Parry who had held the previous record of 483 between the 1948–49 and 1965–66 seasons to finish with 486 League games. Another Hector milestone was his 200th senior goal achieved in a League Cup tie against West Ham United on 6 October 1981 made up of 154 in the League, 12 in the FA Cup, 15 League Cup, four in the European Cup, 12 in the UEFA Cup, two in the Texaco Cup and one in the Charity Shield. His total of League goals in two spells with the club was 155, up to the end of the 1981–82 season.

Doncaster Rovers were involved in the highest scoring Football League game of the 1982–83 season. On 25 September 1982 they beat Reading 7–5 in a Division Three match. The scores went 1–0, 1–1, 2–1, 3–1, 3–2, 4–2, 4–3, 5–3 (at half-time), 5–4, 6–4, 6–5, 7–5. Glyn Snodin scored three for Doncaster, including two penalties, and Kerry Dixon had four of the Reading goals, including one penalty. The attendance was 3118.

Dumbarton achieved promotion as champions of Division Two of the Scottish League in 1971–72 on goal difference from Arbroath and two points ahead of both Stirling Albion and St Mirren. Only Celtic, the Division One champions, scored more goals than Dumbarton's 89 and Kenny Wilson who set up a club record of 38 goals was also the leading League marksman in Scotland.

Dundee failed to win any of their first seven Division One matches in 1980–81 and were bottom of the table. They followed this by being unbeaten for 14 games, dropping only two points in drawn matches before another slump of six games without a win and just two points. But on 11 March they began a run of 12 unbeaten games and only two points dropped which enabled them to finish second and win promotion.

On 27 November 1954 **Dundee United** centre-forward Johnny Coyle was unavailable for the match with Alloa. He was replaced by a trialist

Martin Ferguson (middle, front row) a former Barnsley and Doncaster Rovers forward. *Falkirk Herald*

from the local Osborne club, Billy Boyle who proceeded to score four goals in a 5–4 win for United. Alloa finished two points lower than Dundee United at the end of the season.

Dunfermline Athletic won the Scottish FA Cup for the first time in 1960–61 at the expense of Celtic and under the managership of Jock Stein. Dunfermline's victims were Berwick Rangers, Stranraer, Aberdeen, Alloa Athletic, St Mirren after a replay and Celtic 2–0 also at the second attempt following a goalless draw.

In the week that **East Fife** won the Scottish Cup in 1938 they played four matches. On the Monday they were beaten 2–1 by East Stirling, although they did not include any of the cup side. Two days later they defeated Kilmarnock 4–2 in the Cup Final replay and the following day beat Forfar Athletic 3–0. They completed their successes on Friday with a 7–0 win over Dundee United.

East Stirlingshire manager Martin Ferguson began his appointment with a visit to Montrose in a Scottish League Cup-tie on 8 August 1981. Unfortunately, the team coach broke down at the ground, the replacement at Clackmannan and another vehicle at Perth. The trip was completed by taxi but East Stirling lost 1–0.

Everton have had more seasons in Division One than any other Football League club. Founder members of the competition in 1888, they have had only four seasons in Division Two in 1930–31 and from 1951 to 1954. In 1982–83 they were playing in their 80th season in Division One.

On 14 February 1982 **Exeter City** were beaten 5–1 at Millwall in a Division Three match. The entire team returned two days later to lose a Midweek League game 1–0 at the same venue against Millwall Reserves.

When **Falkirk** defeated Clyde 7–3 on 8 December 1962 in a Division One match in the Scottish League all their goals were scored by Hugh Maxwell, a former Stirling Albion forward who had just returned to Scotland after playing with Bradford (Park Avenue).

Forfar Athletic, as members of Division Two, reached the semi-final of the Scottish Cup in 1981–82 despite being drawn away in each round. They defeated East Fife (Division Two) 3–2 in the second round, drew 0–0 at Hamilton Academical (Division One) in the third and won the replay 3–2 at home. In the fourth round they won 1–0 away to Heart of Midlothian (Division One) and in the quarter-finals won 2–1 at

Queen's Park (Division One). They held Rangers (Premier Division) to a goalless draw at Hampden Park in the semi-final before losing the replay 3–1.

When **Fulham** won the championship of Division Two in 1948–49 all but eight of their 77 goals were scored by their regular forwards: Bob Thomas (23), Arthur Rowley (19), Arthur Stevens (12) plus Jack McDonald and Bedford Jezzard who had 15 goals between them. Twenty players were used but only 13 of them appeared in ten or more games.

Gillingham inside-forward Jimmy Scarth scored three goals in two and a half minutes of a Division Three (Southern) game against Leyton Orient on 1 November 1952. Gillingham led 3–0 at half-time and won 3–2.

On the night before **Grimsby Town** were due to play their FA Cup semi-final with Wolverhampton Wanderers at Old Trafford on 25 March 1939 their goalkeeper George Tweedy was taken ill with influenza. George Moulson had to deputise, but after only 23 minutes of his debut he was concussed diving at the feet of Dickie Dorsett and had to be carried off. Centre-forward Pat Glover went into goal but Grimsby lost 5–0.

Halifax Town finished as runners-up to Doncaster Rovers in 1934–35 just failing to achieve promotion by two points in Division Three (Northern). They suffered only two home defeats, but a mid-season slump in form and poor away results in which they were beaten ten times cost them a chance of a place in Division Two.

The hat-trick achieved by John Brown for **Hamilton Academical** against Berwick Rangers on 9 August 1980 is the only one without the aid of a penalty by a full-back in Scottish League history. Hamilton won 9–1.

Hartlepool United achieved their record total of 60 points in the 1967–68 season, beating their previous best in 1956–57 by one point. They had been runners-up in Division Three (Northern) in 1956–57 scoring a club record 90 goals, 30 more than in 1967–68 when they managed fewer than any of the top ten teams in Division Four.

Heart of Midlothian derived their name from the suggestion of the club's first captain Tom Purdie when they were formed in 1874. It was taken from the local nickname of the old prison demolished 50 years earlier but immortalised by a novel of the same name by Sir Walter Scott.

Above: John Brown (right) of Hamilton Academical on the attack against Motherwell. *Norman Inglis*
Left: Malcolm Brown (Huddersfield Town) who established a record number of consecutive appearances for the Leeds Road club. *Huddersfield Examiner*

Chris Chilton who played 415 League games for Hull City and scored 195 goals. *Hull Daily Mail*

Hereford United became a limited company in 1939 and were elected to the Southern League. The war aborted their first season in the competition and in the second during 1945–46 they finished second to Chelmsford City who were awarded points for cancelled matches.

John Bourke, the Kilmarnock centre-forward, on the attack against Queen's Park. *Gordon Robb*

Hibernian were leading 2–0 in their Scottish League Cup tie at Dundee on 28 August 1950. The match had started with the spectators in shirt sleeves under a sunny sky but by half-time torrential rain had waterlogged the pitch and the match was abandoned. It was not replayed because Hibs had already won their section matches.

Malcolm Brown established a record of consecutive appearances for **Huddersfield Town** in 1981–82, beating the 181 set up by Hugh Turner in the 1920s and 1930s. Right-back Brown began his run in a Division Four game against Doncaster Rovers on 9 September 1978.

Turner, a goalkeeper, had started with Huddersfield in 1926–27 and moved to Fulham in 1937–38 after losing his place to Bob Hesford.

When **Hull City** achieved promotion to Division Two in the 1965–66 season, their centre-forward Chris Chilton played most of the campaign with an egg-sized lump of fat behind a knee. He still managed to score 29 goals and had an operation in the following close season to remove it.

Ipswich Town turned professional in 1936 but too late to be granted exemption from the early rounds of the FA Cup. But they ran up a formidable total of 39 goals, including a record 11–0 win against Cromer.

When **Kilmarnock** won promotion to the Premier Division of the Scottish League for the first time in 1978–79 they went to the top of Division One on 3 February and were never headed. But though the club completed their fixtures on 28 April, Dundee had four games in hand of them and finished one point ahead of Kilmarnock as champions. Kilmarnock's top scorer was John Bourke with 21 goals, though he missed two months and eleven games with injury. Kilmarnock were promoted on goal difference from Clydebank.

Leeds United achieved or equalled nine club records in 1968–69: most points 67; most home points 39; most wins 27; most home wins 18; fewest defeats 2 (both away, another record); unbeaten at home; 26 goals conceded; nine conceded at home.

Leicester City used three different goalkeepers during their sixth round FA Cup match against Shrewsbury Town on 6 March 1982. Goalkeeper Mark Wallington, playing in his 333rd consecutive game, was injured early on and had eight stitches in his right thigh. He conceded two goals, then limped off to be replaced by centre-

Above: Manager Jock Wallace shows concern at the injury to his goalkeeper Mark Wallington. Left: The moment of impact for Wallington. Below right: Hero Alan Young comes off the pitch at the end of a traumatic but successful cup-tie for Leicester City. *Leicester Mercury*

forward Alan Young. But two goals in a minute enabled Leicester to level the scores by half-time.

Two minutes after the interval, Young sustained a head injury and while he was off for ten minutes Steve Lynex temporarily took over in goal.

Jim Melrose who was substitute for the ninth successive time scored twice and Shrewsbury won 5–2. The match lasted 104 minutes with injury time included.

Phil Neale who might be forgiven for wondering where one season ends and another begins.
Lincolnshire Echo

Lincoln City had the distinction in 1982–83 of being captained by Phil Neale who was also the skipper of Worcestershire County Cricket Club.

On 26 December 1981 **Liverpool** lost 3–1 at home to Manchester City and were twelfth in Division One with 24 points from 17 games. But in 1982 they lost only twice in 25 matches to achieve their 13th championship title.

Luton Town provided three players for the Ireland v England international at Windsor Park, Belfast on 22 October 1921, even though they were only members of Division Three (Southern) at the time. Alan Mathieson and Louis Bookman formed the Irish left-wing while Ernest Simms led the England attack in a 1–1 draw.

Manchester City introduced what became known as the Revie Plan in the 1950s. It was a variation of the deep-lying centre-forward game and had been introduced by Johnny Williamson while playing for the club's reserves in a Central League game. He was Don Revie's understudy and when it was tried out in the League side for the first time at Preston on 21 August 1954, City lost 5–0, but they took 12 points from their next seven games.

Manchester United were without a manager from 1938 to 1944. During this period the club's secretary, Walter Crickmer, acted as manager from 6 December 1938 until 16 March 1944 while chief scout Jimmy Porter was in charge of team tactics and training. Scott Duncan had resigned on 9 November 1937 to take charge of Ipswich Town and Matt Busby was appointed in February 1945 taking up his duties in October 1945 after his demobilisation from the Army.

Mansfield Town achieved promotion to Division Three in 1962–63, scoring a club record 108 goals and taking fourth place on goal average from Gillingham. Mansfield's defence conceded 69 goals in the season but their vital games with Gillingham produced just one goal. Mansfield drew 0–0 at home and won 1–0 at Gillingham.

Meadowbank Thistle established their points record in the 1982–83 season. When they beat Stenhousemuir 3–1 on 22 January 1983, they had reached 33 points in their 22nd Division Two match and were top of the table.

Middlesbrough played their first recorded FA Cup tie in 1883 against Staveley. They lost 5–1 and a contemporary report said that nearly the whole of the Middlesbrough team found themselves in hospital after the match.

Before **Millwall** became the first Division Three (Southern) team to reach the FA Cup semi-final in 1936–37, they had twice appeared at this stage of the competition during their Southern League days. In 1900 they beat Jarrow (A) 2–0, Queen's Park Rangers (A) 2–0, Aston Villa 2–1 after 1–1 and 0–0 draws and then lost a semi-final replay 3–0 against Southampton after a 0–0 draw.

In 1903 it was another 3–0 semi-final defeat against Derby County which ended their run after beating Luton (H) 3–0, Preston North End (H) 4–1 and Everton (H) 1–0.

Montrose were unbeaten in 15 Scottish League Division Two matches towards the end of the 1974–75 season but were defeated in their last two games and slipped to third. However, because of reorganization the first six clubs were placed in a new-look Division One which then became the second league in Scotland after the formation of the Premier Division.

Above: Distinguished gathering of Old Trafford 'old boys': (from left to right) Johnny Carey, Jack Rowley, Stan Pearson, Sir Matt Busby, secretary Les Olive who also played for the club plus Manchester Evening News United reporter David Meek. *Manchester Evening News*

Right: Mickey Lawson (left) and Chris Robertson looking forward to putting Meadowbank Thistle on the right rail for 1982–83. *Scotsman Publications Ltd*

Tom Gracie's lamb, the mascot of Morton, a club benevolent enough to allow sheep to graze on their Cappielow Park pitch

During the 1910–11 season, **Morton** players received an unusual offer from Duncan McPhail, a master butcher in Greenock, of a lamb to each player who scored a goal. At one stage several sheep were grazing at Cappielow Park. Centre-forward Tommy Gracie kept one which he christened Toby and it enjoyed the freedom of the ground for some while until coming to a sad and untimely end in the players bath.

Motherwell beat Celtic 8–0 on 30 April 1937 in a Division One match, played on a Friday evening as Celtic were due to visit Wembley the following day for the FA Cup Final between Sunderland and Preston North End.

The goalkeeper for **Newcastle United** in their first match in Division One was Matthew Kingsley who later became their first international. He played against Wolverhampton Wanderers on 3 September 1898 and was capped by England against Wales at Newcastle on 18 March 1901. He made 180 League appearances for Newcastle having previously played for Turton and Darwen. Later Kingsley served West Ham United, Queen's Park Rangers and Rochdale.

When **Newport County** were formed in 1912 the players changed in the King of Prussia (later The King) and walked down Somerton Road to the pitch. Subsequently they changed in a hut in the corner of the field by Baxter's bakery.

Northampton Town enjoyed their most successful season in both League and Cup matches during 1949–50. They had finished 20th the season before in Division Three (Southern) but ended the next season as runners-up in front of Southend United on goal average. It was Bob Dennison's first season as their manager and they also reached the fifth round of the FA Cup, losing 4–2 away to Derby County. Top scorer for them was Adam McCulloch with 16 League and three Cup goals in his first season after being signed from Third Lanark.

Between 1966–67 and 1979–80 **Norwich City** won only six FA Cup matches but during the same period recorded 28 successes in the League Cup.

Nottingham Forest scored five goals in eleven minutes of the second half of their Division Two match at Port Vale on 2 February 1957. Forest opened the scoring in the second minute but Port Vale equalised before the interval. Between the 67th and 78th minutes Forest added five and scored their seventh five minutes before the end.

Adam McCulloch the Third Lanark, Northampton Town, Shrewsbury Town and Aldershot centre-forward

Notts County scored three goals in two minutes in their 4–2 Division One win at West Bromwich Albion on 24 March 1982. Cyrille Regis put Albion ahead after 22 minutes but Iain McCulloch (58 mins), with a header then a shot a minute later followed by another goal from Gordon Mair (60 mins), put Notts 3–1 ahead. Andy King reduced the deficit for West Bromwich after 72 minutes but McCulloch scored his third two minutes from the end.

On 26 December 1981 **Oldham Athletic** were beaten 3–0 by Blackburn Rovers on their own Boundary Park ground. The match had been switched from Blackburn by mutual agreement because Oldham's pitch was playable unlike the Blackburn ground. The Football League at first ruled that the match would still count as a home fixture for Blackburn but altered their decision to record it as a home game for Oldham who up to then had not lost at Boundary Park that season.

When **Orient** reached the semi-final of the FA Cup in the 1977–78 season their nine goals were contributed by two players, Peter Kitchen scoring seven and Joe Mayo two.

When **Oxford United** were known as Headington United and before their election to an enlarged Southern League in 1949, they attracted an attendance in excess of 5000 for the visit of West Ham United 'A' team.

In a ballot for four Southern League places,

The only team carrying a government health warning?

with two clubs seeking re-election and as one of four new applicants, Headington received ten votes, one more than Llanelly— one of the clubs who failed to gain admission.

Although **Partick Thistle** have never appeared in the European Cup, their Firhill Park ground was used for a home game by the Swedish club Djurgaarden against Hibernian in a second round tie on 28 November 1955. The severe weather in Scandinavia made it impossible to play the game in Sweden. Having won 3–1 at Easter Road, Edinburgh on 23 November, Hibs won the second leg 1–0.

Peterborough United played their 1000th League game in Division Four on 3 April 1982 against Bury. They won 1–0 and were then lying third in the table with 74 points from 36 games but obtained only another eight points until the end of the season and missed promotion by one place.

In the early days after **Plymouth Argyle** turned professional in 1903 the club instituted a rule that players were not allowed to smoke four hours prior to kick-off. The fine for breach of the rules was one shilling (5p).

Portsmouth came into being as a professional club in 1898, following the disgrace of Royal Artillery (Portsmouth) Football Club who had forfeited its amateur status by taking its players away for a week's special training prior to an Amateur Cup match against Harwich. Two local sportsmen, G Lewin Oliver (headmaster of 'Olivers', a noted school in the area) and an ex-Warrant Officer of the Royal Engineers, W Wiggington, called a meeting of interested parties which was attended by 70 people. In the course of a few weeks £4950 was raised for the purchase of Fratton Park.

Port Vale was drawn away to Sunderland in the third round of the FA Cup in 1935–36. Vale were bottom but one in Divison Two at the time while Sunderland were the Division One leaders. On 11 January at Roker Park they drew 2–2 and in the replay two days later at Hanley before a crowd of 16 898 Vale won 2–0. But at the end of the season they were relegated from Division Two.

Preston North End were originally a cricket club in 1867 and later indulged in a variety of sports, including athletics and rugby, before taking up soccer in 1879–80. Their first game was said to have been against Eagley who beat them 1–0. An exhibition match against Blackburn Rovers on 26 March 1881 was even more decisive, when Rovers won 16–0.

On 18 October 1981 two teams arrived at the **Queen of the South** ground at Palmerston for a reserve game. Morton's second team thought they were playing the Dumfries club in a Reserve League game and Southern Counties side, Threave Rovers, had arrived for a Challenge Cup tie. In the event Queen's played Morton and Threave sat it out.

The first player thought to have infringed the

amateur status of **Queen's Park** is John McGregor who in 1982–83 was employed as sales representative for the club's lottery and was playing centre-half in their first team.

Queen's Park Rangers became the first Football League club to instal an artificial pitch and it was first used in the 1981–82 season. (For photographs see colour section). The Rangers manager, Terry Venables, had in 1971 combined with Gordon Williams to produce a novel entitled *They used to play on grass*.

Raith Rovers were ordered to replay their Scottish Cup first round tie against 5th King's Rifle Volunteers in the 1894–95 season because they failed to provide goal nets. Having won this match 6–3, they were beaten 4–3 in the replay.

On 22 September 1982 **Rangers** fourth goal in their 6–1 Scottish League Cup quarter-final, first leg win at Kilmarnock, was the club's 11 000th goal. John MacDonald was the milestone marksman.

Reading announced on 13 February 1982 that the referee and linesmen at their home matches would no longer be given biscuits at half-time because of an economy measure. Nicknamed the Royals, Reading had previously been known as The Biscuitmen because of the close proximity of the Huntley and Palmers factory.

The record attendance at **Rochdale** was established on 10 December 1949 for an FA Cup second round tie at Spotland against Notts County. A crowd of 24 231 saw them beaten 2–1. Their previous highest gate had been 20 945 on 30 April 1929 for a Division Three (Northern) match against Bradford City.

When **Rotherham United** were still known as Thornhill United they won the Wharncliffe Charity Cup in the late 1880s. Upon returning to Rotherham they noticed that the sky was lit up, and thinking it was some celebration for their success they were dismayed to discover the town hall on fire.

St Johnstone achieved only eleven points in the Premier Division in 1975–76. They won just three matches all at home, including their opening fixture, and suffered their worst spell between their other two wins, a run of 27 games with 23 defeats.

St Mirren were formed in 1876 when the rugby team decided to switch codes. Their name is derived from the patron saint of Paisley, St

Above: A delight of milestone proportions for Rangers forward John MacDonald
D C Thomson and Co Ltd

Left: Fired with enthusiasm

Mirinus (St Mirren), who is supposed to have been a contemporary of St Columba.

Scunthorpe United became the first Football League club to be eliminated from the FA Cup before the first round proper. In 1950–51 the FA had already completed their Cup plans. Colchester United, Scunthorpe United, Shrewsbury Town and Gillingham were elected to the League but only Gillingham because of a cup run in 1949–50 were excused the qualifying rounds. Shrewsbury withdrew, Colchester played and won their tie leaving Scunthorpe defeated 1–0 at Hereford.

Sheffield United became leading exporters to the North American Soccer League in the late 1970s. In addition to players like Terry Garbett, Tony Field, Keith Eddy, Eddie Colquhoun, Alan Woodward, Colin Franks, Cliff Calvert and Jim Brown, former Manager Ken Furphy and secretary Keith Walker also went to the United States of America.

On 7 December 1974 **Sheffield Wednesday** drew 4–4 at home to Manchester United (the Division Two champions elect) after leading 3–1 at half-time. Wednesday scored only five more goals in their remaining 21 matches and were relegated to Division Three with 21 points. In this period they won only one game 1–0 away to

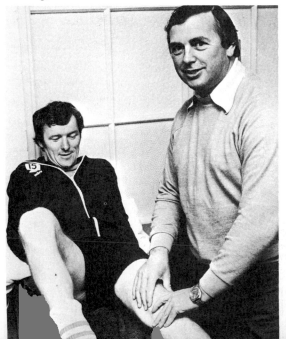

Eric Potts receives treatment during the 1982–83 season from Bury trainer Jack Cunningham. *Gerry McLoughlin*

Southampton with a goal from Eric Potts, the only ever present player for them that season.

Shrewsbury Town twice in three weeks established record receipts for the club. On 6 January 1979 their 3–1 FA Cup win in the third round against Cambridge United produced receipts of £8400, then on 27 January a 2–0 win over Manchester City in the fourth round yielded £18 600.

Southampton became the first English team to visit Argentina when they made the sea journey to South America in 1904.

In the 1980–81 season **Southend United** established 17 club records. They recorded 42 home points; 30 wins including 19 at home; 18 successive home wins; 15 successive home wins from the start of the season; 32 unbeaten home games; 31 goals against; eleven away wins; 25 clean sheets including 17 at home, ten of them successively; ten 'doubles' against other teams; six goals against at home (a new Division Four record); goalkeeper Mervyn Cawston completed 985 minutes without conceding a goal at home between August and December; they were undefeated throughout the season at home; had fewest defeats in a season; and no team completed the 'double' against them. The club were Division Four champions and returned to Division Three after one season in the lowest league.

In the 1960–61 season **Stenhousemuir** finished third in Division Two, four points behind Falkirk the runners-up, achieving 50 points, their highest total and just one goal short of Falkirk's 100, another club record. They lost six of their first 12 matches but were beaten only another four times of their remaining 24, nineteen of them ending in victory. David Campbell with 28 League goals and a further two in the League Cup was their top scorer. Stenhousemuir reached the quarter-finals of the League Cup and finished ahead of Stirling Albion, the ultimate Division Two champions, in their qualifying group.

Stirling Albion competed in the Scottish League Cup before they became members of the Scottish League. In 1945–46 they were included in Section D of the then Scottish Southern League Cup, qualifying competition, Division 'B', finishing second to Dundee who were Division 'B' champions that season.

On 25 April 1981 **Stockport County** arrived at Bury for a Division Four match minus three snowbound players. They played the entire first half with nine men and when they succeeded in

Joe Kasher (left) and Raich Carter. Carter, a former schoolboy international, had been rejected by Leicester City as being too small. *The Evening Chronicle, Newcastle-upon-Tyne*

completing a full side after the break, managed to win the game 1–0.

The first FA Cup meeting between **Stoke City** and Port Vale was held at Stoke on 15 October 1887. It was followed by a court action. Stoke won the match 1–0, but a few weeks later their goalkeeper William Rowley was sued by Vale for a breach of contract along with another player. Stoke had to publish an apology, pay £20 to a Burslem charity, the same amount to Vale for legal fees and release a player to their rivals.

Stranraer were the last Scottish League club to install floodlights. They completed their £20 000 system in June 1981.

Guest of honour for **Sunderland** in their Division One match against Stoke City on 30 October 1982 was Raich Carter (68) on the 50th anniversary of his home debut for the club. Carter who had captained Sunderland in the 1937 FA Cup final was accompanied by Joe Kasher (88), the club's longest surviving ex-player who had also played for Stoke in his career.

Swansea City, when still known as Swansea Town, defeated Real Madrid 3–0 during a close season tour of Spain and Portugal in 1927. They were only the second British club to win there after Nelson's success in 1923.

When **Swindon Town** won the League Cup in 1969 they were unable to enter the Fairs Cup as they were members of Division Three. It was decided to promote an Anglo-Italian competition and Swindon were drawn in the same group as Juventus and Napoli. They beat Juventus 4–0 and Napoli 1–0 and lost respectively to each side 1–0 and 2–1 but qualified for the final also against Napoli. They won it in Italy 3–0, though the match was abandoned after crowd trouble in the 79th minute.

Torquay United were elected to the Football League in 1927. Members of the Southern League at the time they tied with 21 votes with Aberdare Athletic before winning 26–19 on a second ballot.

The new West Stand at White Hart Lane was formally opened by Sir Stanley Rous on 6

Swindon Town skipper Stan Harland with the Anglo-Italian Trophy won in 1970 in Naples. *Wiltshire Newspapers*

Spurs' new stand at White Hart Lane. Note the clever way in which the pitch was bent to fit alongside it . . . *Tommy Hindley*

February 1982. **Tottenham Hotspur** had as their Division One visitors that day Wolverhampton Wanderers, Spurs first visitors at the same ground 74 years earlier.

Tranmere Rovers held the distinction of providing the record attendance at Anfield, Liverpool for 18 years. A crowd of 61 036 watched their fourth round FA Cup tie there on 27 January 1934. Liverpool won 3–1. The figure remained until the same stage of the 1951–52 competition when 61 905 saw Liverpool's cup tie against Wolverhampton Wanderers.

On 26 December 1896 **Walsall** arrived for a Division Two match at Barley Bank, Darwen with only eight men, including a committee member whose registration was rushed through for the game. Four players had missed their connection.

After winning the toss and with the aid of a strong wind and the clever disposition of their players, Walsall managed to work the offside trap holding Darwen at bay for the first 15 minutes. However, once they had broken through the home side quickly scored four times, adding eight after the interval.

Watford scored fewer goals and conceded less than any other team in Division Three (Southern) in 1949–50. Their 45 goals were two fewer than those of the next lowest scores, Port Vale, while the 35 they let in were four less than

Nottingham Forest's total. They finished sixth with 45 points. In 20 matches they kept a clean sheet and between September and November they completed eight successive League games without conceding a goal, a club record.

West Bromwich Albion played their 2000th League game against Manchester United at The Hawthorns on 29 November 1952. It was also Albion's 1000th home game in the competition and they won 3–1 after being a goal down at half-time.

On 26 December 1963 **West Ham United** suffered their heaviest defeat losing 8–2 at home to Blackburn Rovers in Division One. Two days later they won 3–1 at Ewood Park, Blackburn.

Wigan Athletic maintained the record of post-war newcomers to the Football League by winning promotion to Division Three in 1981–82, their fourth season in Division Four. Scunthorpe United figured significantly in Wigan's best sequence of results. After beating them 2–1 at home on 24 October, Wigan remained undefeated for 21 League games, dropping only seven points and ending the run with a 7–2 win at Scunthorpe.

Of the **Wimbledon** players on the active list during 1982–83 only John Leslie remained from their non-league days prior to election to the Football League in 1977. Appropriately he has established two club records: most League goals and appearances.

Wolverhampton Wanderers centre-forward

John Leslie a Wimbledon stalwart of non-league days and record successes in the Football League.
Wimbledon News

George Hedley scored one of the team's goals in their 3–1 FA Cup final win against Newcastle United in 1908. However, the effort split one of his boots which as a pair had 17 patches on them. Still he refused to part with them and declined to change into a new pair brought onto the field by the trainer.

Wrexham were losing 2–0 to Halifax Town in a Division Three (Northern) match on 10 September 1932 with 15 minutes remaining only to recover and win 5–2.

York City celebrated the 50th anniversary of their first match at Bootham Crescent in August 1982. After moving from Fulford Gate they met Stockport County on 31 August 1932. Outside-left Tom Mitchell had scored their first goal in the game and at the age of 83 was invited with his wife Irene (77), who had also been in attendance at the inaugural match, to be York's guests of honour.

These boots were made for . . . something

FA Cup

Forty different teams have won the FA Cup:

7 times—Aston Villa (2–0 West Bromwich Albion; 1–0 West Bromwich Albion; 3–2 Everton; 2–0 Newcastle United; 1–0 Sunderland; 1–0 Huddersfield Town; 2–1 Manchester United). **Tottenham Hotspur** (2–2, 3–1 Sheffield United; 1–0 Wolverhampton Wanderers; 2–0 Leicester City; 3–1 Burnley; 2–1 Chelsea; 1–1, 3–2 Manchester City; 1–1, 1–0 Queen's Park Rangers).

6—Blackburn Rovers (2–1 Queen's Park; 2–0 Queen's Park; 0–0, 2–0 West Bromwich Albion; 6–1 Sheffield Wednesday; 3–1 Notts County; 3–1 Huddersfield Town). **Newcastle United** (1–1, 2–0 Barnsley; 2–0 Aston Villa; 2–1 Arsenal; 2–0 Blackburn Rovers; 1–0 Arsenal; 3–1 Manchester City).

5—Arsenal (2–0 Huddersfield Town; 1–0 Sheffield United; 2–0 Liverpool; 2–1 Liverpool; 3–2 Manchester United). **Wanderers** (1–0 Royal Engineers; 2–0 Oxford University; 1–1, 3–0 Old Etonians; 2–1 Oxford University; 3–1 Royal Engineers). **West Bromwich Albion** (2–1 Preston North End; 3–0 Aston Villa; 2–1 Birmingham City; 3–2 Preston North End; 1–0 Everton). **Manchester United** (1–0 Bristol City; 4–2 Blackpool; 3–1 Leicester City; 2–1 Liverpool; 2–2, 4–0 Brighton and Hove Albion).

4—Bolton Wanderers (2–0 West Ham United; 1–0 Manchester City; 2–0 Portsmouth; 2–0 Manchester United). **Manchester City** (1–0 Bolton Wanderers; 2–1 Portsmouth; 3–1 Birmingham City; 1–0 Leicester City). **Sheffield United** (4–1 Derby County; 1–1, 2–1 Southampton; 3–0 Chelsea; 1–0 Cardiff City). **Wolverhampton Wanderers** (1–0 Everton; 3–1 Newcastle United; 3–1 Leicester City; 3–0 Blackburn Rovers).

3—Everton (1–0 Newcastle United; 3–0 Manchester City; 3–2 Sheffield Wednesday). **Sheffield Wednesday** (2–1 Wolverhampton Wanderers; 2–1 Everton; 4–2 West Bromwich Albion). **West Ham United** (3–2 Preston North End; 2–0 Fulham; 1–0 Arsenal).

2—Bury (4–0 Southampton; 6–0 Derby County). **Nottingham Forest** (3–1 Derby County; 2–1 Luton Town). **Liverpool** (2–1 Leeds United; 3–0 Newcastle United). **Old Etonians** (1–0 Clapham Rovers; 1–0 Blackburn Rovers). **Preston North End** (3–0 Wolverhampton Wanderers; 1–0 Huddersfield Town).

FA CUP Attendances 1971–72 to 1982–83

	1st Rd	2nd Rd	3rd Rd	4th Rd	5th Rd	6th Rd	S/F+F	Total	Matches	Average
1971–72	277 726	236 127	986 094	711 399	468 378	230 292	248 546	3 158 562	**160**	**19 741**
1972–73	259 432	169 114	938 741	735 825	357 386	241 934	226 543	2 928 975	**160**	**18 306**
1973–74	214 236	125 295	840 142	747 909	346 012	233 307	273 051	2 779 952	**167**	**16 646**
1974–75	283 956	170 466	914 994	646 434	393 323	268 361	291 369	2 968 903	**172**	**17 261**
1975–76	255 533	178 099	867 880	573 843	471 925	206 851	205 810	2 759 941	**161**	**17 142**
1976–77	379 230	192 159	942 523	631 265	373 330	205 379	258 216	2 982 102	**174**	**17 139**
1977–78	258 248	178 930	881 406	540 164	400 751	137 059	198 020	2 594 578	**160**	**16 216**
1978–79	243 773	185 343	880 345	537 748	243 683	263 213	249 897	2 604 002	**166**	**15 687**
1979–80	267 121	204 759	804 701	507 725	364 039	157 530	355 541	2 661 416	**163**	**16 328**
1980–81	246 824	194 502	832 578	534 402	320 530	288 714	339 250	2 756 800	**169**	**16 312**
1981–82	236 220	127 300	513 185	356 987	203 334	124 308	279 621	1 840 955	**160**	**11 505**
1982–83	193 461	153 174	669 054	452 623	274 418	193 637	293 162	2 229 529	**157**	**14 200**

Sunderland (3–1 Preston North End; 1–0 Leeds United).

1—Barnsley (0–0, 1–0 West Bromwich Albion). **Blackburn Olympic** (2–1 Old Etonians). **Blackpool** (4–3 Bolton Wanderers). **Bradford City** (0–0, 1–0 Newcastle United). **Burnley** (1–0 Liverpool). **Cardiff City** (1–0 Arsenal). **Charlton Athletic** (1–0 Burnley). **Chelsea** (2–2, 2–1 Leeds United). **Clapham Rovers** (1–0 Oxford University). **Derby County** (4–1 Charlton Athletic). **Huddersfield Town** (1–0 Preston North End). **Ipswich Town** (1–0 Arsenal). **Leeds United** (1–0 Arsenal). **Notts County** (4–1 Bolton Wanderers). **Old Carthusians** (3–0 Old Etonians). **Oxford University** (2–0 Royal Engineers). **Portsmouth** (4–1 Wolverhampton Wanderers). **Royal Engineers** (1–1, 2–0 Old Etonians). **Southampton** (1–0 Manchester United).

Up to and including the 1983 final there have been 114 matches including replays which have produced 302 goals. The successful teams have scored 237 and the beaten sides 65 goals. Fifty-nine defeated teams have failed to score. The most popular result has been 1–0 which has occurred on 31 occasions.

Between 1909 and 1927 there were 15 consecutive finals in which the beaten side failed to score. Three goals is the highest by a defeated side, Bolton losing 4–3 to Blackpool in 1953.

The first match to be screened in colour on Television was the FA Cup Final between Everton and West Bromwich Albion in 1968.

The 1969 FA Cup Final was played on 26 April between Manchester City and Leicester City. There had been no earlier final played since Aston Villa met Newcastle United on 18 April 1905.

Wembley Stadium has housed the FA Cup Final since 1923 and has regularly attracted crowds of 100 000. But in a first round tie in 1980–81 the Wembley Football Club played before the lowest attendance of the competition that season when they attracted only 852 at Enfield.

Sheffield Wednesday were involved in replays in three successive rounds of the FA Cup in 1938–39. In the third round they drew 1–1 at home to Yeovil and Petters United and won the replay 2–1. In the fourth round they drew 1–1 at home to Chester and again 1–1 away after extra time. At Maine Road in a second replay they won 2–0. In the fifth round they drew 1–1 at Chelsea and again 0–0 at home after extra time. In the second replay at Highbury they were beaten 3–1.

Stan Crowther played for Manchester United in the FA Cup in 1957–58 after the Munich air disaster even though he had already played in the competition for Aston Villa. Ernie Taylor was signed by United from Blackpool a week after the air crash but was allowed to play in the fifth round against Sheffield Wednesday on 19 February 1958. The FA waived the rule that a player has to be registered 14 days before the date of the round. Taylor had not played for Blackpool in the FA Cup that season.

The smallest goalkeeper seen in the FA Cup in the post-war era was Norman Preston who stood 5 ft 2 in (1·57 m) tall when he kept goal for Hereford United against Scunthorpe United on 11 December 1952 in a second round tie.

In the 1945–46 season the two-legged FA Cup ties produced one of the most unusual turn round of fortune seen in the competition. Bradford (Park Avenue) were beaten 3–1 at home by Manchester City but won the second leg 8–2 at Maine Road.

Milk Cup
(*formerly League Cup*)

The first 23 League Cup competitions produced 23 different finalists. Aston Villa are the most successful team with three wins in 1961, 1975 and 1977, as well as finishing as runners-up in 1963 and 1971. They were also the first team to play in as many as 100 League Cup games.

Nottingham Forest appeared in three consecutive finals between 1978 and 1980. During this period they were undefeated in 17 ties which incorporated 25 matches. Liverpool emulated their achievement of three successive finals in 1981, 1982 and 1983, winning all three.

Clubs from all four divisions have appeared in the League Cup final and those from three divisions have won it. Non-Division One teams to have achieved this feat have been Norwich City (Division 2) in 1962, Queen's Park Rangers (Division 3) in 1967 and Swindon Town (Division 3) in 1969. Rochdale (Division 4) were the beaten finalists in 1962.

Record score in a League Cup match is Workington 9 Barrow 1 in the first round on 2 September 1964. Neither club is now a member of the Football League. Everton beat Wimbledon 8–0 in the second round on 29 August 1978.

Penalty kicks were first used to decide a League Cup tie in the 1979–80 season. In the first leg of their first round tie at Lincoln on 1 August 1979, Barnsley lost 2–1. At Barnsley, on 14 August, Lincoln were defeated by the same score after extra time. Barnsley won 4–3 on penalty kicks.

Queen's Park Rangers and Derby County were involved in a scoreless tie in the League Cup which had to be decided on penalty kicks. In the second round, first leg, on 26 August 1980, they drew at Loftus Road and again on 3 September at the Baseball Ground after extra time before Rangers won 5–3 on penalties.

The scorer of the first Football League Cup goal was Maurice Cook (Fulham) in the tenth minute of a match against Bristol Rovers on 26 September 1960. Rovers won 2–1.

The League Cup semi-final first leg tie between Sunderland and Aston Villa on 12 January 1963 was unique for two reasons. It was the first occasion in the history of the competition that a game had been played on a Saturday and the first to be broadcast live on BBC's Light Programme.

The Football League Cup and the new Milk Cup first won by Liverpool in 1982 when they took both old and new trophies back to Anfield

The match had been switched because of the unusually severe weather conditions prevailing that winter which had disrupted normal scheduling.

Highest attendance for a Football League Cup game other than the final was 63 418 for the semi-final first leg between Manchester United and Manchester City at Old Trafford on 17 December 1969.

Two weeks before the League Cup final on 13 March 1982, the National Dairy Council concluded a sponsorship deal with the Football League for the League Cup which was then renamed the Milk Cup. Liverpool won and took two trophies back to Anfield after the final.

The following year Liverpool repeated their achievement in what was their third successive and successful appearance in the competition.

Attendances

Season	Entries	Total crowds	Games	Average crowd
1960–61	87	1 204 580	112	10 755
1961–62	82	1 030 534	104	9 909
1962–63	80	1 029 893	102	10 097
1963–64	82	945 265	104	9 089
1964–65	82	962 802	98	9 825
1965–66	83	1 205 876	106	11 376
1966–67	90	1 394 553	118	11 818
1967–68	90	1 671 326	110	15 194
1968–69	91	2 064 647	118	17 497
1969–70	92	2 299 819	122	18 851
1970–71	91	2 038 809	117	17 425
1971–72	92	2 397 154	123	19 489
1972–73	92	1 935 474	120	16 129

League Cup Finals

Year	Winners		Runners-up	
1961	Aston Villa	3	†Rotherham U	2
1962	Norwich C	4	†Rochdale	0
1963	†Birmingham C	3	Aston Villa	1
1964	Leicester C	4	†Stoke C	3
1965	†Chelsea	3	Leicester C	2
1966	West Bromwich A	5	†West Ham U	3
1967	Queen's Park R	3	West Bromwich A	2
1968	Leeds U	1	Arsenal	0*
1969	Swindon T	3	Arsenal	1*
1970	Manchester C	2	West Bromwich A	1
1971	Tottenham H	2	Aston Villa	0
1972	Stoke C	2	Chelsea	1
1973	Tottenham H	1	Norwich C	0
1974	Wolverhampton W	2	Manchester C	1
1975	Aston Villa	1	Norwich C	0
1976	Manchester C	2	Newcastle U	1
1977	Aston Villa (after first replay 1–1*) (after 0–0)	3	Everton	2* ;
1978	Nottingham F (after 0–0*)	1	Liverpool	0
1979	Nottingham F	3	Southampton	2
1980	Wolverhampton W	1	Nottingham F	0
1981	Liverpool (after 1–1*)	2	West Ham U	1
1982	Liverpool	3	Tottenham H	1*
1983	Liverpool	2	Manchester U	1

* after extra time   † home team in first leg

1973–74	92	1 722 629	132	13 050
1974–75	92	1 901 094	127	14 969
1975–76	92	1 841 735	140	13 155
1976–77	92	2 236 636	147	15 215
1977–78	92	2 038 295	148	13 772
1978–79	92	1 827 464	139	13 148
1979–80	92	2 322 866	169	13 745
1980–81	92	2 051 576	161	12 743
1981–82	92	1 880 682	161	11 681
1982–83	92	1 679 756	160	10 498

LEAGUE CUP GOALSCORING
(Leading goalscorers)

1960–61	Gerry Hitchens (Aston Villa)	11
1961–62	Ray Charnley (Blackpool)	6
1962–63	Ken Leek (Birmingham City)	8
1963–64	John Ritchie (Stoke City)	10
1964–65	Tony Hateley (Aston Villa)	10
1965–66	Tony Brown (West Bromwich Albion)	11
	Geoff Hurst (West Ham United)	11
1966–67	Rodney Marsh (Queen's Park Rangers)	11
1967–68	John O'Hare (Derby County)	6
	Jim Fryatt (Torquay United)	6
1968–69	Don Rogers (Swindon Town)	7
1969–70	Jeff Astle (West Bromwich Albion)	5
	John Byrom (Bolton Wanderers)	5
	Francis Lee (Manchester City)	5
	Rodney Marsh (Queen's Park Rangers)	5
1970–71	Martin Chivers (Tottenham Hotspur)	7
1971–72	Martin Chivers (Tottenham Hotspur)	7
1972–73	Kevin Keegan (Liverpool)	5
	Graham Paddon (Norwich City)	5
	Martin Peters (Tottenham Hotspur)	5
1973–74	Francis Lee (Manchester City)	8
1974–75	Lou Macari (Manchester United)	7
1975–76	Dennis Tueart (Manchester City)	8
1976–77	Brian Little (Aston Villa)	10
1977–78	Kenny Dalglish (Liverpool)	6
	Ian Bowyer (Nottingham Forest)	6
1978–79	Garry Birtles (Nottingham Forest)	6
	Bob Latchford (Everton)	6
1979–80	Alan Mayes (Swindon Town)	6
1980–81	Kenny Dalglish (Liverpool)	7
1981–82	Ian Rush (Liverpool)	8
1982–83	Steve Coppell (Manchester United)	6

League Information

Twenty-three different teams have won the Football League championship. Liverpool have been the most successful with 14 titles followed by Arsenal with eight, Manchester United, Everton and Aston Villa with seven each.

The twelve original members of the Football League in 1888 were: Preston North End, Aston Villa, Wolverhampton Wanderers, Blackburn Rovers, Bolton Wanderers, West Bromwich Albion, Accrington, Everton, Burnley, Derby County, Notts County and Stoke, finishing in that order.

Accrington were the first permanent casualty because after being relegated to Division Two in 1893 they resigned before the new season began. (Manchester United had finished five points below them at the bottom of the table.)

However, Stoke were not re-elected in 1890, came back the following year only to be relegated in 1907. After one season in Division Two they resigned for financial reasons but were re-elected to Division Two in 1919.

Notts County were the first team to reach 3000 League matches. They achieved this milestone in a Division Two game against Nottingham Forest on 25 March 1975 which ended in a 2–2 draw. Yet as one of four clubs who were forced to seek re-election to the League after its inaugural season in 1888–89 they received seven votes just two more than Birmingham St George's.

Notts County and Blackburn Rovers were the last two clubs to open their League programme in 1888. While the other ten began on 8 September, County and Rovers started a week later. Notts County played at Everton, Blackburn at home to Accrington.

LEAGUE FEATS

The fewest number of points achieved by a League Championship winning team in a 42-match programme is 52. It has happened on three occasions: Sheffield Wednesday in 1928–29, Arsenal in 1937–38 and Chelsea in 1954–55.

Bristol City were relegated from Division One to Division Four in successive seasons. They finished 20th in Division One in 1979–80, 21st in Division Two in 1980–81 and 23rd in Division Three in 1981–82. On 3 December 1982 Crewe Alexandra drew 1–1 with Torquay United to put Bristol City 24th and bottom of

Division Four because of an inferior goal difference. The following day Bristol City lost 1–0 at Rochdale.

Huddersfield Town (five seasons, in Division 4, 1975–80), Portsmouth (two seasons, 1978–80) and Sheffield United (one season, 1981–82) are the only Division One champions to have played in all four divisions.

Bootle hold the record for the fewest number of Football League matches played. In their only season 1892–93 they finished eighth from their programme of 22 Division Two games.

On 2 May 1960 Burnley defeated Manchester City 2–1 at Maine Road to go to the top of Division One for the first time in the season and became the champions by a point from Wolverhampton Wanderers. They had been beaten 6–1 by Wolves on 30 March 1960.

Leicester City and Manchester City hold the record for Division Two championships with six each.

The fewest number of points to separate the top and bottom teams in any division is 16. It happened in Division One in 1901–02, 1927–28 and 1937–38.

Only five teams have gone through a season without gaining at least one away point. Four of them did so in Division Two: Northwich Victoria in 1893–94, Crewe Alexandra in 1894–95, Loughborough Town in 1899–1900 and Doncaster Rovers in 1904–05. Nelson, the fifth team, equalled the record when they were members of Division Three (Northern) in 1930–31.

Rochdale suffered 13 consecutive home defeats in one season. After beating New Brighton 3–2 on 7 November 1931 they lost their remaining home games. They also lost the first match in 1932–33 to make it 14 defeats, but then drew 0–0 with Barrow who themselves had lost a total of 15 home Division Three (Northern) matches in 1925–26.

Newport County completed 25 Division Four matches in 1970–71 before their first win. The sequence ended on 15 January 1971 when they beat Southend United 3–0 at home following 21 defeats and four draws. Yet they had beaten Reading 2–1 in a Football League Cup tie on 19 August.

Coventry City played eight consecutive away matches in Division One between home fixtures against Middlesbrough on 29 January 1977 and Tottenham Hotspur on 2 April.

Only once since the Second World War have there been more away than home wins in a full day's programme. On 2 February 1957 the 46 matches produced 16 home victories, 18 away and 12 draws.

Of the 32 matches played on 4 February 1954 the only draw in the Football League was recorded between York City and Workington in a Division Three (Northern) match which ended 1–1.

Since the First World War all eleven matches in a single division have resulted in home wins on four occasions: 13 February 1926 in Division One; 3 April 1926 in Division Three (Northern), 14 March 1931 in Division Three (Northern) and 10 December 1955 in Division One.

On Christmas Day 1936, ten of the eleven Division One matches resulted in home wins. The other was drawn. A similar situation occurred on 1 September 1956 and again on 12 September 1964.

On 18 September 1948 there were nine drawn matches in Division One and the entire Football League programme on 13 October 1962 produced 22 draws.

Seven clubs have gone through an entire season without a drawn match in the Football League and they did so in a period of six seasons before the turn of the century: Aston Villa and Sunderland in Division One 1891–92 (26 matches), Small Heath, Division Two 1893–94 (28), Lincoln City and Walsall Town Swifts, Division Two 1894–95 (30), Stoke, Division One 1895–96 (30) and Darwen, Division Two 1896–97 (30).

Torquay United drew eight consecutive Division Three matches between 25 October and 13 December 1969.

The highest number of away wins in any division is eight. This has occurred on three occasions: 27 September 1958 in Division Three; 12 September 1959 in Division Two and 25 November 1967 in Division Two.

The Division One programme on 28 April 1923 comprised ten matches and not a solitary goal was scored by an away team in any of them.

Believed to have been the only Football League match without a corner kick was the Division One game between Newcastle United and Portsmouth on 5 December 1931. It also failed to produce a goal as it ended in a 0–0 draw.

Crewe Alexandra and Hartlepool United have

met in the Football League more times than any other pair of clubs since the first World War. They were founder members of Division Three (Northern) in 1921 and apart from 1963–64 when Crewe were in Division Three, they have been in the same division together ever since.

After losing 2–1 at home to Leicester City on 4 October 1919, Coventry City did not score another goal in Division Two until 25 December 1919 when they defeated Stoke 3–2 at home. They had completed eleven games without scoring.

A common denominator among the seven clubs to have forfeited Football League status for one reason or another since the Second World War—Accrington Stanley, Barrow, Bradford Park Avenue, Gateshead, New Brighton, Southport and Workington—is that they have all come from the north.

In the 1923–24 season Exeter City completed 13 consecutive away matches in Division Three (Southern) without scoring. Mansfield Town failed to score in their first nine home Division Three games of 1971–72.

The eleven clubs to have been admitted to the Football League since the Second World War have been: Colchester United, Gillingham (who had previously been members), Scunthorpe United, Shrewsbury Town, Workington, Peterborough United, Oxford United, Cambridge United, Hereford United, Wimbledon and Wigan Athletic. All of them won promotion at least once, although Workington subsequently lost their place in the competition.

LEAGUE POINTS

Most points in a single season

In the first season under the new system of three points for a win, Sheffield United achieved the highest total among the four divisions with 96 points from their 46 games in Division Four during 1981–82.

All records shown here are under the old system of two points for a win and the unchanged one point for a draw.

Liverpool achieved 68 points in 42 Division One matches in 1978–79. They lost only four games and conceded 16 goals, the lowest for League Champions in a 42-match programme. Unbeaten at home, they dropped only two points to Leeds United and Everton. Liverpool were eight points ahead and achieved their 30th and last win at Elland Road for their eleventh title on 17 May 1979, by 3–0 against Leeds who had held the previous record of 67 points in 1968–69.

Tottenham Hotspur achieved 70 points in 42 Division Two matches in 1919–20. They won their first seven matches and only suffered their initial defeat in the thirteenth at Bury on 8 November. They were also unbeaten at home where only two visitors escaped with a point. Tottenham failed to score in just two matches from a total of 102 goals.

Aston Villa achieved 70 points in 46 Division Three matches in 1971–72. Their most successful spell came from mid-January to mid-March when an unbeaten run produced 19 points out of a possible 22. Their 32 wins was also a record for the division, with 20 of these coming at home.

Nottingham Forest achieved 70 points in 46 Division Three (Southern) matches in 1950–51. Their 110 goals established a club record, while the 30 wins was also a record for the division. Wally Ardron set up a club record with 36 goals.

Bristol City also achieved 70 points in 46 Division Three (Southern) matches in 1954–55. They were champions, nine points ahead of Leyton Orient. Of their 101 goals, John Atyeo scored 28 and Jimmy Rogers 25. City also set up a record of 30 wins for the division. Yet Orient had led the division in mid-season.

Doncaster Rovers achieved 72 points in 42 Division Three (Northern) matches in 1946–47. They completed the double of home and away wins over twelve of their rivals. Five players between them collected 109 of the club's 123 League goals, with Clarrie Jordan top scorer with 42. Two other division records were achieved with 33 wins and only three defeats.

Clarrie Jordan, now reflecting over a pint the points of a previous era. *Doncaster Newspapers Ltd*

Lincoln City achieved 74 points in 46 Division Four matches in 1975–76. They also set up a record of 32 wins and only four defeats. They had two unbeaten runs of 14 matches; the first from mid-October to the end of January, the other from mid-March to the end of the season. Their 111 goals was the first three-figure total in the League since 1966–67. Only once however did the side reach as many as six goals.

Most home points in a single season

Six clubs have achieved maximum points from home matches in the Football League: Sunderland, Division One in 1891–92 (13 games); Liverpool, Division Two in 1893–94 (14); Bury, Division Two in 1894–95 (15); Sheffield Wednesday, Division Two in 1899–1900 (17); Small Heath, Division Two in 1902–3 (17) and Brentford, Division Three (Southern) in 1929–30 (21).

Most away points in a single season

Arsenal achieved 33 points in 21 away Division One matches in 1930–31. They won 14 and drew five of their games. Tottenham Hotspur equalled their performance in 1960–61 obtaining their record with 16 wins and one draw.

Bristol City achieved 31 points in 19 away Division Two matches in 1905–06. They won 13 and drew five of their games.

Oldham Athletic achieved 30 points in 23 away Division Three matches in 1973–74. They won 12 and drew six of their games.

Walsall achieved 32 points in 23 away Division Four matches in 1959–60. They won 14 and drew four of their games.

Nottingham Forest achieved 32 points in 23 away Division Three (Southern) matches in 1950–51. They won 14 and drew four of their games.

Doncaster Rovers achieved 37 points in 21 away Division Three (Northern) matches in 1946–47. They won 18 and drew one of their games.

Fewest points in a single season

Leeds United achieved only 18 points in 42 Division One matches 1946–47. Six matches were won, all at home, and only one draw was achieved away and that to Brentford, the side who were relegated with Leeds but had achieved seven more points than United.

Queen's Park Rangers achieved only 18 points in 42 Division One matches in 1968–69. They had

won promotion from Division Two for the first time the previous season. During the 1968–69 term they equalled their heaviest defeat when beaten 8–1 by Manchester United on 19 March 1969. Their four wins all came at home and only three points were derived away. They finished 12 points beneath the second from bottom club Leicester City.

Glossop only achieved 18 points in 34 Division One matches in 1899–1900. It was their only season in the division and they won just four matches. The club resigned from the League in 1919.

Notts County achieved only 18 points in 34 Division One matches in 1904–05. They won only five matches but despite finishing bottom were re-elected to Division One on its extension of 20 clubs.

Woolwich Arsenal achieved only 18 points in 38 Division One matches in 1912–13. They won only three matches. They did not win promotion to Division One but were elected to it on the extension to 22 clubs in 1919.

Doncaster Rovers achieved only eight points in 34 matches in Division Two in 1904–05. Their nearest rivals were 12 points away. They were not re-elected. Originally they gained admission in 1901 but dropped out two years later only to be re-elected in 1904. Subsequently they returned to the League as members of Division Three (Northern) in 1923.

Loughborough Town achieved only eight points in 34 Division Two matches in 1899–1900. They won only one match and were not re-elected. They conceded 100 goals. Yet the previous season they had beaten Darwen 10–0 for their highest scoring victory.

Rochdale achieved only 21 points in 46 Division Three matches in 1973–74. They won only twice, including once away in September. In February a home match with Cambridge United attracted only 450 spectators.

Merthyr Town achieved only 21 points in 42 Division Three (Southern) matches in 1924–25 and equalled this figure in 1929–30. They won eight matches in the former season suffering 29 defeats but only six in the latter when they conceded a record 135 goals and were not re-elected.

Queen's Park Rangers achieved only 21 points in 42 matches in Division Three (Southern) in 1925–26. They had to apply for re-election for the second time in three years. Their nearest rivals were Charlton Athletic and Exeter City, 14 points above them.

Rochdale achieved only eleven points in 40 matches in Division Three (Northern) in 1931–32. They suffered 33 defeats, including 17 in succession. They also suffered a record 13 in consecutive home defeats after beating New Brighton 3–2 on 7 November 1931. Wigan Borough's withdrawal from the League meant only 40 matches were played that season.

Workington achieved only 19 points in 46 matches in Division Four in 1976–77. Only two points came from their last 13 games and 102 goals were conceded. They finished bottom six points behind their nearest rivals and were not re-elected.

LEAGUE WINS

Most wins in single season

Tottenham Hotspur won 31 of their 42 Division One matches in 1960–61. They finished eight points ahead of Sheffield Wednesday to win the championship with 66 points. Of their 115 goals all but 14 were from their most regularly called upon five forwards. The same season they achieved the League and Cup double, the third team to accomplish the feat. Only four other sides have scored more in Division One.

Tottenham Hotspur also won 32 of their 42 Division Two matches in 1919–20. Nineteen of these came from home wins but it was a 3–1 win, at Stoke on 10 April that ensured the club of winning the championship.

Plymouth Argyle won 30 of their 42 Division Three (Southern) matches in 1929–30. They had finished as runners-up six times in succession during the previous eight seasons. But not until the 19th match did they lose and their total of 68 points was a club record. Yet they had started the season £6000 in debt.

Millwall won 30 of their 42 Division Three (Southern) matches in 1927–28. Nineteen of these came from home wins where only two points were dropped in drawn matches.

Cardiff City won 30 of their 42 Division Three (Southern) matches in 1946–47. Eighteen of these came from home wins where just three points were dropped in drawn matches. Only eleven goals were conceded at home.

Nottingham Forest won 30 of their 46 Division Three (Southern) matches in 1950–51. Sixteen of these came from home wins. Only six matches were lost overall and ten drawn. The club also achieved a record 70 points and a record total of 110 goals. Thirty-two points were contributed from away matches.

Bristol City also won 30 of their 46 Division Three (Southern) matches in 1954–55. Thirteen came from away wins. The club also achieved a record 70 points.

Doncaster Rovers won 33 of their 42 Division Three (Northern) matches in 1946–47. They won 18 away matches, taking 37 points, lost only three times overall and won a record 72 points.

Aston Villa won 32 of their 46 Division Three matches in 1971–72. Twenty matches were won at home including eleven consecutively between October and March.

The Aston Villa first team squad during their successful 1971–72 season. *Terry Weir*

Lincoln City won 32 of their 46 Division Four matches in 1975–76. Twenty-one of these came from home wins. Only two points were dropped in drawn games on their own ground. The club also set records for most wins, most points and fewest defeats in a season in the division.

Record home wins in single season

Brentford won all 21 games in Division Three (Southern) in 1929–30.

Record away wins in single season

Doncaster won 18 of 21 games in Division Three (Northern) in 1946–47.

Most drawn games in single season

Norwich City drew 23 of their 42 Division One matches in 1978–79. They finished 16th in the division, drawing 10 times at home and 13 away in gaining 37 points. In 1978–79 Carlisle United had equalled the previous record of 22 drawn games in Division Three which had been held by three clubs: Tranmere Rovers in Division Three in 1970–71; Aldershot in Divison Four in 1971–72 and Chester in Division Three in 1977–78. Carlisle had finished sixth, with Tranmere (18th), Aldershot (17th) and Chester (fifth).

LEAGUE DEFEATS

Most defeats in single season

Leeds United suffered 30 defeats in 42 Division One matches in 1946–47. Ten came from home matches and 20 away. Only six matches were won all at home. They defeated Huddersfield Town 5–0.

Blackburn Rovers suffered 30 defeats in 42 Division One matches in 1965–66. Fourteen came from home matches and 16 away. Eight matches were won and they included 6–1 and 5–0 wins at home and 4–1 and 3–0 successes away.

Tranmere Rovers suffered 31 defeats in 42 Division Two matches in 1938–39. They finished 14 points beneath their nearest rivals and picked up only one point from away games.

Newport County suffered 31 defeats in 46 Division Three matches in 1961–62. Twelve of these came from home matches. Their heaviest defeat was 8–1 at Notts County.

The Port Vale team which established a fine reputation in defence in the 1953–54 season and also reached the FA Cup semi-final

Merthyr Town suffered 29 defeats in 42 Division Three (Southern) matches in 1924–25. Their 21 points was a record low for the division. They achieved only two points from away games both drawn.

Rochdale suffered 33 defeats in 40 Division Three (Northern) matches in 1931–32. Only eleven points were taken, including just one away from home. 135 goals were conceded and their nearest rivals were 13 points above them.

Workington suffered 32 defeats in 46 Division Four matches in 1975–76. Fourteen of these came from home matches and only 21 points were achieved. The record would have been worse but for recording their only two away wins in the last two games of the season.

Fewest defeats in single season

Preston North End went through 22 Division One matches in 1888–89 without a defeat. Only four points were dropped, including just one at home to Aston Villa on 10 November, the runners-up who finished eleven points behind them.

Leeds United suffered only two defeats in 42 Division One matches in 1968–69. These occurred on 28 September at Manchester City when they lost 3–1 and at Burnley on 19 October when they were beaten 5–1. After this defeat Leeds had a run of 28 undefeated matches until the end of the season.

Liverpool went through 28 Division Two matches without defeat in 1893–94. They won 22 and drew six of their matches. They then won their test match for promotion and drew the first two games of the following season to establish a run of 31 matches without defeat.

Burnley suffered only two defeats in 30 Division Two matches in 1897–98. They won 20 and drew eight of their games. Included among the 80 goals they scored was a 9–3 victory over Loughborough Town.

Bristol City suffered only two defeats in 38 Division Two matches in 1905–06. They won 30 and drew six of their matches. Thirty-one of their points came from away matches which produced 13 wins and five draws. They also won 14 consecutive League matches.

Leeds United suffered only three defeats in 42 Division Two matches in 1963–64. They won 24 matches which was one fewer than runners-up Sunderland who finished two points below them.

Queen's Park Rangers suffered five defeats in 46 Division Three matches in 1966–67. They won 26 and drew 15 of their matches. They finished 12 points ahead of runners-up Middlesbrough and scored 103 goals while conceding only 38. The same season they won the League Cup.

Southampton suffered only four defeats in 42 Division Three (Southern) matches in 1921–22. They conceded just 21 goals, a record for the division. Their 61 points was also a club record. Among their wins was an 8–0 success over Northampton Town. However, they won 23 matches, two fewer than Plymouth Argyle who finished as runners-up on goal average behind them.

Plymouth Argyle suffered only four defeats in 42 Division Three (Southern) matches in 1929–30. Their 68 points was a club record. They conceded only 38 goals and won 30 of their matches.

Port Vale suffered only three defeats in 46 Division Three (Northern) matches in 1953–54. They won 26 matches and drew 17. Both figures were better than those of any of their rivals and they finished eleven points ahead of Barnsley, the runners-up.

Doncaster Rovers suffered only three defeats in 42 Division Three (Northern) matches in 1946–47. Of their record 33 wins, 18 came away and they established a record of 72 points as well.

Wolverhampton Wanderers suffered only three defeats in 42 Division Three (Northern) matches in 1923–24. Twenty-four matches were won, one fewer than achieved by the runners-up Rochdale who finished a point behind. Fifteen matches were drawn by Wolves and only 27 goals conceded, one more than Rochdale.

Lincoln City suffered only four defeats in 46 Division Four matches in 1975–76. They won 32 matches, achieved a record 74 points and scored 111 goals.

Fewest wins in single season

Stoke achieved only three wins in 22 Division One matches in 1889–90. They finished bottom with ten points, only two fewer than the previous season when they had won only four matches. They failed to gain re-election but subsequently returned to the League in 1891 when it was extended to 14 clubs.

Woolwich Arsenal achieved only three wins in 38 Division One matches in 1912–13. They also amassed just 18 points. They scored only 26 goals, finished bottom and were relegated to the Second Division.

Loughborough Town achieved only one win in 34 Divison Two matches in 1899–1900. They drew six games but finished bottom, ten points beneath their nearest rivals Luton Town. They scored only 18 goals and conceded 100. They failed to gain re-election.

Merthyr Town achieved six wins in 42 Division Three (Southern) matches in 1929–30. They won one away game and drew nine overall but finished bottom nine points behind Gillingham.

Rochdale achieved four wins in 40 Division Three (Northern) matches in 1931–32. They suffered 33 defeats, including 17 in succession, as well as a record 13 consecutive home defeats.

Rochdale achieved only two wins in 46 Division Three matches in 1973–74. They played the last 22 matches without a win and achieved only nine points from them in drawn games.

Southport achieved only three wins in 46 matches in Division Four in 1976–77. But they managed to finish six points above the bottom club Workington.

SEQUENCES

After losing 1–0 at Leeds United's Elland Road ground on 19 November 1977, Nottingham Forest completed 42 Division One matches without defeat until losing 2–0 at Anfield against Liverpool on 9 December 1978. They drew 21 and won the other 21 matches. On 30 September 1978 their 2–1 win at Aston Villa had equalled Leeds United's record of 34 matches without defeat, established in the 1968–69 and 1969–70 seasons.

Leeds United were undefeated in the first 29 matches of the 1973–74 season before losing 3–2 at Stoke City on 23 February 1974. This is a Football League record from the start of the season.

Liverpool were unbeaten in all 28 matches (winning 22, drawing six) in Division Two during the 1893–94 season. They also won their 29th match, the extra 'Test Match' (used to decide promotion and relegation between the top two divisions) and the first two matches of the 1894–95 season in Division One before losing 2–1 to Aston Villa on 8 September 1894. In all there had been 31 games without defeat. They

were the first club to win the Division Two championship without losing.

Winning Sequences

Manchester United won 14 successive Division Two matches in the 1904–05 season, an achievement which was equalled by Bristol City in 1905–06 and Preston North End in 1950–51.

Tottenham Hotspur won eleven successive Division One matches from the start of 1960–61. They also achieved eight consecutive away wins and a total of 16 throughout the season.

Huddersfield Town completed 18 away matches in Division One without defeat between 15 November 1924 and 14 November 1925, winning 12 and drawing six.

Losing Sequences

Crewe Alexandra went 30 Division Three (Northern) matches in the 1956–57 season without a win. After defeating Scunthorpe United 2–1 on 19 September they did not achieve victory again until 13 April when they beat Bradford City 1–0. Crewe finished bottom with 21 points and were forced to seek re-election.

Manchester United lost their first 12 matches in Division One during the 1930–31 season. The first win was 2–0 against Birmingham at Old Trafford on 1 November 1930. They did not recover from this disastrous start and finished bottom with 22 points, nine points behind their nearest rivals.

Rochdale lost 17 successive Division Three (Northern) matches in 1931–32. After defeating New Brighton 3–2 on 7 November 1931 they had to wait until drawing 1–1 with the same opposition on 9 March 1932. Rochdale finished bottom with only eleven points from 40 matches, as Wigan Borough had resigned.

Nelson played 24 away matches in Division Three (Northern) without achieving a point. Their 1–1 draw with Halifax Town on 29 March 1930 had been their last away from home because they failed to gain re-election at the end of the 1930–31 season.

Merthyr played 61 away matches in Division Three (Southern) without a win between September 1922 and September 1925. In the 1922–23 season they still finished 17th, were 11th the following season and 13th in 1923–24. But in 1924–25 they were bottom with 21 points.

LEAGUE GOALS

Fewest goals conceded in single season

Liverpool conceded only 16 goals in 42 Division One matches in 1978–79. Goalkeeper Ray Clemence, who played in every match, was beaten three times on one occasion away to Aston Villa on 16 April 1979 in a 3–1 defeat, but did not let more than one goal past him in any other game. On 28 occasions he kept a clean sheet, including 17 times at home where just four goals were conceded. Liverpool were champions eight points ahead of Nottingham Forest who had shared with them the previous lowest-goals total of 24. Liverpool achieved 85 goals themselves, the highest by the League champions since 1967–68. They conceded only seven goals in the last 21 games.

Manchester United conceded only 23 goals in 42 Division Two matches in 1924–25. Only a late revival in which they took as many points in their last six matches as they had achieved in the previous eleven, enabled them to gain promotion in second place. Significantly they drew their last match at Barnsley 0–0.

Southampton conceded 21 goals in 42 Division Three (Southern) matches in 1921–22. They were champions and were promoted, but with two matches remaining Plymouth Argyle had led them by four points. However, while Southampton won twice, Plymouth lost their last two games and were edged out on goal average.

Port Vale conceded 21 goals in 46 Division Three (Northern) matches in 1953–54. The three games they lost also established a record for fewest defeats. Only five goals were conceded at home in four matches. Port Vale kept a clean sheet in 30 games overall. And in winning the championship they had an 11 point lead over runners-up Barnsley.

Rotherham United conceded 32 goals in 46 Division Three matches in 1980–81. They were champions finishing two points ahead of Barnsley and Charlton Athletic. Though they had as many as three goals scored against them on two occasions they kept their goal intact 24 times, including six successive games all of which were won. However, in their first 13 matches they had let in 13 goals and a new record seemed unlikely at the time.

Lincoln City conceded 25 goals in 46 Division Four matches in 1980–81. They were runners-up two points behind the champions Southend United who conceded only 31 goals themselves. Two goals were the most City let in during any one match and this occurred just four times in

Tottenham Hotspur in 1961, taking the opportunity of some Middle East sun during a break from the rigours of the Football League. *Bill Nicholson*

the season. They kept their goal intact on 25 occasions. From December to mid-March they also completed 14 matches without defeat.

Fewest goals scored in single season

Leicester City scored only 26 goals in 42 Division One matches in 1977–78. Three goals on one occasion was their highest total. They failed to score at all in 23 matches. They finished bottom, with an inferior goal difference to Newcastle United and ten points beneath the third relegated club West Ham United.

Watford scored only 24 goals in 42 Division Two matches in 1971–72. They also failed to score more than two goals in any one match and did not score at all in 23. In the second half of the season they achieved only six goals in 21 matches.

Crystal Palace scored only 33 goals in 42 Division Three (Southern) matches in 1950–51. Though they reached four goals in two occasions, they failed to score at all in 24 games.

Crewe Alexandra scored only 32 goals in 42 Division Three (Northern) matches in 1923–24. They did however manage to achieve 27 points, two more than the bottom two clubs.

Stockport County scored only 27 goals in 46 Division Three matches in 1969–70. Three goals on one occasion was their highest total. They failed to score at all in 25 matches. They finished bottom, seven points beneath their nearest rivals Barrow.

Crewe Alexandra achieved only 29 goals in Division Four during 1981–82. They failed to score at all in 23 matches, exactly half of their programme. They managed three goals on one occasion when they beat Scunthorpe United 3–0 on 10 October 1981, their first League win after eight consecutive defeats. Only ten goals were scored away and they were bottom of the table for most of the season, reaching 22nd place just for two weeks in November.

Most goals scored in single season (Team)

Aston Villa scored 128 goals in 42 Division One matches during 1930–31. They scored in every home match and failed in only three away. Eighty-six goals came at home and in 20 games four goals or more were recorded. At Villa Park, Middlesbrough were beaten 8–1; Manchester United 7–0; Huddersfield Town 6–1 and Arsenal 5–1. Villa also won 6–1 at Huddersfield

and 4–0 at Birmingham. Top scorer was Pongo Waring with 49 goals, while Eric Houghton had 30. Yet Villa could only finish runners-up, seven points behind Arsenal.

Middlesbrough scored 122 goals in 42 Division Two matches during 1926–27. On three occasions they scored seven goals: against Portsmouth and Swansea at home and also at Grimsby, while they managed six on two other occasions. Portsmouth in fact finished eight points behind them but were also promoted. Yet Middlesbrough took only one point and scored just one goal in their first four League matches. In the fourth they brought in George Camsell who ended the season as their top scorer with 59 goals. His total included eight hat-tricks.

Millwall scored 127 goals in 42 Division Three (Southern) matches in 1927–28. Unbeaten at home where they dropped only two points, Millwall also won eleven times away and finished ten points ahead of second placed Northampton Town. Millwall achieved 9–1 wins against Torquay United and Coventry City as well as scoring seven goals once and six on four occasions including once away. However, they themselves were also beaten 5–0 and 6–1 away.

Bradford City scored 128 goals in 42 Division Three (Northern) matches in 1928–29. They managed double figures in their opening League game at home to Rotherham United whom they defeated 11–1, in what proved to be the club's record victory. Promotion was not decided until the last match of the season, however, with Stockport County finishing one point behind them. Top scorer Albert Whitehurst, secured during the season, was leading scorer with 24 goals in only 15 matches, including seven in succession against Tranmere Rovers on 6 March 1929 in an 8–0 win.

City not only habitually scored more goals than the opposition but they were so often in total command that they prevented their opponents from scoring. In one run of five League games during March that season they reached a total of 29 goals without reply in this sequence: 8–0, 8–0, 5–0, 5–0 and 3–0. Indeed, around this period this astonishing team netted 43 goals in 12 games during which they conceded only two goals and not more than one in a particular game. Yet the club had faced liquidation at the end of the previous season and was almost wound up.

Queen's Park Rangers scored 111 goals in 46 Division Three matches in 1961–62. On three occasions they scored six goals but also lost 6–3 at home to Reading. They could finish no higher than fourth and Bournemouth who were third edged them out on goal average despite scoring 42 fewer goals.

Peterborough United scored 134 goals in 46 Division Four matches in 1960–61. Seven goals were reached twice, six on four occasions including once away at Stockport, who were ironically the only side to prevent Peterborough from scoring at home during the season. Terry Bly was top scorer with 52 League goals, a record for the division. The second best supported team in the division at home with an average of 14 222, Peterborough produced the highest support away with 12 182 on average in their first season in the Football League.

Most goals against in single season (Team)

Blackpool conceded 125 goals in 42 Division One matches during 1930–31. Their heaviest defeat, 10–1, a club record, was against Huddersfield Town on 13 December 1930. Seven goals were conceded on three occasions, including at home to Leeds United in a 7–3 defeat. But Blackpool escaped relegation by one point, finishing above Leeds. The previous season they had won promotion as Division Two champions with record points and goals.

Darwen conceded 141 goals in 34 Division Two matches during 1898–99. It proved the last season in the club's eventful eight seasons in the League and they suffered three 10–0 defeats away, gathering only nine points from a possible 68 and were not re-elected.

Merthyr Town conceded 135 goals in 42 Division Three (Southern) matches in 1929–30. They were bottom, nine points beneath their nearest rivals. Coventry City still have the cheque they received as their share of the receipts from a midweek match at Merthyr's Penydarren Park in April 1930 which amounted to 18s. 4d (92p). Merthyr were not re-elected in what was their third plea for re-admission. Between September 1922 and September 1925 they had created a Football League record with a run of 61 away games without a win. And in 1924–25 they suffered 29 defeats overall in 42 matches, a record for the division.

Nelson conceded 136 goals in 42 Division Three (Northern) matches in 1927–28. These included conceding nine goals in one match, eight in another and seven in a third. But they had had

their own scoring successes earlier. In 1924–25 they scored seven on two occasions, while in their most prolific season 1926–27 a total of 104 goals included two more scores of seven. In 1925–26 they also scored seven goals in successive games.

Accrington Stanley conceded 123 goals in 46 Division Three matches in 1959 60. But only once did they concede as many as six goals. And they took more points (14) from away matches than at home.

Hartlepool United conceded 109 goals in 46 Division Four matches in 1959–60. Seven goals were conceded once and six on two occasions.

Bristol Derby Matches

BRISTOL CITY v BRISTOL ROVERS

Bristol City were founded in 1894 as Bristol South End and became known under their present title in 1897. Bristol Rovers were founded in 1883 as Black Arabs, changed to Eastville Rovers in 1884, Bristol Eastville Rovers in 1897 and became known as Bristol Rovers in 1898.

League meetings between the two clubs have resulted in Bristol City winning 24 matches, Rovers 14 with the other 20 drawn.

Bristol City's home games with their score first:

Season	Score
1922–23	0–1
1924–25	2–0
1925–26	0–0
1926–27	3–1
1932–33	3–1
1933–34	0–3
1934–35	1–1
1935–36	0–2
1936–37	4–1
1937–38	0–0
1938–39	2–1
1946–47	4–0

*Bristol Derby
Matches continued*

1947–48	5–2
1948–49	1–1
1949–50	1–2
1950–51	1–0
1951–52	1–1
1952–53	0–0
1955–56	1–1
1956–57	5–3
1957–58	3–2
1958–59	1–1
1959–60	2–1
1962–63	4–1
1963–64	3–0
1964–65	2–1
1974–75	1–1
1975–76	1–1
1981–82	1–2

Bristol City's Ashton Gate ground, complete with sprinkler in action. *Peter Bateman*

Bristol Rovers' home games with their score first:

Season	Score
1922–23	1–2
1924–25	0–0
1925–26	0–1
1926–27	0–5
1932–33	1–1
1933–34	5–1
1934–35	2–2
1935–36	1–1
1936–37	3–1
1937–38	1–0
1938–39	1–1
1946–47	0–3
1947–48	0–2
1948–49	3–1
1949–50	2–3
1950–51	2–1
1951–52	2–0
1952–53	0–0
1955–56	0–3
1956–57	0–0
1957–58	3–3
1958–59	1–2
1959–60	2–1
1962–63	1–2
1963–64	4–0
1964–65	1–1
1974–75	1–4
1975–76	0–0
1981–82	1–0

Bristol Rovers Eastville ground with open-air terracing on one side. *Peter Bateman*

Queen's Park Rangers' decision
to instal an artificial pitch at
Loftus Road was rewarded at the
end of the season when they won
promotion to Division One.
Right: a section of the Omniturf
with its foam underlay. **Above:**
the practice of using legs on the
surface itself is something which
provided ample photographic
coverage in the testing stages.
Keith Creckendon

The Auld Firm derby is one of the most absorbing contests anywhere in the soccer calendar and New Year's Day 1983 was no exception to this scenario. Celtic won this time, beating Rangers 2–1 at Ibrox. Our pictures capture the flavour of the occasion. *J. Hendry*

Cup tie day at Old Trafford and Manchester United have the plum tie of the Third Round against West Ham United in January 1983. Below the Souvenir Shop is a point of focus before the afternoon matches, while the United bench with assistant manager Mick Brown and substitute Lou Macari are obviously pleased with what they see. *Geoff Roberts*

Above: Waiting for a corner can be fatal for defenders and attackers alike, a moment's lack of concentration can lead to either a goal or a missed opportunity of scoring; below: the West Ham bench is less happy with the outcome of events with Manager John Lyall (centre). But to a youthful fan the magic of the day is obvious. *Geoff Roberts*

Rivalry in the Merseyside derby (above) has a touch of friendly assistance by an Evertonian for a youthful Liverpool fan while the souvenirs have their appeal, all of which is in contrast to beach soccer at the Copacabana in Brazil. *Tommy Hindley*

Football League Goalscorers

(Division One from 1888–89, other divisions since 1919–20 because of the difficulty in checking earlier scorers).

Ted Drake (Arsenal)

Ginger Richardson (West Bromwich Albion)

LEADING LEAGUE GOALSCORERS 1888–1915

Season	Leading scorer	Team	Goals
1888–89	John Goodall	Preston NE	21
1889–90	Jimmy Ross	Preston NE	24
1890–91	Jack Southworth	Blackburn Rovers	26
1891–92	John Campbell	Sunderland	32
1892–93	John Campbell	Sunderland	31
1893–94	Jack Southworth	Everton	27
1894–95	John Campbell	Sunderland	22
1895–96	Johnny Campbell	Aston Villa	20
	Steve Bloomer	Derby County	20
1896–97	Steve Bloomer	Derby County	22
1897–98	Fred Wheldon	Aston Villa	21
1898–99	Steve Bloomer	Derby County	23
1899–1900	Bill Garratt	Aston Villa	27
1900–01	Steve Bloomer	Derby County	24
1901–02	James Settle	Everton	18
	Fred Priest	Sheffield Utd	18
1902–03	Alec Raybould	Liverpool	31
1903–04	Steve Bloomer	Derby County	20
1904–05	Arthur Brown	Sheffield Utd	23
1905–06	Bullet Jones	Birmingham	26
	Albert Shepherd	Bolton W	26
1906–07	Alec Young	Everton	30
1907–08	Enoch West	Nottingham F	27
1908–09	Bert Freeman	Everton	38
1909–10	John Parkinson	Liverpool	29
1910–11	Albert Shepherd	Newcastle Utd	25
1911–12	Harold Hampton	Aston Villa	25
	Dave McLean	Sheffield Wed	25
	George Holley	Sunderland	25
1912–13	David McLean	Sheffield Wed	30
1913–14	George Elliot	Middlesbrough	31
1914–15	Bobby Parker	Everton	35

DIVISION ONE 1919–39

Season	Leading scorer	Team	Goals
1919–20	Fred Morris	WBA	37
1920–21	Joe Smith	Bolton W	38
1921–22	Andy Wilson	Middlesbrough	31
1922–23	Charlie Buchan	Sunderland	30
1923–24	Wilf Chadwick	Everton	28
1924–25	Fred Roberts	Manchester City	31
1925–26	Ted Harper	Blackburn Rovers	43
1926–27	Jimmy Trotter	Sheffield Wed	37
1927–28	Dixie Dean	Everton	60
1928–29	Dave Halliday	Sunderland	43
1929–30	Vic Watson	West Ham Utd	41
1930–31	Pongo Waring	Aston Villa	49
1931–32	Dixie Dean	Everton	44
1932–33	Jack Bowers	Derby County	35
1933–34	Jack Bowers	Derby County	35
1934–35	Ted Drake	Arsenal	42
1935–36	Ginger Richardson	WBA	39
1936–37	Freddie Steele	Stoke City	33
1937–38	Tommy Lawton	Everton	28
1938–39	Tommy Lawton	Everton	35

DIVISION ONE 1946–83

Season	Leading scorer	Team	Goals
1946–47	Dennis Westcott	Wolverhampton W	37
1947–48	Ronnie Rooke	Arsenal	33
1948–49	Willie Moir	Bolton W	25
1949–50	Dickie Davis	Sunderland	25
1950–51	Stan Mortensen	Blackpool	30
1951–52	George Robledo	Newcastle U	33
1952–53	Charlie Wayman	Preston NE	24
1953–54	Jimmy Glazzard	Huddersfield Town	29
	Johnny Nicholls	WBA	29
1954–55	Ronnie Allen	WBA	27
1955–56	Nat Lofthouse	Bolton W	33
1956–57	John Charles	Leeds United	38
1957–58	Bobby Smith	Tottenham Hotspur	36
1958–59	Jimmy Greaves	Chelsea	32
1959–60	Dennis Viollet	Manchester United	32
1960–61	Jimmy Greaves	Chelsea	41
1961–62	Ray Crawford	Ipswich Town	33
	Derek Kevan	WBA	33
1962–63	Jimmy Greaves	Tottenham Hotspur	37
1963–64	Jimmy Greaves	Tottenham Hotspur	35
1964–65	Jimmy Greaves	Tottenham Hotspur	29
	Andy McEvoy	Blackburn Rovers	29

1965–66	Roger Hunt	Liverpool	30
1966–67	Ron Davies	Southampton	37
1967–68	George Best	Manchester United	28
	Ron Davies	Southampton	28
1968–69	Jimmy Greaves	Tottenham Hotspur	27
1969–70	Jeff Astle	WBA	25
1970–71	Tony Brown	WBA	28
1971–72	Francis Lee	Manchester City	33
1972–73	Bryan Robson	West Ham United	28
1973–74	Mick Channon	Southampton	21
1974–75	Malcolm Macdonald	Newcastle U	21
1975–76	Ted MacDougall	Norwich City	23
1976–77	Malcolm Macdonald	Arsenal	25
	Andy Gray	Aston Villa	25
1977–78	Bob Latchford	Everton	30
1978–79	Frank Worthington	Bolton W	24
1979–80	Phil Boyer	Southampton	23
1980–81	Steve Archibald	Tottenham Hotspur	20
	Peter Withe	Aston Villa	20
1981–82	Kevin Keegan	Southampton	26
1982–83	Luther Blissett	Watford	27

DIVISION TWO 1919–39

Season	Leading scorer	Team	Goals
1919–20	Sam Taylor	Huddersfield Town	35
1920–21	Syd Puddefoot	West Ham United	29
1921–22	Jimmy Broad	Stoke City	25
1922–23	Harry Bedford	Blackpool	32
1923–24	Harry Bedford	Blackpool	34
1924–25	Arthur Chandler	Leicester City	33
1925–26	Bob Turnbull	Chelsea	39
1926–27	George Camsell	Middlesbrough	59
1927–28	Jimmy Cookson	WBA	38
1928–29	Jimmy Hampson	Blackpool	40
1929–30	Jimmy Hampson	Blackpool	45
1930–31	Dixie Dean	Everton	39
1931–32	Cyril Pearce	Swansea Town	35
1932–33	Ted Harper	Preston NE	37
1933–34	Pat Glover	Grimsby Town	42
1934–35	Jack Milsom	Bolton W	31
1935–36	Jock Dodds	Sheffield Utd	34
	Bob Finan	Blackpool	34
1936–37	Jack Bowers	Leicester City	33
1937–38	George Henson	Bradford PA	27
1938–39	Hugh Billington	Luton Town	28

DIVISION TWO 1946–83

Season	Leading scorer	Team	Goals
1946–47	Charlie Wayman	Newcastle U	30
1947–48	Eddie Quigley	Sheffield W	23
1948–49	Charlie Wayman	Southampton	32
1949–50	Tommy Briggs	Grimsby Town	35
1950–51	Cecil McCormack	Barnsley	33
1951–52	Derek Dooley	Sheffield W	46
1952–53	Arthur Rowley	Leicester City	39
1953–54	John Charles	Leeds United	42
1954–55	Tommy Briggs	Blackburn Rovers	33
1955–56	Bill Gardiner	Leicester City	34
1956–57	Arthur Rowley	Leicester City	44
1957–58	Tom Johnston	Leyton Orient (35) and Blackburn Rovers (8)	43
1958–59	Brian Clough	Middlesbrough	42
1959–60	Brian Clough	Middlesbrough	39
1960–61	Ray Crawford	Ipswich Town	39
1961–62	Roger Hunt	Liverpool	41
1962–63	Bobby Tambling	Chelsea	35
1963–64	Ron Saunders	Portsmouth	33
1964–65	George O'Brien	Southampton	34
1965–66	Martin Chivers	Southampton	30
1966–67	Bobby Gould	Coventry City	24
1967–68	John Hickton	Middlesbrough	24
1968–69	John Toshack	Cardiff City	22
1969–70	John Hickton	Middlesbrough	24
1970–71	John Hickton	Middlesbrough	25
1971–72	Bob Latchford	Birmingham City	23
1972–73	Don Givens	QPR	23
1973–74	Duncan McKenzie	Nottingham Forest	26
1974–75	Brian Little	Aston Villa	20
1975–76	Derek Hales	Charlton Athletic	28
1976–77	Mickey Walsh	Blackpool	26
1977–78	Bob Hatton	Blackpool	22
1978–79	Bryan Robson	West Ham United	24
1979–80	Clive Allen	QPR	28
1980–81	David Cross	West Ham United	22
1981–82	Ronnie Moore	Rotherham United	22
1982–83	Gary Lineker	Leicester City	26

DIVISION THREE (SOUTH) 1920–39

Season	Leading scorer	Team	Goals
1920–21	John Connor	Crystal Palace	28
	Ernie Simms	Luton Town	28
	George Whitworth	Northampton Town	28
1921–22	Frank Richardson	Plymouth Argyle	31
1922–23	Fred Pagnam	Watford	30
1923–24	Billy Haines	Portsmouth	28
1924–25	Jack Fowler	Swansea Town	28
1925–26	Jack Cock	Plymouth Argyle	32
1926–27	Harry Morris	Swindon Town	47
1927–28	Harry Morris	Swindon Town	38
1928–29	Andrew Rennie	Luton Town	43
1929–30	George Goddard	QPR	37
1930–31	Peter Simpson	Crystal Palace	46
1931–32	Clarrie Bourton	Coventry City	49
1932–33	Clarrie Bourton	Coventry City	40
1933–34	Albert Dawes	Northampton T (11) and Crystal Palace (16)	27
1934–35	Ralph Allen	Charlton Athletic	32
1935–36	Albert Dawes	Crystal Palace	38
1936–37	Joe Payne	Luton Town	55
1937–38	Harry Crawshaw	Mansfield Town	25
1938–39	Ben Morton	Swindon Town	28

**Pat Glover
(Grimsby Town)**

DIVISION THREE (SOUTH) 1946–58

Season	Leading scorer	Team	Goals
1946–47	Don Clark	Bristol City	36
1947–48	Len Townsend	Bristol City	29
1948–49	Don McGibbon	Bournemouth	30
1949–50	Tommy Lawton	Notts County	31
1950–51	Wally Ardron	Nottingham Forest	36
1951–52	Ronnie Blackman	Reading	39
1952–53	Geoff Bradford	Bristol Rovers	33
1953–54	Jack English	Northampton Town	28
1954–55	Ernie Morgan	Gillingham	31
1955–56	Sammy Collins	Torquay United	40
1956–57	Ted Phillips	Ipswich Town	41
1957–58	Sam McCrory	Southend United	31
	Derek Reeves	Southampton	31

DIVISION THREE (NORTH) 1921–39

Season	Leading scorer	Team	Goals
1921–22	Jim Carmichael	Grimsby Town	37
1922–23	George Beel	Chesterfield	23
	Jim Carmichael	Grimsby Town	23
1923–24	David Brown	Darlington	27
1924–25	David Brown	Darlington	39
1925–26	Jimmy Cookson	Chesterfield	44
1926–27	Albert Whitehurst	Rochdale	44
1927–28	Joe Smith	Stockport County	38
1928–29	Jimmy McConnell	Carlisle United	43
1929–30	Frank Newton	Stockport County	36
1930–31	Jimmy McConnell	Carlisle United	37
1931–32	Alan Hall	Lincoln City	42
1932–33	Bill McNaughton	Hull City	39
1933–34	Alf Lythgoe	Stockport County	46
1934–35	Gilbert Alsop	Walsall	40
1935–36	Bunny Bell	Tranmere Rovers	33
1936–37	Ted Harston	Mansfield Town	55
1937–38	John Roberts	Port Vale	28
1938–39	Sam Hunt	Carlisle United	32

DIVISION THREE (NORTH) 1946–58

Season	Leading scorer	Team	Goals
1946–47	Clarrie Jordan	Doncaster Rovers	42
1947–48	Jimmy Hutchinson	Lincoln City	32
1948–49	Wally Ardron	Rotherham United	29
1949–50	Peter Doherty	Doncaster Rovers	26
	Reg Phillips	Crewe Alex	26
1950–51	Jack Shaw	Rotherham United	37
1951–52	Andy Graver	Lincoln City	36
1952–53	Jimmy Whitehouse	Carlisle United	29
1953–54	Jack Connor	Stockport County	31
1954–55	Jack Connor	Stockport County	30
	Arthur Bottom	York City	30
	Don Travis	Oldham Athletic	30
1955–56	Bob Crosbie	Grimsby Town	36
1956–57	Ray Straw	Derby County	37
1957–58	Alf Ackerman	Carlisle United	35

DIVISION THREE 1958–83

Season	Leading scorer	Team	Goals
1958–59	Jim Towers	Brentford	32
1959–60	Derek Reeves	Southampton	39
1960–61	Tony Richards	Walsall	36
1961–62	Cliff Holton	Northampton T (36) and Walsall (1)	37
1962–63	George Hudson	Coventry City	30
1963–64	Alf Biggs	Bristol Rovers	30
1964–65	Ken Wagstaff	Mansfield Town (8) and Hull City (23)	31
1965–66	Les Allen	QPR	30
1966–67	Rodney Marsh	QPR	30
1967–68	Don Rogers	Swindon Town	25
	Bobby Owen	Bury	25
1968–69	Brian Lewis	Luton Town	22
	Don Rogers	Swindon Town	22
1969–70	George Jones	Bury	26
1970–71	Gerry Ingram	Preston NE	22
	Dudley Roberts	Mansfield Town	22
1971–72	Ted MacDougall	Bournemouth	35
	Alf Wood	Shrewsbury Town	35
1972–73	Bruce Bannister	Bristol Rovers	25
	Arthur Horsfield	Charlton Athletic	25
1973–74	Billy Jennings	Watford	26
1974–75	Dixie McNeil	Hereford United	31
1975–76	Dixie McNeil	Hereford United	35
1976–77	Peter Ward	Brighton & HA	32
1977–78	Alex Bruce	Preston NE	27
1978–79	Ross Jenkins	Watford	29
1979–80	Terry Curran	Sheffield Wed	22
1980–81	Tony Kellow	Exeter City	25
1981–82	Gordon Davies	Fulham	24
1982–83	Kerry Dixon	Reading	26

DIVISION FOUR 1958–83

Season	Leading scorer	Team	Goals
1958–59	Arthur Rowley	Shrewsbury Town	37
1959–60	Cliff Holton	Watford	42
1960–61	Terry Bly	Peterborough U	52
1961–62	Bobby Hunt	Colchester United	41
1962–63	Ken Wagstaff	Mansfield Town	34
	Colin Booth	Doncaster Rovers	34
1963–64	Hugh McIlmoyle	Carlisle United	39
1964–65	Alick Jeffrey	Doncaster Rovers	36
1965–66	Kevin Hector	Bradford PA	44
1966–67	Ernie Phythian	Hartlepools United	23
1967–68	Roy Chapman	Port Vale	25
	Les Massie	Halifax Town	25
1968–69	Gary Talbot	Chester	22
1969–70	Albert Kinsey	Wrexham	27
1970–71	Ted MacDougall	Bournemouth	42
1971–72	Peter Price	Peterborough U	28
1972–73	Fred Binney	Exeter City	28
1973–74	Brian Yeo	Gillingham	31
1974–75	Ray Clarke	Mansfield Town	28
1975–76	Ronnie Moore	Tranmere Rovers	34
1976–77	Brian Joicey	Barnsley	25
1977–78	Steve Phillips	Brentford	32
	Alan Curtis	Swansea City	32
1978–79	John Dungworth	Aldershot	26
1979–80	Colin Garwood	Portsmouth (17) and Aldershot (10)	27
1980–81	Alan Cork	Wimbledon	23
1981–82	Keith Edwards	Sheffield United	36
1982–83	Steve Cammack	Scunthorpe United	25

The four goals scored by **Ian Rush** for Liverpool against Everton in Division One on 6 November 1982 at Goodison Park in a 5–0 win was the first time a player had scored as many goals in a Merseyside derby since **Freddie Howe** for Liverpool against Everton at Anfield on 7 September 1935 in a 6–0 win in Division One.

Howe had started his career with Wilmslow before joining Stockport County during 1931–32. He made one League appearance in each of these two seasons before moving to Hyde in 1933. A friendship with Tommy 'Tosh' Johnson of Everton resulted in his joining Liverpool in 1934 and he scored 37 League goals in 89 League appearances during the next three seasons, including 16 in 1937–38.

A natural opportunist, his scoring feats then took him to Manchester City but after only six games and five goals he moved to Grimsby Town making 29 League appearances and scoring 15 goals.

Howe continued his goalscoring during wartime regional football and joined Oldham Athletic in 1946 for his last League season finishing with 21 goals in 30 League games.

Dick Black scored three goals in each of two Scottish League Division One matches for Morton against Celtic in the 1931–32 season. On 19 September he scored all three in a 3–3 draw at home and again on 30 January when Celtic won 6–3 at Parkhead. He scored 38 League goals that season in 37 games.

On 4 September 1982 **Bob Latchford** scored three goals for Swansea City in a Division One match against Norwich City at Vetch Field in a 4–0 win. It was his 12th hat-trick. The others had occurred with Birmingham City (five times), Everton (five) and Swansea (once previously).

4.9.71 Birmingham v Charlton Athletic, *Division Two*
28.9.71 Birmingham v Watford, *Division Two*
9.9.72 Birmingham v Manchester City, *Division One*
21.11.73 Ipswich Town v Birmingham, *League Cup 4th Round*
24.11.73 Birmingham v Leicester City, *Division One*
8.10.77 Queen's Park Rangers v Everton, *Division One*
26.11.77 Everton v Coventry City, *Division One*
29.8.78 Everton v Wimbledon, *League Cup 2nd round*
13.11.79 Everton v Leeds United, *Division One*
20.9.80 Everton v Crystal Palace, *Division One*
29.8.81 Swansea v Leeds United, *Division One*
4.9.82 Swansea v Norwich City, *Division One*

Peter Withe scored his 100th League goal for Aston Villa v Brighton and Hove Albion on 13 November 1982 in a Division One game after two and a half years at Villa Park, his longest

Bob Latchford (no. 11) celebrates with another hat-trick for Swansea City against Norwich City. *South Wales Evening Post*

Tony Brown (arm raised in delight) scores for West Bromwich Albion against Manchester City in October 1969

spell among spells with ten previous clubs: Southport, Preston North End (on loan), Barrow, Port Elizabeth City and Arcadia Shepherds (both South Africa), Wolverhampton Wanderers, Portland Timbers (USA), Birmingham City, Nottingham Forest and Newcastle United. He achieved his century in 291 League appearances having scored his first League goal for Wolves against Ipswich Town. Withe's first honour had come with another club Skelmersdale when he won a Northern Floodlit Cup winners medal. He was capped for England on six occasions.

Of players appearing in the Football League during the 1982–83 season only **Bob Hatton** had scored goals for as many as nine different clubs: Wolverhampton Wanderers, Bolton Wanderers, Northampton Town, Carlisle United, Birmingham City, Blackpool, Luton Town, Sheffield United and Cardiff City. At the end of the 1981–82 season he had reached 207 League goals.

An experimental game with no offside decisions was played at Tynecastle on 19 June 1965, Heart of Midlothian, beating Kilmarnock 8–2 with **Donald Ford** scoring five for Hearts.

Billy Meredith scored his first goal at St James Park in 1894 and his 200th on the same ground on 12 October 1907.

Of the players active in the Football League during the 1982–83 season, the most prolific marksman among them was **Bryan Robson** with Chelsea. On 20 April 1982 he had achieved his 250th League goal for Carlisle United against Exeter City in a Division Three game. He celebrated the occasion by adding two more goals for a hat-trick in Carlisle's 3–2 win.

Robson had started his scoring exploits with Newcastle United and continued them with two spells each for Sunderland and West Ham United.

Craig Madden (Bury) who established a new club goalscoring record in 1981–82. *Bury Times*

The leading marksman in Football League matches during 1981–82 was **Keith Edwards** with 36. He achieved 35 in 41 matches for Sheffield United after scoring just once in five games for Hull City at the start of the season.

The leading marksman in League and Cup games during 1981–82 was **Craig Madden** with 42 for Bury. He achieved 35 in the club's Division Four total of 90 and would have equalled Edwards's effort but for a missed penalty at Hartlepool on 8 May 1982.

Harry Stapley was a member of probably the only amateur forward line to play regularly in the Football League when he led the Glossop attack in the years before World War One.

A London-born schoolmaster he played for Bromley, Norwich CEYMS, Reading, West Ham United and Glossop. He was leading scorer for West Ham in the Southern League for three seasons 1905–06 to 1907–08 inclusive before joining Glossop.

A frail-looking centre-forward he had no shot of strength but used to roll the ball in and was a master of the swerve. He also played 12 times for England in Amateur Internationals plus three times for Great Britain in the 1908 Olympic Games.

The all-amateur Glossop attack was J E Raine, Christopher Porter, Harry Stapley, Tom Fitchie and Ivan Sharpe and Stapley scored 90 goals in seven seasons, finishing leading marksman in five of them including one as joint leader.

Percy Varco was an instant success as a goal-scorer for Norwich City after joining them in 1927. He scored ten goals in his first seven matches and finished the season with a club record 32 goals, including 29 in the League. Injury limited his appearances after this and in January 1930 he left on a free transfer for Exeter City, having scored 47 goals in 65 League and Cup matches.

With Exeter he twice returned to Norwich and scored on each occasion. But it was a broken kneecap received earlier with Queen's Park Rangers which was aggravated at Norwich which led to his removal to Exeter where he still managed to score goals. In 1930–31 he registered 23 for them in the League and 16 the following term before a brief spell with Brighton ended his career.

He had started in his native Cornwall and played for Torquay United before moving to Aston Villa for £200 in December 1923 and QPR in 1926.

He helped Exeter to reach the sixth round of the FA Cup in 1930–31, scoring five of their 17 goals. After retiring in 1933 he became a fish merchant and served two spells as Mayor of Fowey in Cornwall while running the town's Aquarium.

The first player to score 200 post-war League goals was **Wally Ardron** who had actually started his Football League career with Rotherham United, in 1938–39 making one appearance. They had signed him from Denaby United for £100 but finance of a more modest figure had nearly ended his career as a schoolboy in Swinton, Lancashire. His schoolteacher supplied the team with boots at six shillings (30p) a pair which the players had to repay at 6d (2½p) a week. Ardron paid one shilling (5p) but found the payments a problem and decided to return the boots.

The master told him to score three goals and he could keep the boots which he did.

In 1946–47 he scored 38 League goals, a club record, for Rotherham combining his football with work as a railway fireman. A fitness fanatic he had a gymnasium rigged in a bedroom in his house and excelled at weight-lifting, boxing and swimming.

He produced 27 goals in 1947–48 and was the leading scorer in Division Three (Northern) the following season with 29 goals.

Transferred to Nottingham Forest, he was their leading marksman with 25 League goals in 1949–50 and top scorer in Division Three (Southern) the following term with 36 goals, a Forest record.

He added 29 in 1951–52 and reached his double century during the following term. His League career ended after 305 League matches and 217 goals in 1954–55.

Andy Wilson scored only 13 League goals during the 1923–24 season but was leading marksman for two clubs: eight with Middlesbrough and five with Chelsea.

Les Mutrie scored in nine successive League games for Hull City during 1981–82. During this spell he achieved 14 goals and finished as leading scorer for the club in Division Four with 27.

Luton Town and Sheffield United respectively were champions of Divisions Two and Four in 1981–82. Luton scored 86 goals, Sheffield United 94 and both clubs failed to score in five matches and were each involved in four goalless draws.

Jim Forrest scored 56 goals in the 1964–65 season for Rangers. These were made up of 30 in the League, 17 in the League Cup, six in the European Cup and three in the Scottish Cup.

Wally Ardron, a prolific goalscorer in the post-war years of the Football League.
Forman Newspapers Ltd

Peter Davenport made his Football League debut for Nottingham Forest at Liverpool on 1 May 1982 in a 2–0 defeat. He failed to score in his next two outings at centre-forward but opened his account in a 2–0 win against Tottenham Hotspur and in the last League game of the season produced a hat-trick in a 3–1 win at Ipswich.

Born at Birkenhead he joined Wrexham as a schoolboy aged 14, but left three years later. After taking 'A' levels he worked with the Land Registry at Birkenhead before signing amateur forms for Everton.

But it was with Cammell Laird in the West Cheshire League that he began scoring goals and his brother Paul wrote to Nottingham Forest suggesting he was worth a trial.

Davenport scored on his Central League debut and in five months produced 22 goals in 20 outings.

Football League Club directory

(Three points for a win was only introduced from the start of the 1981–82 season; thus the relevant club records retained here are for two points. Sheffield United achieved 96 Division Four points in 1981–82, 36 more than their previous record.)

Ground	Capacity & record	League career		Honours (domestic) League	Cup

ALDERSHOT (1926) Red-blue stripes, blue trim/blue

Ground	Capacity & record	League career		League	Cup
Recreation Ground High Street Aldershot GU11 1TW 117 × 76 yd	16 000 19 138 v Carlisle FA Cup 4th Rd replay, 28 January 1970	1932–58 Div. 3 (S) 1958–73 Div. 4 1973–76 Div. 3	1976– Div 4	Highest placing 8th Div. 3 1974	FA Cup never past 5th Rd League Cup never past 2nd Rd

ARSENAL (1886) Red, white sleeves/white

Ground	Capacity & record	League career	League	Cup
Arsenal Stadium Highbury London N5 1BU 110 × 71 yd	60 000 73 295 v Sunderland Div. 1 9 March 1935	1893–1904 Div. 2 1904–13 Div. 1 1913–15 Div. 2 1919– Div. 1	Div. 1 Champions 1931, 1933, 1934, 1935, 1938, 1948, 1953, 1971 Runners-up 1926, 1932, 1973, Div 2 runners-up 1904	FA Cup winners 1930, 1936, 1950, 1971, 1979 Runners-up 1927, 1932, 1952, 1972, 1978, 1980 League Cup runners-up 1968, 1969

ASTON VILLA (1874) Claret, light blue trim/white

Ground	Capacity & record	League career		League	Cup
Villa Park Trinity Road Birmingham B6 6HE 115 × 75 yd	48 000 76 588 v Derby Co FA Cup 6th Rd 2 March 1946	1888 (founder member of League) 1936–38 Div. 2 1938–59 Div. 1 1959–60 Div. 2 1960–67 Div. 1	1967–70 Div. 2 1970–72 Div. 3 1972–75 Div. 2 1975– Div. 1	Div. 1 Champions 1864, 1896, 1897, 1899, 1900, 1910, 1981 Runners-up 1889, 1903, 1908, 1911, 1913, 1914, 1931, 1933 Div. 2 Champions 1938, 1960 Runners-up 1975 Div. 3 Champions 1972	FA Cup winners 1887,1895, 1897, 1905, 1913, 1920 1957 (joint record) Runners-up 1892, 1924 League Cup winners 1961, 1975, 1977 Runners-up 1963, 1971

BARNSLEY (1887) Red/White

Ground	Capacity & record	League career		League	Cup
Oakwell Ground Grove Street Barnsley S71 1ET 111 × 75 yd	35 554 40 255 v Stoke City FA Cup 5th Rd 15 February 1936	1898 elected to Div. 2 1932–34 Div. 3 (N) 1934–38 Div. 2 1938–39 Div. 3 (N) 1946–53 Div. 2 1953–55 Div. 3 (N)	1955–59 Div. 2 1959–65 Div. 3 1965–68 Div. 4 1968–72 Div. 3 1972–79 Div. 4 1979–81 Div. 3 1981– Div. 2	Div. 3 (N) Champions 1934, 1939, 1955 Runners-up 1954 Div. 3 Runners-up 1981 Div. 4 runners-up 1968	FA Cup winners 1912 Runners-up 1910 League Cup never past 5th Rd

Most League points	goals	Record win	Highest number of League goals in total	by season	Most League appearances	Most capped player
						ALDERSHOT
57, Div. 4 1978–79	83, Div. 4 1963–64	8–1 Gateshead Div. 4 13 September 1958	Jack Howarth 171, 1965–71 1972–77	John Dungworth 26 Div. 4 1978–79	Murray Brodie, 461, 1970–83	Peter Scott, 1, N. Ireland 1979
						ARSENAL
66, Div. 1 1930–31	127, Div. 1 1930–31	12–0 v Loughborough T. Div. 2 12 March 1900	Cliff Bastin 150, 1930–47	Ted Drake 42 Div. 1 1934–35	George Armstrong 500, 1960–77	Pat Rice 49, N. Ireland 1968–80
						ASTON VILLA
70, Div. 3 1971–72	128, Div.1 1930–31	13–0 v Wednesbury Old Athletic FA Cup 1st Rd 30 October 1886	Harry Hampton 213, 1904–20 Billy Walker 213, 1919–34	Pongo Waring 49 Div. 1 1930–31	Charlie Aitken 560, 1961–76	Peter McParland 33, N. Ireland 1954–61
						BARNSLEY
67, Div. 3 (N) 1938–39	118, Div. 3 (N) 1933–34	9–0 v Loughborough T Div. 2 28 January 1899 Accrington Stanley Div. 3 (N) 3 February 1934	Ernest Hine 123, 1921–26 1934–38	Cecil McCormack 33 Div. 2 1950–51	Barry Murphy 514, 1962–78	Eddie McMorran 9, N. Ireland 1950–52

Ground	Capacity & record	League career		Honours (domestic) League	Cup

BIRMINGHAM CITY (1875) Blue, white trim/white, blue trim

Ground	Capacity & record	League career		Honours (domestic) League	Cup
St Andrews Birmingham B9 4NH 115 × 75 yd	44 500 66 844 v Everton FA Cup 5th Rd 11 February 1939	1892–94 Div. 2 1894–96 Div. 1 1896–1901 Div. 2 1901–02 Div. 1 1902–03 Div. 2 1903–08 Div. 1 1908–21 Div. 2 1921–39 Div. 1	1946–48 Div. 2 1948–50 Div. 1 1950–55 Div. 2 1955–65 Div. 1 1965–72 Div. 2 1972–79 Div. 1 1979–80 Div. 2 1980– Div. 1	Div. 2 Champions 1893, 1921, 1948, 1955 Runners-up 1894, 1901, 1903, 1972	FA Cup runners-up 1931, 1956 League Cup winners 1963

BLACKBURN ROVERS (1875) Blue-white halves/white

Ground	Capacity & record	League career		Honours (domestic) League	Cup
Ewood Park Blackburn BB2 4JF 116 × 72 yd	25 000 61 783 v Bolton W FA Cup 6th Rd 2 March 1929	1888 (founder member of League) 1936–39 Div. 2 1946–47 Div. 1 1947–57 Div. 2 1957–66 Div. 1	1966–71 Div. 2 1971–75 Div. 3 1975–79 Div. 2 1979–80 Div. 3 1980– Div. 2	Div. 1 Champions 1912, 1914 Div. 2 Champions 1939 Runners-up 1958 Div. 3 Champions 1975 Runners-up 1980	FA Cup winners 1884, 1885, 1886 1890, 1891, 1928 Runners-up 1882, 1960 League Cup semi-finalists 1962

BLACKPOOL (1887) Tangerine, white trim/white

Ground	Capacity & record	League career		Honours (domestic) League	Cup
Bloomfield Road Blackpool FY1 6JJ 111 × 73 yd	18 000 39 118 v Manchester U Div. 1 19 April 1952	1896 elected to Div. 2 1899 failed re-election 1900 re-elected 1900–30 Div. 2 1930–33 Div. 1	1933–37 Div. 2 1937–67 Div. 1 1967–70 Div. 2 1970–71 Div. 1 1971–78 Div. 2 1978–81 Div. 3 1981– Div. 4	Div. 1 runners-up 1956 Div. 2 Champions 1930 Runners-up 1937, 1970	FA Cup winners 1953 Runners-up 1948, 1951 League Cup semi-finalists 1962

BOLTON WANDERERS (1874) White/navy blue

Ground	Capacity & record	League career		Honours (domestic) League	Cup
Burnden Park Bolton BL3 2QR 113 × 76 yd	43 000 69 912 v Manchester C FA Cup 5th Rd 18 February 1933	1888 (founder member of League) 1899–1900 Div. 2 1900–03 Div. 1 1903–05 Div. 2 1905–08 Div. 1 1908–09 Div. 2 1909–10 Div. 1	1910–11 Div. 2 1911–33 Div. 1 1933–35 Div. 2 1935–64 Div. 1 1964–71 Div.2 1971–73 Div. 3 1973–78 Div. 2 1978–80 Div. 1 1980–83 Div. 2 1983– Div. 3	Div. 2 Champions 1909, 1978 Runners-up 1900, 1905, 1911, 1935 Div. 3 Champions 1973	FA Cup winners 1923, 1926, 1929, 1958 Runners-up 1894, 1904, 1953 League Cup semi-finalists 1977

AFC BOURNEMOUTH (1899) All red

Ground	Capacity & record	League career		Honours (domestic) League	Cup
Dean Court Ground Bournemouth Dorset BH7 7AF 112 × 75 yd	19 175 28 799 v Manchester U FA Cup 6th Rd 2 March 1957	1923 elected to Div. 3(S) 1970–71 Div. 4 1971–75 Div. 3 1975–82 Div. 4 1982– Div. 3		Div. 3(S) runners-up 1948 Div. 4 runners-up 1971	FA Cup never past 6th Rd League Cup never past 4th Rd

BRADFORD CITY (1903) White with claret and amber trim/white

Ground	Capacity & record	League career		Honours (domestic) League	Cup
Valley Parade Ground Bradford BD8 7DY 110 × 76 yd	16 000 39 146 v Burnley FA Cup 4th Rd 11 March 1911	1903 elected to Div. 2 1908–22 Div. 1 1922–27 Div. 2 1927–29 Div. 3(N) 1929–37 Div. 2	1937–61 Div. 3 1961–69 Div. 4 1969–72 Div. 3 1972–77 Div. 4 1977–78 Div. 3 1978–82 Div. 4 1982– Div. 3	Div. 2 Champions 1908 Div. 3(N) Champions 1929 Div. 4 runners-up 1982	FA Cup winners 1911 League Cup never past 5th Rd

Most League points	goals	Record win	Highest number of League goals in total	by season	Most League appearances	Most capped player
						BIRMINGHAM CITY
59, Div. 2 1947–48	103, Div. 2 1893–94	12–0 v Walsall Town Swifts Div. 2 17 December 1892 Doncaster Rovers Div. 2 11 April 1903	Joe Bradford 249, 1920–35	Joe Bradford 29 Div. 1 1927–28	Gil Merrick 486, 1946–60	Malcolm Page 28, Wales 1971–79
						BLACKBURN ROVERS
60, Div. 3 1974–75	114, Div. 2 1954–55	11–0 v Rossendale United FA Cup 1st Rd 25 October 1884	Tommy Briggs 140, 1952–58	Ted Harper 43 Div. 1 1925–26	Ronnie Clayton 580, 1950–69	Bob Crompton 41, England 1902–14
						BLACKPOOL
58, Div. 2 1929–30 & 1967–68	98, Div. 2 1929–30	10–0 v Lanerossi Vicenza Anglo-Italian tournament 10 June 1972	Jimmy Hampson 247, 1927–38	Jimmy Hampson 45 Div. 2 1929–30	Jimmy Armfield 568, 1952–71	Jimmy Armfield 43, England 1959–66
						BOLTON WANDERERS
61, Div. 3 1972–73	96, Div. 2 1934–35	13–0 v Sheffield United FA Cup 2nd Rd 1 February 1890	Nat Lofthouse 255, 1946–61	Joe Smith 38 Div. 1 1920–21	Eddie Hopkinson 519, 1956–70	Nat Lofthouse 33, England 1951–58
						AFC BOURNEMOUTH
62, Div. 3 1971–72	88, Div. 3(S) 1956–57	11–0 v Margate FA Cup 1st Rd 20 November 1971	Ron Eyre 202, 1924–33	Ted MacDougall 42 Div. 4 1970–71	Ray Bumstead 412, 1958–70	Tommy Godwin 4, Eire 1956–58
						BRADFORD CITY
63, Div. 3(N) 1928–29	128, Div. 3(N) 1928–29	11–1 v Rotherham United Div. 3(N) 25 August 1928	Frank O'Rourke 88, 1906–13	David Layne 34 Div. 4 1961–62	Ian Cooper 443, 1965–77	Harry Hampton 9, N. Ireland 1911–14

Ground	Capacity & record	League career		Honours (domestic) League	Cup

BRENTFORD (1889) Red-white stripes/black

| Griffin Park
Braemar Road
Brentford
Middlesex
TW8 0NT
114 × 75 yd | 37 000
39 626 v
Preston NE
FA Cup 6th Rd
5 March 1938 | 1920 (founder
member of Div. 3)
1921–33 Div 3(S)
1933–35 Div. 2
1935–47 Div. 1
1947–54 Div. 2 | 1962–63 Div. 4
1963–66 Div. 3
1966–72 Div. 4
1972–73 Div. 3
1973–78 Div. 4
1978– Div. 3 | Div. 2 Champions
1935
Div. 3(S)
Champions 1933
Runners–up
1930, 1958 | FA Cup never
past 6th Rd
League Cup
never past
4th Rd |

BRIGHTON & HOVE ALBION (1900) All blue

| The Goldstone Ground
Old Shoreham Road
Hove, Sussex
BN3 7DE
112 × 75yd | 32 500
36 747 v
Fulham Div. 2
27 December 1958 | 1920 (founder
member of Div. 3)
1921–58 Div. 3(S)
1958–62 Div. 2
1962–63 Div. 3
1963–65 Div. 4 | 1965–72 Div. 3
1972–73 Div. 2
1973–77 Div. 3
1977–79 Div. 2
1979–83 Div. 1
1983– Div. 2 | Div. 2 Runners-up
1979
Div. 3(S)
Champions 1958
Runners-up
1954, 1956
Div. 3 runners-up
1972, 1977
Div. 4 Champions
1965 | FA Cup
runners-up
1983
League Cup
never past
5th Rd |

BRISTOL CITY (1894) Red/white

| Ashton Gate
Bristol
BS3 2EJ
115 × 75 yd | 30 868
43 335 v
Preston NE
FA Cup 5th Rd
16 February 1935 | 1901 elected
to Div. 2
1906–11 Div. 1
1911–22 Div. 2
1922–23 Div. 3(S)
1923–24 Div. 2
1924–27 Div. 3(S) | 1927–32 Div. 2
1932–55 Div. 3(S)
1955–60 Div. 2
1960–65 Div. 3
1965–76 Div. 2
1976–80 Div. 1
1980–81 Div. 2
1981–82 Div. 3
1982– Div. 4 | Div. 1 runners-up
1907
Div. 2 champions
1906
Runners-up 1976
Div. 3(S)
Champions 1923,
1927, 1955
Runners-up 1938
Div. 3 runners-up
1965 | FA Cup
runners-up
1909
League Cup
semi-finalists
1971 |

BRISTOL ROVERS (1883) Blue-white quarters/blue

| Bristol Stadium
Eastville
Bristol BS5 6NN
110 × 70 yd | 12 500
38 472 v
Preston NE
FA Cup 4th Rd
30 January 1960 | 1920 (founder
member of Div. 3)
1921–53 Div. 3(S)
1953–62 Div. 2 | 1962–74 Div. 3
1974–81 Div. 2
1981– Div. 3 | Div. 3(S)
Champions 1953
Div. 3 runners-up
1974 | FA Cup never
past 6th Rd
League Cup
never past
5th Rd |

BURNLEY (1882) Claret/Blue

| Turf Moor
Burnley
BB10 4BX
115 × 73 yd | 23 000
54 775 v
Huddersfield T
FA Cup 3rd Rd
23 February 1924 | 1888 (founder
member of
League)
1897–98 Div. 2
1898–1900 Div. 1
1900–13 Div. 2
1913–30 Div. 1 | 1930–47 Div. 2
1947–71 Div. 1
1971–73 Div. 2
1973–76 Div. 1
1976–80 Div. 2
1980–82 Div. 3
1982–83 Div. 2
1983– Div. 3 | Div. 1 Champions
1921, 1960
Runners-up
1920, 1962
Div. 2 Champions
1898, 1973
Runners-up
1913, 1947
Div. 3 Champions
1982 | FA Cup winners
1914
Runners-up
1947, 1962
League Cup
semi-finalists
1961, 1969 |

Most League points	goals	Record win	Highest number of League goals in total	by season	Most League appearances	Most capped player

BRENTFORD

| 62, Div. 3(S) 1932–33 Div. 4 1962–63 | 98, Div. 4 1962–63 | 9–0 v Wrexham Div. 3 15 October 1963 | Jim Towers 153, 1954–61 | Jack Holliday 38 Div. 3(S) 1932–33 | Ken Coote 514, 1949–64 | Idris Hopkins 12, Wales 1934–39 |

BRIGHTON & HOVE ALBION

| 65, Div. 3(S) 1955–56 Div. 3 1971–72 | 112, Div. 3(S) 1955–56 | 10–1 v Wisbech FA Cup 1st Rd 13 November 1965 | Tommy Cook 113, 1922–29 | Peter Ward 32 Div. 3 1976–77 | Tug Wilson 509, 1922–36 | Mark Lawrenson 13, Eire 1979–81 |

BRISTOL CITY

| 70, Div. 3(S) 1954–55 | 104, Div. 3(S) 1926–27 | 11–0 v Chichester FA Cup 1st Rd 5 November 1960 | John Atyeo 315, 1951–66 | Don Clark 36 Div. 3(S) 1946–47 | John Atyeo 597, 1951–66 | Billy Wedlock 26, England 1907–14 |

BRISTOL ROVERS

| 64, Div. 3(S) 1952–53 | 92, Div 3(S) 1952–53 | 7–0 v Swansea T Div. 2 2 Oct. 1954 Brighton & HA Div. 3(S) 29 Nov. 1952 Shrewsbury T Div. 3, 21 Mar. 1964 | Geoff Bradford 245, 1949–64 | Geoff Bradford 33 Div. 3(S) 1952–53 | Stuart Taylor 545, 1966–79 | Matt O'Mahoney 6, Eire; 1, N Ireland 1938–39 |

BURNLEY

| 62, Div. 2 1972–73 | 102, Div. 1 1960–61 | 9–0 v Darwen Div. 1 9 January 1892 Crystal Palace FA Cup 2nd Rd replay 27 January 1909 New Brighton FA Cup 4th Rd 26 January 1957 | George Beel 178, 1923–32 | George Beel 35 Div. 1 1927–28 | Jerry Dawson 530, 1906–29 | Jimmy McIlroy 52, N. Ireland 1951–63 |

Ground	Capacity & record	League career		Honours (domestic) League	Cup

BURY (1885) White/royal blue

| Gigg Lane
Bury
BL9 9HR
112 × 72 yd | 35 000
35 000 v
Bolton W
FA Cup 3rd Rd
9 January 1960 | 1894 elected
to Div. 2
1895–1912 Div. 1
1912–24 Div. 2
1924–29 Div. 1
1929–57 Div. 2
1957–61 Div. 3 | 1961–67 Div. 2
1967–68 Div. 3
1968–69 Div. 2
1969–71 Div. 3
1971–74 Div. 4
1974– Div. 3 | Div. 2 Champions
1895
Runners-up
1924
Div. 3 Champions
1961
Runners-up 1968 | FA Cup winners
1900, 1903
League Cup
semi-finalists
1963 |

CAMBRIDGE UNITED (1919) Amber/black

| Abbey Stadium
Newmarket Road
Cambridge CB5 8LL
115 × 75 yd | 12 500
14 000 v
Chelsea
Friendly
1 May 1970 | 1970 elected
to Div. 4
1973–74 Div. 3
1974–77 Div. 4 | 1977–78 Div. 3
1978– Div. 2 | Div. 4 Champions
1977
Div. 3 runners-up
1978 | FA Cup never
past 5th Rd
League Cup
never past
4th Rd |

CARDIFF CITY (1899) Blue/blue

| Ninian Park
Cardiff
CF1 8SX
114 × 78 yd | 43 000
57 800 v
Arsenal Div. 1
22 April 1953 | 1920 elected
to Div. 2
1921–29 Div. 1
1929–31 Div. 2
1931–47 Div. 3(S)
1947–52 Div. 2
1952–57 Div. 1 | 1957–60 Div. 2
1960–62 Div. 1
1962–75 Div. 2
1975–76 Div. 3
1982–83 Div. 3
1983– Div. 2 | Div. 1 runners-up
1924
Div. 2 runners-up
1921, 1952, 1960
Div. 3(S)
Champions 1947
Div. 3 runners-up
1976 | FA Cup winners
1927
Runners-up
1925
League Cup
semi-finalists
1966 |

CARLISLE UNITED (1904) Blue with red and white trim/blue

| Brunton Park
Carlisle
CA1 1LL
117 × 78 yd | 25 000
27 500 v
Birmingham C
FA Cup 3rd Rd
5 January 1957
and Middlesbrough
FA Cup 5th Rd
7 February 1970 | 1928 elected
to Div. 3(N)
1958–62 Div. 4
1962–63 Div. 3
1963–64 Div. 4
1964–65 Div. 3 | 1965–74 Div. 2
1974–75 Div. 1
1975–77 Div. 2
1977–82 Div. 3
1982– Div. 2 | Promoted to
Div. 1 1974
Div. 3 Champions
1965
Runners-up 1982
Div. 4 runners-up
1964 | FA Cup never
past 6th Rd
League Cup
semi-finalists
1970 |

CHARLTON ATHLETIC (1905) Red/white

| The Valley
Floyd Road
Charlton
London SE7 8AW
114 × 78 yd | 20 000
75 031 v
Aston Villa
FA Cup 5th Rd
12 February 1938 | 1921 elected
to Div. 3(S)
1929–33 Div. 2
1933–35 Div. 3(S)
1935–36 Div. 2 | 1936–57 Div. 1
1957–72 Div. 2
1972–75 Div. 3
1975–80 Div. 2
1980–81 Div. 3
1981– Div. 2 | Div. 1 runners-up
1937
Div. 2 runners-up
1936
Div. 3(S)
Champions 1929,
1935 | FA Cup winners
1947
Runners-up
1946
League Cup
never past
4th Rd |

CHELSEA (1905) Blue/blue

| Stamford Bridge
London SW6 1HS
114 × 71 yd | 45 000
82 905 v
Arsenal Div. 1
12 October 1935 | 1905 elected
to Div. 2
1907–10 Div. 1
1910–12 Div. 2
1912–24 Div. 1
1924–30 Div. 2 | 1930–62 Div. 1
1962–63 Div. 2
1963–75 Div. 1
1975–77 Div. 2
1977–79 Div. 1
1979– Div. 2 | Div. 1 Champions
1955
Div. 2 runners-up
1907, 1912, 1930,
1963, 1977 | FA Cup winners
1970
Runners-up
1915, 1967
League Cup
winners 1965
Runners-up
1972 |

Most League points	goals	Record win	Highest number of League goals in total	by season	Most League appearances	Most capped player
						BURY
68, Div. 3 1960–61	108, Div. 3 1960–61	12–1 v Stockton FA Cup 1st Rd replay 2 February 1897	Norman Bullock 124, 1920–35	Craig Madden 35 Div. 4 1981–82	Norman Bullock 506, 1920–35	Bill Gorman 11, Eire 1936–38
						CAMBRIDGE UNITED
65, Div. 4 1976–77	87, Div. 4 1976–77	6–0 v Darlington Div. 4 18 September 1971	Alan Biley 75, 1975–79	Alan Biley 21 Div. 3 1977–78	Steve Fallon 338, 1975–83	Tom Finney 7, N. Ireland 1979–80
						CARDIFF CITY
66, Div. 3(S) 1946–47	93, Div. 3(S) 1946–47	9–2 v Thames Div. 3(S) 6 February 1932	Len Davies 127, 1921–29	Stan Richards 31 Div. 3(S) 1946–47	Tom Farquharson 445, 1922–35	Alf Sherwood 39, Wales 1946–56
						CARLISLE UNITED
62, Div. 3(N) 1950–51	113, Div. 4 1963–64	8–0 v Hartlepool United Div. 3(N) 1 September 1928 Scunthorpe United Div. 3(N) 25 December 1952	Jimmy McConnell 126, 1928–32	Jimmy McConnell 42 Div. 3(N) 1928–29	Alan Ross 466, 1963–79	Eric Welsh 4, N Ireland 1966–67
						CHARLTON ATHLETIC
61, Div. 3(S) 1934–35	107, Div. 2 1957–58	8–1 Middlesbrough Div. 1 12 September 1953	Stuart Leary 153, 1953–62	Ralph Allen 32 Div. 3(S) 1934–35	Sam Bartram 583, 1934–56	John Hewie 19, Scotland 1956–60
						CHELSEA
57, Div. 2 1906–07	98, Div. 1 1960–61	13–0 v Jeunesse Hautcharage Cup-Winners' Cup 1st Rd 29 September 1971	Bobby Tambling 164, 1958–70	Jimmy Greaves 41 Div. 1 1960–61	Ron Harris 655, 1962–80	Ray Wilkins 24, England 1976–79

Ground	Capacity & record	League career		Honours (domestic) League	Cup

CHESTER (1884) Royal blue-white stripes/blue

Ground	Capacity & record	League career		League	Cup
The Stadium Sealand Road Chester CH1 4LW 114 × 76 yd	20 000 20 500 v Chelsea FA Cup 3rd Rd replay 16 January 1952	1931 elected to Div. 3(N) 1958–75 Div. 4 1975–82 Div. 3 1982– Div. 4		Div. 3(N) runners-up 1936	FA Cup never past 5th Rd League Cup semi-finalists 1975

CHESTERFIELD (1866) Royal blue/white

| Recreation Ground Chesterfield S40 4SX 114 × 72 yd | 19 750 30 968 v Newcastle U Div. 2 7 April 1939 | 1899 elected to Div. 2 1909 failed re-election 1921 elected to Div. 3(N) 1931–33 Div. 2 | 1933–36 Div. 3(N) 1936–51 Div. 2 1951–58 Div. 3(N) 1958–61 Div. 3 1970–83 Div. 3 1983– Div. 4 | Div. 3(N) Champions 1931, 1936 Runners-up 1934 Div. 4 Champions 1970 | FA Cup never past 5th Rd League Cup never past 4th Rd |

COLCHESTER UNITED (1937) Blue-white stripes/blue

| Layer Road Ground Colchester CO2 7JJ 110 × 71 yd | 16 150 19 072 v Reading FA Cup 1st Rd 27 November 1948 | 1950 elected to Div. 3(S) 1958–61 Div. 3 1961–62 Div. 4 1962–65 Div. 3 1965–66 Div. 4 | 1966–68 Div. 3 1968–74 Div. 4 1974–76 Div. 3 1976–77 Div. 4 1977–81 Div. 3 1981– Div.4 | Div. 4 runners-up 1962 | FA Cup never past 6th Rd League Cup never past 5th Rd |

COVENTRY CITY (1883) Sky blue/sky blue

| Highfield Road Coventry CV2 4GU 110 × 75 yd | 20 000* 51 457 v Wolverhampton W Div. 2 29 April 1967 | 1919 elected to Div. 2 1925–26 Div. 3(N) 1926–36 Div. 3(S) 1936–52 Div. 2 1952–58 Div. 3(S) | 1958–59 Div. 4 1959–64 Div. 3 1964–67 Div. 2 1967– Div. 1 | Div. 2 Champions 1967 Div. 3 Champions 1964 Div. 3(S) Champions 1936 Runners-up 1934 Div. 4 runners-up 1959 | FA Cup never past 6th Rd League Cup semi-finalists 1981 |

*all seated

CREWE ALEXANDRA (1877) Red/white

| Football Ground Gresty Road Crewe CW2 6EB 112 × 74 yd | 17 000 20 000 v Tottenham H FA Cup 4th Rd 30 January 1960 | 1892 (founder member of Div. 2) 1896 failed re-election 1921 re-elected to Div. 3(N) | 1958–63 Div. 4 1963–64 Div. 3 1964–68 Div. 4 1968–69 Div. 3 1969– Div. 4 | Highest placing 10th Div. 2 1893 | FA Cup semi-finalists 1888 League Cup never past 3rd Rd |

CRYSTAL PALACE (1905) White with red over blue diagonal band/white

| Selhurst Park London SE25 6PU 112 × 74 yd | 38 500 51 801 v Burnley Div. 2 11 May 1979 | 1920 (founder member of Div. 3) 1921–25 Div. 2 1925–58 Div. 3(S) 1958–61 Div. 4 1961–64 Div. 3 | 1964–69 Div. 2 1969–73 Div. 1 1973–74 Div. 2 1974–77 Div. 3 1977–79 Div. 2 1979–81 Div. 1 1981– Div. 2 | Div. 2 Champions 1979 runners-up 1969 Div. 3 runners-up 1964 Div. 3(S) Champions 1921 Runners-up 1929, 1931, 1939 Div. 4 Runners-up 1961 | FA Cup semi-finalists 1976 League Cup never past 5th Rd |

Most League points	Most League goals	Record win	Highest number of League goals		Most League appearances	Most capped player
			in total	by season		
			CHESTER			
56, Div. 3(N) 1946–47 Div. 4 1964–65	119, Div. 4 1964–65	12–0 v York City Div. 3(N) 1 February 1936	Gary Talbot 83, 1963–67 1968–70	Dick Yates 36 Div. 3(N) 1946–47	Ray Gill 408, 1951–62	Bill Lewis 9, Wales 1894–96
			CHESTERFIELD			
64, Div. 4 1969–70	102, Div. 3(N) 1930–31	10–0 v Glossop North End Div. 2 17 January 1903	Ernie Moss 127, 1969–76, 1979–81	Jimmy Cookson 44 Div. 3(N) 1925–26	Dave Blakey 613, 1948–67	Walter McMillen 4, N Ireland 1937–38
			COLCHESTER UNITED			
60, Div. 4 1973–74	104, Div. 4 1961–62	9–1 v Bradford City Div. 4 30 December 1961	Martyn King 131, 1959–65	Bobby Hunt 37 Div. 4 1961–62	Micky Cook 577, 1969–83	None
			COVENTRY CITY			
60, Div. 4 1958–59 Div. 3 1963–64	108, Div. 3(S) 1931–32	9–0 v Bristol City Div. 3(S) 28 April 1934	Clarrie Bourton 171, 1931–37	Clarrie Bourton 49 Div. 3(S) 1931–32	George Curtis 486, 1956–70	Dave Clements 21, N Ireland 1965–71
			CREWE ALEXANDRA			
59, Div. 4 1962–63	95, Div. 3(N) 1931–32	8–0 v Rotherham United Div. 3(N) 1 October 1932	Bert Swindells 126, 1928–37	Terry Harkin 34 Div. 4 1964–65	Tommy Lowry 436, 1966–78	Bill Lewis 12, Wales 1890–92
			CRYSTAL PALACE			
64, Div. 4 1960–61	110, Div. 4 1960–61	9–0 v Barrow Div. 4 10 October 1959	Peter Simpson 154, 1930–36	Peter Simpson 46 Div. 3(S) 1930–31	Terry Long 432, 1956–69	Ian Evans 13, Wales 1975–77 Peter Nicholas 13, Wales 1979–81

Ground	Capacity & record	League career		Honours (domestic) League	Cup

DARLINGTON (1883) White with black trim/black

Ground	Capacity & record	League career		Honours (domestic) League	Cup
Feethams Ground Darlington DL1 5JB 110 × 74 yd	20 000 21 023 Bolton W League Cup 3rd Rd 14 November 1960	1921 (founder member of Div. 3(N) 1925–27 Div. 2 1927–58 Div. 3(N)	1958–66 Div. 4 1966–67 Div. 3 1967– Div. 4	Div. 3(N) Champions 1925 Runners-up 1922 Div. 4 runners-up 1966	FA Cup never past 5th Rd League Cup never past 5th Rd

DERBY COUNTY (1884) White/blue

Ground	Capacity & record	League career		Honours (domestic) League	Cup
Baseball Ground Shaftesbury Crescent Derby DE3 8NB 110 × 71 yd	33 000 41 826 v Tottenham H Div. 1 20 September 1969	1888 (founder member of League) 1907–12 Div. 2 1912–14 Div. 1 1914–15 Div. 2 1915–21 Div. 1	1921–26 Div. 2 1926–53 Div. 1 1953–55 Div. 2 1955–57 Div. 3(N) 1957–69 Div. 2 1969–80 Div. 1 1980– Div. 2	Div. 1 Champions 1972, 1975 Runners-up 1896, 1930, 1936 Div. 2 Champions 1912, 1915, 1969 Runners-up 1926 Div. 3(N) Champions 1957 Runners-up 1956	FA Cup winners 1946 Runners-up 1898, 1899, 1903 League Cup semi-finalists 1968

DONCASTER ROVERS (1879) White with red trim/white

Ground	Capacity & record	League career		Honours (domestic) League	Cup
Belle Vue Ground Doncaster DN4 5HT 110 × 77 yd	21 150 37 149 v Hull City Div. 3(N) 2 October 1948	1901 elected to Div. 2 1903 failed re-election 1904 re-elected 1905 failed re-election 1923 re-elected to Div. 3(N) 1935–37 Div. 2	1937–47 Div. 3(N) 1947–48 Div. 2 1948–50 Div. 3(N) 1950–58 Div. 2 1958–59 Div. 3 1959–66 Div. 4 1966–67 Div. 3 1967–69 Div. 4 1969–71 Div. 3 1971–81 Div. 4 1981–83 Div. 3 1983– Div. 4	Div. 3(N) Champions 1935, 1947, 1950 Runners-up 1938–1939 Div. 4 Champions 1966, 1969	FA Cup never past 5th Rd League Cup never past 5th Rd

EVERTON (1878) Blue/white

Ground	Capacity & record	League career		Honours (domestic) League	Cup
Goodison Park Liverpool L4 4EL 112 × 78 yd	53 091 78 299 v Liverpool Div. 1 18 September 1948	1888 (founder member of League) 1930–31 Div. 2 1931–51 Div. 1 1951–54 Div. 2 1954– Div. 1		Div. 1 Champions 1891, 1915, 1928, 1932, 1939, 1963, 1970 Runners-up 1890, 1895, 1902, 1905, 1909, 1912 Div. 2 Champions 1931 Runners-up 1954	FA Cup winners 1906, 1933, 1966 Runners-up 1893, 1897, 1907, 1968 League Cup runners-up 1977

EXETER CITY (1904) Red-white stripes/black

Ground	Capacity & record	League career		Honours (domestic) League	Cup
St James Park Exeter EX4 6PX 114 × 73 yd	17 500 20 984 v Sunderland FA Cup 6th Rd replay 4 March 1931	1920 elected to Div. 3 1921–58 Div. 3(S) 1958–64 Div. 4 1964–66 Div. 3	1966–77 Div. 4 1977– Div. 3	Div. 3(S) runners-up 1933 Div. 4 runners-up 1977	FA Cup never past 6th Rd League Cup never past 4th Rd

Most League points	goals	Record win	Highest number of League goals in total	by season	Most League appearances	Most capped player
						DARLINGTON
59, Div. 4 1965–66	108, Div. 3(N) 1929–30	9–2 v Lincoln City Div. 3(N) 7 January 1928	David Brown 74, 1923–26	David Brown 39 Div. 3(N) 1924–25	Ron Greener 442, 1955–68	None
						DERBY COUNTY
63, Div. 2 1968–69 Div. 3(N) 1955–56, 1956–57	111, Div. 3(N) 1956–57	12–0 v Finn Harps UEFA Cup 3rd Rd First leg 15 September 1976	Steve Bloomer 291, 1892–1906 1910–14	Jack Bowers 37 Div. 1 1930–31 Ray Straw 37 Div. 3(N) 1956–57	Kevin Hector 486, 1966–78, 1980–82	Roy McFarland 28, England 1971–76
						DONCASTER ROVERS
72, Div. 3(N) 1946–47	123, Div. 3(N) 1946–47	10–0 v Darlington Div. 4 25 January 1964	Tom Keetley 180, 1923–29	Clarrie Jordan 42 Div. 3(N) 1946–47	Fred Emery 406, 1925–36	Len Graham 14, N Ireland 1951–58
						EVERTON
66, Div. 1 1969–70	121, Div. 2 1930–31	11–2 v Derby County FA Cup 1st Rd 18 January 1890	Dixie Dean 349, 1925–37	Dixie Dean 60 Div. 1 1927–28	Ted Sagar 465, 1929–53	Alan Ball 39, England 1966–71
						EXETER CITY
62, Div. 4 1976–77	88, Div. 3(S) 1932–33	8–1 v Coventry City Div. 3(S) 4 December 1926 Aldershot Div. 3(S) 4 May 1935	Alan Banks 105, 1963–66, 1967–73	Fred Whitlow 34 Div. 3(S) 1932–33	Arnold Mitchell 495, 1952–66	Dermot Curtis 1, Eire 1963

Ground	Capacity & record	League career	Honours (domestic) League	Cup

FULHAM (1879) White/black

| Craven Cottage
Stevenage Road
Fulham
London SW6 6HH
110 × 75 yd | 20 000
49 335 v
Millwall Div. 2
8 October 1938 | 1907 elected
to Div. 2
1928–32 Div. 3(S)
1932–49 Div. 2
1949–52 Div. 1
1952–59 Div. 2 | 1959–68 Div. 1
1968–69 Div. 2
1969–71 Div. 3
1971–80 Div. 2
1980–82 Div. 3
1982– Div. 2 | Div. 2 Champions
1949
Runners-up 1959
Div. 3(S)
Champions 1932
Div. 3 runners-up
1971 | FA Cup
runners-up 1975
League Cup
never past
5th Rd |

GILLINGHAM (1893) Blue/white

| Prestfield Stadium
Gillingham
114 × 75 yd | 22 000
23 002 v
QPR
FA Cup 3rd Rd
10 January 1948 | 1920 (founder
member of Div. 3)
1921 Div. 3(S)
1938 failed
re-election
1950 re-elected
to Div. 3(S) | 1958–64 Div. 4
1964–71 Div. 3
1971–74 Div. 4
1974– Div. 3 | Div. 4 Champions
1964
Runners-up 1974 | FA Cup never
past 5th Rd
League Cup
never past
4th Rd |

GRIMSBY TOWN (1878) Black-white stripes/black

| Blundell Park
Cleethorpes
South Humberside
DN35 7PY
111 × 74 yd | 22 000
31 657 v
Wolverhampton W
FA Cup 5th Rd
20 February 1937 | 1892 (founder
member of Div. 2)
1901–03 Div. 1
1903–10 Div. 2
1910 failed
re-election
1911 re-elected
to Div. 2
1920–21 Div. 3
1921–26 Div. 3(N)
1926–29 Div. 2
1929–32 Div. 1 | 1932–34 Div. 2
1934–48 Div. 1
1948–51 Div. 2
1951–56 Div. 3(N)
1956–59 Div. 2
1959–62 Div. 3
1962–64 Div. 2
1964–68 Div. 3
1968–72 Div. 4
1972–77 Div. 3
1977–79 Div. 4
1979–80 Div. 3
1980– Div. 2 | Div. 2 Champions
1901, 1934
Runners-up 1929
Div. 3(N)
Champions
1926, 1956
Runners-up 1952
Div. 3 Champions
1980
Div. 3 runners-up
1962
Div. 4 Champions
1972
Runners-up 1979 | FA Cup
semi-finalists
1936, 1939
League Cup
never past
5th Rd |

HALIFAX TOWN (1911) Royal blue with white trim/white

| Shay Ground
Halifax
HX1 2YS
110 × 70 yd | 16 500
36 885 v
Tottenham H
FA Cup 5th Rd
14 February 1953 | 1921 (founder
member of
Div. 3(N))
1958–63 Div. 3
1963–69 Div. 4 | 1969–76 Div. 3
1976– Div. 4 | Div. 3(N)
runners-up 1935
Div. 4 runners-up
1969 | FA Cup never
past 5th Rd
League Cup
never past
4th Rd |

HARTLEPOOL UNITED (1908) Blue/white

| The Victoria Ground
Hartlepool
113 × 77 yd | 18 000
17 426 v
Manchester U
FA Cup 3rd Rd
5 January 1957 | 1921 (founder
member of
Div. 3(N))
1958–68 Div. 4 | 1968–69 Div. 3
1969– Div. 4 | Div. 3(N)
runners-up 1957 | FA Cup never
past 4th Rd
League Cup
never past
4th Rd |

HEREFORD UNITED (1924) White with black and red trim/black

| Edgar Street
Hereford HR4 9JU
111 × 80 yd | 17 500
18 114 v
Sheffield W
FA Cup 3rd Rd
4 January 1958 | 1972 elected to
Div. 4
1973–76 Div. 3
1976–77 Div. 2 | 1977–78 Div. 3
1978– Div. 4 | Div. 3 Champions
1976
Div. 4 runners-up
1973 | FA Cup never
past 4th Rd
League Cup
never past
3rd Rd |

Most League points	goals	Record win	Highest number of League goals in total	by season	Most League appearances	Most capped player
						FULHAM
60, Div. 2 1958–59 Div. 3 1970–71	111, Div. 3(S) 1931–32	10–1 v Ipswich Town Div. 1 26 December 1963	Bedford, Jezzard 154, 1948–56	Frank Newton 41 Div. 3(S) 1931–32	Johnny Haynes 594, 1952–70	Johnny Haynes 56, England 1954–62
						GILLINGHAM
62, Div. 4 1973–74	90, Div. 4 1973–74	10–1 v Gorleston FA Cup 1st Rd 16 November 1957	Brian Yeo 135, 1963–75	Ernie Morgan 31 Div. 3(S) 1954–55 Brian Yeo 31 Div. 4 1973–74	John Simpson 571, 1957–72	Damien Richardson 2, Eire 1973–79
						GRIMSBY TOWN
68, Div. 3(N) 1955–56	103, Div. 2 1933–34	9–2 v Darwen Div. 2 15 April 1899	Pat Glover 182, 1930–39	Pat Glover 42 Div. 2 1933–34	Keith Jobling 448, 1953–69	Pat Glover 7, Wales 1931–39
						HALIFAX TOWN
57, Div. 4 1968–69	83, Div. 3(N) 1957–58	7–0 v Bishop Auckland FA Cup 2nd Rd replay 10 January 1967	Ernest Dixon 129, 1922–30	Albert Valentine 34 Div. 3(N) 1934–35	John Pickering 367, 1965–74	None
						HARTLEPOOL UNITED
60, Div. 4 1967–68	90, Div. 3(N) 1956–57	10–1 v Barrow Div. 4 4 April 1959	Ken Johnson 98, 1949–64	William Robinson 28 Div. 3(N) 1927–28	Wattie Moore 448, 1948–64	Ambrose Fogarty 1, Eire 1964
						HEREFORD UNITED
63, Div. 3 1975–76	86, Div. 3 1975–76	11–0 v Thynnes FA Cup qualifying rd 13 September 1947	Dixie McNeil 88, 1974–77 1982	Dixie McNeil 35 Div. 3 1975–76	Tommy Hughes 240, 1973–82	Brian Evans 1, Wales 1973

Ground	Capacity & record	League career		Honours (domestic) League	Cup

HUDDERSFIELD TOWN (1908) Blue-white stripes/white

| Leeds Road Huddersfield HD1 6PE 115 × 75 yd | 48 000 67 037 v Arsenal FA Cup 6th Rd 27 February 1932 | 1910 elected to Div. 2 1920–52 Div. 1 1952–53 Div. 2 1953–56 Div. 1 1956–70 Div. 2 | 1970–72 Div. 1 1972–73 Div. 2 1973–75 Div. 3 1975–80 Div. 4 1980–83 Div. 3 1983– Div. 2 | Div. 1 Champions 1924, 1925, 1926 Runners-up 1927, 1928, 1934 Div. 2 Champions 1970 Runners-up 1920, 1953 Div. 4 Champions 1980 | FA Cup winners 1922 Runners-up 1920, 1928, 1930, 1938, League Cup semi-finalists 1968 |

HULL CITY (1904) Black-amber stripes/black

| Boothberry Park Hull HU4 6EU 112 × 75 yd | 42 000 55 019 v Manchester U FA Cup 6th Rd 26 February 1949 | 1905 elected to Div. 2 1930–33 Div. 3(N) 1933–36 Div. 2 1936–49 Div. 3(N) 1949–56 Div. 2 1956–58 Div. 3(N) | 1958–59 Div. 3 1959–60 Div. 2 1960–66 Div. 3 1966–78 Div. 2 1978–81 Div. 3 1981–83 Div. 4 1983– Div. 3 | Div. 3(N) Champions 1933, 1949 Div. 3 Champions 1966 Runners-up 1959 | FA Cup semi-finalists 1930 League Cup never past 4th Rd |

IPSWICH TOWN (1887) Blue/white

| Portman Road Ipswich Suffolk IP1 2DA 112 × 72 yd | 37 000 38 010 v Leeds United FA Cup 6th Rd 8 March 1975 | 1938 elected to Div. 3(S) 1954–55 Div. 2 1955–57 Div. 3(S) 1957–61 Div. 2 | 1961–64 Div. 1 1964–68 Div. 2 1968– Div. 1 | Div. 1 Champions 1962 Runners-up 1981, 1982 Div. 2 Champions 1961, 1968 Div. 3(S) Champions 1954, 1957 | FA Cup winners 1978 League Cup semi-finalists 1982 |

LEEDS UNITED (1919) White/white

| Elland Road Leeds LS11 0ES 117 × 76 yd | 43 900 57 892 v Sunderland FA Cup 5th Rd replay 15 March 1967 | 1920 elected to Div. 2 1924–27 Div. 1 1927–28 Div. 2 1928–31 Div. 1 1931–32 Div. 2 | 1932–47 Div. 1 1947–56 Div. 2 1956–60 Div. 1 1960–64 Div. 2 1964–82 Div. 1 1982– Div. 2 | Div. 1 Champions 1969, 1974 Runners-up 1965, 1966, 1970, 1971, 1972 Div. 2 Champions 1924, 1964 Runners-up 1928, 1932, 1956 | FA Cup winners 1972 Runners-up 1965, 1970, 1973 League Cup winners 1968 |

LEICESTER CITY (1884) Blue/white

| City Stadium Filbert Street Leicester LE2 7FL 112 × 75 yd | 32 000 47 298 v Tottenham H FA Cup 5th Rd 18 February 1928 | 1894 elected to Div. 2 1908–09 Div. 1 1909–25 Div. 2 1925–35 Div. 1 1935–37 Div. 2 1937–39 Div. 1 | 1946–54 Div. 2 1954–55 Div. 1 1955–57 Div. 2 1957–69 Div. 1 1969–71 Div. 2 1971–78 Div. 1 1978–80 Div. 2 1980–81 Div. 1 1981–83 Div. 2 1983– Div. 1 | Div. 1 runners-up 1929 Div. 2 Champions 1925, 1937, 1954, 1957, 1971, 1980 Runners-up 1908 | FA Cup runners up 1949, 1961, 1963, 1969 League Cup winners 1964 Runners-up 1965 |

Most League points	Most League goals	Record win	Highest number of League goals in total	Highest number of League goals by season	Most League appearances	Most capped player

HUDDERSFIELD TOWN

Most League points	Most League goals	Record win	in total	by season	Most League appearances	Most capped player
66, Div. 4 1979–80	101, Div. 4 1979–80	10–1 v Blackpool Div. 1 13 December 1930	George Brown 142, 1921–29	Sam Taylor 35 Div. 2 1919–20 George Brown 35 Div. 1 1925–26	Billy Smith 520, 1914 34	Jimmy Nicholson 31, N Ireland 1965–71

HULL CITY

69, Div. 3 1965–66	109, Div. 3 1965–66	11–1 v Carlisle United Div. 3(N) 14 January 1939	Chris Chilton 195, 1960–71	Bill McNaughton 39 Div. 3(N) 1932–33	Andy Davidson 511, 1952–67	Terry Neill 15, N Ireland 1970–73

IPSWICH TOWN

64, Div. 3(S) 1953–54 1955–56	106, Div. 3(S) 1955–56	10–0 v Floriana (Malta) Euro. Cup 1st Rd 25 September 1962	Ray Crawford 203, 1958–63, 1966–69	Ted Phillips 41 Div. 3(S) 1956–57	Mick Mills 591, 1966–82	Allan Hunter 47, N Ireland 1972–80

LEEDS UNITED

67, Div. 1 1968–69	98, Div. 2 1927–28	10–0 v Lyn Oslo (Norway) Euro. Cup 1st Rd First leg 17 September 1969	John Charles 154, 1948–57 1962	John Charles 42 Div. 2 1953–54	Jack Charlton 629, 1953–73	Billy Bremner 54, Scotland 1965–75

LEICESTER CITY

61, Div. 2 1956–57	109, Div. 2 1956–57	10–0 v Portsmouth Div. 1 20 October 1928	Arthur Chandler 262, 1923–25	Arthur Rowley 44 Div. 2 1956–57	Adam Black 530, 1920–35	Gordon Banks 37, England 1963–66

Ground	Capacity & record	League career		Honours (domestic) League	Cup

LINCOLN CITY (1883) Red-white stripes/black

| Sincil Bank
Lincoln LN5 8LD
110 × 75 yd | 16 225
23 196 v
Derby Co
League Cup 4th Rd
15 November 1967 | 1892 (founder member of Div. 2)
1908 failed re-election
1909 re-elected
1911 failed re-election
1912 re-elected
1920 failed re-election
1921 re-elected | 1921–32 Div. 3(N)
1932–34 Div. 2
1934–38 Div. 3(N)
1948–49 Div. 2
1949–52 Div. 3(N)
1952–61 Div. 2
1961–62 Div. 3
1962–76 Div. 4
1976–79 Div. 3
1979–81 Div. 4
1981– Div. 3 | Div. 3(N) Champions 1932, 1948, 1952
Runners-up 1928, 1931, 1937
Div. 4 Champions 1976
Runners-up 1981 | FA Cup never past 5th Rd (equivalent)
League Cup never past 4th Rd |

LIVERPOOL (1892) Red/red

| Anfield Road
Liverpool L4 0TH
110 × 75 yd | 45 000
61 905 v
Wolverhampton W
FA Cup 4th Rd
2 February 1952 | 1893 elected to Div. 2
1894–95 Div. 1
1895–96 Div. 2
1896–1904 Div. 1 | 1904–05 Div. 2
1905–54 Div. 1
1954–62 Div. 2
1962– Div. 1 | Div. 1 Champions 1901, 1906, 1922, 1923, 1947, 1964, 1966, 1973, 1976, 1977, 1979, 1980, 1982, 1983 (record)
Runners-up 1899, 1910, 1969, 1974, 1975, 1978
Div. 2 Champions 1894, 1896, 1905, 1962 | FA Cup winners 1965, 1974
Runners-up 1914, 1950, 1971, 1977
League Cup winners 1981
Runners-up 1978
Milk Cup 1982, 1983 |

LUTON TOWN (1885) White with navy blue and orange trim/white

| 70–72 Kenilworth Road
Luton LU1 1DH
112 × 72 yd | 22 601
30 069 v
Blackpool
FA Cup 6th Rd replay
4 March 1959 | 1897 elected to Div. 2
1900 failed re-election
1920 elected to Div. 3
1921–37 Div. 3(S)
1937–55 Div. 2
1955–60 Div. 1 | 1960–63 Div. 2
1963–65 Div. 3
1965–68 Div. 4
1968–70 Div. 3
1970–74 Div. 2
1974–75 Div. 1
1975–82 Div. 2
1982– Div. 1 | Div. 2 Champions 1982
Runners-up 1955, 1974
Div. 3 runners-up 1970
Div. 4 Champions 1968
Div. 3(S) Champions 1937
Runners-up 1936 | FA Cup runners-up 1959
League Cup never past 5th Rd |

MANCHESTER CITY (1887) Sky blue/sky blue

| Maine Road
Moss Side
Manchester M14 7WN
119 × 79 yd | 52 500
84 569 v
Stoke City
FA Cup 6th Rd
3 March 1934 | 1892 elected to Div. 2 as Ardwick FC
1894 elected to Div. 2 as Manchester C
1899–1902 Div. 1
1902–03 Div. 2
1903–09 Div. 1
1909–10 Div. 2 | 1910–26 Div. 1
1926–28 Div. 2
1928–38 Div. 1
1938–47 Div. 2
1947–50 Div. 1
1950–51 Div. 2
1951–63 Div. 1
1963–66 Div. 2
1966–83 Div. 1
1983– Div. 2 | Div. 1 Champions 1937, 1968
Runners-up 1904, 1921, 1977
Div. 2 Champions 1899, 1903, 1910, 1928, 1947, 1966
Runners-up 1896, 1951 | FA Cup winners 1904, 1934, 1956, 1969
Runners-up 1926, 1933, 1955, 1981
League Cup winners 1970, 1976
Runners-up 1974 |

Most League points	goals	Record win	Highest number of League goals in total	by season	Most League appearances	Most capped player
						LINCOLN CITY
74, Div. 4 1975–76	121, Div. 3(N) 1951–52	11–1 v Crewe Alexandra Div. 3(N) 29 September 1951	Andy Graver 144, 1950–55, 1958–61	Allan Hall 42 Div. 3(N) 1931–32	Tony Emery 402, 1946–59	David Pugh 3, Wales, 1900–01 Con Moulson 3, Eire 1936–37 George Moulson 3, Eire 1948
						LIVERPOOL
68, Div. 1 1978–79	106, Div. 2 1895–96	11–0 v Stromsgodset (Norway) Cup Winners' Cup 17 September 1974	Roger Hunt 245, 1959–69	Roger Hunt 41 Div. 2 1961–62	Ian Callaghan 640, 1960–1978	Emlyn Hughes 59, England 1970–79
						LUTON TOWN
66, Div. 4 1967–68	103, Div. 3(S) 1936–37	12–0 v Bristol Rovers Div. 3(S) 13 April 1936	Gordon Turner 243, 1949–64	Joe Payne 55 Div. 3(S) 1936–37	Bob Morton 494, 1948–64	George Cummins 19, Eire 1953–61
						MANCHESTER CITY
62, Div. 2 1946–47	108, Div. 2 1926–27	11–3 v Lincoln City Div. 2 23 March 1895	Tommy Johnson 158, 1919–30	Tommy Johnson 38 Div. 1 1928–29	Alan Oakes 565, 1959–76	Colin Bell 48, England 1968–75

Ground	Capacity & record	League career		Honours (domestic) League	Cup

MANCHESTER UNITED (1878) Red/white

| Old Trafford Manchester M16 0RA 116 × 76 yd | 58 504 70 504 v Aston Villa Div. 1 27 December 1920 | 1892 elected to Div. 1 as Newton Heath. Changed name 1902 1894–1906 Div. 2 1906–22 Div. 1 1922–25 Div. 2 1925–31 Div. 1 | 1931–36 Div. 2 1936–37 Div. 1 1937–38 Div. 2 1938–74 Div. 1 1974–75 Div. 2 1975– Div. 1 | Div. 1 Champions 1908, 1911, 1952, 1956, 1957, 1965, 1967 Runners-up 1947, 1948, 1949, 1951, 1959, 1964, 1968, 1980 Div. 2 Champions 1936, 1975 Runners-up 1897, 1906, 1925, 1938 | FA Cup winners 1909, 1948, 1963, 1977, 1983 Runners-up 1957, 1958, 1976, 1979 League Cup semi-finalists 1970, 1971, 1975 Milk Cup runners-up 1983 |

MANSFIELD TOWN (1905) Amber/blue

| Field Mill Ground Quarry Lane Mansfield Notts 115 × 72 yd | 23 500 24 467 v Nottingham F FA Cup 3rd Rd 10 January 1953 | 1931 elected to Div. 3(S) 1932–37 Div. 3(N) 1937–47 Div. 3(S) 1947–58 Div. 3(N) 1958–60 Div. 3 1960–63 Div. 4 | 1963–72 Div. 3 1972–75 Div. 4 1975–77 Div. 3 1977–78 Div. 2 1978–80 Div. 3 1980– Div. 4 | Div. 3 Champions 1977 Div. 4 Champions 1975 Div. 3(N) Runners-up 1951 | FA Cup never past 6th Rd League Cup never past 5th Rd |

MIDDLESBROUGH (1876) Red with white trim/red

| Ayresome Park Middlesbrough Teesside 115 × 75 yd | 42 000 53 596 v Newcastle U Div. 1 27 December 1949 | 1899 elected to Div. 2 1902–24 Div. 1 1924–27 Div 2 1927–28 Div. 1 1928–29 Div. 2 | 1929–54 Div. 1 1954–66 Div. 2 1966–67 Div. 3 1967–74 Div. 2 1974–82 Div. 1 1982– Div. 2 | Div. 2 Champions 1927, 1929, 1974 Runners-up 1902 Div. 3 runners-up 1967 | FA Cup never past 6th Rd League Cup semi-finalists 1976 |

MILLWALL (1885) Blue/white

| The Den Cold Blow Lane London SE14 5RH 112 × 74 yd | 32 000 48 672 v Derby Co FA Cup 5th Rd 20 February 1937 | 1920 (founder members of Div. 3) 1921 Div. 3(S) 1928–34 Div. 2 1934–38 Div. 3(S) 1938–48 Div. 2 1948–58 Div. 3(S) 1958–62 Div. 4 | 1962–64 Div. 3 1964–65 Div. 4 1965–66 Div. 3 1966–75 Div. 2 1975–76 Div. 3 1976– Div. 2 | Div. 3(S) Champions 1928, 1938 Div. 3 runners-up 1966 Div. 4 Champions 1962 Runners-up 1965 | FA Cup semi-finalists 1900, 1903, 1937 League Cup never past 5th Rd |

NEWCASTLE UNITED (1882) Black-white stripes/black

| St James' Park Newcastle-upon-Tyne NE1 4ST 115 × 75 yd | 38 008 68 386 v Chelsea Div. 1 3 September 1930 | 1893 elected to Div. 2 1898–1934 Div. 1 1934–48 Div. 2 1948–61 Div. 1 | 1961–65 Div 2 1965–78 Div. 1 1978– Div. 2 | Div. 1 Champions 1905, 1907, 1909, 1927 Div. 2 Champions 1965 Runners-up 1898, 1948 | FA Cup winners 1910, 1924, 1932, 1951, 1952, 1955 Runners-up 1905, 1906, 1908, 1911, 1974 League Cup runners-up 1976 |

Most League points	Most League goals	Record win	Highest number of League goals		Most League appearances	Most capped player
			in total	by season		
MANCHESTER UNITED						
64, Div. 1 1956–57	103, Div. 1 1956–57 1958–59	10–0 v Anderlecht (Belgium) European Cup Prelim Rd 26 September 1956	Bobby Charlton 198, 1956–73	Dennis Viollet 32 Div. 1 1959–60	Bobby Charlton 606, 1956–73	Bobby Charlton 106, England 1958–70
MANSFIELD TOWN						
68, Div. 4 1974–75	108, Div. 4 1962–63	9–2 v Rotherham United Div. 3(N) 27 December 1932 Hounslow Town replay 5 November 1962	Harry Johnson 104, 1931–36	Ted Harston 55 Div. 3(N) 1936–37	Sandy Pate 413, 1967–78	John McClelland 6, N Ireland 1980–81
MIDDLESBROUGH						
65, Div. 2 1973–74	122, Div. 2 1926–27	9–0 v Brighton & HA Div. 2 23 August 1958	George Camsell 326, 1925–39	George Camsell 59 Div. 2 1926–27	Tim Williamson 563, 1902–23	Wilf Mannion 26, England 1946–51
MILLWALL						
65, Div. 3(S) 1927–28 Div. 3 1965–66	127, Div. 3(S) 1927–28	9–1 v Torquay United Div. 3(S) 29 August 1927 Coventry City Div. 3(S) 19 November 1927	Derek Possee 79, 1967–73	Richard Parker 37 Div. 3(S) 1926–27	Barry Kitchener 523, 1967–82	Eamonn Dunphy, 22 Eire 1966–71
NEWCASTLE UNITED						
57, Div. 2 1964–65	98, Div. 1 1951–52	13–0 v Newport County Div. 2 5 October 1946	Jackie Milburn 178, 1946–57	Hughie Gallacher 36 Div. 1 1926–27	Jim Lawrence 432, 1904–22	Alf McMichael 40, N Ireland 1949–60

Ground	Capacity & record	League career		Honours (domestic) League	Cup

NEWPORT COUNTY (1912) Amber/black

| Somerton Park
Newport
Gwent
110 × 75 yd | 18 000
24 268 v
Cardiff City
Div. 3(S)
16 October 1937 | 1920 (founder
member of Div. 3)
1921 Div. 3(S)
1931 dropped out
of League
1932 re-elected | 1932–39 Div. 3(S)
1946–47 Div. 2
1947–58 Div. 3(S)
1958–62 Div. 3
1962–80 Div. 4
1980– Div. 3 | Div. 3(S)
Champions 1939 | FA Cup never
past 5th Rd
League Cup
never past
3rd Rd |

NORTHAMPTON TOWN (1897) White with claret trim/claret

| County Ground
Abington Avenue
Northampton
NN1 4PS
120 × 75 yd | 17 000
24 523 v
Fulham Div. 1
23 April 1966 | 1920 (founder
member of Div. 3)
1921 Div. 3(S)
1958–61 Div. 4
1961–63 Div. 3
1963–65 Div. 2
1965–66 Div. 1 | 1966–67 Div. 2
1967–68 Div. 3
1968–76 Div. 4
1976–77 Div. 3
1977– Div. 4 | Div. 2 runners-up
1965
Div. 3 Champions
1963
Div. 3(S)
runners-up
1928, 1950
Div. 4 runners-up
1976 | FA Cup never
past 5th Rd
League Cup
never past
5th Rd |

NORWICH CITY (1905) Yellow/green

| Carrow Road
Norwich
NR1 1JE
114 × 74 yd | 29 000
43 984 v
Leicester City
FA Cup 6th Rd
30 March 1963 | 1920 (founder
member of Div. 3)
1921 Div. 3(S)
1934–39 Div. 2
1946–58 Div. 3(S) | 1958–60 Div. 3
1960–72 Div. 2
1972–74 Div. 1
1974–75 Div. 2
1975–81 Div. 1
1981–82 Div. 2
1982– Div. 1 | Div. 2 Champions
1972
Div. 3(S)
Champions 1934
Div. 3 runners-up
1960 | FA Cup
semi-finalists
1959
League Cup
winners 1962
Runners-up
1973, 1975 |

NOTTINGHAM FOREST (1865) Red/white

| City Ground
Nottingham
NG2 5FJ
115 × 78 yd | 35 000
49 945 v
Manchester U
Div. 1
28 October 1967 | 1892 elected to
Div. 1
1906 Div. 2
1907 Div. 1
1911–22 Div. 2
1922–25 Div. 1
1925–49 Div. 2 | 1949–51 Div. 3(S)
1951–57 Div. 2
1957–72 Div. 1
1972–77 Div. 2
1977– Div. 1 | Div. 1 Champions
1978, Runners-up
1967, 1979
Div. 2 Champions
1907, 1922
Runners-up 1957
Div. 3(S)
Champions 1951 | FA Cup winners
1898, 1959
League Cup
winners 1978,
1979
Runners-up 1980 |

NOTTS COUNTY (1862) Black-white stripes/black

| County Ground
Meadow Lane
Nottingham
NG2 3HJ
117 × 76 yd | 23 680
47 310 v
York City
FA Cup 6th Rd
12 March 1955 | 1888 (founder
member of
League)
1893–97 Div. 2
1897–1913 Div. 1
1913–14 Div. 2
1914–20 Div. 1
1920–23 Div. 2
1923–26 Div. 1
1926–30 Div. 2 | 1930–31 Div. 3(S)
1931–35 Div. 2
1935–50 Div. 3(S)
1950–58 Div. 2
1958–59 Div. 3
1959–60 Div. 4
1960–64 Div. 3
1964–71 Div. 4
1971–73 Div. 3
1973–81 Div. 2
1981– Div. 1 | Div. 2 Champions
1897, 1914, 1923
Runners-up 1895,
1981
Div. 3(S)
Champions
1931, 1950
Runners-up 1937
Div. 4 Champions
1971
Runners-up 1960 | FA Cup winners
1894
Runners-up
1891
League Cup
never past
5th Rd |

Most League points	Most League goals	Record win	Highest number of League goals in total	Highest number of League goals by season	Most League appearances	Most capped player

NEWPORT COUNTY

| 61, Div. 4 1979–80 | 85, Div. 4 1964–65 | 10–0 v Merthyr Town Div. 3(S) 10 April 1930 | Reg Parker 99, 1948–54 | Tudor Martin 34 Div. 3(S) 1929–30 | Len Weare 526, 1955–70 | (All 2 for Wales) Fred Cook 1925, Steve Lowndes 1983, Jack Nicholls 1924, Alf Sherwood 1956, Bill Thomas 1930, Nigel Vaughan 1983, Harold Williams 1949 |

NORTHAMPTON TOWN

| 68, Div. 4 1975–76 | 109, Div. 3 1962–63 Div. 3(S) 1952–53 | 10–0 v Walsall Div. 3(S) 5 November 1927 | Jack English 135, 1947–60 | Cliff Holton 36 Div. 3 1961–62 | Tommy Fowler 521, 1946–61 | E Lloyd Davies 12, Wales 1908–14 |

NORWICH CITY

| 64, Div. 3(S) 1950–51 | 99, Div. 3(S) 1952–53 | 10–2 v Coventry City Div. 3(S) 15 March 1930 | Johnny Gavin 122, 1945–54, 1955–58 | Ralph Hunt 31 Div. 3(S) 1955–56 | Ron Ashman 590, 1947–64 | Martin O'Neill 18, N Ireland 1981, 1982–83 |

NOTTINGHAM FOREST

| 70, Div. 3(S) 1950–51 | 110, Div. 3(S) 1950–51 | 14–0 v Clapton FA Cup 1st Rd 17 January 1891 | Grenville Morris 199, 1898–1913 | Wally Ardron 36 Div. 3(S) 1950–51 | Bob McKinlay 614, 1951–70 | Martin O'Neill 36, N Ireland 1972–80 |

NOTTS COUNTY

| 69, Div. 4 1970–71 | 107, Div. 4 1959–60 | 15–0 v Thornhill United FA Cup 1st Rd 24 October 1885 | Les Bradd 125, 1967–78 | Tom Keetley 39 Div. 3(S) 1930–31 | Albert Iremonger 564, 1904–26 | Bill Fallon 7, Eire 1934–38 |

Ground	Capacity & record	League career		Honours (domestic) League	Cup

OLDHAM ATHLETIC (1894) Blue/white

| Boundary Park
Oldham
110 × 74 yd | 26 324
47 671 v
Sheffield W
FA Cup 4th Rd
25 January 1930 | 1907 elected
to Div. 2
1910–23 Div. 1
1923–35 Div. 2
1935–53 Div. 3(N)
1953–54 Div. 2
1954–58 Div. 3(N) | 1958–63 Div. 4
1963–69 Div. 3
1969–71 Div. 4
1971–74 Div. 3
1974– Div. 2 | Div. 1 runners-up
1915
Div. 2 runners-up
1910
Div. 3(N)
Champions 1953
Div. 3 Champions
1974
Div. 4 runners-up
1963 | FA Cup
semi-finalists
1913
League Cup
never past
3rd Rd |

ORIENT (1881) All red

| Leyton Stadium
Brisbane Road
Leyton
London E10 5NE
110 × 75 yd | 26 500
34 345 v
West Ham U
FA Cup 4th Rd
25 January 1964 | 1905 elected
to Div. 2
1929–56 Div. 3(S)
1956–62 Div. 2
1962–63 Div. 1 | 1963–66 Div. 2
1966–70 Div. 3
1970–82 Div. 2
1982– Div. 3 | Div. 2 runners-up
1962
Div. 3 Champions
1970
Div. 3(S)
Champions 1956
Runners-up 1955 | FA Cup
semi-finalists
1978
League Cup
never past
5th Rd |

OXFORD UNITED (1896) Yellow/blue

| Manor Ground
Beech Road
Headington
Oxford OX3 7RS
112 × 78 yd | 17 350
22 730 v
Preston NE
FA Cup 6th Rd
29 February 1964 | 1962 elected
to Div. 4
1965–68 Div. 3 | 1968–76 Div. 2
1976– Div. 3 | Div. 3 Champions
1968 | FA Cup never
past 6th Rd
League Cup
never past
5th Rd |

PETERBOROUGH UNITED (1923) Blue/white

| London Road Ground
Peterborough
PE2 8AL
112 × 76 yd | 30 000
30 096 v
Swansea T
FA Cup 5th Rd
20 February 1965 | 1960 elected
to Div. 4
1961–68 Div. 3
1968 demoted
for financial
irregularities | 1968–74 Div. 4
1974–79 Div. 3
1979– Div. 4 | Div. 4 Champions
1961, 1974 | FA Cup never
past 6th Rd
League Cup
semi-finalists
1966 |

PLYMOUTH ARGYLE (1886) White with green trim/white

| Home Park
Plymouth
Devon PL2 1DQ
112 × 75 yd | 38 000
43 596 v
Aston Villa Div. 2
10 October 1936 | 1920 (founder
member of Div. 3)
1921–30 Div. 3(S)
1930–50 Div. 2
1950–52 Div. 3(S)
1952–56 Div. 2
1956–58 Div. 3(S) | 1958–59 Div. 3
1959–68 Div. 2
1968–75 Div. 3
1975–77 Div. 2
1977– Div. 3 | Div. 3(S)
Champions
1930, 1952
Runners-up
1922, 1923, 1924
1925, 1926, 1927
Div. 3 Champions
1959
Runners-up 1975 | FA Cup never
past 5th Rd
League Cup
semi-finalists
1965, 1974 |

PORTSMOUTH (1898) Blue/white

| Fratton Park
Frogmore Road
Portsmouth
PO4 8RA
116 × 73 yd | 40 000
51 385 v
Derby Co
FA Cup 6th Rd
26 February 1949 | 1920 (founder
member of Div. 3)
1921–24 Div. 3(S)
1924–27 Div. 2
1927–59 Div. 1
1959–61 Div. 2 | 1961–62 Div. 3
1962–76 Div. 2
1976–78 Div. 3
1978–80 Div. 4
1980–83 Div. 3
1983– Div. 2 | Div. 1 Champions
1949, 1950
Div. 2 runners-up
1927
Div. 3(S)
Champions 1924
Div. 3 Champions
1962 | FA Cup winners
1939
Runners-up
1929, 1934
League Cup
never past
5th Rd |

Most League points	Most League goals	Record win	Highest number of League goals in total	Highest number of League goals by season	Most League appearances	Most capped player

OLDHAM ATHLETIC

| 62, Div. 3 1973-74 | 95, Div. 4 1962-63 | 11-0 v Southport Div. 4 26 December 1962 | Eric Gemmell 110, 1947-54 | Tom Davis 33 Div. 3(N) 1936-37 | Ian Wood 525, 1966-80 | Albert Gray 9, Wales 1924-27 |

ORIENT

| 66, Div. 3(S) 1955-56 | 106, Div. 3(S) 1955-56 | 9-2 v Aldershot Div. 3(S) 10 February 1934 Chester League Cup 3rd Rd 15 October 1962 | Tom Johnston 121, 1956-58, 1959-61 | Tom Johnston 35 Div. 2 1957-58 | Peter Allen 431, 1965-78 | Tony Grealish 8, Eire 1976-79 |

OXFORD UNITED

| 61, Div. 4 1964-65 | 87, Div. 4 1964-65 | 7-1 v Barrow Div. 4 19 December 1964 | Graham Atkinson 73, 1962-73 | Colin Booth 23 Div. 4 1964-65 | John Shuker 480, 1962-77 | David Roberts 6, Wales 1973-74 |

PETERBOROUGH UNITED

| 66, Div. 4 1960-61 | 134, Div. 4 1960-61 | 8-1 v Oldham Athletic Div. 4 26 November 1969 | Jim Hall 120, 1967-75 | Terry Bly 52 Div. 4 1960-61 | Tommy Robson 482, 1968-81 | Ollie Conmy 5, Eire 1965-69 |

PLYMOUTH ARGYLE

| 68, Div. 3(S) 1929-30 | 107, Div. 3(S) 1925-26, 1951-52 | 8-1 v Millwall Div. 2 16 January 1932 | Sammy Black 180, 1924-38 | Jack Cock 32 Div. 3(S) 1925-26 | Sammy Black 470, 1924-38 | Moses Russell 20, Wales 1920-28 |

PORTSMOUTH

| 65, Div. 3 1961-62 | 91, Div. 4 1979-80 | 9-1 v Notts County Div. 2 9 April 1927 | Peter Harris 194, 1946-60 | Billy Haines 40 Div. 2 1926-27 | Jimmy Dickinson 764, 1946-65 | Jimmy Dickinson 48, England 1949-56 |

Ground	Capacity & record	League career		Honours (domestic) League	Cup

PORT VALE (1876) White/black

Vale Park Burslem Stoke-on-Trent ST6 1AW 116 × 76 yd	35 000 50 000 v Aston Vila FA Cup 5th Rd 20 February 1960	1892 (founder member of Div. 2) 1896 failed re-election 1898 re-elected 1907 resigned 1919 returned in October and took over the fixtures of Leeds City 1929–30 Div. 3(N)	1930–36 Div. 2 1936–38 Div. 3(N) 1938–52 Div. 3(S) 1952–54 Div. 3(N) 1954–57 Div. 2 1957–58 Div. 3(S) 1958–59 Div. 3 1959–65 Div. 3 1965–70 Div. 4 1970–78 Div. 3 1978–83 Div. 4 1983– Div. 3	Div. 3(N) Champions 1930, 1954 Runners-up 1953 Div. 4 Champions 1959	FA Cup semi-finalists 1954 League Cup never past 2nd Rd

PRESTON NORTH END (1881) White/navy blue

Deepdale Preston PR1 6RU 112 × 78 yd	25 000 42 684 v Arsenal Div. 1 23 April 1938	1888 (founder member of League) 1901–04 Div. 2 1904–12 Div. 1 1912–13 Div. 2 1913–14 Div. 1 1914–15 Div. 2 1919–25 Div. 1 1925–34 Div. 2	1934–49 Div. 1 1949–51 Div. 2 1951–61 Div. 1 1961–70 Div. 2 1970–71 Div. 3 1971–74 Div. 2 1974–78 Div. 3 1978– Div. 2	Div. 1 Champions 1889, 1890 Runners-up 1891, 1892, 1893, 1906, 1953, 1958 Div. 2 Champions 1904, 1913, 1951 Runners-up 1915, 1934 Div. 3 Champions 1971	FA Cup winners 1889, 1938 Runners-up 1888, 1922, 1937, 1954, 1964 League Cup never past 4th Rd

QUEEN'S PARK RANGERS (1885) Blue-white hoops/white

South Africa Road London W12 7PA 112 × 72 yd	30 000 35 353 v Leeds U Div. 1 28 April 1974	1920 (founder member of Div. 3 1921–48 Div. 3(S) 1948–52 Div. 2 1952–58 Div. 3(S) 1958–67 Div. 3	1967–68 Div. 2 1968–69 Div. 1 1969–73 Div. 2 1973–79 Div. 1 1979–83 Div. 2 1983– Div. 1	Div. 1 runners-up 1976 Div. 2 runners-up 1968, 1973 Div. 3(S) Champions 1948 Runners-up 1947 Div. 3 Champions 1967	FA Cup runners-up 1982 League Cup winners 1967

READING (1871) Blue-white hoops/white

Elm Park Norfolk Road Reading RG3 2EF 112 × 77 yd	27 200 33 042 v Brentford FA Cup 5th Rd 19 February 1927	1920 (founder member of Div. 3) 1921–26 Div. 3(S) 1926–31 Div. 2 1931–58 Div. 3(S)	1958–71 Div. 3 1971–76 Div. 4 1976–77 Div.3 1977–79 Div. 4 1979–83 Div. 3 1983– Div. 4	Div. 3(S) Champions 1926 Runners-up 1932, 1935, 1949, 1952 Div. 4 Champions 1979	FA Cup semi-finalists 1927 League Cup never past 4th Rd

ROCHDALE (1907) Blue/white

Spotland Sandy Lane Rochdale OL11 5DS 113 × 75 yd	28 000 24 231 v Notts Co FA Cup 2nd Rd 10 December 1949	1921 elected to Div. 3(N) 1958–59 Div. 3 1959–69 Div. 4	1969–74 Div. 3 1974– Div. 4	Div. 3(N) runners-up 1924, 1927	FA Cup never past 4th Rd League Cup runners-up 1962

Most League points	Most League goals	Record win	Highest number of League goals		Most League appearances	Most capped player
			in total	by season		
PORT VALE						
69, Div. 3(N) 1953–54	110, Div. 4 1958–59	9–1 v Chesterfield Div. 2 24 September 1932	Wilf Kirkham 154, 1923–29, 1931–33	Wilf Kirkham 38 Div. 2 1926–27	Roy Sproson 762, 1950–72	Sammy Morgan 7, N Ireland 1972–73
PRESTON NORTH END						
61, Div. 3 1970–71	100, Div. 2 1927–28 Div. 1 1957–58	26–0 v Hyde FA Cup 1st series 1st Rd 15 October 1887	Tom Finney 187, 1946–60	Ted Harper 37 Div. 2 1932–33	Alan Kelly 447, 1961–75	Tom Finney 76, England 1946–58
QUEEN'S PARK RANGERS						
67, Div. 3 1966–67	111, Div. 3 1961–62	9–2 v Tranmere Rovers Div. 3 3 December 1960	George Goddard 172, 1926–34	George Goddard 37 Div. 3(S) 1929–30	Tony Ingham 519, 1950–63	Don Givens 26, Eire 1973–78
READING						
65, Div. 4 1978–79	112, Div. 3(S) 1951–52	10–2 v Crystal Palace Div. 3(S) 4 September 1946	Ronnie Blackman 156, 1947–54	Ronnie Blackman 39 Div. 3(S) 1951–52	Steve Death 471, 1969–82	Pat McConnell 8, N Ireland 1925–28
ROCHDALE						
62, Div. 3(N) 1923–24	105, Div. 3(N) 1926–27	8–1 v Chesterfield Div. 3(N) 18 December 1926	Reg Jenkins 119, 1964–73	Albert Whitehurst 44 Div. 3(N) 1926–27	Graham Smith 317, 1966–74	None

Ground	Capacity & record	League career	Honours (domestic) League	Cup

ROTHERHAM UNITED (1884) Red, white sleeves/white

Ground	Capacity & record	League career	League	Cup
Millmoor Ground Rotherham 115 × 76 yd	21 000 25 000 v Sheffield U Div. 2 13 December 1952 and Sheffield W Div. 2 26 January 1952	1919 elected to Div. 2	1923–51 Div. 3(N) 1951–68 Div. 2 1968–73 Div. 3 1973–75 Div. 4 1975–81 Div. 2 1981–83 Div. 2 1983– Div. 3	Div. 3(N) Champions 1951 Runners-up 1947, 1948, 1949 Div. 3 Champions 1981	FA Cup never past 5th Rd League Cup runners-up 1961

SCUNTHORPE UNITED (1904) Sky blue with claret trim/sky blue

Ground	Capacity & record	League career	League	Cup
Old Show Ground Scunthorpe South Humberside DN15 7RH 112 × 78 yd	25 000 23 935 v Portsmouth FA Cup 4th Rd 30 January 1954	1950 elected to Div. 3(N) 1958–64 Div. 2 1964–68 Div. 3	1968–72 Div. 4 1972–73 Div. 3 1973–83 Div. 4 1983– Div. 3	Div. 3(N) Champions 1958	FA Cup never past 5th Rd League Cup never past 3rd Rd

SHEFFIELD UNITED (1889) Red-white stripes/black

Ground	Capacity & record	League career	League	Cup
Bramall Lane Ground Sheffield S2 4SU 117 × 75 yd	49 000 68 287 v Leeds U FA Cup 5th Rd 15 February 1936	1892 elected to Div. 2 1893–1934 Div. 1 1934–39 Div. 2 1946–49 Div. 1 1949–53 Div. 2 1953–56 Div. 1	1956–61 Div. 2 1961–68 Div. 1 1968–71 Div. 2 1971–76 Div. 1 1976–79 Div. 2 1979–81 Div. 3 1981–82 Div. 4 1982– Div. 3	Div. 1 Champions 1898 Runners-up 1897, 1900 Div. 2 Champions 1953 Runners-up 1893 1939, 1961, 1971 Div. 4 Champions 1982	FA Cup winners 1899, 1902, 1915, 1925 Runners-up 1901, 1936 League Cup never past 5th Rd

SHEFFIELD WEDNESDAY (1867) Blue-white stripes/blue

Ground	Capacity & record	League career	League	Cup
Hillsborough Sheffield S6 1SW 115 × 75 yd	50 174 72 841 v Manchester C FA Cup 5th Rd 17 February 1934	1892 elected to Div. 1 1899–1900 Div. 2 1900–20 Div. 1 1920–26 Div. 2 1926–37 Div. 1 1937–50 Div. 2 1950–51 Div. 1	1951–52 Div. 2 1952–55 Div. 1 1955–56 Div. 2 1956–58 Div. 1 1958–59 Div. 2 1959–70 Div. 1 1970–75 Div. 2 1975–80 Div. 3 1980– Div. 2	Div. 1 Champions 1903, 1904, 1929, 1930 Runners-up 1961 Div. 2 Champions 1900, 1926, 1952, 1956, 1959 Runners-up 1950	FA Cup winners 1896, 1907, 1935 Runners-up 1890, 1966 League Cup never past 5th Rd

SHREWSBURY TOWN (1886) Amber-blue stripes/blue

Ground	Capacity & record	League career	League	Cup
Gay Meadow Shrewsbury 116 × 76 yd	18 000 18 917 v Walsall Div. 3 26 April 1961	1950 elected to Div. 3(N) 1951–58 Div. 3(S) 1958–59 Div. 4	1959–74 Div. 3 1974–75 Div. 4 1975–79 Div. 3 1979– Div. 2	Div. 3 Champions 1979 Div. 4 runners-up 1975	FA Cup never past 6th Rd League Cup semi-finalists 1961

SOUTHAMPTON (1885) Red-white stripes/black

Ground	Capacity & record	League career	League	Cup
The Dell Milton Road Southampton SO9 4XX 110 × 72 yd	25 000 31 044 v Manchester U Div. 1 8 October 1969	1920 (founder member of Div. 3) 1921–22 Div. 3(S) 1922–53 Div. 2 1953–58 Div. 3(S) 1958–60 Div. 3	1960–66 Div. 2 1966–74 Div. 1 1974–78 Div. 2 1978– Div. 1	Div. 2 runners-up 1966, 1978 Div. 3(S) Champions 1922 Runners-up 1921 Div. 3 Champions 1960	FA Cup winners 1976 Runners-up 1900, 1902 League Cup runners-up 1979

Most League points	goals	Record win	Highest number of League goals in total	by season	Most League appearances	Most capped player
						ROTHERHAM UNITED
71, Div. 3(N) 1950–51	114, Div. 3(N) 1946–47	8–0 v Oldham Athletic Div. 3(N) 26 May 1947	Gladstone Guest 130, 1946–56	Wally Ardron 38 Div. 3(N) 1946–47	Danny Williams 459, 1946–62	Harold Millership 6, Wales 1920–21
						SCUNTHORPE UNITED
66, Div. 3(N) 1957–58	88, Div. 3(N) 1957–58	9–0 v Boston United FA Cup 1st Rd 21 November 1953	Barrie Thomas 92, 1959–62, 1964–66	Barrie Thomas 31 Div. 2 1961–62	Jack Brownsword 600, 1950–65	None
						SHEFFIELD UNITED
60, Div. 2 1952–53	102, Div. 1 1925–26	11–2 v Cardiff City Div. 1 1 January 1926	Harry Johnson 205, 1919–30	Jimmy Dunne 41 Div. 1 1930–31	Joe Shaw 629, 1948–66	Billy Gillespie 25, N Ireland 1913–30
						SHEFFIELD WEDNESDAY
62, Div. 2 1958–59	106, Div. 2 1958–59	12–0 v Halliweil FA Cup 1st Rd 17 January 1891	Andy Wilson 200, 1900–20	Derek Dooley 46 Div 2 1951–52	Andy Wilson 502, 1900–20	Ron Springett 33, England 1959–66
						SHREWSBURY TOWN
62, Div. 4 1974–75	101, Div. 4 1958–59	7–0 v Swindon Town Div. 3(S) 6 May 1955	Arthur Rowley 152, 1958–65	Arthur Rowley 38 Div. 4 1958–59	Ken Mulhearn 370, 1971–80	Jimmy McLaughlin 5, N Ireland 1961–63
						SOUTHAMPTON
61, Div. 3(S) 1921–22 Div. 3 1959–60	112, Div. 3(S) 1957–58	11–0 v Northampton Town Southern League 28 December 1901	Mike Channon 182, 1966–77 1979–82	Derek Reeves 39 Div. 3 1959–60	Terry Paine 713, 1956–74	Mike Channon 45, England 1972–77

Ground	Capacity & record	League career		Honours (domestic) League	Cup

SOUTHEND UNITED (1906) White with blue trim/blue

Ground	Capacity & record	League career		Honours (domestic) League	Cup
Roots Hall Ground Victoria Avenue Southend-on-Sea SS2 6NQ 110 × 74 yd	32 000 31 036 v Liverpool FA Cup 3rd Rd 10 January 1979	1920 (founder member of Div. 3) 1921–58 Div. 3(S) 1958–66 Div. 3	1966–72 Div. 4 1972–76 Div. 3 1976–78 Div. 4 1978–80 Div. 3 1980–81 Div. 4 1981– Div. 3	Div. 4 champions 1981 Runners-up 1972, 1978	FA Cup never past 5th Rd League Cup never past 3rd Rd

STOCKPORT COUNTY (1883) Royal blue-white stripes/white

Ground	Capacity & record	League career		Honours (domestic) League	Cup
Edgeley Park Stockport Cheshire SK3 9DD 110 × 75 yd	16 500 27 833 v Liverpool FA Cup 5th Rd 11 February 1950	1900 elected to Div. 2 1904 failed re-election 1905 re-elected to Div. 2 1905–21 Div. 2 1921–22 Div. 3(N)	1922–26 Div. 2 1926–37 Div. 3(N) 1937–38 Div. 2 1938–58 Div. 3(N) 1958–59 Div. 3 1959–67 Div. 4 1967–70 Div. 3 1970– Div. 4	Div. 3(N) Champions 1922, 1937 Runners-up 1929, 1930 Div. 4 Champions 1967	FA Cup never past 5th Rd League Cup never past 4th Rd

STOKE CITY (1863) Red-white stripes/white

Ground	Capacity & record	League career		Honours (domestic) League	Cup
Victoria Ground Stoke-on-Trent 116 × 75 yd	35 000 51 380 v Arsenal Div. 1 29 March 1937	1888 (founder member of League) 1890 not re-elected 1891 re-elected 1907–08 Div. 2 1908 resigned 1919 re-elected to Div. 2	1922–23 Div. 1 1923–26 Div. 2 1926–27 Div. 3(N) 1927–33 Div. 2 1933–53 Div. 1 1953–63 Div. 2 1963–77 Div. 1 1977–79 Div. 2 1979– Div. 1	Div. 2 Champions 1933, 1963 Runner-up 1922 Div. 3(N) Champions 1927	FA Cup semi-finalists 1899, 1971, 1972 League Cup winners 1927

SUNDERLAND (1879) Red-white stripes/black

Ground	Capacity & record	League career		Honours (domestic) League	Cup
Roker Park Sunderland Tyne & Wear 113 × 74 yd	47 000 75 118 v Derby Co FA Cup 6th Rd replay 8 March 1933	1890 elected to Div. 1 1958–64 Div. 2 1964–70 Div. 1 1970–76 Div.2 1976–77 Div. 1 1977–80 Div. 2 1980– Div. 1		Div. 1 Champions 1892, 1893, 1895, 1902, 1913, 1936 Runners-up 1894, 1898, 1901, 1923, 1935 Div. 2 Champions 1976 Runners-up 1964, 1980	FA Cup winners 1937, 1973 Runners-up 1913 League Cup semi-finalists 1963

SWANSEA CITY (1900) White/white

Ground	Capacity & record	League career		Honours (domestic) League	Cup
Vetch Field Swansea Glamorgan SA1 3SU 110 × 70 yd	26 496 32 796 v Arsenal FA Cup 4th Rd 17 February 1968	1920 (founder member of Div. 3) 1921–25 Div. 3(S) 1925–47 Div. 2 1947–49 Div. 3(S) 1949–65 Div. 2	1965–67 Div. 3 1967–70 Div. 4 1970–73 Div. 3 1973–78 Div. 4 1978–79 Div. 3 1979–81 Div. 2 1981–83 Div. 1 1983– Div. 2	Div. 3 runners-up 1979 Div. 3(S) Champions 1925, 1949	FA Cup semi-finalists 1926, 1964 League Cup never past 4th Rd

SWINDON TOWN (1881) Red/white

Ground	Capacity & record	League career		Honours (domestic) League	Cup
County Ground Swindon Wiltshire SN1 2ED 114 × 72 yd	26 000 32 000 v Arsenal FA Cup 3rd Rd 17 January 1972	1920 (founder member of Div. 3) 1921–58 Div. 3(S) 1958–63 Div. 3 1963–65 Div. 2	1965–69 Div. 3 1969–74 Div. 2 1974–82 Div. 3 1982– Div. 4	Div. 3 runners-up 1963, 1969	FA Cup semi-finalists 1910, 1912 League Cup winners 1969

Most League points	goals	Record win	Highest number of League goals in total	by season	Most League appearances	Most capped player

SOUTHEND UNITED

Most League points	goals	Record win	Highest number of League goals in total	by season	Most League appearances	Most capped player
67, Div. 4 1980–81	92, Div. 3(S) 1950–51	10–1 v Golders Green FA Cup 1st Rd 24 November 1934 Brentwood FA Cup 2nd Rd 7 December 1968	Roy Hollis 122, 1953–60	Jim Shankly 31 Div. 3(S) 1928–29 Sammy McCrory 31 Div. 3(S) 1957–58	Sandy Anderson 451, 1950–63	George Mackenzie 9, Eire 1937–39

STOCKPORT COUNTY

| 64, Div. 4 1966–67 | 115, Div. 3(N) 1933–34 | 13–0 v Halifax Town Div. 3(N) 6 January 1934 | Jackie Connor 132, 1951–56 | Alf Lythgoe 46 Div. 3(N) 1933–34 | Bob Murray 465, 1952–63 | Harry Hardy 1, England 1924 |

STOKE CITY

| 63, Div. 3(N) 1926–27 | 92, Div. 3(N) 1926–27 | 10–3 v West Bromwich Albion Div. 1 4 February 1937 | Freddie Steele 142, 1934–49 | Freddie Steele 33 Div. 1 1936–37 | Eric Skeels 506, 1958–76 | Gordon Banks 36, England 1967–72 |

SUNDERLAND

| 61, Div. 2 1963–64 | 109, Div. 1 1935–36 | 11–1 v Fairfield FA Cup 1st Rd 2 February 1895 | Charlie Buchan 209, 1911–25 | Dave Halliday 43 Div. 1 1928–29 | Jim Montgomery 537, 1962–77 | Billy Bingham 33, N Ireland 1951–58 Martin Harvey 33, N Ireland 1961–71 |

SWANSEA CITY

| 62, Div. 3(S) 1948–49 | 90, Div. 2 1956–57 | 8–0 v Hartlepool United Div. 4 1 April 1978 | Ivor Allchurch 166, 1949–58, 1965–68 | Cyril Pearce 35 Div. 2 1931–32 | Wilfred Milne 585, 1919–37 | Ivor Allchurch 42, Wales 1950–58 |

SWINDON TOWN

| 64, Div. 3 1968–69 | 100, Div. 3(S) 1926–27 | 10–1 v Farnham United Breweries FA Cup 1st Rd 28 November 1925 | Harry Morris 216, 1926–33 | Harry Morris 47 Div. 3(S) 1926–27 | John Trollope 770, 1960–80 | Rod Thomas 30, Wales 1967–73 |

Ground	Capacity & record	League career		Honours (domestic) League	Cup

TORQUAY UNITED (1898) White with blue and yellow trim/white

| Plainmoor Ground Torquay Devon TQ1 3PS 112 × 74 yd | 22 000 21 908 v Huddersfield T FA Cup 4th Rd 29 January 1955 | 1927 elected to Div. 3(S) 1958–60 Div. 4 1960–62 Div. 3 | 1962–66 Div. 4 1966–72 Div. 3 1972– Div. 4 | Div. 3(S) runners-up 1957 | FA Cup never past 4th Rd League Cup never past 3rd Rd |

TOTTENHAM HOTSPUR (1882) White/blue

| 748 High Road Tottenham London N17 0AP 110 × 73 yd | 50 000 75 038 v Sunderland FA Cup 6th Rd 5 March 1938 | 1908 elected to Div. 2 1909–15 Div. 1 1919–20 Div. 2 1920–28 Div. 1 1928–33 Div. 2 | 1933–35 Div. 1 1935–50 Div. 2 1950–77 Div. 1 1977–78 Div. 2 1978– Div. 1 | Div. 1 Champions 1951, 1961 Runners-up 1922 1952, 1957, 1963 Div. 2 Champions 1920, 1950 Runners-up 1909, 1933 | FA Cup winners 1901, 1921, 1961, 1962, 1967, 1981, 1982 (joint record) League Cup winners 1971, 1973 Milk Cup runners-up 1982 |

TRANMERE ROVERS (1883) Royal blue/white

| Prenton Park Prenton Road West Birkenhead 112 × 74 yd | 18 000 24 424 v Stoke City FA Cup 4th Rd 5 February 1972 | 1921 (founder member of Div. 3(N) 1938–39 Div. 2 1946–58 Div. 3(N) 1958–61 Div. 3 | 1961–67 Div. 4 1967–75 Div. 3 1975–76 Div. 4 1976–79 Div. 3 1979– Div. 4 | Div. 3(N) Champions 1938 | FA Cup never past 5th Rd League Cup never past 4th Rd |

WALSALL (1888) Red/white

| Fellows Park Walsall WS2 9DB 113 × 73 yd | 24 100 25 453 v Newcastle U Div. 2 29 August 1961 | 1892 elected to Div. 2 1895 failed re-election 1896–1901 Div. 2 1901 failed re-election 1921 (founder member of Div. 3(N)) | 1927–31 Div. 3(S) 1931–36 Div. 3(N) 1936–58 Div. 3(S) 1958–60 Div. 4 1960–61 Div. 3 1961–63 Div. 2 1963–79 Div. 3 1979–80 Div. 4 1980– Div. 3 | Div. 4 Champions 1960 Runners-up 1980 Div. 3 runners-up 1961 | FA Cup never past 5th Rd League Cup never past 4th Rd |

WATFORD (1891) Yellow with black-red trim/red

| Vicarage Road Watford WD1 8ER 113 × 73 yd | 28 000 34 099 v Manchester U FA Cup 4th Rd 3 February 1969 | 1920 (founder member of Div. 3) 1921–58 Div. 3(S) 1958–60 Div. 4 1960–69 Div. 3 | 1969–72 Div. 2 1972–75 Div. 3 1975–78 Div. 4 1978–79 Div. 3 1979–82 Div. 2 1982– Div. 1 | Div. 2 runners-up 1982 Div. 3 Champions 1969 Runners-up 1979 Div. 4 Champions 1978 | FA Cup semi-finalists 1970 League Cup semi-finalists 1979 |

WEST BROMWICH ALBION (1879) Blue-white stripes/white

| The Hawthorns West Bromwich B71 4LF 115 × 75 yd | 38 600 64 815 v Arsenal FA Cup 6th Rd 6 March 1937 | 1888 (founder member of League) 1901–02 Div. 2 1902–04 Div. 1 1904–11 Div. 2 1911–27 Div. 1 | 1927–31 Div. 2 1931–38 Div. 1 1938–49 Div. 2 1949–73 Div. 1 1973–76 Div. 2 1976– Div. 1 | Div. 1 Champions 1920 Runners-up 1925, 1954 Div. 2 Champions 1902, 1911 Runners-up 1931, 1949 | FA Cup winners 1888, 1892, 1931, 1954, 1968 Runners-up 1886, 1887, 1895, 1912, 1935 League Cup winners 1966 Runners-up 1967, 1970 |

Most League points	Most League goals	Record win	Highest number of League goals in total	Highest number of League goals by season	Most League appearances	Most capped player
						TORQUAY UNITED
60, Div. 4 1959–60	89, Div. 3(S) 1956–57	9–0 v Swindon Town Div. 3(S) 8 March 1952	Sammy Collins 204, 1948–58	Sammy Collins 40 Div. 3(S) 1955–56	Dennis Lewis 443, 1947–59	None
						TOTTENHAM HOTSPUR
70, Div. 2 1919–20	115, Div. 1 1960–61	13–2 v Crewe Alexandra FA Cup 4th Rd replay 3 February 1960	Jimmy Greaves 220, 1961–70	Jimmy Greaves 37 Div. 1 1962–63	Steve Perryman 549, 1969–83	Pat Jennings 66, N Ireland 1964–77
						TRANMERE ROVERS
60, Div. 4 1964–65	111, Div. 3(N) 1930–31	13–4 v Oldham Athletic Div. 3(N) 26 December 1935	Bunny Bell 104, 1931–36	Bunny Bell 35 Div. 3(N) 1933–34	Harold Bell 595, 1946–64	Albert Gray 3, Wales 1931
						WALSALL
65, Div. 4 1959–60	102, Div. 4 1959–60	10–0 v Darwen Div. 2 4 March 1899	Tony Richards 184, 1954–63 Colin Taylor 184, 1958–63, 1964–68, 1969–73	Gilbert Alsop 40 Div. 3(N) 1933–34, 1934–35	Colin Harrison 467, 1964–82	Mick Kearns 15, Eire 1973–79
						WATFORD
71, Div. 4 1977–78	92, Div. 4 1959–60	10–1 v Lowestoft Town FA Cup 1st Rd 27 November 1926	Tom Barnett 144, 1928–39	Cliff Holton 42 Div. 4 1959–60	Duncan Welbourne 411, 1963–74	Gerry Armstrong 21, N Ireland 1980–83
						WEST BROMWICH ALBION
60, Div. 1 1919–20	105, Div. 2 1929–30	12–0 v Darwen Div. 1 4 April 1892	Tony Brown 218, 1963–79	William Richardson 39 Div. 1 1935–36	Tony Brown 574, 1963–80	Stuart Williams 33, Wales 1954–62

Ground	Capacity & record	League career		Honours (domestic) League	Cup

WEST HAM UNITED (1900) Claret with blue sleeves/white

| Boleyn Ground
Green Street
Upton Park
London E13 9AZ
110 × 72 yd | 35 500
42 322 v
Tottenham H
Div. 1
17 October 1970 | 1919 elected
to Div. 2
1923–32 Div. 1
1932–58 Div. 2 | 1958–78 Div. 1
1978–81 Div. 2
1981– Div. 1 | Div. 2 Champions
1958, 1981
Runners-up 1923 | FA Cup winners
1964, 1975, 1980
Runners-up 1923
League Cup
runners-up 1966,
1981 |

WIGAN ATHLETIC (1932) Blue-white stripes/blue

| Springfield Park
Wigan
117 × 73 yd | 30 000
27 500 v
Hereford U
FA Cup 2nd Rd
12 December 1953 | 1978 elected to Div. 4
1982– Div. 3 | | Promoted to
Div. 3 1982 | FA Cup never
past 4th Rd
League Cup
never past
4th Rd |

WIMBLEDON (1889) Blue with yellow trim/blue

| Plough Lane Ground
Durnsford
Wimbledon
London SW19
110 × 85 yd | 15 000
18 000 v
HMS Victory
FA Amateur Cup
3rd Rd
23 February 1935 | 1977 elected
to Div. 4
1979–80 Div. 3
1980–81 Div. 4
1981–82 Div. 3
1982–83 Div. 4
1983– Div. 3 | | Promoted to
Div. 3 1979,
1981 | FA Cup never
past 4th Rd
League Cup
never past
4th Rd |

WOLVERHAMPTON WANDERERS (1877) Gold/black

| Molineux Grounds
Wolverhampton
WV1 4QR
115 × 72 yd | 41 074
61 315 v
Liverpool
FA Cup 5th Rd
11 February 1939 | 1888 (founder
member of
League)
1906–23 Div. 2
1923–24 Div. 3(N)
1924–32 Div. 2 | 1932–65 Div. 1
1965–67 Div. 2
1967–76 Div. 1
1976–77 Div. 2
1977–82 Div. 1
1982–83 Div. 2
1983– Div. 1 | Div. 1 Champions
1954, 1958, 1959
Runners-up
1938, 1939, 1950,
1955, 1960
Div. 2 Champions
1932, 1977
Runners-up 1967
Div. 3(N)
Champions 1924 | FA Cup winners
1893, 1908, 1949,
1960
Runners-up
1889, 1896, 1921,
1939
League Cup
winners 1974, 1980 |

WREXHAM (1873) Red/white

| Racecourse Ground
Mold Road
Wrexham
117 × 75 yd | 30 000
34 445 v
Manchester U
FA Cup 4th Rd
26 January 1957 | 1921 (founder
member of
Div. 3(N)
1958–60 Div. 3
1960–62 Div. 4 | 1962–64 Div. 3
1964–70 Div. 4
1970–78 Div. 3
1978–82 Div. 2
1982–83 Div. 3
1983– Div. 4 | Div. 3 Champions
1978
Div. 3(N)
runners-up 1933
Div. 4 runners-up
1970 | FA Cup never
past 6th Rd
League Cup
never past
5th Rd |

YORK CITY (1922) Red/navy blue

| Bootham Crescent
York YO3 7AQ
115 × 75 yd | 16 529
28 123 v
Huddersfield T
FA Cup 5th Rd
5 March 1938 | 1929 elected
to Div. 3(N)
1958–59 Div. 4
1959–60 Div. 3
1960–65 Div. 4
1965–66 Div. 3 | 1966–71 Div. 4
1971–74 Div. 3
1974–76 Div. 2
1976–77 Div. 3
1977– Div. 4 | Highest placing
15th Div. 2
1975 | FA Cup
semi-finalists
1955
League Cup
never past
5th Rd |

Most League points	goals	Record win	Highest number of League goals in total	by season	Most League appearances	Most capped player
						WEST HAM UNITED
66, Div. 2 1980–81	101, Div. 2 1957–58	8–0 v Rotherham United Div. 2 8 March 1958 Sunderland Div. 1 19 October 1968	Vic Watson 306, 1920–35	Vic Watson 41 Div. 1 1929–30	Billy Bonds 575, 1967–83	Bobby Moore 108, England 1962–73
						WIGAN ATHLETIC
55, Div. 4 1978–79, 1979–80	80, Div. 4 1981–82	7–2 v Scunthorpe United 12 March 1982	Peter Houghton 61, 1978–83	Les Bradd 19, Div. 4 1981–82	Peter Houghton 179, 1978–83	None
						WIMBLEDON
61, Div. 4 1978–79	96, Div. 4 1982–83	15–2 v Polytechnic FA Cup Pr Rd 7 February 1929	John Leslie 87, 1977–83	Alan Cork 23, Div. 4 1980–81 John Leslie 23, Div. 4 1982–83	John Leslie 253, 1977–82	None
						WOLVERHAMPTON WANDERERS
64, Div. 1 1957–58	115, Div. 2 1931–32	14–0 v Crosswell's Brewery FA Cup 2nd Rd 13 November 1886	Bill Hartill 164, 1928–35	Dennis Westcott 37 Div. 1 1946–47	Derek Parkin 501, 1968–82	Billy Wright 105, England 1946–59
						WREXHAM
61, Div. 4 1969–70 Div. 3 1977–78	106, Div. 3(N) 1932–33	10–1 v Hartlepool United Div. 4 3 March 1962	Tom Bamford 175, 1928–34	Tom Bamford 44 Div. 3(N) 1933–34	Arfon Griffiths 592, 1959–61 1962–79	Dai Davies 28, Wales 1977–81
						YORK CITY
62, Div. 4 1964–65	92, Div. 3(N) 1954–55	9–1 v Southport Div. 3(N) 2 February 1957	Norman Wilkinson 125, 1954–66	Bill Fenton 31 Div. 3(N) 1951–52 Arthur Bottom 31 Div. 3(N) 1955–56	Barry Jackson 481, 1958–70	Peter Scott 7, N Ireland 1976–78

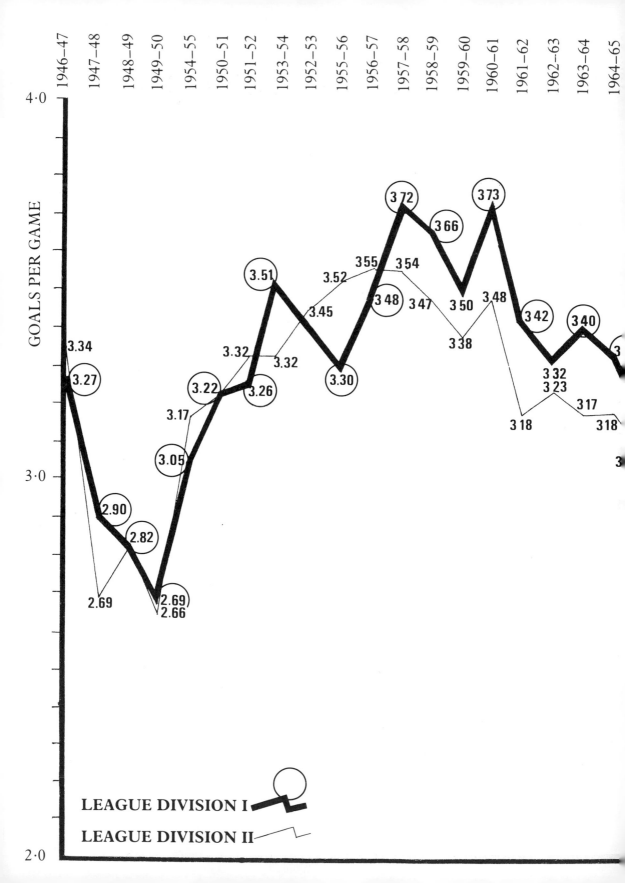

GOALS PER GAME

1946–47 1947–48 1948–49 1949–50 1954–55 1950–51 1951–52 1953–54 1952–53 1955–56 1956–57 1957–58 1958–59 1959–60 1960–61 1961–62 1962–63 1963–64 1964–65

4.0

3.0

2.0

3.34
3.27
2.90
2.82
2.69
2.66
2.69
3.05
3.22
3.17
3.26
3.32
3.32
3.51
3.45
3.30
3.52
3.55
3.48
3.54
3.47
3.50
3.72
3.66
3.38
3.48
3.73
3.42
3.32
3.23
3.18
3.40
3.17
3.18

LEGEND DIVISION I
LEAGUE DIVISION II

1966–67 1967–68 1968–69 1969–70 1970–71 1971–72 1972–73 1973–74 1974–75 1975–76 1976–77 1977–78 1978–79 1979–80 1980–81 1981–82 1982–83

AVERAGE NUMBER OF GOALS
PER GAME IN
THE FOOTBALL LEAGUE

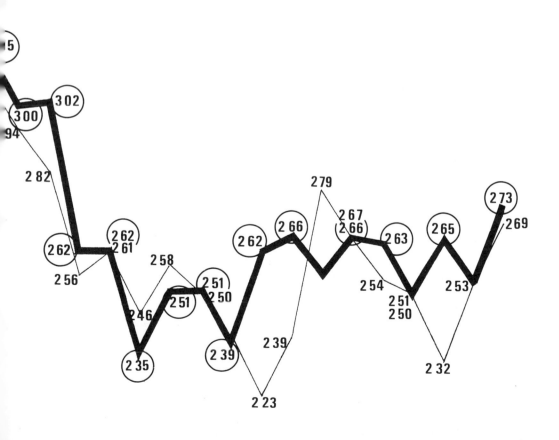

Scottish League Information

LEAGUE POINTS

Most points in a single season

Rangers achieved 76 points in 42 Division One matches in 1920–21. They finished ten points ahead of Celtic, the runners-up, and 26 points in front of Hearts who finished in third place. Rangers' only defeat was 2–0 at home to Celtic on New Year's Day when Rangers were weakened by injuries. Only the previous season they had established a new record with a total of 71 points. During these two seasons they lost only three of the 84 League matches played and enjoyed one spell of 56 consecutive games in which they were beaten only once, a 2–1 home defeat by Clydebank.

Morton achieved 69 points in 38 Division Two matches in 1966–67. They finished eleven points ahead of Raith Rovers, the runners-up. Morton scored 113 goals that season.

Fewest points in a single season

Abercorn achieved only three points in 18 Division One matches in 1896–97. Renton managed only four from the same number of matches in 1893–94, as did Dundee in 1898–99 and Clyde in 1899–1900.

Stirling Albion achieved only six points in 30 Division One matches in 1954–55. They suffered nine defeats of four or more goals during the season.

Vale of Leven achieved only five points in 22 Division One matches in 1891–92. They failed to win any of their matches and are the only Scottish League club to have completed a season without a single win. They conceded 101 goals.

Edinburgh City achieved only seven points in 34 Division Two matches in 1936–37. They won only two games and conceded 120 goals.

League points deducted

In the 1893–94 season Port Glasgow Athletic had seven points deducted, a record for the Scottish League. They had three points deducted for those achieved in games against Northern and Clyde for fielding an unregistered player and a further four for the infringement itself.

LEAGUE GOALS

Most goals scored in a single season (Team)

Heart of Midlothian scored 132 goals in 34 Division One matches during 1957–58. They were League champions by a margin of 13 points over the runners-up, Rangers. They suffered only one defeat 2–1 away to Clyde and collected a club record 62 points. Hearts beat East Fife 9–0, Falkirk 9–1 and Queen's Park 8–0.

Raith Rovers scored 142 goals in 34 Division Two matches during 1937–38. They never failed to score in any of their games and achieved five scores of six goals or more at home. Away they won 8–2 at Brechin City, 8–1 at East Stirling and 8–3 at Alloa. Norman Haywood and Tommy Gilmour scored 73 League goals between them and Haywood's total of 38 established a club record.

Most goals against in a single season (Team)

Edinburgh City conceded 146 goals in 38 Division Two matches during 1931–32. They finished bottom, eight points below their nearest rivals. Though they scored as many as 78 goals themselves they managed to keep their goal intact in only two games. Their heaviest defeats were 8–2 at Alloa and 8–4 at home to Queen of the South.

Leith Athletic conceded 137 goals in 38 Division One matches during 1931–32. They were relegated having finished bottom, three points behind Dundee United. Leith won six and drew four of their matches.

Fewest goals scored in a single season (Team)

Morton scored only 18 goals in 18 Division One matches in 1901–02. They achieved seven points, won only one game and finished bottom, six points behind their nearest rivals.

Stirling Albion scored only 18 goals in 39 Division One matches in 1980–81. They achieved 23 points including 6 wins, 2 of which were away. Their highest win was 4–2 at home to East Stirling but overall they failed to score in 27 games. They were relegated but finished one point above Berwick Rangers.

Lochgelly United scored only 20 goals in 38 Division Two matches in 1923–24. They finished bottom with 12 points from four wins and four draws and were 19 points away from their nearest rivals.

Albion scored only 19 goals in 22 Division Two matches in 1911–12 while Johnstone (not to be confused with St Johnstone) scored 20 from 22 games in the same division in 1913–14.

Fewest goals conceded in a single season

Celtic conceded only 14 goals in 38 Divison One matches in 1913–14. They kept their goal intact in 26 games and only Hearts were able to score more than a single goal against them when they won 2–0 at Tynecastle. To appreciate this performance it should be remembered that 14 represents the lowest total of goals conceded in any Scottish League season however few matches might have been played.

LEAGUE WINS

Most wins in a single season

Rangers won 35 of their 42 Division One matches in 1920–21. They began with a 4–1 win over Airdrieonians and were undefeated in their first 23 games, dropping only two points (at Aberdeen and Ayr) before losing 2–0 at home to Celtic in their only defeat. From the end of September until mid-December they had a winning run of 12 matches.

Morton won 33 of their 38 Division Two matches in 1966–67. They finished as champions, having lost only two matches and conceded only 20 goals.

LEAGUE DEFEATS

Most defeats in a single season

St Mirren suffered 31 defeats in 42 Division One matches in 1920–21. They did win seven games and for much of the season kept just ahead of Dumbarton until a slump in their last 15 games produced 13 defeats and they finished six points behind Dumbarton in last place. Their goals against total of 92 was the worst in either the Scottish League or Football League that season. Fourteen of their defeats were at home.

Brechin City suffered 30 defeats in 36 Division Two matches in 1962–63. They finished bottom 14 points behind their nearest rivals. Their nine points came from three wins and three draws and they lost 13 home games.

Fewest defeats in a single season

Celtic went through 18 Division One matches in 1897–98 without a defeat. Only three points were dropped. In 1898–99 Rangers won all their Division One matches, while in the same season

Kilmarnock were undefeated in Division Two dropping only four points in 18 games.

Rangers suffered only one defeat in 42 Division One matches in 1920–21. Celtic beat them 2–0 on New Year's Day with inside-left Joe Cassidy scoring both goals. Heart of Midlothian suffered only one defeat in 34 Division One matches in 1957–58, as did both Rangers and Celtic in 1967–68. That season Celtic were champions, two points ahead of Rangers.

Fewest wins in a single season

Vale of Leven failed to win any of their 22 Division One matches in 1891–92. They achieved only five points and were not re-elected.

Ayr United achieved only one win in 34 Division One matches in 1966–67. That solitary success came from a penalty from centre-half Eddie Monan at home to St Johnstone.

Forfar Athletic achieved only one win in 38 Division Two matches in 1974–75. They finished 12 points behind their nearest rivals at the bottom of the table. Only one point came from their last 15 games.

SEQUENCES

After losing 2–0 at Tyncastle to Hearts on 13 November 1915, Celtic completed 62 Division One matches without defeat until losing 2–0 at home to Kilmarnock on 21 April 1917. They won 49 and drew 13 of their games. In 1915–16 they won the championship by a margin of eleven points and retained their title the following season by ten points.

Rangers won all 18 of their Division One matches in 1898–99. That season lasted only four and a half months from the end of August until the beginning of January and when Rangers resumed in August 1899 they took their sequence to 22 consecutive wins before dropping a point at Tynecastle where Hearts held them in a 1–1 draw.

Morton won the last two League games in Division Two during 1962–63 and then 23 consecutive matches at the start of 1963–64 until losing 3–1 to East Fife on 1 February 1964.

LEAGUE DRAWS

Hibernian drew 18 of their 36 Premier Division matches in 1976–77. They drew ten at home and eight away and had one run of eight games which

Eddie Monan, the tallest man in the back row of the Ayr United blazers with Ally MacLeod on his left.
Ayr Advertiser

produced seven draws . They scored 34 goals and conceded 35.

PREMIER LEAGUE RECORDS

Celtic achieved two records in 1980–81: 56 points and 84 goals. They were top after winning their first two games but did not regain first place until 31 January. They lost only once in 1981, their last League game 3–1 at St Mirren whom they had beaten 7–0 earlier in the season for their highest win. Celtic dropped only four points out of their last possible 32.

In 1982–83 Celtic scored 90 goals when finishing runners-up to champions Dundee United who also achieved 90 goals. United also equalled Celtic's 56 points of two seasons earlier.

Motherwell conceded 86 goals in 1978–79. Their heaviest defeat 8–0 at Aberdeen is the record for the Premier Division. Only on three occasions did they prevent the opposition from scoring.

St Johnstone achieved only eleven points in 1975–76. Kilmarnock scored only 23 goals in 1980–81 and Clydebank 23 in 1977–78.

Rangers, Celtic, Aberdeen and Dundee United are the only sides never to be relegated from the Premier Division.

The first season in which the promoted clubs stayed up was in 1981–82 when Hibernian and Dundee retained their places. Previously at least one club had always returned to Division One after one season.

The first Premier Division goal was scored by Bobby Ford after one and a half minutes of the Dundee v Aberdeen game on 30 August 1975. It proved a decisive goal as Dundee won 3–2.

Ian Redford was the youngest player to score a hat-trick when he registered four goals for Dundee against St Mirren on 18 August 1979. He was 19 years 135 days old.

Celtic goalkeeper Peter Latchford kept six successive clean sheets in 1975–76 from 7 February to 3 April.

The highest score in a Premier Division match is eight. Aberdeen beat Motherwell 8–0 on 26 March 1979 and Rangers won 8–1 at Kilmarnock on 20 September 1980.

Dundee Derby Matches

DUNDEE v DUNDEE UNITED

Dundee were founded in 1893 and Dundee United in 1909 as Dundee Hibernians; they became known as Dundee United in 1923.

League meetings between the two clubs have resulted in Dundee United winning 28 times to Dundee's 20 with 10 drawn matches.

Dundee's home games with their score first:

Season	Score
1925–26	0–0
1926–27	5–0
1929–30	1–0
1931–32	1–1
1938–39	2–0
1946–47	2–0
1960–61	3–0
1961–62	4–1
1962–63	1–2
1963–64	1–1
1964–65	2–4
1965–66	0–5
1966–67	2–3
1967–68	2–2
1968–69	1–2
1969–70	1–2
1970–71	2–3
1971–72	6–4
1972–73	3–0
1973–74	0–1
1974–75	2–0
1975–76	0–0
	2–1
1979–80	1–0
	1–1
1981–82	1–3
	0–2
1982–83	0–2
	1–2

Dundee United's home games with their score first:

Season	Score
1925–26	0–1
1926–27	1–0
1929–30	0–1
1931–32	0–3
1938–39	3–0
1946–47	1–2
1960–61	3–1
1961–62	1–2
1962–63	1–1
1963–64	2–1
1964–65	1–4
1965–66	2–1
1966–67	1–4
1967–68	0–0
1968–69	3–1
1969–70	4–1
1970–71	3–2
1971–72	1–1
1972–73	2–1
1973–74	1–2
1974–75	3–0
1975–76	1–2
	1–0
1979–80	3–0
	2–0
1981–82	5–2
	1–1
1982–83	1–0
	5–3

Dundee derby day with the Dens Park side in dark shirts attacking United.
D C Thomson & Co Ltd

Scottish League Directory

| Ground | Honours (domestic) | | |
	League	Cup	

ABERDEEN (1903) Scarlet/scarlet

Pittodrie Park Aberdeen AB2 1QH 110 × 71 yd	Premier Div. Champions 1979–80 Premier Div. runners-up 1977–78, 1980–81, 1981–82 Div. 1 Champions 1954–55 Runners-up 1910–11, 1936–37, 1955–56, 1970–71, 1971–72	FA Cup Winners 1947, 1970, 1982, 1983 Runners-up 1937, 1953, 1954, 1959, 1967, 1978	League Cup Winners 1956, 1977 Runners-up 1979, 1980

AIRDRIEONIANS (1878) White/white

Broomfield Park Airdrie Lanarkshire ML6 9JL 112 × 68 yd	Div. 1 runners-up 1922–23, 1923–24, 1924–25, 1925–26, 1979–80 Div. 2 Champions 1902–03 1954–55, 1973–74 Runners-up 1900–01, 1946–47, 1949–50, 1965–66	FA Cup Winners 1924 Runners-up 1975

ALBION ROVERS (1882) Primrose/red

Cliftonhill Park Coatbridge M15 9XX 110 × 74 yd	Div. 2 Champions 1933–34 Runners-up 1913–14, 1937–38, 1947–48	FA Cup Runners-up 1920

ALLOA (1883) Gold/black

Recreation Ground Alloa FK10 110 × 75 yd	Div. 2 Champions 1921–22 Runners-up 1938–39, 1976–77, 1981–82

ARBROATH (1878) Maroon/white

Gayfield Park Arbroath DD11 12B 115 × 73 yd	Div. 2 runners-up 1934–35, 1958–59, 1967–68, 1971–72

AYR UNITED (1910) White/black

Somerset Park Ayr KA8 9NB 111 × 75 yd	Div. 2 Champions 1911–12, 1912–13, 1927–28, 1936–37, 1958–59, 1965–66 Runners-up 1910–11, 1955–56, 1968–69

BERWICK RANGERS (1881) Gold/black

Shielfield Park Tweedmouth Berwick-on-Tweed TD15 2EF 112 × 76 yd	Div. 2 Champions 1978–79

League career			Record win	Most League points	Highest number of individual League goals

ABERDEEN

League career			Record win	Most League points	Highest number of individual League goals
1904–05 Div. 2 1905–17 Div. 1	1919–75 Div. 1	1975– Pr. Div	13–0 v Peterhead, Scottish Cup, 3rd Rd 10 February 1923	61, Div. 1, 1935–36	Benny Yorston, 38, 1929–30

AIRDRIEONIANS

League career			Record win	Most League points	Highest number of individual League goals
1894–1903 Div. 2 1903–36 Div. 1 1936–47 Div. 2 1947–48 Div. 1	1948–50 Div. 2 1950–54 Div.1 1954–55 Div. 2 1955–65 Div. 1	1965–66 Div. 2 1966–73 Div. 1 1973–74 Div. 2 1974–80 Div. 1 1980–82 Pr. Div. 1982– Div. 1	15–1 v Dundee Wanderers, Div. 2, 1 December 1894	60, Div. 2, 1973–74	Bert Yarnall, 39 1916–17

ALBION ROVERS

League career			Record win	Most League points	Highest number of individual League goals
1903–15 Div. 2 1919–23 Div. 1 1923–34 Div. 2	1934–37 Div. 1 1937–38 Div. 2 1938–39 Div. 1	1946–48 Div. 2 1948–49 Div. 1 1949– Div. 2	12–0 v Airdriehill, Scottish Cup, 1st Rd 3 September 1897	54, Div. 2, 1929–30	Jim Renwick, 41 1932–33

ALLOA

League career			Record win	Most League points	Highest number of individual League goals
1921–22 Div. 2 1922–23 Div. 1	1923–77 Div. 2 1977–78 Div. 1	1978–82 Div. 2, 1982– Div. 1	9–2 v Forfar, Div. 2 18 March 1933	60, Div. 2, 1921–22	Wee Crilley, 49, 1921–22

ARBROATH

League career			Record win	Most League points	Highest number of individual League goals
1921–35 Div. 2 1935–39 Div. 1 1946–59 Div. 2	1959–60 Div. 1 1960–68 Div. 2 1968–69 Div. 1	1969–72 Div. 2 1972–80 Div. 1 1980– Div. 2	36–0 v Bon Accord, Scottish Cup, 12 September 1885	57, Div. 2, 1966–67	Dave Easson, 45, 1958–59

AYR UNITED

League career			Record win	Most League points	Highest number of individual League goals
1897–1913 Div. 2 1913–25 Div. 1 1925–28 Div. 2 1928–36 Div. 1 1936–37 Div. 2 1937–39 Div. 1	1946–56 Div 2 1956–57 Div. 1 1957–59 Div. 2 1959–61 Div. 1 1961–66 Div. 2 1966–67 Div. 1	1967–69 Div. 2 1969–75 Div. 1 1975–78 Pr. Div. 1978– Div. 1	11–1 v Dumbarton, League Cup, 13 August 1952	60, Div. 2, 1958–59	Jimmy Smith, 66, 1927–28

BERWICK RANGERS

League career			Record win	Most League points	Highest number of individual League goals
1955–79 Div. 2	1979–81 Div. 1	1981– Div. 2	8–1 v Forfar Athletic, Div. 2, 25 December 1965 8–1 v Vale of Leithen, Scottish Cup Pr. Rd 30 September 1967	54, Div. 2, 1978–79	Ken Bowron, 38 1963–64

	Honours (domestic)		
Ground	**League**	**Cup**	

BRECHIN CITY (1906) Red/red

Glebe Park Brechin DD9 6BJ 110 × 67 yd	Div. 2 Champions 1982–83	

CELTIC (1888) Green, white/white

Celtic Park Parkhead Glasgow G40 3RE 115 × 75 yd	Prem. Div. Champions 1976–77, 1978–79, 1980–81, 1981–82 Premier Div. runners-up 1975–76, 1979–80, 1982–83 Div. 1 Champions 1892–93, 1893–94, 1895–96, 1897–98, 1904–05, 1905–06, 1906–07, 1907–08, 1908–09, 1909–10, 1913–14, 1914–15, 1915–16, 1916–17, 1918–19, 1921–22,	1925–26, 1935–36, 1937–38, 1953–54, 1965–66, 1966–67, 1967–68,1968–69,1969–70, 1970–71, 1971–72, 1972–73, 1973–74 Runners-up 16 times FA Cup Winners 1892, 1899, 1900, 1904, 1907, 1908, 1911, 1912, 1914,	1923, 1925, 1927, 1931, 1933, 1937, 1951, 1954, 1965, 1967 1969, 1971, 1972, 1974, 1975, 1977, 1980 Runners-up 14 times League Cup Winners 1957, 1958, 1966, 1967, 1968, 1969, 1970, 1975, 1983 Runners-up 8 times

CLYDE (1878) White/black

Shawfield Stadium Glasgow G5 0AN 110 × 70 yd	Div. 2 Champions 1904–05 1951–52, 1956–57, 1961–62, 1972–73, 1977–78, 1981–82 Runners-up 1903–04, 1905–06, 1925–26, 1963–64	FA Cup Winners 1939, 1955, 1958 Runners-up 1910, 1912, 1949

CLYDEBANK (1965) White/white

Kilbowie Park Clydebank G81 2PB 110 × 68 yd	Div. 1 runners-up 1976–77 Div. 2 Champions 1975–76	

COWDENBEATH (1881) Blue/white

Central Park Cowdenbeath KY4 9NP 110 × 70 yd	Div. 2 Champions 1913–14, 1914–15, 1938–39 Runners-up 1921–22, 1923–24, 1969–70	

DUMBARTON (1872) White/white

Boghead Park Dumbarton G82 2JA 112 × 74 yd	Div. 1 Champions 1890–91 (shared) 1891–92 Div. 2 Champions 1910–11, 1971–72 Runners-up 1907–08	FA Cup Winners 1883 Runners-up 1881, 1882, 1887, 1891, 1897

DUNDEE (1893) Blue/white

Dens Park Dundee DD1 1RQ 113 × 73 yd	Div. 1 Champions 1961–62, 1978–79 Runners-up 1902–03, 1906–07, 1908–09, 1948–49, 1980–81 Div. 2 Champions 1946–47	FA Cup Winners 1910 Runners-up 1925, 1952, 1964	League Cup Winners 1952, 1953, 1974 Runners-up 1968, 1981

League career			Record win	Most League points	Highest number of individual League goals
					BRECHIN CITY
1929–39 Div. 2	1954–83 Div. 2 1983– Div. 1		12–1 v Thornhill, Scottish Cup, 1st Rd 28 January 1926	55, Div. 2, 1982–83	Willie McIntosh, 26, 1959–60
					CELTIC
1890–1975 Div. 1	1975– Pr. Div.		11–0 v Dundee, Div. 1, 26 October 1895	67, Div. 1, 1915–16 1921–22	Jimmy McGrory, 50, 1935–36
					CLYDE
1891–93 Div. 1 1893–94 Div. 2 1894–1900 Div. 1 1900–06 Div. 2 1906–24 Div. 1 1924–26 Div. 2 1926–51 Div. 1	1951–52 Div. 2 1952–56 Div. 1 1956–57 Div. 2 1957–61 Div. 1 1961–62 Div. 2 1962–63 Div. 1 1963–64 Div. 2	1964–72 Div. 1 1972–73 Div. 2 1973–76 Div. 1 1976–78 Div. 2 1978–80 Div. 1 1980–82 Div. 2 1982– Div. 1	11–1 v Cowdenbeath, Div. 2, 6 October 1951	64, Div. 2, 1956–57	Bill Boyd, 32, 1932–33
					CLYDEBANK
1966–76 Div. 2 1976–77 Div. 1	1977–78 Pr. Div.	1978– Div. 1	8–1 v Arbroath, Div. 1, 3 January 1977	58, Div. 1 1976–77	Blair Millar, 28, 1978–79
					COWDENBEATH
1905–24 Div. 2 1924–34 Div. 1	1934–70 Div. 2 1970–71 Div. 1	1971– Div. 2	12–0 v St Johnstone, Scottish Cup, 1st Rd 21 January 1928	60, Div. 2, 1938–39	Willie Devlin, 40, 1925–26
					DUMBARTON
1890–96 Div. 1 1896–97 Div.2 1906–13 Div. 2	1913–22 Div. 1 1922–54 Div. 2 1955–72 Div. 2	1972– Div. 1	13–1 v Kirkintilloch Central, Scottish Cup, 1st Rd 1 September 1888	52, Div. 2, 1971–72	Kenny Wilson, 38, 1971–72
					DUNDEE
1893–1917 Div. 1 1919–38 Div. 1 1938–47 Div. 2	1947–75 Div. 1 1975–76 Pr. Div. 1976–79 Div. 1	1979–80 Pr. Div. 1980–81 Div. 1 1981– Pr. Div.	10–0 v Alloa, Div. 2, 8 March 1947 and v Dunfermline, Div. 2, 22 March 1947	55, Div. 1, 1978–79	Dave Halliday, 38, 1923–24

| | Honours (domestic) | | |
| Ground | League | Cup | |

DUNDEE UNITED (1910) Tangerine/black

Tannadice Park Dundee DD3 7JW 110 × 74 yd	Prem. Div. Champions 1982–83 Div. 2 Champions 1924–25, 1928–29 Runners-up 1930–31, 1959–60	FA Cup Runners-up 1974, 1981	League Cup Winners 1980, 1981 Runners-up 1982

DUNFERMLINE ATHLETIC (1885) White, black/white

East End Park Dunfermline Fife KY12 7RB 114 × 72 yd	Div. 2 Champions 1925–26 Runners-up 1912–13, 1933–34, 1954–55, 1957–58, 1972–73, 1978–79	FA Cup Winners 1961, 1968 Runners-up 1965	League Cup Runners-up 1950

EAST FIFE (1903) Black, white/white

Bayview Park Methil Fife KY8 3AG 110 × 71 yd	Div. 2 Champions 1947–48 Runners-up 1929–30, 1970–71	FA Cup Winners 1938 Runners-up 1927, 1950	League Cup Winners 1948, 1950, 1954

EAST STIRLINGSHIRE (1881) Black, white/black

Firs Park Falkirk FK2 7AY 112 × 72 yd	Div. 2 Champions 1931–32 Runners-up 1962–63, 1979–80		

FALKIRK (1876) Blue/white

Brockville Park Falkirk FK1 5AX 100 × 70 yd	Div. 1 runners.up 1907–08, 1909–10 Div. 2 Champions 1935–36, 1969–70, 1974–75, 1979–80 Runners-up 1904–05, 1951–52, 1960–61	FA Cup Winners 1913, 1957	League Cup Runners-up 1948

FORFAR ATHLETIC (1884) Blue/white

Station Park Forfar DD8 1DA 116 × 69 yd	Highest League placing 3rd, Div. 2, 1979–80		

HAMILTON ACADEMICAL (1875) Red, white/white

Douglas Park Hamilton ML3 0DF 104 × 72 yd	Div. 2 Champions 1903–04 Runners-up 1952–53, 1964–65	FA Cup Runners-up 1911, 1935	

HEART OF MIDLOTHIAN (1874) Maroon/white

Tynecastle Park Edinburgh EH11 2NL 110 × 76 yd	Div. 1 Champions 1894–95, 1896–97, 1957–58, 1959–60, 1979–80 Runners-up 1893–94, 1898–99, 1903–04, 1905–06, 1914–15, 1937–38, 1953–54, 1956–57, 1958–59, 1964–65, 1977–78, 1982–83	FA Cup Winners 1891, 1896, 1901, 1906, 1956 Runners-up 1903, 1907, 1968, 1976	League Cup Winners 1955, 1959, 1960, 1963 Runners-up 1962

League career		Record win	Most League points	Highest number of individual League goals
				DUNDEE UNITED
1910–15 Div. 2 1923–25 Div. 2 1925–27 Div. 1 1927–29 Div. 2	1929–30 Div. 1 1930–31 Div. 2 1931–32 Div. 1 1932–60 Div. 2	1960–75 Div. 1 1975– Pr. Div.	14–0 v Nithsdale Wanderers, Scottish Cup, 1st Rd 17 January 1931	56, Pr. Div., 1982–83	John Coyle, 41, 1955–56
				DUNFERMLINE ATHLETIC
1912–15 Div. 2 1921–26 Div. 2 1926–28 Div. 1 1928–34 Div. 2 1934–37 Div. 1	1937–55 Div. 2 1955–57 Div. 1 1957–58 Div. 2 1958–72 Div. 1 1972–73 Div. 2 1973–76 Div. 1	1976–79 Div. 2 1979–83 Div. 1 1983– Div. 2	11–2 v Stenhousemuir, Div. 2, 27 September 1930	59, Div. 2, 55, 1925–26	Bobby Skinner, 55 1925–26
				EAST FIFE
1921–30 Div. 2 1930–31 Div. 1 1931–48 Div. 2	1948–58 Div. 1 1958–71 Div. 2 1971–74 Div. 1	1974–75 Div. 2 1975–78 Div. 1 1978– Div. 2	13–2 v Edinburgh City, Div. 2, 11 December 1937	57, Div. 2 1929–30	Henry Morris, 41, 1947–48
				EAST STIRLINGSHIRE
1900–15 Div. 2 1921–23 Div. 2	1924–39 Div. 2 1955–63 Div. 2	1963–64 Div. 1 1964–80 Div. 2 1980–82 Div. 1 1982– Div. 2	10–1 v Stenhousemuir, Scottish Cup, 1st Rd 1 September 1888	55, Div. 2, 1931–32	Malcolm Morrison, 36, 1938–39
				FALKIRK
1902–05 Div. 2 1905–35 Div. 1 1935–36 Div. 1 1936–51 Div. 1 1951–52 Div. 2	1952–59 Div. 1 1959–61 Div. 2 1961–69 Div. 1 1969–70 Div. 2 1970–74 Div. 1	1974–75 Div. 2 1975–77 Div. 1 1977–80 Div. 2 1980– Div. 1	12–1 v Laurieston, Scottish Cup, 2nd Rd 23 March 1893	59, Div. 2, 1935–36	Evelyn Morrison, 43, 1928–29
				FORFAR ATHLETIC
1921–25 Div. 2	1926–39 Div. 2	1949– Div. 2	14–1 v Lindertis, Scottish Cup, 1st Rd 1 September 1888	48, Div. 2, 1982–83	Davie Kilgour, 45, 1929–30
				HAMILTON ACADEMICAL
1897–1906 Div. 2 1906–47 Div. 1 1947–53 Div. 2	1953–54 Div. 1 1954–65 Div. 2 1965–66 Div. 1	1966–75 Div. 2 1975– Div. 1	10–2 v Cowdenbeath, Div. 1, 15 October 1932	55, Div. 2, 1973–74	David Wilson, 34, 1936–37
				HEART OF MIDLOTHIAN
1890–1975 Div. 1 1975–77 Pr. Div.	1977–78 Div. 1 1978–79 Pr. Div.	1979–80 Div. 1 1980–81 Pr. Div. 1981–83 Div. 1 1983– Pr. Div.	15–0 v King's Park, Scottish Cup, 13 March 1937	62, Div. 1, 1957–58	Barney Battles, 44, 1930–31

Ground	Honours (domestic) League	Cup	

HIBERNIAN (1875) Green/white

| Easter Road Park Edinburgh EH7 5QG 112 × 74 yd | Div. 1 Champions 1902–03, 1947–48, 1950–51, 1951–52, 1980–81. Runners-up 1896–97, 1946–47, 1949–50, 1952–53, 1973–74, 1974–75. Div. 2 Champions 1893–94, 1894–95, 1932–33 | FA Cup Winners 1887, 1902 Runners-up 1896, 1914, 1923, 1924, 1947, 1958, 1972, 1979 | League Cup Winners 1973 Runners-up 1951, 1969, 1975 |

KILMARNOCK (1869) Blue, white/blue

| Rugby Park Kilmarnock KA1 2DP 115 × 75 yd | Div. 1 Champions 1964–65 Runners-up 1959–60, 1960–61, 1962–63, 1963–64, 1975–76, 1978–79, 1981–82. Div. 2 Champions 1897–98, 1898–99. Runners-up 1953–54, 1973–74 | FA Cup Winners 1920, 1929 Runners-up 1898, 1932, 1938, 1957, 1960 | League Cup Runners-up 1953, 1961, 1963 |

MEADOWBANK THISTLE (1974) Amber/black

| Meadowbank Stadium Edinburgh EH7 6AE 105 × 72 yd | Div. 2 runners-up 1982–83 | | |

MONTROSE (1879) White/white

| Links Park Montrose DD10 8QD 114 × 66 yd | Highest League placing 3rd, Div. 1, 1975–76 | | |

MORTON (1874) Blue, white/white

| Cappielow Park Greenock PA15 2TY 110 × 71 yd | Div. 1 Champions 1977–78 Runners-up 1916–17. Div. 2 Champions 1949–50, 1963–64, 1966–67. Runners-up 1899–1900, 1928–29, 1936–37 | FA Cup Winners 1922 Runners-up 1948 | League Cup Runners-up 1964 |

MOTHERWELL (1886) Amber, claret/amber

| Fir Park Motherwell ML1 2QN 110 × 72 yd | Div. 1 Champions 1931–32, 1981–82. Runners-up 1926–27, 1929–30, 1932–33, 1933–34. Div. 2 Champions 1953–54, 1968–69. Runners-up 1894–95, 1902–03 | FA Cup Winners 1952 Runners-up 1931, 1933, 1939, 1951 | League Cup Winners 1951 Runners-up 1955 |

PARTICK THISTLE (1876) Red, yellow/red

| Firhill Park Glasgow G20 7AL 110 × 71 yd | Div. 1 Champions 1975–76 Div. 2 Champions 1896–97 1899–1900, 1970–71 Runners-up 1901–02 | FA Cup Winners 1921 Runners-up 1930 | League Cup Winners 1972 Runners-up 1954, 1957, 1959 |

League career		Record win	Most League points	Highest number of individual League goals

HIBERNIAN

1893–95 Div. 2	1931–33 Div. 2	1975–80 Pr. Div. 15–1 v Peebles Rovers,	57, Div. 1,	Joe Baker, 42,
1895–1931 Div. 1	1933–75 Div. 1	1980–81 Div. 1 Scottish Cup, 2nd Rd	1980–81	1959–60
		1981– Pr. Div. 11 February 1961		

KILMARNOCK

1895–99 Div. 2	1954–73 Div. 1	1976–77 Pr. Div. 13–2 v Saltcoats Victoria,	54, Div. 1,	Peerie
1899–1947 Div. 1	1973–74 Div. 2	1977–79 Div. 1 Scottish Cup, 2nd Rd	1978–79	Cunningham, 35,
1947–54 Div. 2	1974–76 Div. 1	1979–81 Pr. Div. 12 September 1896		1927–28
		1981–82 Div. 1		
		1982–83 Pr. Div.		
		1983– Div. 1		

MEADOWBANK THISTLE

| 1974–83 Div. 2 | | 6–1 v Stenhousemuir, | 54, Div. 2 | John Jobson, 17, |
| 1983– Div. 1 | | Div. 2, 6 February 1982 | 1982–83 | 1979–80 |

MONTROSE

1929–39 Div. 2	1975–79 Div. 1	1979– Div. 2 12–0 v Vale of Leithen,	53, Div. 2,	Brian Third, 29,
1955–75 Div. 2		Scottish Cup, 2nd Rd	1974–75	1972–73
		4 January 1975		

MORTON

1893–1900 Div. 2	1937–38 Div. 1	1952–64 Div. 2 11–0 v Carfin Shamrock,	69, Div. 2,	Allan McGraw,
1900–27 Div. 1	1938–39 Div. 2	1964–66 Div. 1 Scottish Cup, 1st Rd	1966–67	41,
1927–29 Div. 2	1946–49 Div. 1	1966–67 Div. 2 13 November 1886		1963–64
1929–33 Div. 1	1949–50 Div. 2	1967–78 Div. 1		
1933–37 Div. 2	1950–52 Div. 1	1978–83 Pr. Div.		
		1983– Div. 1		

MOTHERWELL

1893–1903 Div. 2	1954–68 Div. 1	1975–79 Pr. Div 12–1 v Dundee United,	66, Div. 1,	Willie McFadyen,
1903–53 Div. 1	1968–69 Div. 2	1979–82 Div. 1 Div. 2, 23 January 1954	1931–32	52,
1953–54 Div. 2	1969–75 Div. 1	1982– Pr. Div.		1931–32

PARTICK THISTLE

1893–97 Div. 2	1900–01 Div. 1	1970–71 Div. 2 16–0 v Royal Albert,	56, Div. 2,	Alec Hair, 41,
1897–99 Div. 1	1901–02 Div. 2	1971–76 Div. 1 Scottish Cup, 17 January	1970–71	1926–27
1899–1900 Div. 2	1902–70 Div. 1	1976–82 Pr. Div. 1931		
		1982– Div. 1		

Ground	Honours (domestic)		
	League	Cup	

QUEEN OF THE SOUTH (1919) Blue/white

| Palmerston Park
Dumfries DG2 9BA
111 × 73 yd | Div. 2 Champions 1950–51
Runners-up 1932–33, 1961–62,
1974–75, 1980–81 | | |

QUEEN'S PARK (1867) Black, white/white

| Hampden Park
Glasgow G42 2BA
115 × 75 yd | Div. 2 Champions 1922–23,
1955–56, 1980–81 | FA Cup
Winners 1874, 1875, 1876, 1880,
1881, 1882, 1884, 1886, 1890,
1893
Runners-up 1892, 1900 | English FA Cup runners-up
1884, 1885 |

RAITH ROVERS (1893) Blue/white

| Stark's Park
Kirkcaldy KY1 1SA
113 × 67 yd | Div. 2 Champions 1907–08,
1909–10 (shared), 1937–38,
1948–49
Runners-up 1908–09, 1926–27,
1966–67, 1975–76, 1977–78 | FA Cup
Runners-up 1913 | League Cup
Runners-up 1949 |

RANGERS (1873) Blue/white

| Ibrox Stadium
Glasgow G51 2XD
115 × 75 yd | Premier Div. Champions
1975–76, 1977–78
Premier Div. Runners-up
1976–77, 1978–79
Div. 1 Champions 1890–91
(shared), 1898–99, 1899–1900,
1900–01, 1901–02, 1910–11,
1911–12, 1912–13, 1917–18,
1919–20, 1920–21, 1922–23,
1923–24, 1924–25, 1926–27,
1927–28, 1928–29, 1929–30,
1930–31, 1932–33, 1933–34,
1934–35, 1936–37, 1938–39,
1946–47, 1948–49, 1949–50,
1952–53, 1955–56, 1956–57,
1958–59, 1960–61, 1962–63,
1963–64, 1974–75
Runners-up 21 times | FA Cup
Winners 1894, 1897, 1898, 1903,
1928, 1930, 1932, 1934, 1935,
1936, 1948, 1949, 1950, 1953,
1960, 1962, 1963, 1964, 1966,
1973, 1976, 1978, 1979
Runners-up 14 times | League Cup
Winners 1947, 1949, 1961, 1962,
1964, 1965, 1971, 1976, 1978,
1979, 1982
Runners-up 6 times |

ST JOHNSTONE (1884) Blue/white

| Muirton Park
Perth PH1 5AP
109 × 74 yd | Div. 1 Champions 1982–83
Div. 2 Champions 1923–24,
1959–60, 1962–63
Runners-up 1931–32 | | League Cup
Runners-up 1970 |

ST MIRREN (1876) Black, white/black

| St Mirren Park
Paisley PA3 2EJ
115 × 74 yd | Div. 1 Champions 1976–77
Div. 2 Champions 1967–68
Runners-up 1935–36 | FA Cup
Winners 1926, 1959
Runners-up 1908, 1934, 1962 | League Cup
Runners-up 1956 |

League career			Record win	Most League points	Highest number of individual League goals

QUEEN OF THE SOUTH

League career			Record win	Most League points	Highest number of individual League goals
1925–33 Div. 2	1951–59 Div. 1	1964–75 Div. 2	11–1 v Stranraer, Scottish Cup, 16 January 1932	53, Div. 2, 1961–62	Jimmy Gray, 33, 1927–28
1933–50 Div. 1	1959–62 Div. 2	1976–79 Div. 1			
1950–51 Div. 2	1962–64 Div. 1	1979–81 Div. 2			
		1981–82 Div. 1			
		1982– Div. 2			

QUEEN'S PARK

1900–22 Div. 1	1923–48 Div. 1	1956–58 Div. 1	16–0 v St Peter's, Scottish Cup, 1st Rd 12 September 1885	57, Div. 2, 1922–23	Willie Martin, 30, 1937–38
1922–23 Div. 2	1948–56 Div. 2	1958–81 Div. 2			
		1981–83 Div. 1			
		1983– Div. 2			

RAITH ROVERS

1902–10 Div. 2	1929–38 Div. 2	1967–70 Div. 1	10–1 v Coldstream, Scottish Cup, 2nd Rd 13 March 1954	59, Div. 2, 1937–38	Norman Haywood, 38, 1937–38
1910–17 Div. 1	1938–39 Div. 1	1970–76 Div. 2			
1919–26 Div. 1	1946–49 Div. 2	1976–77 Div. 1			
1926–27 Div. 2	1949–63 Div. 1	1977–78 Div. 1			
1927–29 Div. 1	1963–67 Div. 2	1978– Div. 1			

RANGERS

1890–1975 Div. 1	1975– Pr. Div.		14–2 v Whitehill, Scottish Cup, 2nd Rd, 22 September 1883; v Blairgowrie Scottish Cup, 1st Rd, 20 January 1934	76, Div. 1, 1920–21	Sam English, 44, 1931–32

ST JOHNSTONE

1911–15 Div. 2	1932–39 Div. 1	1963–75 Div. 1	8–1 v Partick Thistle, League Cup, 16 August 1969	56, Div. 2, 1923–24	Jimmy Benson, 36 1931–32
1921–24 Div. 2	1946–60 Div. 2	1975–76 Pr. Div.			
1924–30 Div. 1	1960–62 Div. 1	1976–83 Div. 1			
1930–32 Div. 2	1962–63 Div. 2	1983– Pr. Div.			

ST MIRREN

1890–1935 Div. 1	1967–68 Div. 2	1975–77 Div. 1	15–0 v Glasgow University, Scottish Cup, 1st Rd 10 January 1960	62, Div. 2, 1967–68 Div. 1, 1976–77	Dunky Walker, 45, 1921–22
1935–36 Div. 2	1968–71 Div. 1	1977– Pr. Div.			
1936–67 Div. 1	1971–75 Div. 2				

| Ground | Honours (domestic) | |
	League	Cup

STENHOUSEMUIR (1884) Maroon/white

Ochilview Park
Larbert FK5 4QL
110 × 72 yd

Highest League placing
3rd, Div. 2, 1958–59, 1960–61

STIRLING ALBION (1945) Red/red

Annfield Park
Stirling S7K 83D
110 × 74 yd

Div. 2 Champions 1952–53
1957–58, 1960–61, 1964–65,
1976–77
Runners-up 1948–49, 1950–51

STRANRAER (1870) Blue/white

Stair Park
Stranraer
110 × 70 yd

Highest League placing
4th, Div. 2, 1960–61, 1976–77

Wales

Billy Meredith was selected for Wales on 71 consecutive international matches between 1895 and 1920, but was released to play in only 48 plus three Victory internationals in 1919. He even played in two of these while suspended by his club, Manchester United.

He had been offered maximum wages by the club but refused to sign and was placed on the transfer list. The Football League suggested that he be granted a free transfer but United turned it down. There was a dispute over what he was owed in benefit.

But on 22 December 1919 the Football Association confirmed the benefit at £762.18.3d (£762.91¼p) and that the player could not demand a free transfer.

United agreed to pay him this balance and the maximum £10 per week. He re-signed on 23 December returning to the side against Liverpool on Boxing Day in a goalless draw. Meredith asked for his back pay for the first part of the season but since he had refused to join the Football Association would not sanction this payment although the club had agreed to pay it.

During this period he had twice turned out for Wales on 11 October at Cardiff in a 2–1 win over England and seven days later at Stoke when England won 2–0.

At the end of 1920–21 it was reported that Manchester United would not engage Meredith unless he signed for £5 per week. They agreed to give him a free transfer to any club other than Manchester City. Despite this he signed for City in July 1921.

He was born 200 yards over the English border.

Northern Ireland

Pat Jennings the Irish international goalkeeper who started his career with Newry Town has played for three Football League clubs in the London area: Watford, Tottenham Hotspur and

League career			Record win	Most League points	Highest number of individual League goals
					STENHOUSEMUIR
1921– Div. 2			9–2 v Dundee United, Div. 2, 17 April 1937	50, Div. 2, 1960–61	Evelyn Morrison, 29, 1927–28 and Bobby Murray, 29, 1936–37
					STIRLING ALBION
1947–49 Div. 2	1953–56 Div. 1	1962–65 Div. 2	7–0 v Albion Rovers, Div. 2, 19 November 1947; v Montrose, Div. 2, 28 September 1957; v St Mirren, Div. 1, 5 March 1960 and v Arbroath, Div. 2, 11 March 1961	59, Div. 2, 1964–65	Michael Lawson, 26, 1975–76
1949–50 Div. 1	1956–58 Div. 2	1965–68 Div. 1			
1950–51 Div. 2	1958–60 Div. 1	1968–77 Div. 2			
1951–52 Div. 1	1960–61 Div. 2	1977–81 Div. 1			
1952–53 Div. 2	1961–62 Div. 1	1981– Div. 2			
					STRANRAER
1955– Div. 2			7–0 v Brechin City, Div. 2, 6 February 1965	44, Div. 2, 1960–61 1971–72	Derek Frye, 27, 1977–78

Arsenal and made his debut against a fourth, Queen's Park Rangers on a London ground where comparatively few other players have appeared.

This was at the White City in April 1963 where Rangers were experimenting with home fixtures. The game ended in a 2–2 draw.

Jennings completed his 1000th first class games on 26 February 1983 in a Division One match for Arsenal against West Bromwich Albion. It was also his 695th League game and his other appearances had been as follows:

Northern Ireland 95
FA Cup 81
League/Milk Cup 65
European matches 55
Others... 9

(These other 9 games include Charity Shield, Texaco Cup, Anglo-Italian Cup Winner's Cup, Great Britain and Under-23 internationals)

His 66 international appearances while with Tottenham made him their most capped player and his 472 League games for them was a record until the 1981–82 season.

He is also Northern Ireland's most capped international player, having made his initial appearance while still with Watford on 15 April 1964 against Wales in a 3–2 win at Swansea.

Pat Jennings on the occasion of his 1000th first-class game. *ASP*

Managers

POST WAR TITLE WINNERS, WITH MANAGERS AND THEIR FORMER PLAYING POSITIONS.

key to positions: glk.—goalkeeper; r.b.—right-back; l.b.—left-back; f.b.—full-back; r.h.—right-half; c.h.—centre-half; l.h.—left-half; o.r.—outside-right; i.r.—inside-right; c.f.—centre-forward; i.l.—inside-left; o.l.—outside-left; i.f.—inside-forward; w.h.—wing-half; h.b.—half-back; m.f.—midfield.
(h)—Honorary position as director-manager.

1946–47	FA Cup	Charlton Athletic **Jimmy Seed** *i.r.*
	Div. 1	Liverpool **George Kay** *c.h.*
	Div. 2	Manchester City **Sam Cowan** *c.h.*
	Div 3S	Cardiff City **Billy McCandless** *l.b.*
	Div. 3N	Doncaster Rovers **Jackie Bestall** *i.r.*
1947–48	FA Cup	Manchester United **Matt Busby** *r.h.*
	Div. 1	Arsenal **Tom Whittaker** *l.b.*
	Div. 2	Birmingham City **Harry Storer** *l.h.*
	Div. 3S	Queen's Park Rangers **David Mangnall** *c.f.*
	Div. 3N	Lincoln City **Bill Anderson** *r.b.*
1948–49	FA Cup	Wolves **Stan Cullis** *c.h.*
	Div. 1	Portsmouth **Bob Jackson** *c.f.*
	Div. 2	Fulham **Frank Osborne** *c.f.*
	Div 3S	Swansea Town **Billy McCandless** *l.b.*
	Div. 3N	Hull City **Raich Carter** *i.f.*
1949–50	FA Cup	Arsenal **Tom Whittaker** *l.b.*
	Div. 1	Portsmouth **Bob Jackson** *c.f.*
	Div. 2	Tottenham Hotspur **Arthur Rowe** *c.h.*
	Div. 3S	Notts County **Eric Houghton** *o.l.*
	Div. 3N	Doncaster Rovers **Peter Doherty** *i.l.*
1950–51	FA Cup	Newcastle United **Stanley Seymour** (h) *o.l.*
	Div. 1	Tottenham Hotspur **Arthur Rowe** *c.h.*
	Div. 2	Preston North End **Will Scott** *l.h.*
	Div. 3S	Nottingham Forest **Billy Walker** *i.l.*
	Div. 3N	Rotherham United **Reg Freeman** *l.b.*
1951–52	FA Cup	Newcastle United **Stanley Seymour** (h) *o.l.*
	Div. 1	Manchester United **Matt Busby** *r.h.*
	Div. 2	Sheffield Wednesday **Eric Taylor** *not a player*
	Div. 3S	Plymouth Argyle **Jimmy Rae** *l.b.*
	Div. 3N	Lincoln City **Bill Anderson** *r.b.*
1952–53	FA Cup	*Blackpool* **Joe Smith** *i.l.*
	Div. 1	Arsenal **Tom Whittaker** *l.b.*
	Div. 2	Sheffield United **Reg Freeman** *l.b.*
	Div. 3S	Bristol Rovers **Bert Tann** *c.h.*
	Div. 3N	Oldham Athletic **George Hardwick** *l.b.*
1953–54	FA Cup	West Bromwich Albion **Vic Buckingham** *w.h.*
	Div. 1	Wolves **Stan Cullis** *c.h.*
	Div. 2	Leicester City **Norman Bullock** *c.f.*
	Div. 3S	Ipswich Town **Scott Duncan** *o.r.*
	Div. 3N	Port Vale **Freddie Steele** *c.f.*
1954–55	FA Cup	Newcastle United **Duggie Livingstone** *l.b.*

Dave Mackay (left) and Roy McFarland (Derby County). Mackay later led Derby to the Championship as manager and McFarland rejoined them as assistant during 1982–83.

	Div. 1	Chelsea **Ted Drake** *c.f.*
	Div. 2	Birmingham City **Arthur Turner** *c.h.*
	Div. 3S	Bristol City **Pat Beasley** *o.l.*
	Div. 3N	Barnsley **Tim Ward** *r.h.*
1955–56	FA Cup	Manchester City **Les McDowall** *c.h.*
	Div. 1	Manchester United **Matt Busby** *r.h.*
	Div. 2	Sheffield Wednesday **Eric Taylor** *not a player*
	Div. 3S	Leyton Orient **Alec Stock** *i.r.*
	Div. 3N	Grimsby Town **Allenby Chilton** *c.h.*
1956–57	FA Cup	Aston Villa **Eric Houghton** *o.l.*
	Div. 1	Manchester United **Matt Busby** *r.h.*
	Div. 2	Leicester City **David Halliday** *c.f.*
	Div. 3S	Ipswich Town **Alf Ramsey** *r.b.*
	Div. 3N	Derby County **Harry Storer** *l.h.*
1957–58	FA Cup	Bolton Wanderers **Bill Ridding** *c.f.*
	Div. 1	Wolves **Stan Cullis** *c.h.*
	Div. 2	West Ham United **Ted Fenton** *l.h.*
	Div. 3S	Brighton and H.A. **Billy Lane** *c.f.*
	Div. 3N	Scunthorpe United **Tony McShane** *h.b.*
1958–59	FA Cup	Nottingham Forest **Billy Walker** *i.l.*
	Div. 1	Wolves **Stan Cullis** *c.h.*
	Div. 2	Sheffield Wednesday **Harry Catterick** *c.f.*
	Div. 3	Plymouth Argyle **Jack Rowley** *c.f.*
	Div. 4	Port Vale **Norman Low** *c.h.*
1959–60	FA Cup	Wolves **Stan Cullis** *c.h.*
	Div. 1	Burnley **Harry Potts** *i.f.*
	Div. 2	Aston Villa **Joe Mercer** *l.h.*
	Div. 3	Southampton **Ted Bates** *i.l.*
	Div. 4	Walsall **Billy Moore** *l.h.*
1960–61	FA Cup	Tottenham Hotspur **Bill Nicholson** *r.h.*
	FL Cup	Aston Villa **Joe Mercer** *l.h.*
	Div. 1	Tottenham Hotspur **Bill Nicholson** *r.h.*
	Div. 2	Ipswich Town **Alf Ramsey** *r.b.*
	Div. 3	Bury **David Russell** *r.h.*
	Div. 4	Peterborough United **Jimmy Hagan** *i.l.*
1961–62	FA Cup	Tottenham Hotspur **Bill Nicholson** *r.h.*
	FL Cup	Norwich City **Willie Reid** *i.f.*
	Div. 1	Ipswich Town **Alf Ramsey** *r.b.*
	Div. 2	Liverpool **Bill Shankly** *r.h.*
	Div. 3	Portsmouth **George Smith** *c.h.*
	Div. 4	Millwall **Ron Gray** *i.f.*
1962–63	FA Cup	Manchester United **Matt Busby** *r.h.*
	FL Cup	Birmingham City **Gil Merrick** *glk.*
	CW Cup	Tottenham Hotspur **Bill Nicholson** *r.h.*
	Div. 1	Everton **Harry Catterick** *c.f.*
	Div. 2	Stoke City **Tony Waddington** *i.f.*
	Div. 3	Northampton Town **Dave Bowen** *l.h.*
	Div. 4	Brentford **Malcolm McDonald** *r.b.*
1963–64	FA Cup	West Ham United **Ron Greenwood** *c.h.*
	FL Cup	Leicester City **Matt Gillies** *c.h.*
	Div. 1	Liverpool **Bill Shankly** *r.h.*
	Div. 2	Leeds United **Don Revie** *i.r.*
	Div. 3	Coventry City **Jimmy Hill** *i.r.*
	Div. 4	Gillingham **Freddie Cox** *o.r.*
1964–65	FA Cup	Liverpool **Bill Shankly** *r.h.*
	FL Cup	Chelsea **Tommy Docherty** *r.h.*
	CW Cup	West Ham United **Ron Greenwood** *c.h.*
	Div. 1	Manchester United **Matt Busby** *r.h.*
	Div. 2	Newcastle United **Joe Harvey** *r.h.*
	Div. 3	Carlisle United **Alan Ashman** *c.f.*
	Div. 4	Brighton and H.A. **Archie Macaulay** *r.h.*
1965–66	FA Cup	Everton **Harry Catterick** *c.f.*
	FL Cup	West Bromwich Albion **Jimmy Hagan** *i.l.*

	Div. 1	Liverpool **Bill Shankly** *r.h.*	
	Div. 2	Manchester City **Joe Mercer** *l.h.*	
	Div. 3	Hull City **Cliff Britton** *r.h.*	
	Div. 4	Doncaster Rovers **Jackie Bestall** *i.r.*	
1966–67	FA Cup	Tottenham Hotspur **Bill Nicholson** *r.h.*	
	FL Cup	Queen's Park Rangers **Alec Stock** *i.r.*	
	Div. 1	Manchester United **Matt Busby** *r.h.*	
	Div. 2	Coventry City **Jimmy Hill** *i.r.*	
	Div. 3	Queen's Park Rangers **Alec Stock** *i.r.*	
	Div. 4	Stockport County **Jimmy Meadows** *r.b.*	
1967–68	FA Cup	West Bromwich Albion **Alan Ashman** *c.f.*	
	FL Cup	Leeds United **Don Revie** *i.r.*	
	E. Cup	Manchester United **Matt Busby** *r.h.*	
	Fairs Cup	Leeds United **Don Revie** *i.r.*	
	Div. 1	Manchester City **Joe Mercer** *l.h.*	
	Div. 2	Ipswich Town **Bill McGarry** *r.h.*	
	Div. 3	Oxford United **Arthur Turner** *c.h.*	
	Div. 4	Luton Town **Allan Brown** *i.r.*	
1968–69	FA Cup	Manchester City **Joe Mercer** *l.h.*	
	FL Cup	Swindon Town **Danny Williams** *l.h.*	
	Fairs Cup	Newcastle United **Joe Harvey** *r.h.*	
	Div. 1	Leeds United **Don Revie** *i.r.*	
	Div. 2	Derby County **Brian Clough** *c.f.*	
	Div. 3	Watford **Ken Furphy** *r.h.*	
	Div. 4	Doncaster Rovers **Lawrie McMenemy** *c.h.*	
1969–70	FA Cup	Chelsea **Dave Sexton** *i.f.*	
	FL Cup	Manchester City **Joe Mercer** *l.h.*	
	CW Cup	Manchester City **Joe Mercer** *l.h.*	
	Fairs Cup	Arsenal **Bertie Mee** *i.f.*	
	Div. 1	Everton **Harry Catterick** *c.f.*	
	Div. 2	Huddersfield Town **Ian Greaves** *r.b.*	
	Div. 3	Orient **Jimmy Bloomfield** *i.r.*	
	Div. 4	Chesterfield **Jimmy McGuigan** *o.r.*	
1970–71	FA Cup	Arsenal **Bertie Mee** *i.f.*	
	FL Cup	Tottenham Hotspur **Bill Nicholson** *r.h.*	
	CW Cup	Chelsea **Dave Sexton** *i.f.*	
	Fairs Cup	Leeds United **Don Revie** *i.r.*	
	Div. 1	Arsenal **Bertie Mee** *i.f.*	
	Div. 2	Leicester City **Frank O'Farrell** *l.h.*	
	Div. 3	Preston North End **Alan Ball** *h.b.*	
	Div. 4	Notts County **Jimmy Sirrel** *i.r.*	
1971–72	FA Cup	Leeds United **Don Revie** *i.r.*	
	FL Cup	Stoke City **Tony Waddington** *i.f.*	
	UEFA Cup	Tottenham Hotspur **Bill Nicholson** *r.h.*	
	Div. 1	Derby County **Brian Clough** *c.f.*	
	Div. 2	Norwich City **Ron Saunders** *c.f.*	
	Div. 3	Aston Villa **Vic Crowe** *l.h.*	
	Div. 4	Grimsby Town **Lawrie McMenemy** *c.h.*	
1972–73	FA Cup	Sunderland **Bob Stokoe** *c.h.*	
	FL Cup	Tottenham Hotspur **Bill Nicholson** *r.h.*	
	UEFA Cup	Liverpool **Bill Shankly** *r.h.*	
	Div. 1	Liverpool **Bill Shankly** *r.h.*	
	Div. 2	Burnley **Jimmy Adamson** *r.h.*	
	Div. 3	Bolton Wanderers **Jimmy Armfield** *r.b.*	
	Div. 4	Southport **Jimmy Meadows** *r.b.*	
1973–74	FA Cup	Liverpool **Bill Shankly** *r.h.*	
	FL Cup	Wolves **Bill McGarry** *r.h.*	
	Div. 1	Leeds United **Don Revie** *i.r.*	
	Div. 2	Middlesbrough **Jack Charlton** *c.h.*	
	Div. 3	Oldham Athletic **Jimmy Frizzell** *i.r.*	
	Div. 4	Peterborough United **Noel Cantwell** *l.b.*	
1974–75	FA Cup	West Ham United **John Lyall** *l.b.*	
	FL Cup	Aston Villa **Ron Saunders** *c.f.*	
	Div. 1	Derby County **Dave Mackay** *l.h.*	
	Div. 2	Manchester United **Tommy Docherty** *r.h.*	
	Div. 3	Blackburn Rovers **Gordon Lee** *r.b.*	
	Div. 4	Mansfield Town **Dave Smith** *r.b.*	
1975–76	FA Cup	Southampton **Lawrie McMenemy** *c.h.*	
	FL Cup	Manchester City **Tony Book** *r.b.*	
	UEFA Cup	Liverpool **Bob Paisley** *r.h.*	
	Div. 1	Liverpool **Bob Paisley** *r.h.*	
	Div. 2	Sunderland **Bob Stokoe** *c.h.*	
	Div. 3	Hereford United **John Sillett** *r.b.*	
	Div. 4	Lincoln City **Graham Taylor** *r.b.*	
1976–77	FA Cup	Manchester United **Tommy Docherty** *r.h.*	
	FL Cup	Aston Villa **Ron Saunders** *c.f.*	
	E. Cup	Liverpool **Bob Paisley** *r.h.*	
	Div. 1	Liverpool **Bob Paisley** *r.h.*	
	Div. 2	Wolves **Sammy Chung** *i.f.*	
	Div. 3	Mansfield Town **Peter Morris** *h.b.*	
	Div. 4	Cambridge United **Ron Atkinson** *r.h.*	
1977–78	FA Cup	Ipswich Town **Bobby Robson** *r.h.*	
	FL Cup	Nottingham Forest **Brian Clough** *c.f.*	
	E. Cup	Liverpool **Bob Paisley** *r.h.*	
	Div. 1	Nottingham Forest **Brian Clough** *c.f.*	
	Div. 2	Bolton Wanderers **Ian Greaves** *l.b.*	
	Div. 3	Wrexham **Arfon Griffiths** *i.r.*	
	Div. 4	Watford **Graham Taylor** *r.b.*	
1978–79	FA Cup	Arsenal **Terry Neill** *c.h.*	
	FL Cup	Nottingham Forest **Brian Clough** *c.f.*	
	E. Cup	Nottingham Forest **Brian Clough** *c.f.*	
	Div. 1	Liverpool **Bob Paisley** *r.h.*	
	Div. 2	Crystal Palace **Terry Venables** *i.f.*	
	Div. 3	Shrewsbury Town **Graham Turner** *w.h.*	
	Div. 4	Reading **Maurice Evans** *i.f.*	
1979–80	FA Cup	West Ham United **John Lyall** *l.b.*	
	FL Cup	Wolves **John Barnwell** *i.r.*	
	E. Cup	Nottingham Forest **Brian Clough** *c.f.*	
	Div. 1	Liverpool **Bob Paisley** *r.h.*	
	Div. 2	Leicester City **Jock Wallace** *glk.*	
	Div. 3	Grimsby Town **George Kerr** *i.f.*	
	Div. 4	Huddersfield Town **Mick Buxton** *r.b.*	
1980–81	FA Cup	Tottenham Hotspur **Keith Burkinshaw** *w.h.*	
	FL Cup	Liverpool **Bob Paisley** *r.h.*	
	E. Cup	Liverpool **Bob Paisley** *r.h.*	
	UEFA Cup	Ipswich Town **Bobby Robson** *r.h.*	
	Div. 1	Aston Villa **Ron Saunders** *c.f.*	
	Div. 2	West Ham United **John Lyall** *l.b.*	
	Div. 3	Rotherham United **Ian Porterfield** *i.f.*	
	Div. 4	Southend United **Dave Smith** *f.b.*	
1981–82	FA Cup	Tottenham Hotspur **Keith Burkinshaw** *w.h.*	
	FL Cup	Liverpool **Bob Paisley** *r.h.*	
	E. Cup	Aston Villa **Tony Barton** *o.r.*	
	Div. 1	Liverpool **Bob Paisley** *r.h.*	
	Div. 2	Luton Town **David Pleat** *o.l.*	
	Div. 3	Burnley **Brian Miller** *l.h.*	
	Div. 4	Sheffield United **Ian Porterfield** *i.f.*	
1982–83	FA Cup	Manchester United **Ron Atkinson** *w.h.*	
	FL Cup	Liverpool **Bob Paisley** *r.h.*	
	Div. 1	Liverpool **Bob Paisley** *r.h.*	
	Div. 2	Queen's Park Rangers **Terry Venables** *i.f.*	
	Div. 3	Portsmouth **Bobby Campbell** *r.h.*	
	Div. 4	Wimbledon **Dave Bassett** *m.f.*	

British International Championship

The British International Championship began when all four home countries started playing each other. Previously matches between some of them had only been regarded as friendlies. The tournament itself began in 1883–84. If countries were level on points at the top they shared the title, as goal average or goal difference did not count in determining the winner until the latter system was introduced in 1978–79.

England have won the title outright on 34 occasions, Scotland 24, Wales seven and Ireland twice. England have been concerned in all the 20 shared titles, Scotland 17, Wales and Ireland in five each.

In the overall record of matches between the four home countries, in addition to the friendlies played before the International Championship started, England and Wales met each other twice in qualifying matches for the 1974 World Cup, as did Scotland and Wales in the 1978 World Cup, Scotland played England as part of their Centenary in 1973 and Wales met England in their Centenary match in 1976.

England also played Ireland in the qualifying competition of the 1980 European Championship and Scotland were drawn with Ireland in the same World Cup group for the 1982 finals.

In 1980–81 both England and Wales declined to play in Northern Ireland and the championship was not completed.

England v Scotland

First match	Scotland 0 England 0 30 November 1872 Glasgow
Overall record	101 matches: Scotland 39 wins, England 40, drawn 22. Goals: England 182, Scotland 165
Record win	England 9 Scotland 3 15 April 1961, Wembley
Best individual performance	Dennis Wilshaw (England) 4 goals v Scotland, 2 April 1955, Wembley
Most appearances	Billy Wright (England) 13

Wales v Scotland

First match	Scotland 4 Wales 0 25 March 1876 Glasgow
Overall record	98 matches: Scotland 59 wins, Wales 17, drawn 22. Goals: Scotland 235, Wales 108
Record win	Scotland 9 Wales 0 23 March 1878 Old Hampden
Best individual performance	Willie Paul (Scotland) 4 goals v Wales, 22 March 1890, Paisley. John Madden (Scotland) 4 goals v Wales, 18 March 1883, Wrexham
Most appearances	Billy Meredith (Wales), 12, Ivor Allchurch (Wales) 12

England v Wales

First match	England 2 Wales 1 18 January 1879 Kennington Oval
Overall record	96 matches: England 62 wins, Wales 13, drawn 21. Goals: England 239, Wales 89
Record win	Wales 1 England 9 16 March 1896 Cardiff
Best individual performance	Steve Bloomer (England) 5 goals v Wales, 16 March 1896, Cardiff
Most appearances	Billy Meredith (Wales) 20

Ireland v Wales

First match	Wales 7 Ireland 1 25 February 1882 Wrexham
Overall record	89 matches: Wales 42 wins, Ireland 27, drawn 20. Goals: Wales 180, Ireland 125
Record win	Wales 11 Ireland 0 3 March 1888 Wrexham
Best individual performance	Joe Bambrick (Ireland) 6 goals v Wales, 1 February 1930, Belfast
Most appearances	Billy Meredith (Wales) 16

Ireland v England

First match	Ireland 0 England 13 18 February 1882 Belfast
Overall record	91 matches: England 70 wins, Ireland 6, drawn 15. Goals: England 312, Ireland 80
Record win	Ireland 0 England 13 18 February 1882 Belfast
Best individual performance	Willie Hall (England) 5 goals v Ireland, 16 November 1938, Old Trafford
Most appearances	Pat Jennings (Ireland) 18

Scotland v Ireland

First match	Ireland 0 Scotland 5 26 January 1884 Belfast
Overall record	90 matches: Scotland 60 wins, Ireland 14, drawn 16. Goals: Scotland 253, Ireland 79
Record win	Scotland 11 Ireland 0 23 February 1901 Hampden Park
Best individual performance	Charles Heggie (Scotland) 5 goals v Ireland, 20 March 1886, Belfast
Most appearances	Danny Blanchflower (Ireland) 13

Youngest international players

England:	Duncan Edwards (Manchester United) 18 years 183 days, left-half v Scotland, 2 April 1955
Ireland:	Norman Kernaghan (Belfast Celtic) 17 years 80 days, outside-right v Wales, 11 March 1936
Scotland:	Johnny Lambie (Queen's Park), 17 years 92 days, inside-forward v Ireland, 20 March 1886
Wales:	John Charles (Leeds United) 18 years 71 days, centre-half v Ireland, 8 March 1950

Full International Record of the Home Countries

ENGLAND

Opponents	P	W	D	L	F	A
Argentina	8	4	3	1	12	7
Austria	15	8	3	4	54	25
Australia	4	2	2	0	4	2
Belgium	17	12	4	1	66	24
Bohemia	1	1	0	0	4	0
Brazil	12	1	4	7	9	19
Bulgaria	5	3	2	0	7	1
Chile	2	2	0	0	4	1
Colombia	1	1	0	0	4	0
Cyprus	2	2	0	0	6	0
Czechoslovakia	10	6	2	2	19	11
Denmark	8	6	2	0	23	9
Ecuador	1	1	0	0	2	0
Finland	6	6	0	0	26	4
France	19	14	2	3	60	25
East Germany (GDR)	3	2	1	0	6	3
West Germany	16	8	3	5	31	21
Greece	4	3	1	0	8	0
Hungary	14	9	0	5	42	27
Iceland	1	0	1	0	1	1
Northern Ireland	91	70	15	6	312	80
Republic of Ireland	8	4	3	1	14	7
Italy	14	6	4	4	23	18
Kuwait	1	1	0	0	1	0
Luxembourg	6	6	0	0	34	3
Malta	2	2	0	0	6	0
Mexico	4	2	1	1	11	2
Netherlands (Holland)	7	4	2	1	13	5
Norway	6	5	0	1	25	4
Peru	2	1	0	1	5	4
Poland	4	1	2	1	3	4
Portugal	14	8	5	1	35	16
Rumania	6	2	3	1	5	3
Scotland	101	40	22	39	182	165
Spain	15	9	2	4	31	17
Sweden	10	6	2	2	23	13
Switzerland	14	9	2	3	36	12
USA	4	3	0	1	24	5
USSR	7	3	3	1	14	7
Uruguay	6	2	2	2	7	8
Wales	96	62	21	13	239	89
Yugoslavia	11	2	5	4	15	18
Rest of Europe	1	1	0	0	3	0
FIFA	1	0	1	0	4	4
Rest of the World	1	1	0	0	2	1

SCOTLAND

Opponents	P	W	D	L	F	A
Argentina	2	0	1	1	2	4
Austria	14	3	4	7	18	28
Belgium	9	3	0	6	13	15
Brazil	6	0	2	4	2	9
Bulgaria	1	1	0	0	2	1
Canada	3	3	0	0	7	0
Cyprus	2	2	0	0	13	0
Chile	1	1	0	0	4	2
Czechoslovakia	10	5	1	4	18	16
Denmark	9	8	0	1	17	5
England	101	39	22	40	165	182
Finland	4	4	0	0	13	3
France	7	5	0	2	10	6
East Germany (GDR)	3	2	0	1	5	2

	P	W	D	L	F	A
West Germany	9	3	4	2	16	13
Hungary	6	1	2	3	11	15
Northern Ireland	90	60	16	14	253	79
Republic of Ireland	4	2	1	1	8	3
Italy	3	1	0	2	1	6
Iran	1	0	1	0	1	1
Israel	2	2	0	0	4	1
Luxembourg	1	1	0	0	6	0
Netherlands (Holland)	8	5	1	2	13	10
New Zealand	1	1	0	0	5	2
Norway	8	6	1	1	27	12
Paraguay	1	0	0	1	2	3
Peru	3	1	1	2	4	4
Poland	5	1	1	3	6	8
Portugal	11	4	2	5	13	11
Rumania	2	0	2	0	2	2
Spain	7	2	2	3	13	14
Sweden	6	3	1	2	10	7
Switzerland	9	5	1	3	15	13
Turkey	1	0	0	1	2	4
Uruguay	2	0	0	2	2	10
USA	1	1	0	0	6	0
USSR	3	0	1	2	2	5
Wales	98	59	22	17	235	108
Yugoslavia	5	1	4	0	8	6
Zaire	1	1	0	0	2	0
Kuwait	2	0	2	0	0	0
Malta	2	2	0	0	9	0
Mexico	2	0	1	1	2	3
Norway	1	1	0	0	1	0
Poland	2	1	0	1	2	3
Portugal	2	1	0	1	4	4
Rumania	2	0	1	1	0	2
Scotland	98	17	22	59	108	235
Spain	3	0	2	1	3	4
Sweden	1	0	1	0	0	0
Switzerland	2	1	0	1	3	6
Turkey	4	3	0	1	9	1
Rest of UK	2	1	0	1	3	3
USSR	4	1	1	2	3	6
Yugoslavia	5	0	2	3	8	15

WALES

Opponents	P	W	D	L	F	A
Austria	4	1	0	3	3	6
Belgium	2	1	0	1	6	4
Brazil	6	0	1	5	4	12
Bulgaria	1	1	0	0	1	0
Chile	1	0	0	1	0	2
Czechoslovakia	7	3	0	5	6	9
Denmark	2	1	0	1	4	3
England	96	13	21	62	89	239
Finland	2	2	0	0	4	0
France	4	1	1	2	4	9
East Germany (GDR)	4	1	0	3	7	8
West Germany	6	0	3	3	4	12
Greece	2	1	0	1	4	3
Hungary	7	3	2	2	11	10
Iceland	2	1	1	0	6	2
Luxembourg	2	2	0	0	8	1
Northern Ireland	89	42	20	27	180	125
Republic of Ireland	3	3	0	0	8	4
Iran	1	1	0	0	1	0
Israel	2	2	0	0	4	0
Italy	3	0	0	3	2	9

NORTHERN IRELAND

Opponents	P	W	D	L	F	A
Albania	4	2	2	0	6	2
Argentina	1	0	0	1	1	3
Australia	3	2	1	0	5	3
Austria	2	0	1	1	2	4
Belgium	2	1	0	1	3	2
Bulgaria	4	2	1	1	4	3
Cyprus	4	3	0	1	11	1
Czechoslovakia	2	2	0	0	3	1
Denmark	2	1	0	1	2	5
England	91	6	15	70	80	312
France	5	0	1	4	4	17
Greece	2	1	0	1	3	2
Netherlands (Holland)	5	1	2	2	4	8
Honduras	1	0	1	0	1	1
Israel	4	2	2	0	5	3
Iceland	2	1	0	1	2	1
Republic of Ireland	2	1	1	0	1	0
Italy	4	1	1	2	6	7
Mexico	1	1	0	0	4	1
Norway	2	1	0	1	4	2
Poland	2	2	0	0	4	0
Portugal	6	2	3	1	7	4
Scotland	90	14	16	60	79	253
Spain	6	1	2	3	5	12
Sweden	4	2	0	2	6	3
Switzerland	2	1	0	1	2	2
Turkey	3	3	0	0	9	2
Uruguay	1	1	0	0	3	0
USSR	4	0	2	2	1	4
Wales	89	27	20	42	125	180
West Germany	6	1	1	4	7	15
Yugoslavia	3	1	1	1	1	1

International Appearances of the Home Countries

INTERNATIONAL APPEARANCES (ENGLAND) 50 or more

		Int. Champ.	Others	Total
Bobby Moore (West Ham United)	1962–1973	30	78	108
Bobby Charlton (Manchester United)	1958–1970	32	74	106
Billy Wright (Wolverhampton Wanderers)	1946–1959	38	67	105
Tom Finney (Preston North End)	1946–1956	29	47	76
Gordon Banks (Leicester City, Stoke City)	1963–1972	23	50	73
Alan Ball (Blackpool, Everton, Arsenal)	1965–1975	20	52	72
Martin Peters (West Ham United, Tottenham Hotspur)	1966–1974	19	48	67
Dave Watson (Sunderland, Manchester City, Werder Bremen, Southampton, Stoke City)	1974–1982	18	47	65
Ray Wilson (Huddersfield Town, Everton)	1960–1968	15	48	63

INTERNATIONAL APPEARANCES (ENGLAND) 50 or more (continued)

		Int. Champ.	Others	Total
Kevin Keegan (Liverpool, Hamburg, Southampton)	1972–1982	13	50	63
Emlyn Hughes (Liverpool, Wolverhampton Wanderers)	1969–1980	21	41	62
Ray Clemence (Liverpool)	1972–	14	46	60
Jimmy Greaves (Chelsea, Tottenham Hotspur)	1959–1967	14	43	57
Johnny Haynes (Fulham)	1954–1962	16	40	56
Stanley Matthews (Stoke City, Blackpool)	1934–1957	24	30	54*
Ray Wilkins (Chelsea, Manchester United)	1976–	14	40	54
Peter Shilton (Leicester City, Stoke City, Nottingham Forest, Southampton)	1970–	15	38	53

* Matthews' total does not include the 29 war-time and Victory internationals in which he appeared.

INTERNATIONAL APPEARANCES (SCOTLAND) 50 or more

		Int. Champ.	Others	Total
Kenny Dalglish (Celtic, Liverpool)	1971–	26	64	90
Danny McGrain (Celtic)	1973–1982	22	40	62
Denis Law (Huddersfield T, Manchester City, Torino, Manchester Utd)	1958–1974	26	29	55
Billy Bremner (Leeds United)	1965–1976	19	35	54
George Young (Rangers)	1946–1957	29	24	53

INTERNATIONAL APPEARANCES (NORTHERN IRELAND) 50 or more

		Int. Champ.	Others	Total
Pat Jennings (Watford, Tottenham Hotspur, Arsenal)	1964–	46	53	99
Sammy McIlroy (Manchester United, Stoke City)	1972–	29	40	69
Terry Neill (Arsenal, Hull City)	1961–1973	30	30	60
Martin O'Neill (Distillery, Nottingham Forest, Norwich City, Manchester City, Norwich City)	1971–	18	38	56
Jimmy Nichol (Manchester United, Toronto Blizzard, Sunderland, Toronto Blizzard)	1976–	19	37	56
Danny Blanchflower (Barnsley, Aston Villa, Tottenham Hotspur)	1949–1962	37	19	56
Billy Bingham (Sunderland, Luton Town, Everton)	1951–1963	34	22	56
Jimmy McIlroy (Burnley)	1951–1965	36	19	55
Allan Hunter (Blackburn Rovers, Ipswich Town)	1969–1980	23	30	53
Sammy Nelson (Arsenal, Brighton & HA)	1970–1982	18	33	51
Bryan Hamilton (Linfield, Ipswich Town, Everton, Millwall, Swindon Town)	1968–1980	22	28	50

INTERNATIONAL APPEARANCES (WALES) 50 or more

		Int. Champ.	Others	Total
Ivor Allchurch (Swansea, Newcastle United, Cardiff City)	1950–1966	37	31	68
Cliff Jones (Swansea, Tottenham Hotspur, Fulham)	1954–1969	31	28	59
Terry Yorath (Leeds United, Coventry City, Tottenham Hotspur)	1969–	27	32	59
Brian Flynn (Burnley, Leeds United, Burnley)	1974–	26	32	58
Leighton Phillips (Cardiff City, Aston Villa, Swansea City)	1971–	23	33	56
Leighton James (Burnley, Derby County, Burnley, Swansea City)	1971–	25	29	54
Joey Jones (Liverpool, Wrexham, Chelsea)	1975–	22	30	52
Dai Davies (Everton, Wrexham, Swansea City)	1975–	21	31	52
John Mahoney (Stoke City, Middlesbrough, Swansea City)	1967–	22	29	51

British International Soccer

Scotland's most successful run began in the late 1870s and 1880s when they had 13 wins in a row, beating Wales six times, England five and Ireland twice. They actually went 22 games without defeat after beating Wales 3–0 on 7 April 1880 and ended it with a 5–1 win against Wales on 10 March 1888.

England's most successful run came in the fol-lowing decade. It started when they beat Wales 3–1 on 15 March 1890 and ended after they again defeated the Welsh 9–1 on 16 March 1896, fol-lowing a sequence of 20 matches. It comprised 16 wins and four draws and at one time produced nine successive wins.

Nothern Ireland's best sequence of results began on 1 May 1957 against Portugal in a 3–0 win and ended after a 1–0 win against Czechoslovakia in the World Cup on 8 June 1958. It produced four wins and three draws.

Wales' best sequence started on 13 November 1957 with a 1–1 draw against Scotland and ended with a 2–1 win over Hungary in the World Cup finals in Sweden on 17 June 1958. It produced three wins and five draws.

Above: Neil Franklin who played in the first 27 post-war internationals for England pictured (left). *Staffordshire Evening Sentinel*. **Left: Former England international stars at the Thwaites Open Classic Bowling competition: Tom Finney (left) and Bryan Douglas.** *Wally Talbot*

Tom Finney was the highest scoring winger for England in the post-war period with 30 goals in 76 appearances. He made his last appearance as a right-winger in the 1956–57 season when Bryan Douglas took over from him. Finney continued in his other regular berth on the left-wing afterwards.

Neil Franklin was centre-half for England in their first 27 post-war international games and received an award. His career was interrupted when he was suspended for playing illegally in Colombia in 1950 and he did not play for England again.

England scored seven goals in each of two suc-cessive games against Northern Ireland although they had to wait eight years between the matches. On 16 November 1938 England won 7–0 at Old Trafford and on 28 September 1946 they beat the Irish 7–2 at Windsor Park, Belfast.

Billy Foulkes (Newcastle United) scored with his first kick on his international debut for Wales against England at Ninian Park, Cardiff on 20 October 1951. The game ended in a 1–1 draw.

At Wrexham on 17 March 1937 in the Wales v Northern Ireland international all the players from the Welsh team were taken from clubs outside the country and all but two of the Irish team, Fulton and Banks both amateurs, were similarly drawn from abroad. Wales won 4–1.

The receipts for the 100th international between Scotland and England at Hampden Park on 29 May 1982 were £500 000 from a crowd of 80 529. The first official game between the two countries on 30 November 1872 on the ground of the West of Scotland Cricket Club in Glasgow produced a total of £103 from a 4000 attendance. The profit from the game was £33.

The lowest attendance for a British International Championship match since before the First World War was at Wrexham on 27 May 1982

Wembley on 15 December 1982 it was the highest score recorded in a European Championship match. On the afternoon of the same day Yugoslavia drew 4–4 with Wales in Titograd in the same competition for the highest scoring draw.

Luther Blissett scored a hat-trick for England in the match against Luxembourg, the first black player to score for England in a full international. In the same match Mark Chamberlain became the second. It was also the first time that as many as seven different players figured on the scoresheet including one own goal, in a full England international match.

Ivor and Len Allchurch and John and Mel Charles all played in the same Welsh team on three occasions: against Northern Ireland on 20 April 1955, against Israel on 15 January 1958 and against Brazil on 12 May 1962.

Kenny Dalglish completed his 90th international appearance for Scotland against Switzerland on 30 March 1983 at Hampden Park. The striker had established himself as Scotland's most experienced international in 1978 when he overtook Denis Law's record of 55 appearances. Dalglish made his first appearance as substitute against Belgium on 10 November 1971. Dalglish also holds the record of consecutive appearances for Scotland, making 43 between 1976 and 1981.

Gordon Banks appeared in 73 international matches for England. His first game was against Scotland on 6 April 1963 at Wembley and his last was also against the Scots at Hampden Park on 27 May 1972. He established himself as England's most experienced goalkeeper.

Alan Rough appeared in goal for Scotland on 51 occasions. His first game was against Switzerland on 7 April 1976 at Hampden Park and his last match was against the USSR in Malaga on 22 June 1982 in the World Cup.

Hungary are the only Continental country to have scored as many as six and seven goals in full international matches against England. They won 6–3 at Wembley on 25 November 1953 and 7–1 in Budapest on 23 May 1954.

During the 1980–81 season England had a run of six matches without a win, losing four times. Between March and May 1981 they had five successive games at Wembley losing three, drawing the other two and scoring just one goal. In the period from May to October 1958 they had seven games without a win, drawing five and losing two.

Top left: Budapest in May 1954 and Ferenc Puskas (dark shirt) prepares to torment Billy Wright (4). **Bottom left:** November 1953 at Wembley and the white-shirted England defence is under pressure from the Hungarians. Harry Johnston (right) and goalkeeper Gil Merrick have to keep their eyes on the ball. **Above:** England centre-forward Stan Mortensen is carried off by Hungarians Gyula Lorant (centre) and Gyula Grosics while trainer Jimmy Trotter attends to him.

when Wales and Northern Ireland played before a crowd of 2315. On the same day there was live television coverage of the FA Cup Final replay.

When England beat Luxembourg 9–0 at

Arsenal and Wales international goalkeeper Jack Kelsey, a former blacksmith who made 327 League appearances and played on 41 occasions for his country.

Pat Jennings completed his 95th international appearance for Northern Ireland in goal against France on 4 July 1982 in Madrid in the World Cup. His first had been against Wales on 15 April 1964 at Swansea and he has played in more matches for his country than any other player.

Dai Davies overtook Jack Kelsey's record of 41 international appearances in goal for Wales during the 1980–81 season. Davies made his first against Hungary on 16 April 1975 and reached his 51st on 2 June 1982 at Toulouse against France. Kelsey had played between 1954 and 1962.

Awards

FOOTBALLER OF THE YEAR

The Football Writers Association, founded in 1947, has elected a Footballer of the Year at the end of each season since 1947–48.

1947–48	Stanley Matthews (Blackpool)
1948–49	Johnny Carey (Manchester United)
1949–50	Joe Mercer (Arsenal)
1950–51	Harry Johnston (Blackpool)
1951–52	Billy Wright (Wolverhampton Wanderers)
1952–53	Nat Lofthouse (Bolton Wanderers)
1953–54	Tom Finney (Preston North End)
1954–55	Don Revie (Manchester City)
1955–56	Bert Trautmann (Manchester City)
1956–57	Tom Finney (Preston North End)
1957–58	Danny Blanchflower (Tottenham Hotspur)
1958–59	Syd Owen (Luton Town)
1959–60	Bill Slater (Wolverhampton Wanderers)
1960–61	Danny Blanchflower (Tottenham Hotspur)
1961–62	Jimmy Adamson (Burnley)
1962–63	Stanley Matthews (Stoke City)
1963–64	Bobby Moore (West Ham United)
1964–65	Bobby Collins (Leeds United)
1965–66	Bobby Charlton (Manchester United)
1966–67	Jackie Charlton (Leeds United)
1967–68	George Best (Manchester United)
1968–69	Dave Mackay (Derby County) and Tony Book (Manchester City)
1969–70	Billy Bremner (Leeds United)
1970–71	Frank McLintock (Arsenal)
1971–72	Gordon Banks (Stoke City)
1972–73	Pat Jennings (Tottenham Hotspur)
1973–74	Ian Callaghan (Liverpool)
1974–75	Alan Mullery (Fulham)
1975–76	Kevin Keegan (Liverpool)
1976–77	Emlyn Hughes (Liverpool)
1977–78	Kenny Burns (Nottingham Forest)
1978–79	Kenny Dalglish (Liverpool)
1979–80	Terry McDermott (Liverpool)
1980–81	Frans Thijssen (Ipswich Town)
1981–82	Steve Perryman (Tottenham Hotspur)
1982–83	Kenny Dalglish (Liverpool)

Since 1974 the Professional Footballers Association have given their own Footballer of the Year award.

1974	Andy Gray (Aston Villa)
1975	Pat Jennings (Tottenham Hotspur)
1976	Colin Todd (Derby County)
1977	Norman Hunter (Leeds United)
1978	Peter Shilton (Nottingham Forest)
1979	Liam Brady (Arsenal)
1980	Terry McDermott (Liverpool)
1981	John Wark (Ipswich Town)
1982	Kevin Keegan (Southampton)
1983	Kenny Dalglish (Liverpool)

Major Records

AGE

Albert Geldard and Ken Roberts are believed to have been the youngest players to appear in Football League matches. Geldard was 15 years 158 days old when he made his debut for Bradford Park Avenue against Millwall on 16 September 1929, in a Division Two match. Roberts was exactly the same age on his first appearance for Wrexham against Bradford (Park Avenue) on 1 September 1951 in a Division Three (Northern) match.

Neil McBain was the oldest player to have appeared in a Football League match. He was 52 years 4 months old when, as manager of New Brighton, he had to select himself to play in goal in an emergency against Hartlepool United on 15 March 1947 in a Division Three (North) match.

Scott Endersby was the youngest player to appear in the FA Cup proper when he kept goal for Kettering against Tilbury in the first round on 26 November 1977, when he was 15 years 288 days old.

Billy Meredith was the oldest player to appear in the FA Cup proper when he played for Manchester City against Newcastle United on 29 March 1924 at the age of 49 years 8 months.

Paul Allen at 17 years 256 days was the youngest FA Cup finalist when he played for West Ham United against Arsenal in 1980. The youngest scorer was Norman Whiteside for Manchester United against Brighton and Hove Albion in 1983 when 18 years 18 days.

Walter Hampson at 41 years 8 months was the oldest FA Cup finalist when he played for Newcastle United against Aston Villa in 1924.

APPEARANCES

The record for Football League appearances is 824 by Terry Paine for Southampton and Hereford United from 1957 to 1977.

THE DOUBLE

Only four clubs have won the Football League championship and the FA Cup in the same season: Preston North End 1888–89, Aston Villa in 1896–97, Tottenham Hotspur in 1960–61 and Arsenal in 1970–71.

GOALSCORING

Highest scorer in one match in Britain at first-class level: John Petrie 13 goals for Arbroath v Bon Accord, Scottish Cup first round, 5 September 1885.

Career total in world: Artur Friedenreich, 1329 goals in Brazilian football between 1910–1930.

Highest scores:

First-class match: Arbroath 36 Bon Accord 0, Scottish Cup first round, 5 September 1885

International: England 13 Northern Ireland 0, 18 February 1882

FA Cup: Preston North End 26 Hyde United 0, first round, 15 October 1887

Football League: Newcastle United 13 Newport County 0, Division Two, 5 October 1946; Stockport County 13 Halifax Town 0, Division Three (Northern), 6 January 1934

Scottish League: Celtic 11 Dundee 0, Division One, 26 October 1895; East Fife 13 Edinburgh City 2, Division Two, 11 December 1937

Aggregate: Tranmere Rovers 13 Oldham Athletic 4, Division Three (Northern), 26 December 1935

Most in one season:

Football League: 134 goals by Peterborough United, Division Four, 1960–61 in 46 matches.

Scottish League: 142 goals by Raith Rovers, Division Two, 1937–38 in 34 matches.

Quickest goals; in 6 seconds by:
Albert Mundy, Aldershot against Hartlepool United, *Division Four*, 25 October 1958
Barrie Jones, Notts County against Torquay United, *Division Three*, 31 March 1962
Keith Smith, Crystal Palace against Derby County, *Division Two*, 12 December 1964
Tommy Langley, Queen's Park Rangers against Bolton Wanderers, *Division Two*, 11 October 1980

Individual record in Football League:
Joe Payne, ten goals for Luton Town against Bristol Rovers, Division Three (Southern), 13 April 1936

Individual record in FA Cup:
Ted MacDougall, nine goals for Bournemouth against Margate, FA Cup first round, 20 November 1971

Leading aggregate scorers in Football League and Scottish League games:
Arthur Rowley (West Bromwich Albion, Leicester City, Shrewsbury Town) 434 goals 1946–65.

Jimmy McGrory (Celtic, Clydebank) 410 goals 1922–38.

LONG SERVICE

The Football League record for long-service among players is held by Ted Sagar who joined Everton on 26 March 1929 and retired in May 1953 after 24 years 1 month.

TRANSFERS

Diego Maradona was transferred from Boca Juniors to Barcelona for £4 235 000 on 28 May 1982.

ATTENDANCE RECORDS

Any match

205 000 (199 854 paid) for the Brazil v Uruguay match in the 1950 World Cup final series on 16 July 1950 at the Maracana Stadium, Rio de Janeiro.

European Cup

136 505 for the Celtic v Leeds United semi-final at Hampden Park, Glasgow, on 15 April 1970.

International

149 547 for the Scotland v England international at Hampden Park, Glasgow, on 17 April 1937.

FA Cup final

160 000 (estimated) for the Bolton Wanderers v West Ham United match at Wembley on 28 April 1923 (counted admissions were 126 047).

Scottish Cup final

146 433 for the Celtic v Aberdeen final at Hampden Park, Glasgow, on 24 April 1937.

Football League

Division One: Manchester United v Arsenal at Maine Road, 17 January 1948, 83 260.

Division Two: Aston Villa v Coventry City at Villa Park, 30 October 1937, 68 029.

Division Three (Southern): Cardiff City v Bristol City at Ninian Park, 7 April 1947, 51 621.

Division Three (Northern): Hull City v Rotherham United at Boothferry Park, 25 December 1948, 49 655.

Division Three: Sheffield Wednesday v Sheffield United at Hillsborough, 26 December 1979, 49 309.

Division Four: Crystal Palace v Millwall at Selhurst Park, 31 March 1961, 37 774.

Scottish League: Rangers v Celtic, Ibrox Park, 2 January 1939, 118 567.

Low attendances

The smallest recorded attendance for a Division One match is believed to have been 4554 for the Arsenal v Leeds United game at Highbury on 5 May 1966. On the same evening, during which rain fell heavily, there was live television coverage of the Cup-Winners' Cup Final between Liverpool and Borussia Dortmund. Leeds, who were second in the League at the time, won 3–0.

Attendances in Football League matches of under 500 have been as follows: 484, Gateshead v Accrington Stanley, Division Three (Northern) 26 March 1952; 469 Thames v Luton Town, Division Three (Southern), 6 December 1930 and 450, Rochdale v Cambridge United, Division Three, 5 February 1974.

Although the attendance for the Stockport County v Leicester City match in Division Two at Old Trafford on 7 May 1921 was said to have been as low as 13, contemporary reports put the crowd at 'about 1000' and it seems likely that the figure given was underestimated.

Two English clubs have played European cup matches behind closed doors. West Ham United met Castilla in the Cup-Winners' Cup at Upton Park on 1 October 1980 and Aston Villa played Besiktas, in the European Cup at Villa Park on 15 September 1982. In both instances UEFA had ordered the clubs to ban spectators because of previous crowd trouble, ironically involving away matches in Madrid and Brussels respectively.

The official attendance for the FA Cup third round second replay between Bradford City and Norwich City at Lincoln in 1915 was nil. It was played behind closed doors so that it did not interfere with war work in nearby munitions factories. However, several hundred spectators gained access to the ground without paying.

Meadowbank Thistle had an attendance of 80 for their Scottish League, Division Two match against Stenhousemuir on 22 December 1979.

EUROPEAN SOCCER

Goalscoring in European Competitions

Alfredo di Stefano scored 49 goals for Real Madrid in the European Cup between 1955–56 and 1963–64. **Eusebio** (Benfica) scored 46 between 1961–62 and 1973–74 and **Gerd Muller** (Bayern Munich) 36 between 1969–70 and 1976–77.

The highest individual aggregate of goals for one season in the European Cup was achieved by **Jose Altafini** (AC Milan) with 14 goals in the 1962–63 season. **Lothar Emmerich** (Borussia Dortmund) scored 14 in the 1965–66 Cup-Winners' Cup.

Feyenoord beat KR Reykjavik 12–2 in a European Cup first round match on 17 September 1969 and Dynamo Bucharest beat Crusaders 11–0 in a European Cup first round match on 3 October 1973. **Sporting Lisbon** beat Apoel Nicosia 16–1 in a Cup-Winner's Cup first round match on 13 November 1963. **FC Cologne** beat Union Luxembourg 13–0 in a first round Fairs Cup match on 5 October 1965.

A number of British clubs have reached double figures in one leg of a European match. **Chelsea** beat Jeunesse Hautcharage (Luxembourg) 13–0 on 29 September 1971 in a Cup-Winners' Cup game; **Derby County** beat Finn Harps (Eire) 12–0 on 15 September 1976 in the UEFA Cup; **Ipswich Town** beat Floriana (Malta) 10–0 on 25 September 1962 in the European Cup; **Leeds United** beat Lyn Oslo (Norway) 10–0 on 17 September 1969 in the European Cup; **Liverpool** beat Stromsgodset (Norway) 11–0 on 17 September 1974 in the Cup-Winners' Cup and Dundalk (Eire) 10–0 on 16 September 1969 in the Fairs Cup as well as Oulun Palloseura 10–1 on 1 October 1980 in the European Cup; **Manchester United** beat Anderlecht (Belgium) 10–0 on 26 September 1956 in the European Cup; **Aberdeen** beat KR Reykjavik (Iceland) 10–1 on 6 September 1967 in the Cup-Winners' Cup; **Dunfermline Athletic** beat Apoel Nicosia (Cyprus) 10–1 on 18 September 1968 in the Cup-Winners' Cup; **Swansea City** beat Sliema Wanderers (Malta) 12–0 on 15 September 1982 in the Cup-Winners' Cup.

Liverpool have been the only British club to have reached double figures in a European match on more than one occasion.

The highest aggregate of goals scored by one British player in the three European competitions: European Cup, Cup-Winners' Cup and Fairs/UEFA Cup was achieved by **Peter Lorimer** who scored 30 for Leeds United between 1965–66 and 1976–77.

Denis Law scored 28 goals for Manchester United in European Cup, Cup-Winners' Cup and Fairs Cup matches between 1963–64 and 1968–69.

John Wark (Ipswich Town) became the first British player to score from as many as three penalties in one European match when he hit three against Aris Salonika (Greece) on 17 September 1980 in the UEFA Cup. Wark scored four goals in this match.

Ray Crawford scored five goals for Ipswich Town against Floriana (Malta) on 25 September

1962 in the European Cup, and **Peter Osgood** scored five for Chelsea against Jeunesse Hautcharage (Luxembourg) on 29 September 1971 in the Cup-Winners' Cup.

The highest individual score in either the European Champions Cup or the Cup-Winners' Cup is six goals. **Lothar Emmerich** scored six for Borussia Dortmund against Floriana in the first round of the Cup-Winners' Cup on 10 October 1965. **Kiril Milanov** scored six for Levski Spartak against Reipas Lahden in a Cup-Winners' Cup match in 1976–77.

Stan Bowles registered eleven goals for Queen's Park Rangers, including three goals in each of two successive UEFA Cup matches against Brann Bergen in the 1976–77 season.

Kevin Hector scored seven goals on two UEFA Cup matches for Derby County against Finn Harps in 1976–77, including five in the first leg.

Trevor Whymark scored four goals on two occasions for Ipswich Town in the UEFA Cup. The first occasion was on 24 October 1973 against Lazio and the second against Landskrona Bois on 28 September 1977.

Right: Peter Osgood who scored 16 goals in Europe for Chelsea and another two for Southampton. Signalling practice for Ray Crawford (Kettering Town) with instruction from Mel Nurse (Swansea City) in white. Crawford scored 289 Football League goals. He also hit eight for Ipswich in Europe.

European Cup Records

EUROPEAN CHAMPION CLUBS CUP

The European Cup is discovered at last—at a hostelry in the midlands. *Foxless, Tamworth*

Season	Games	Goals	The Final	Attendances Overall	Average
1955–56	29	127	13.6.56, Paris, 38 000 **Real Madrid (2) 4, Stade de Reims (2) 3** Di Stefano, Rial 2, Marquitos; Leblond, Templin, Hidalgo	912 000	31 450
1956–57	44	170	30.5.57, Madrid, 124 000 **Real Madrid (0) 2, Fiorentina (0) 0** Di Stefano (pen), Gento	1 786 000	40 590
1957–58	48	189	28.5.58, Brussels, 67 000 **Real Madrid (0) (2) 3, AC Milan (0) (2) 2 (a.e.t.)** Di Stefano, Rial, Gento; Schiaffino, Grillo	1 790 000	37 290
1958–59	55	199	2.6.59, Stuttgart, 80 000 **Real Madrid (1) 2, Stade de Reims (0) 0** Mateos, Di Stefano	2 010 000	36 545
1959–60	52	218	18.5.60, Glasgow, 135 000 **Real Madrid (3) 7, Eintracht Frankfurt (1) 3** Di Stefano 3, Puskas 4; Kress, Stein 2	2 780 000	50 545
1960–61	51	166	31.3.61, Berne, 28 000 **Benfica (2) 3, Barcelona (1) 2** Aguas, Ramallets (og), Coluna; Kocsis, Czibor	1 850 000	36 274
1961–62	55	221	2.5.62, Amsterdam, 65 000 **Benfica (2) 5, Real Madrid (3) 3** Aguas, Cavem, Coluna, Eusebio 2; Puskas 3	2 135 000	45 727
1962–63	59	214	22.5.63, London, 45 000 **AC Milan (0) 2, Benfica (1) 1** Altafini 2; Eusebio	2 158 000	36 593
1963–64	61	212	27.5.64, Vienna, 74 000 **Inter Milan (1) 3, Real Madrid (0) 1** Mazzola 2, Milani; Felo	2 180 000	35 737
1964–65	62	215	28.5.65, Milan, 80 000 **Inter Milan (1) 1, Benfica (0) 0** Jair	2 577 000	41 564
1965–66	58	234	11.5.66, Brussels, 55 000 **Real Madrid (0) 2, Partizan Belgrade (1) 1** Amancio, Serena; Vasovic	2 112 000	36 431
1966–67	65	211	25.5.67, Lisbon, 56 000 **Celtic (0) 2, Inter Milan (1) 1** Gemmell, Chalmers; Mazzola (pen)	2 248 000	34 584
1967–68	60	162	29.5.68, London, 100 000 **Manchester United (0) (1) 4, Benfica (0) (1) 1 (a.e.t)** Charlton 2, Best, Kidd; Graca	2 544 000	42 500
1968–69	52	176	28.5.69, Madrid, 50 000 **AC Milan (2) 4, Ajax (0) 1** Prati 3, Sormani; Vasovic (pen)	2 056 000	39 540
1969–70	63	202	6.5.70, Milan, 50 000 **Feyenoord (1) (1) 2, Celtic (1) (1) 1 (a.e.t.)** Israel, Kindvall; Gemmell	2 345 000	37 222
1970–71	63	210	2.6.71, London, 90 000 **Ajax (1) 2, Panathinaikos (0) 0** Van Dijk, Kapsis (og)	2 124 000	33 714
1971–72	64	175	31.5.72, Rotterdam, 67 000 **Ajax (0) 2, Inter Milan (0) 0** Cruyff 2	2 066 976	32 280
1972–73	58	160	30.5.73, Belgrade, 93 500 **Ajax (0) 1, Juventus (0) 0** Rep	1 712 277	30 000
1973–74	60	180	15.5.74, Brussels, 65 000 **Bayern Munich (0) (0) 1, Atletico Madrid (0) (0) 1 (a.e.t.)** Schwarzenbeck; Luis	1 586 852	26 448
		replay:	17.5.74, Brussels, 65 000 **Bayern Munich (1) 4, Atletico Madrid (0) 0** Muller 2, Hoeness 2		
1974–75	55	174	28.5.75, Paris, 50 000 **Bayern Munich (0) 2, Leeds United (0) 0** Roth, Muller	1 380 254	25 096
1975–76	61	202	12.5.76, Glasgow, 54 864 **Bayern Munich (0) 1, St Etienne (0) 0** Roth	1 736 087	28 460
1976–77	61	155	25.5.77, Rome, 57 000 **Liverpool (1) 3, Borussia Moenchengladbach (0) 1** McDermott, Smith, Neal (pen); Simonsen	2 010 000	34 325
1977–78	59	172	10.5.78, London, 92 000 **Liverpool (0) 1, FC Bruges (0) 0** Dalglish	1 509 471	25 584
1978–79	63	185	30.5.79, Munich, 57 500 **Nottingham Forest (1) 1, Malmo (0) 0** Francis	1 511 291	23 988
1979–80	63	185	28.5.80, Madrid, 50 000 **Nottingham Forest (1) 1, SV Hamburg (0) 0** Robertson	1 729 415	27 451
1980–81	63	166	27.5.81, Paris, 48 360 **Liverpool (0) 1, Real Madrid (0) 0** Kennedy A.	1 166 593	26 374
1981–82	63	170	26.5.82, Rotterdam, 46 000 **Aston Villa (0) 1, Bayern Munich (0) 0** Withe	1 530 082	24 287
1982–83	61	180	25.5.83, Athens, 75 000 **SV Hamburg (1) 1, Juventus (0) 0** Magath (figures not to hand at press time)		

EUROPEAN CUP-WINNERS' CUP

Season	Games	Goals	The Final	Attendances Overall	Average
1960–61	18	60	1st leg, 17.5.61, Glasgow, 80 000 **Rangers (0) 0, Fiorentina (1) 2** Milan 2		
			2nd leg, 27.5.61, Florence, 50 000 **Fiorentina (1) 2, Rangers (1) 1** Milan, Hamrin; Scott	290 000	16 111
1961–62	44	174	10.5.62, Glasgow, 27 389 **Fiorentina (1) 1, Atletico Madrid (1) 1** Hamrin; Piero		
		replay:	5.9.62, Stuttgart, 45 000 **Atletico Madrid (2) 3, Fiorentina (0) 0** Jones, Mendonca, Piero	650 000	14 733
1962–63	48	169	15.5.63, Rotterdam, 25 000 **Tottenham Hotspur (2) 5, Atletico Madrid (0) 1** Greaves 2, White, Dyson 2; Collar (pen)	1 100 000	22 916
1963–64	62	202	13.5.64, Brussels, 9 000 **MTK Budapest (1) (3) 3, Sporting Lisbon (1) (3) 3 (a.e.t.)** Sandor 2, Kuti; Figueiredo 2, Dansky (og)		
		replay:	15.5.64, Antwerp, 18 000 **Sporting Lisbon (1) 1, MTK Budapest (0) 0** Mendes	1 300 000	20 967
1964–65	61	163	19.5.65, London, 100 000 **West Ham United (0) 2, Munich 1860 (0) 0** Sealey 2	1 100 000	18 032
1965–66	59	188	5.5.66, Glasgow, 41 657 **Borussia Dortmund (0) (1) 2, Liverpool (0) (1) 1 (a.e.t.)** Held, Yeats (og); Hunt	1 546 000	26 203
1966–67	61	170	31.5.67, Nuremberg, 69 480 **Bayern Munich (0) (0) 1, Rangers (0) (0) 0 (a.e.t.)** Roth	1 556 000	25 508
1967–68	64	200	23.5.68, Rotterdam, 60 000 **AC Milan (2) 2, SV Hamburg (0) 0** Hamrin 2	1 683 000	26 269
1968–69	51	157	21.5.69, Basle, 40 000 **Slovan Bratislava (3) 3, Barcelona (1) 2** Cvetler, Hrivnak, Jan Capkovic; Zaldua, Rexach	957 000	18 765
1969–70	64	179	29.4.70, Vienna, 10 000 **Manchester City (2) 2, Gornik Zabrze (0) 1** Young, Lee (pen); Ozlizlo	1 675 000	25 890
1970–71	67	203	19.5.71, Athens, 42 000 **Chelsea (0) (1) 1, Real Madrid (0) (1) 1** Osgood; Zoco		
		replay:	21.5.71, Athens, 24 000 **Chelsea (2) 2, Real Madrid (0) 1** Dempsey, Osgood; Fleitas	1 570 000	23 582
1971–72	65	186	24.5.72, Barcelona, 35 000 **Rangers (2) 3, Dynamo Moscow (0) 2** Stein, Johnston 2; Estrekov, Makovikov	1 145 211	17 615
1972–73	61	174	16.5.73, Salonika, 45 000 **AC Milan (1) 1, Leeds United (0) 0** Chiarugi	908 564	15 000
1973–74	61	169	8.5.74, Rotterdam, 5000 **FC Magdeburg (1) 2, AC Milan (0) 0** Lanzi (og), Seguin	1 105 494	18 123
1974–75	59	177	14.5.75, Basle, 13 000 **Dynamo Kiev (2) 3, Ferencvaros (0) 0** Onischenko 2, Blokhin	1 298 850	22 014
1975–76	61	189	5.5.76, Brussels, 58 000 **Anderlecht (1) 4, West Ham United (1) 2** Rensenbrink 2 (1 pen), Van der Elst 2; Holland, Robson	1 128 962	18 508
1976–77	63	198	11.5.77, Amsterdam, 65 000 **SV Hamburg (0) 2, Anderlecht (0) 0** Volkert (pen), Magath	1 537 000	24 400
1977–78	63	179	3.5.78, Amsterdam, 48 679 **Anderlecht (3) 4, Austria/WAC (0) 0** Rensenbrink 2 (1 pen), Van Binst 2	1 161 383	18 434
1978–79	59	160	16.5.79, Basle, 58 000 **Barcelona (2) (2) 4, Fortuna Dusseldorf (2) (2) 3 (a.e.t.)** Sanchez, Asensi, Rexach, Krankl; Klaus Allofs, Seel 2	1 041 135	17 646
1979–80	63	176	14.5.80, Brussels, 40 000 **Valencia (0) 0, Arsenal (0) 0 (a.e.t.)** (Valencia won 5–4 on penalties)	1 193 682	18 947
1980–81	65	176	13.5.81, Dusseldorf, 9000 **Dynamo Tbilisi (0) 2, Carl Zeiss Jena (0) 1** Gutsayev, Daraselia; Hoppe	1 239 795	19 074
1981–82	63	176	12.5.82, Barcelona, 100 000 **Barcelona (1) 2, Standard Liege (1) 1** Simonsen, Quini; Vandersmissen	1 504 023	23 873
1982–83	65	198	11.5.83, Gothenburg, 17 804 **Aberdeen (1) 2, Real Madrid (1) 1 (a.e.t.)** Black, Hewitt; Juanito (pen)	(figures not to hand at press time)	

FAIRS CUP/UEFA CUP

Season	Final		
1955–58	First leg:	5.3.58, London, 45 466 **London (1) 2, Barcelona (2) 2** Greaves, Langley (pen); Tejada, Martinez	
	Second leg:	1.5.58, Barcelona, 62 000 **Barcelona (3) 6, London (0) 0** Suarez 2, Evaristo 2, Martinez, Verges	
1958–60	First leg:	29.3.60, Birmingham, 40 500 **Birmingham City (0) 0, Barcelona (0) 0**	

Season	Final		
	Second leg:	4.5.60, Barcelona, 70 000 **Barcelona (2) 4, Birmingham City (0) 1** Martinez, Czibor 2, Coll; Hooper	
1960–61	First leg:	27.9.61, Birmingham, 21 005 **Birmingham City (0) 2, AS Roma (1) 2** Hellawell, Orritt; Manfredini 2	
	Second leg:	11.10.61, Rome, 60 000 **AS Roma (0) 2, Birmingham City (0) 0** Farmer (og), Pestrin	

Season	Final	
1961-62	First leg:	8.9.62, Valencia, 65 000
		Valencia 6, Barcelona 2
		Yosu 2, Guillot 3, Nunez; Kocsis 2
	Second leg:	12.9.62, Barcelona, 60 000
		Barcelona 1, Valencia 1
		Kocsis; Guillot
1962-63	First leg:	12.6.63, Zagreb, 40 000
		Dynamo Zagreb (1) 1, Valencia (0) 2
		Zambata; Waldo, Urtiaga
	Second leg:	26.6.63, Valencia, 55 000
		Valencia (1) 2, Dynamo Zagreb (0) 0
		Mano, Nunez
1963-64	Final:	24.6.64, Barcelona, 50 000
		Real Zaragoza (1) 2, Valencia (1) 1
		Villa, Marcelino; Urtiaga
1964-65	Final:	23.6.65, Turin, 25 000
		Ferencvaros (1) 1, Juventus (0) 0
		Fenyvesi
1965-66	Fist leg:	14.9.66, Barcelona, 70 000
		Barcelona (0) 0, Real Zaragoza (1) 1
		Canario
	Second leg:	21.9.66, Zaragoza, 70 000
		Real Zaragoza (1) 2, Barcelona (1) 4
		Marcelino 2; Pujol 3, Zabella
1966-67	First leg:	30.8.67, Zagreb, 40 000
		Dynamo Zagreb (1) 2, Leeds United (0) 0
		Cercer 2
	Second leg:	6.9.67, Leeds, 35 604
		Leeds United (0) 0, Dynamo Zagreb (0) 0
1967-68	First leg:	7.8.68, Leeds, 25 368
		Leeds United (1) 1, Ferencvaros (0) 0
		Jones
	Second leg:	11.9.68, Budapest, 70 000
		Ferencvaros (0) 0, Leeds United (0) 0
1968-69	First leg:	25.5.69, Newcastle, 60 000
		Newcastle United (0) 3, Ujpest Dozsa (0) 0
		Moncur 2, Scott
	Second leg:	11.6.69, Budapest, 37 000
		Ujpest Dozsa (2) 2; Newcastle United (0) 3
		Bene, Gorocs; Moncur, Arentoft, Foggon
1969-70	First leg:	22.4.70, Brussels, 37 000
		Anderlecht (2) 3, Arsenal (0) 1
		Devrindt, Mulder 2; Kennedy
	Second leg:	28.4.70, London, 51 612
		Arsenal (1) 3, Anderlecht (0) 0
		Kelly, Radford, Sammels
1970-71	First leg:	26.5.71, Turin, 65 000
		Juventus (0) 0, Leeds United (0) 0
		(game abandoned after 51 minutes)
		28.5.71, Turin, 65 000
		Juventus (1) 2, Leeds United (0) 2
		Bettega, Capello; Madeley, Bates
	Second leg:	3.6.71, Leeds, 42 483
		Leeds United (1) 1, Juventus (1) 1
		Clarke; Anastasi
		Leeds won on away goals rule.
1971-72	First leg:	3.5.72, Wolverhampton, 45 000
		Wolverhampton Wanderers (0) 1, Tottenham Hotspur (0) 2
		McCalliog; Chivers 2

Season	Final	
	Second Leg:	17.5.72, London, 48 000
		Tottenham Hotspur (1) 1, Wolverhampton Wanderers (0) 1
		Mullery; Wagstaffe
1972-73	First Leg:	10.5.73, Liverpool, 41 169
		Liverpool (3) 3, Borussia Moenchengladbach (0) 0
		Keegan 2, Lloyd
	Second leg:	25.5.73, Moenchengladbach, 35 000
		Borussia Moenchengladbach (2) 2, Liverpool (0) 0
		Heynckes 2
1973-74	First leg:	21.5.74, London, 46 281
		Tottenham Hotspur (1) 2, Feyenoord (1) 2
		England, Van Daele (og); Van Hanegem, De Jong
	Second leg:	29.5.74, Rotterdam, 68 000
		Feyenoord (1) 2, Tottenham Hotspur (0) 0
		Rijsbergen, Ressel
1974-75	First leg:	7.5.75, Dusseldorf, 45 000
		Borussia Moenchengladbach (0) 0, Twente Enschede (0) 0
	Second leg:	21.5.75, Enschede, 24 500
		Twente Enschede (0) 1, Borussia Moenchengladbach (2) 5
		Drost; Heynckes 3, Simonsen 2 (1 pen)
1975-76	First leg:	28.4.76, Liverpool, 56 000
		Liverpool (0) 3, Bruges (2) 2
		Kennedy, Case, Keegan (pen); Lambert, Cools
	Second leg:	19.5.76, Bruges, 32 000
		Bruges (1) 1, Liverpool (1) 1
		Lambert (pen), Keegan
1976-77	First leg:	4.5.77, Turin, 75 000
		Juventus (1) 1, Athletic Bilbao (0) 0
		Tardelli
	Second leg:	18.5.77, Bilbao, 43 000
		Athletic Bilbao (1) 2, Juventus (1) 1
		Iruerta, Carlos; Bettega
1977-78	First leg:	26.4.78, Bastia, 15 000
		Bastia (0) 0, PSV Eindhoven (0) 0
	Second leg:	9.5.78, Eindhoven, 27 000
		PSV Eindhoven (1) 3, Bastia (0) 0
		Willy Van der Kerkhof, Deijkers, Van der Kuylen
1978-79	First leg:	9.5.79, Belgrade, 87 500
		Red Star Belgrade (1) 1, Borussia Moenchengladbach (0) 1
		Sestic; Jurisic (og)
	Second leg:	23.5.79, Dusseldorf, 45 000
		Borussia Moenchengladbach (1) 1, Red Star Belgrade (0) 0
		Simonsen
1979-80	First leg:	7.5.80, Moenchengladbach, 25 000
		Borussia Moenchengladbach (1) 3, Eintracht Frankfurt (1) 2
		Kulik 2, Matthaus; Karger, Holzenbein
	Second leg:	21.5.80, Frankfurt, 60 000
		Eintracht Frankfurt (0) 1, Borussia Moenchengladbach (0) 0
		Schaub
		(Eintracht won on away goals rule)

Season	Final	
1980–81	First leg:	6.5.81, Ipswich, 27 532
		Ipswich Town (1) 3, AZ 67 Alkmaar (0) 0 Wark (pen), Thijssen, Mariner
	Second leg:	20.5.81, Amsterdam, 28 500
		AZ 67 Alkmaar (3) 4, Ipswich Town (2) 2 Welzl, Metgod, Tol, Jonker; Thijssen, Wark
1981–82	First leg:	5.5.82, Gothenburg, 42 548
		IFK Gothenburg (0) 1, SV Hamburg, (0) 0 Tord Holmgren
	Second leg:	19.5.82, Hamburg, 60 000
		SV Hamburg (0) 0, IFK Gothenburg (1) 3 Corneliusson, Nilsson, Fredriksson (pen)
1982–83	First leg:	4.5.83, Brussels, 45 000
		Anderlecht (1) 1, Benfica (0) 0 Brylle
	Second leg:	18.5.83, Lisbon, 80 000
		Benfica (1) 1, Anderlecht (1) 1 Sheu; Lozano

UEFA Cup attendances

The aggregate attendances for the 1979–80 season were 2 927 601 at 126 matches for an average of 23 235 compared with 2 826 679 for the same number of games in 1978–79 for an average of 22 433.

In 1980–81, attendances were 2 192 169 at 126 games for an average of 17 398 while in 1981–82 they were 2 247 173 for the same number of matches at an average of 17 835.

UEFA Cup goalscoring

In 1982–83 the 126 matches in the UEFA Cup produced a total of 352 goals.

EUROPEAN CHAMPIONSHIP FINALS

Series	Final							No of entries		
1958–60	(10 July 1960, Paris att. 17 966)									
	USSR (Metreveli, Ponedelnik)	(0)	(1)	2	**Yugoslavia** (Netto o.g.)	(1)	(1)	1	**17**	
1962–64	(21 June 1964, Madrid att. 120 000)									
	Spain (Pereda, Marcelino)		(1)	2	**USSR** (Khusainov)		(1)	1	**29**	
1966–68	(8 June 1968, Rome att. 75 000)									
	Italy (Domenghini)	(0)	(1)	1	**Yugoslavia** (Dzajic)	(1)	(1)	1	**31**	
Replay	(10 June 1968, Rome att. 60 000)									
	Italy (Riva, Anastasi)		(2)	2	**Yugoslavia**		(0)	0		
1970–72	(18 June 1972, Brussels att. 43 437)									
	West Germany (Muller (G) 2, Wimmer)		(1)	3	**USSR**		(0)	0	**32**	
1974–76	(20 June 1976, Belgrade att. 45 000)									
	Czechoslovakia (Svehlik, Dobias)	(2)	(2)	2	**West Germany** (Muller (D), Holzenbein)	(1)	(2)	2	**32**	
	Czechoslovakia won 5–3 on penalties									
1978–80	(22 June 1980, Rome att. 47 864)									
	West Germany (Hrubesch 2)		(1)	2	**Belgium** (Vandereycken)		(0)	1	**32**	

British Clubs in Europe

*won on away goals counting double
†won on penalties
‡won on the toss of a coin

FOOTBALL LEAGUE CLUBS

Season	Competition	Round	Date	Opponents (Country)	Venue	Result		Scorers
ARSENAL								
1971–72	European Cup	1	15. 9.71	Stromsgodset (Norway)	A	W	3–1	Simpson, Marinello, Kelly
			29. 9.71		H	W	4–0	Kennedy, Radford 2, Armstrong
		2	20.10.71	Grasshoppers	A	W	2–0	Kennedy, Graham
			3.11.71	(Switzerland)	H	W	3–0	Kennedy, George, Radford
		QF	8. 3.72	Ajax (Holland)	A	L	1–2	Kennedy
			22. 3.72		H	L	0–1	
1979–80	Cup-Winners' Cup	1	19. 9.79	Fenerbahce (Turkey)	H	W	2–0	Sunderland, Young
			3.10.79		A	D	0–0	
		2	24.10.79	Magdeburg (East	H	W	2–1	Young, Sunderland
			7.11.79	Germany)	A	D	2–2	Price, Brady
		QF	5. 3.80	Gothenburg (Sweden)	H	W	5–1	Sunderland 2, Price, Brady, Young
			19. 3.80		A	D	0–0	
		SF	9. 4.80	Juventus (Italy)	H	D	1–1	own goal
			23. 4.80		A	W	1–0	Vaessen
		F	14. 5.80	Valencia (Spain)†	N	D	0–0	
1963–64	Fairs Cup	1	25. 9.63	Staevnet (Denmark)	A	W	7–1	Strong 3, Baker 3, MacLeod
			22.10.63		H	L	2–3	Skirton, Barnwell
		2	13.11.63	Liege (Belgium)	H	D	1–1	Anderson
			18.12.63		A	L	1–3	McCullough
1969–70	Fairs Cup	1	9. 9.69	Glentoran (Northern	H	W	3–0	Graham 2, Gould
			29. 9.69	Ireland)	A	L	0–1	
		2	29.10.69	Sporting Lisbon (Portugal)	A	D	0–0	
			26.11.69		H	W	3–0	Radford, Graham 2
		3	17.12.69	Rouen (France)	A	D	0–0	
			13. 1.70		H	W	1–0	Sammels
		QF	11. 3.70	Dynamo Bacau	A	W	2–0	Sammels, Radford
			18. 3.70	(Rumania)	H	W	7–1	George 2, Sammels 2, Radford 2, Graham
		SF	8. 4.70	Ajax (Holland)	H	W	3–0	George 2 (1 pen), Sammels
			15. 4.70		A	L	0–1	
		F	22. 4.70	Anderlecht (Belgium)	A	L	1–3	Kennedy
			28. 4.70		H	W	3–0	Kelly, Radford, Sammels
1970–71	Fairs Cup	1	16. 9.70	Lazio (Italy)	A	D	2–2	Radford 2
			23. 9.70		H	W	2–0	Radford, Armstrong
		2	21.10.70	Sturm Graz (Austria)	A	L	0–1	
			4.11.70		H	W	2–0	Storey (pen), Kennedy
		3	2.12.70	Beveren (Belgium)	H	W	4–0	Graham, Kennedy 2, Sammels
			16.12.70		A	D	0–0	
		QF	9. 3.71	IFC Cologne (West	H	W	2–1	McLintock, Storey
			23. 3.71	Germany)*	A	L	0–1	
1978–79	UEFA Cup	1	13. 9.78	Lokomotive Leipzig (East	H	W	3–0	Stapleton 2, Sunderland
			27. 9.78	Germany)	A	W	4–1	Brady (pen), Stapleton 2, Sunderland
		2	18.10.78	Hajduk Split	A	L	1–2	O'Leary
			1.11.78	(Yugoslavia)	H	W	1–0	Young
		3	22.11.78	Red Star Belgrade	A	L	0–1	
			6.12.78	(Yugoslavia)	H	D	1–1	Sunderland
1981–82	UEFA Cup	1	16. 9.81	Panathinaikos (Greece)	A	W	2–0	McDermott, Meade
			30. 9.81		H	W	1–0	Talbot
		2	20.10.81	Winterslag (Belgium)*	A	L	0–1	
			3.11.81		H	W	2–1	Hollins, Rix
1982–83	UEFA Cup	1	14. 9.82	Moscow Spartak	A	L	2–3	Robson, Chapman
			29. 9.82	(USSR)	H	L	2–5	Chapman, own goal

Season	Competition	Round	Date	Opponents (Country)	Venue	Result		Scorers

ASTON VILLA

Season	Competition	Round	Date	Opponents (Country)	Venue	Result		Scorers
1975–76	UEFA Cup	1	17. 9.75	Antwerp (Belgium)	A	L	1–4	Graydon
			1.10.75		H	L	0–1	
1977–78	UEFA Cup	1	14. 9.77	Fenerbahce (Turkey)	H	W	4–0	Gray, Deehan 2, Little
			28. 9.77		A	W	2–0	Deehan, Little
		2	19.10.77	Gornik Zabrze (Poland)	H	W	2–0	McNaught 2
			2.11.77		A	D	1–1	Gray
		3	23.11.77	Athletic Bilbao (Spain)	H	W	2–0	own goal, Deehan
			7.12.77		A	D	1–1	Mortimer
		QF	1. 3.78	Barcelona (Spain)	H	D	2–2	McNaught, Deehan
			15. 3.78		A	L	1–2	Little
1981–82	European Cup	1	16. 9.81	Valur (Iceland)	H	W	5–0	Morley, Withe 2, Donovan 2
			30. 9.81		A	W	2–0	Shaw 2
		2	21.10.81	Dynamo Berlin	A	W	2–1	Morley 2
			4.11.81	(East Germany)	H	L	0–1	
		QF	3. 3.82	Dynamo Kiev	A	D	0–0	
			17. 3.82	(USSR)	H	W	2–0	Shaw, McNaught
		SF	7. 4.82	Anderlecht (Belgium)	H	W	1–0	Morley
			21. 4.82		A	D	0–0	
		F	26. 5.82	Bayern Munich (West Germany)	N	W	1–0	Withe
1982–83	European Cup	1	15. 9.82	Besiktas (Turkey)	H	W	3–1	Withe, Morley, Mortimer
			29. 9.82		A	D	0–0	
		2	20.10.82	Dynamo Bucharest	A	W	2–0	Shaw 2
			3.11.82	(Rumania)	H	W	4–2	Shaw 3, Walters
		QF	2. 3.83	Juventus (Italy)	H	L	1–2	Cowans
			16. 3.83		A	L	1–3	Withe
1982–83	Super Cup	F	19. 1.83	Barcelona (Spain)	A	L	0–1	
			26. 1.83		H	W	3–0	Shaw, Cowans, McNaught

BIRMINGHAM CITY

Season	Competition	Round	Date	Opponents (Country)	Venue	Result		Scorers
1955–58	Fairs Cup	Gp.D	15. 5.56	Inter-Milan (Italy)	A	D	0–0	
			17. 4.57		H	W	2–1	Govan 2
			22. 5.56	Zagreb (Yugoslavia)	A	W	1–0	Brown
			3.12.56		H	W	3–0	Orritt, Brown, Murphy
		SF	23.10.57	Barcelona (Spain)	H	W	4–3	Murphy 2, Brown, Orritt
			13.11.57		A	L	0–1	
			26.11.57		N	L	1–2	Murphy
1958–60	Fairs Cup	1	14.10.58	IFC Cologne (West Germany)	A	D	2–2	Neal, Hooper
			11.11.58		H	W	2–0	Larkin, Taylor
		QF	6. 5.59	Zagreb (Yugoslavia)	H	W	1–0	Larkin
			25. 5.59		A	D	3–3	Larkin 2, Hooper
		SF	7.10.59	Union St Gilloise (Belgium)	A	W	4–2	Hooper, Gordon, Barrett, Taylor
			11.11.59		H	W	4–2	Gordon 2, Larkin, Hooper
		F	29. 3.60	Barcelona (Spain)	H	D	0–0	
			4. 5.60		A	L	1–4	Hooper
1960–61	Fairs Cup	1	19.10.60	Ujpest Dozsa (Hungary)	H	W	3–2	Gordon 2, Astall
			26.10.60		A	W	2–1	Rudd, Singer
		QF	23.11.60	Copenhagen (Denmark)	A	D	4–4	Gordon 2, Singer 2
			7.12.60		H	W	5–0	Stubbs 2, Harris, Hellawell, own goal
		SF	19. 4.61	Inter-Milan (Italy)	A	W	2–1	Harris, own goal
			3. 5.61		H	W	2–1	Harris 2
		F	27. 9.61	AS Roma (Italy)	H	D	2–2	Hellawell, Orritt
			11.10.61		A	L	0–2	
1961–62	Fairs Cup	1		bye				
		2	15.11.61	Espanol (Spain)	A	L	2–5	Bloomfield, Harris (pen)
			7.12.61		H	W	1–0	Auld

Season	Competition	Round	Date	Opponents (Country)	Venue	Result		Scorers

BURNLEY

Season	Competition	Round	Date	Opponents (Country)	Venue	Result		Scorers
1960–61	European Cup	Pr		bye				
		1	16.11.60	Reims (France)	H	W	2–0	Robson, McIlroy
			30.11.60		A	L	2–3	Robson, Connelly
		QF	18. 1.61	SV Hamburg (West	H	W	3–1	Pilkington 2, Robson
			15. 3.61	Germany)	A	L	1–4	Harris
1966–67	Fairs Cup	1	20. 9.66	Stuttgart (West Germany)	A	D	1–1	Irvine
			27. 9.66		H	W	2–0	Coates, Lochhead
		2	10.10.66	Lausanne (Switzerland)	A	W	3–1	Coates, Harris, Lochhead
			25.10.66		H	W	5–0	Lochhead 3, O'Neill, Irvine
		3	18. 1.67	Napoli (Italy)	H	W	3–0	Coates, Latcham, Lochhead
			8. 2.67		A	D	0–0	
		QF	4. 4.67	Eintracht Frankfurt	A	D	1–1	Miller
			18. 4.67	(West Germany)	H	L	1–2	Miller

CARDIFF CITY

Season	Competition	Round	Date	Opponents (Country)	Venue	Result		Scorers
1964–65	Cup Winners' Cup	1	9. 9.64	Esbjerg (Denmark)	A	D	0–0	
			13.10.64		H	W	1–0	King
		2	16.12.64	Sporting Lisbon (Portugal)	A	W	2–1	Farrell, Tapscott
			23.12.64		H	D	0–0	
		QF	20. 1.65	Real Zaragoza (Spain)	A	D	2–2	Williams, King
			3. 2.65		H	L	0–1	
1965–66	Cup Winners' Cup	1	8. 9.65	Standard Liege (Belgium)	H	L	1–2	Johnston
			20.10.65		A	L	0–1	
1967–68	Cup Winners' Cup	1	20. 9.67	Shamrock Rovers (Eire)	A	D	1–1	King
			4.10.67		H	W	2–0	Toshack, Brown (pen)
		2	15.11.67	NAC Breda (Holland)	A	D	1–1	King
			29.11.67		H	W	4–1	Brown, Barrie Jones, Clark, Toshack
		QF	6. 3.68	Moscow Torpedo	H	W	1–0	Barrie Jones
			19. 3.68	(USSR)	A	L	0–1	
			3. 4.68		H	W	1–0	Dean
		SF	24. 4.68	SV Hamburg (West	A	D	1–1	Dean
			1. 5.68	Germany)	H	L	2–3	Dean, Harris
1968–69	Cup Winners' Cup	1	18. 9.68	Porto (Portugal)	H	D	2–2	Toshack, Bird (pen)
			2.10.68		A	L	1–2	Toshack
1969–70	Cup Winners' Cup	1	17. 9.69	Mjondalen (Norway)	A	W	7–1	Clark 2, Toshack 2, Lea, Sutton, King
			1.10.69		H	W	5–1	King 2, Allan 3
		2	12.11.69	Goztepe Izmir (Turkey)	A	L	0–3	
			16.11.69		H	W	1–0	Bird
1970–71	Cup-Winners' Cup	1	16. 9.70	Pezoporikos (Cyprus)	H	W	8–0	Toshack 2, Clark 2, Sutton, Gibson, King, Woodruff
			30. 9.70		A	D	0–0	
		2	21.10.70	Nantes (France)	H	W	5–1	Toshack 2, Gibson, King, Phillips
			4.11.70		A	W	2–1	Toshack, Clark
		QF	10. 3.70	Real Madrid (Spain)	H	W	1–0	Clark
			24. 3.71		A	L	0–2	
1971–72	Cup-Winners' Cup	1	15. 9.71	Dynamo Berlin (East	A	D	1–1	Gibson
			29. 9.71	Germany)†	H	D	1–1	Clark
1973–74	Cup-Winners' Cup	1	19. 9.73	Sporting Lisbon (Portugal)	H	D	0–0	
			3.10.73		A	L	1–2	Vincent
1974–75	Cup-Winners' Cup	1	18. 9.74	Ferencvaros (Hungary)	A	L	0–2	
			2.10.74		H	L	1–4	Dwyer
1976–77	Cup-Winners' Cup	Pr	4. 8.76	Servette (Switzerland)	H	W	1–0	Evans
			11. 8.76		A	L	1–2*	Showers
		1	15. 9.76	Dynamo Tbilisi (USSR)	H	W	1–0	Alston
			29. 9.76		A	L	0–3	
1977–78	Cup-Winners' Cup	1	14. 9.77	Austria/WAC (Austria)	H	D	0–0	
			28. 9.77		A	L	0–1	

Season	Competition	Round	Date	Opponents (Country)	Venue	Result		Scorers

CHELSEA

Season	Competition	Round	Date	Opponents (Country)	Venue	Result		Scorers
1970–71	Cup-Winners' Cup	1	16. 9.70	Aris Salonika (Greece)	A	D	1–1	Hutchinson
			30. 9.70		H	W	5–1	Hutchinson 2, Hollins 2, Hinton
		2	21.10.70	CSKA Sofia (Bulgaria)	A	W	1–0	Baldwin
			4.11.70		H	W	1–0	Webb
		QF	10. 3.71	FC Bruges (Belgium)	A	L	0–2	
			24. 3.71		H	W	4–0	Houseman, Osgood 2, Baldwin
		SF	14. 4.71	Manchester City	H	W	1–0	Smethurst
			28. 4.71	(England)	A	W	1–0	Weller
		F	19. 5.71	Real Madrid (Spain)	N	D	1–1	Osgood
			21. 5.71		N	W	2–1	Dempsey, Osgood
1971–72	Cup-Winners' Cup	1	15. 9.71	Jeunesse Hautcharage (Luxembourg)	A	W	8–0	Osgood 3, Houseman 2, Hollins, Webb, Baldwin
			29. 9.71		H	W	13–0	Osgood 5, Baldwin 3, Hollins (pen), Hudson, Webb, Houseman, Harris
		2	20.10.71	Atvidaberg (Sweden)*	A	D	0–0	
			3.11.71		H	D	1–1	Hudson
1958–59	Fairs Cup	1	30. 9.58	Frem Copenhagen	A	W	3–1	Harrison, Greaves, Nicholas
			4.11.58	(Denmark)	H	W	4–1	Greaves 2, Sillett (P), own goal
		QF	29. 4.59	Belgrade (Yugoslavia)	H	W	1–0	Brabrook
			13. 5.59		H	L	1–4	Brabrook
1965–66	Fairs Cup	1	22. 9.65	AS Roma (Italy)	H	W	4–1	Venables 3, Graham
			6.10.65		A	D	0–0	
		2	17.11.65	Weiner SK (Austria)	A	L	0–1	
			1.12.65		H	W	2–0	Murray, Osgood
		3	9. 2.66	AC Milan (Italy)	A	L	1–2	Graham
			16. 2.66		H	W	2–1	Graham, Osgood
			2. 3.66		A	D	1–1‡	Bridges
		QF	15. 3.66	Munich 1860 (West Germany)	A	D	2–2	Tambling 2
			29. 3.66		H	W	1–0	Osgood
		SF	27. 4.66	Barcelona (Spain)	A	L	0–2	
			11. 5.66		H	W	2–0	own goals 2
			25. 5.66		A	L	0–5	
1968–69	Fairs Cup	1	18. 9.68	Morton (Scotland)	H	W	5–0	Osgood, Birchenall, Cooke, Boyle, Hollins
			30. 9.68		A	W	4–3	Baldwin, Birchenall, Houseman, Tambling
		2	23.10.68	DWS Amsterdam	H	D	0–0	
			30.10.68	(Holland)‡	A	D	0–0	

COVENTRY CITY

Season	Competition	Round	Date	Opponents (Country)	Venue	Result		Scorers
1970–71	Fairs Cup	1	16. 9.70	Trakia Plovdiv (Bulgaria)	A	W	4–1	O'Rourke 3, Martin
			30. 9.70		H	W	2–0	Joicey, Blockley
		2	20.10.70	Bayern Munich (West Germany)	A	L	1–6	Hunt
			3.11.70		H	W	2–1	Martin, O'Rourke

DERBY COUNTY

Season	Competition	Round	Date	Opponents (Country)	Venue	Result		Scorers
1972–73	European Cup	1	13. 9.72	Zeljeznicar (Yugoslavia)	H	W	2–0	McFarland, Gemmill
			27. 9.72		A	W	2–1	Hinton, O'Hare
		2	25.10.72	Benfica (Portugal)	H	W	3–0	McFarland, Hector, McGovern
			8.11.72		A	D	0–0	
		QF	7. 3.73	Spartak Trnava (Czechoslovakia)	A	D	0–0	
			21. 3.73		H	W	2–0	Hector 2
		SF	11. 4.73	Juventus (Italy)	A	L	1–3	Hector
			25. 4.73		H	D	0–0	
1975–76	European Cup	1	17. 9.75	Slovan Bratislava (Czechoslovakia)	A	L	0–1	
			1.10.75		H	W	3–0	Bourne, Lee 2
		2	22.10.75	Real Madrid (Spain)	H	W	4–1	George 3 (2 pen), Nish
			5.11.75		A	L	1–5	George

Season	Competition	Round	Date	Opponents (Country)	Venue	Result		Scorers
1974–75	UEFA Cup	1	18. 9.74	Servette (Switzerland)	H	W	4–1	Hector 2, Daniel, Lee
			2.10.74		A	W	2–1	Lee, Hector
		2	23.10.74	Atletico Madrid (Spain)	H	D	2–2	Nish, Rioch (pen)
			6.11.74		A	D	2–2†	Rioch, Hector
		3	27.11.74	Velez (Yugoslavia)	H	W	3–1	Bourne 2, Hinton
			11.12.74		A	L	1–4	Hector
1976–77	UEFA Cup	1	15. 9.76	Finn Harps (Eire)	H	W	12–0	Hector 5, James 3, George 3,
			29. 9.76		A	W	4–1	Hector 2, George 2
		2	20.10.76	AEK Athens (Greece)	A	L	0–2	
			3.11.76		H	L	2–3	George, Rioch

EVERTON

Season	Competition	Round	Date	Opponents (Country)	Venue	Result		Scorers
1963–64	European Cup	1	18. 9.63	Inter-Milan (Italy)	H	D	0–0	
			25. 9.63		A	L	0–1	
1970–71	European Cup	1	16. 9.70	Keflavik (Iceland)	H	W	6–2	Ball 3, Royle 2, Kendall
			30. 9.70		A	W	3–0	Royle 2, Whittle
		2	21.10.70	Borussia Moenchenglad-	A	D	1–1	Kendall
			4.11.70	bach (West Germany)	H	D	1–1†	Morrissey
		QF	9. 3.71	Panathinaikos (Greece)×	H	D	1–1	Johnson
			24. 3.71		A	D	0–0	
1966–67	Cup-Winners' Cup	1	28. 9.66	Aalborg (Denmark)	A	D	0–0	
			11.10.66		H	W	2–1	Morrissey, Ball
		2	9.11.66	Real Zaragoza (Spain)	A	L	0–2	
			23.11.66		H	W	1–0	Brown
1962–63	Fairs Cup	1	24.10.62	Dumfermline Athletic	H	W	1–0	Stevens
			31.10.62	(Scotland)	A	L	0–2	
1964–65	Fairs Cup	1	23. 9.64	Valerengen (Norway)	A	W	5–2	Pickering 2, Harvey, Temple 2
			14.10.64		H	W	4–2	Young 2, Vernon, own goal
		2	11.11.64	Kilmarnock (Scotland)	A	W	2–0	Temple, Morrissey
			23.11.64		H	W	4–1	Harvey, Pickering 2, Young
		3	20. 1.65	Manchester United	A	D	1–1	Pickering
			9. 2.65	(England)	H	L	1–2	Pickering
1965–66	Fairs Cup	1	28. 9.65	IFC Nuremberg (West	A	D	1–1	Harris
			12.10.65	Germany)	H	W	1–0	Gabriel
		2	3.11.65	Ujpest Dozsa (Hungary)	A	L	0–3	
			16.11.65		H	W	2–1	Harris, own goal
1975–76	UEFA Cup	1	17. 9.75	AC Milan (Italy)	H	D	0–0	
			1.10.75		A	L	0–1	
1978–79	UEFA Cup	1	12. 9.78	Finn Harps (Eire)	A	W	5–0	Thomas, King 2, Latchford, Walsh
			26. 9.78		H	W	5–0	King, Latchford, Walsh, Ross, Dobson
		2	18.10.78	Dukla Prague	H	W	2–1	Latchford, King
			1.11.78	(Czechoslovakia)	A	L	0–1	
1979–80	UEFA Cup	1	19. 9.79	Feyenoord (Holland)	A	L	0–1	
			3.10.79		H	L	0–1	

IPSWICH TOWN

Season	Competition	Round	Date	Opponents (Country)	Venue	Result		Scorers
1962–63	European Cup	Pr	18. 9.62	Floriana (Malta)	A	W	4–1	Crawford 2, Phillips 2
			25. 9.62		H	W	10–0	Crawford 5, Moran 2, Phillips 2, Elsworthy
		1	14.11.62	AC Milan (Italy)	A	L	0–3	
			28.11.62		H	W	2–1	Crawford, Blackwood
1978–79	Cup-Winners' Cup	1	13. 9.78	AZ 67 (Holland)	A	D	0–0	
			27. 9.78		H	W	2–0	Mariner, Wark (pen)
		2	18.10.78	SW Innsbruck (Austria)	H	W	1–0	Wark (pen)
			1.11.78		A	D	1–1	Burley
		QF	7. 3.79	Barcelona (Spain)	H	W	2–1	Gates 2
			21. 3.79		A	L	0–1	
1973–74	UEFA Cup	1	19. 9.73	Real Madrid (Spain)	H	W	1–0	own goal
			3.10.73		A	D	0–0	
		2	24.10.73	Lazio (Italy)	H	W	4–0	Whymark 4
			7.11.73		A	L	2–4	Viljoen (pen), Johnson

Season	Competition	Round	Date	Opponents (Country)	Venue	Result		Scorers
		3	28.11.73	Twente Enschede	H	W	1–0	Whymark
			12.12.73	(Holland)	A	W	2–1	Morris, Hamilton
		QF	6. 3.74	Lokomotive Leipzig	H	W	1–0	Beattie
			20. 3.74	(East Germany)†	H	L	0–1	
1974–75	UEFA Cup	1	18. 9.74	Twente Enschede	H	D	2–2	Hamilton, Talbot
			2.10.74	(Holland)*	A	D	1–1	Hamilton
1975–76	UEFA Cup	1	17. 9.75	Feyenoord (Holland)	A	W	2–1	Whymark, Johnson
			1.10.75		H	W	2–0	Woods, Whymark
		2	22.10.75	FC Bruges (Belgium)	H	W	3–0	Gates, Peddelty, Austin
			5.11.75		A	L	0–4	
1977–78	UEFA Cup	1	14. 9.77	Landskrona (Sweden)	A	W	1–0	Whymark
			28. 9.77		H	W	5–0	Whymark 4 (1 pen), Mariner
		2	19.10.77	Las Palmas (Spain)	H	W	1–0	Gates
			2.11.77		A	D	3–3	Mariner 2, Talbot
		3	23.11.77	Barcelona (Spain)	H	W	3–0	Gates, Whymark, Talbot
			7.12.77		A	L	0–3†	
1979–80	UEFA Cup	1	19. 9.79	Skeid Oslo (Norway)	A	W	3–1	Mills, Turner, Mariner
			3.10.79		H	W	7–0	Muhren 2, McCall 2, Wark, Thijssen, Mariner
		2	24.10.79	Grasshoppers*	A	D	0–0	
			7.11.79	(Switzerland)	H	D	1–1	Beattie
1980–81	UEFA Cup	1	17. 9.80	Aris Salonika	H	W	5–1	Wark 4 (3 pens), Mariner
			1.10.80	(Greece)	A	L	1–3	Gates
		2	22.10.80	Bohemians	H	W	3–0	Wark 2, Beattie
			5.11.80	(Czechoslovakia)	A	L	0–2	
		3	26.11.80	Widzew Lodz	H	W	5–0	Wark 3, Brazil, Mariner
			10.12.80	(Poland)	A	L	0–1	
		QF	4. 3.81	St Etienne	A	W	4–1	Mariner 2, Wark, Brazil
			18. 3.81	(France)	H	W	3–1	Butcher, Wark (pen), Mariner
		SF	8. 4.81	IFC Cologne	H	W	1–0	Wark
			22. 4.81	(West Germany)	A	W	1–0	Butcher
		F	6. 5.81	AZ 67 (Holland)	H	W	3–0	Wark (pen), Thijssen, Mariner
			20. 5.81		A	L	2–4	Thijssen, Wark
1981–82	UEFA Cup	1	16. 9.81	Aberdeen (Scotland)	H	D	1–1	Thijssen
			30. 9.81		A	L	1–3	Wark (pen)
1982–83	UEFA Cup	1	15. 9.82	AS Roma (Italy)	A	L	0–3	
			29. 9.82		H	W	3–1	Gates, McCall, Butcher

LEEDS UNITED

Season	Competition	Round	Date	Opponents (Country)	Venue	Result		Scorers
1969–70	European Cup	1	17. 9.69	Lyn Oslo (Norway)	H	W	10–0	Jones 3, Clarke 2, Giles 2, Bremner 2, O'Grady
			1.10.69		A	W	6–0	Belfitt 2, Hibbitt 2, Jones, Lorimer
		2	12.11.69	Ferencvaros (Hungary)	H	W	3–0	Giles, Jones 2
			26.11.69		A	W	3–0	Jones 2, Lorimer
		QF	4. 3.70	Standard Liege (Belgium)	A	W	1–0	Lorimer
			18. 3.70		H	W	1–0	Giles (pen)
		SF	1. 4.70	Celtic (Scotland)	H	L	0–1	
			15. 4.70		A	L	1–2	Bremner
1974–75	European Cup	1	28. 9.74	Zurich (Switzerland)	H	W	4–1	Clarke 2, Lorimer (pen), Jordan
			2.10.74		A	L	1–2	Clarke
		2	23.10.74	Ujpest Dozsa (Hungary)	A	W	2–1	Lorimer, McQueen
			6.11.74		H	W	3–0	McQueen, Bremner, Yorath
		QF	5. 3.75	Anderlecht (Belgium)	H	W	3–0	Jordan, McQueen, Lorimer
			19. 3.75		A	W	1–0	Bremner
		SF	9. 4.75	Barcelona (Spain)	H	W	2–1	Bremner, Clarke
			24. 4.75		A	D	1–1	Lorimer
		F	28. 5.75	Bayern Munich (West Germany)	N	L	0–2	
1972–73	Cup-Winners' Cup	1	13. 9.72	Ankaragucu (Turkey)	A	D	1–1	Jordan
			28. 9.72		H	W	1–0	Jones
		2	25.10.72	Carl Zeiss Jena (East Germany)	A	D	0–0	
			8.11.72		H	W	2–0	Cherry, Jones
		QF	7. 3.73	Rapid Bucharest (Rumania)	H	W	5–0	Giles, Clarke, Lorimer 2, Jordan
			23. 3.73		A	W	3–1	Jones, Jordan, Bates

Season	Competition	Round	Date	Opponents (Country)	Venue	Result		Scorers
		SF	11. 4.73	Hajduk Split (Yugoslavia)	H	W	1–0	Clarke
			25. 4.73		A	D	0–0	
		F	16. 5.73	AC Milan (Italy)	N	L	0–1	
1965–66	Fairs Cup	1	29. 9.65	Torino (Italy)	H	W	2–1	Bremner, Peacock
			6.10.65		A	D	0–0	
		2	24.11.65	Lokomotive Leipzig	A	W	2–1	Lorimer, Bremner
			1.12.65	(East Germany)	H	D	0–0	
		3	2. 2.66	Valencia (Spain)	H	D	1–1	Lorimer
			16. 2.66		A	W	1–0	O'Grady
		QF	2. 3.66	Ujpest Dozsa (Hungary)	H	W	4–1	Cooper, Bell, Storrie, Bremner
			9. 3.66		A	D	1–1	Lorimer
		SF	20. 4.66	Real Zaragoza (Spain)	A	L	0–1	
			27. 4.66		H	W	2–1	Johanneson, Charlton
			11. 5.66		N	L	1–3	Charlton
1966–67	Fairs Cup	1		bye				
		2	18.10.66	DWS Amsterdam	A	W	3–1	Bremner, Johanneson, Greenhoff
			26.10.66	(Holland)	H	W	5–1	Johanneson 3, Giles, Madeley
		3	18. 1.67	Valencia (Spain)	H	D	1–1	Greenhoff
			8. 2.67		A	W	2–0	Giles, Lorimer
		QF	22. 3.67	Bologna (Italy)	A	L	0–1	
			19. 4.67		H	W	1–0‡	Giles (pen)
		SF	19. 5.67	Kilmarnock (Scotland)	H	W	4–2	Belfitt 3, Giles (pen)
			24. 5.67		A	D	0–0	
		F	30. 8.67	Dynamo Zagreb	A	L	0–2	
			6. 9.67	(Yugoslavia)	H	D	0–0	
1967–68	Fairs Cup	1	3.10.67	Spora Luxembourg	A	W	9–0	Lorimer 4, Greenhoff 2, Madeley, Jones, Bremner
			17.10.67	(Luxembourg)	H	W	7–0	Johanneson 3, Greenhoff 2, Cooper, Lorimer
		2	29.11.67	Partizan Belgrade	A	W	2–1	Lorimer, Belfitt
			6.12.67	(Yugoslavia)	H	D	1–1	Lorimer
		3	20.12.67	Hibernian (Scotland)	H	W	1–0	Gray (E)
			10. 1.68		A	D	0–0	
		QF	26. 3.68	Rangers (Scotland)	A	D	0–0	
			9. 4.68		H	W	2–0	Lorimer, Giles (pen)
		SF	1. 5.68	Dundee (Scotland)	A	D	1–1	Madeley
			15. 5.68		H	W	1–0	Gray (E)
		F	7. 8.68	Ferencvaros (Hungary)	H	W	1–0	Charlton
			11. 9.68		A	D	0–0	
1968–69	Fairs Cup	1	18. 9.68	Standard Liege (Belgium)	A	D	0–0	
			23.10.68		H	W	3–2	Charlton, Lorimer, Bremner
		2	13.11.68	Napoli (Italy)	H	W	2–0	Charlton 2
			27.11.68		A	L	0–2‡	
		3	18.12.68	Hanover 96 (West	H	W	5–1	O'Grady, Hunter, Lorimer 2, Charlton
			4. 2.69	Germany)	A	W	2–1	Belfitt, Jones
		QF	5. 3.69	Ujpest Dozsa (Hungary)	A	L	0–1	
			19. 3.69		A	L	0–2	
1970–71	Fairs Cup	1	15. 9.70	Sarpsborg (Norway)	H	W	1–0	Lorimer
			29. 9.70		H	W	5–0	Charlton 2, Bremner 2, Lorimer
		2	21.10.70	Dynamo Dresden	A	W	1–0	Lorimer
			4.11.70	(East Germany)	A	L	1–2*	Jones
		3	2.12.70	Sparta Prague	H	W	6–0	Clarke, Bremner, Gray (E) 2, Charlton, own goal
			9.12.70	(Czechoslovakia)	A	W	3–2	Gray (E), Clarke, Belfitt
		QF	10. 3.71	Setubal (Portugal)	H	W	2–1	Lorimer, Giles (pen)
			24. 3.71		A	D	1–1	Lorimer
		SF	14. 4.71	Liverpool (England)	A	W	1–0	Bremner
			28. 4.71		H	D	0–0	
		F	28. 5.71	Juventus (Italy)	A	D	2–2	Madeley, Bates
			3. 6.71		H	D	1–1*	Clarke
1971–72	UEFA Cup	1	15. 9.71	Lierse (Belgium)	A	W	2–0	Galvin, Lorimer
			29. 9.71		H	L	0–4	
1973–74	UEFA Cup	1	19. 9.73	Stromsgodset (Norway)	A	D	1–1	Clarke
			3.10.73		H	W	6–1	Clarke 2, Jones 2, Gray (F), Bates

Season	Competition	Round	Date	Opponents (Country)	Venue	Result		Scorers
		2	24.10.73	Hibernian (Scotland)	H	D	0-0	
			7.11.73		A	D	0-0†	
		3	28.11.73	Setubal (Portugal	H	W	1-0	Cherry
			12.12.73		A	L	1-3	Liddell
1979-80	UEFA Cup	1	19. 9.79	Valletta (Malta)	A	W	4-0	Graham 3, Hart
			3.10.79		H	W	3-0	Curtis, Hankin, Hart
		2	24.10.79	Uni. Craiova (Rumania)	A	L	0-2	
			7.11.79		H	L	0-2	

N.B. Leeds met Barcelona in Spain on 22.9.71 in a match to determine who should hold the Fairs Cup trophy permanently. Barcelona, the first winners beat Leeds, the holders 2-1 (Jordan was the United scorer).

LEICESTER CITY

Season	Competition	Round	Date	Opponents (Country)	Venue	Result		Scorers
1961-62	Cup-Winners' Cup	1	13. 9.61	Glenavon (Northern Ireland)	A	W	4-1	Walsh 2, Appleton, Keyworth
			27. 9.61		H	W	3-1	Wills, Keyworth, McIlmoyle
		2	25.10.61	Atletico Madrid (Spain)	H	D	1-1	Keyworth
			15.11.61		A	L	0-2	

LIVERPOOL

Season	Competition	Round	Date	Opponents (Country)	Venue	Result		Scorers
1964-65	European Cup	Pr	17. 8.64	KR Reykjavik (Iceland)	A	W	5-0	Wallace 2, Hunt 2, Chisnall
			14. 9.64		H	W	6-1	Byrne, St John 2, Graham, Hunt, Stevenson
		1	25.11.64	Anderlecht (Belgium)	H	W	3-0	St John, Hunt, Yeats
			16.12.64		A	W	1-0	Hunt
		QF	10. 2.65	IFC Cologne (West Germany)	A	D	0-0	
			17. 3.65		H	D	0-0	
			24. 3.65		N	D	2-2‡	St John, Hunt
		SF	4. 5.65	Inter-Milan (Italy)	H	W	3-1	Hunt, Callaghan, St John
			12. 5.65		A	L	0-3	
1966-67	European Cup	1	28. 9.66	Petrolul Ploesti (Rumania)	H	W	2-0	St John, Callaghan
			12.10.66		A	L	1-3	Hunt
			19.10.66		N	W	2-0	St John, Thompson (P)
		2	7.12.66	Ajax (Holland)	A	L	1-5	Lawler
			14.12.66		H	D	2-2	Hunt 2
1973-74	European Cup	1	19. 9.73	Jeunesse D'Esch (Luxembourg)	A	D	1-1	Hall
			3.10.73		H	W	2-0	Toshack, own goal
		2	24.10.73	Red Star Belgrade (Yugoslavia)	A	L	1-2	Lawler
			6.11.73		H	L	1-2	Lawler
1976-77	European Cup	1	14. 9.76	Crusaders (Northern Ireland)	H	W	2-0	Neal (pen), Toshack
			28. 9.76		A	W	5-0	Johnson 2, Keegan, McDermott, Heighway
		2	20.10.76	Trabzonspor (Turkey)	A	L	0-1	
			3.11.76		H	W	3-0	Heighway, Johnson, Keegan
		QF	2. 3.77	St Etienne (France)	A	L	0-1	
			16. 3.77		H	W	3-1	Keegan, Kennedy, Fairclough
		SF	6. 4.77	Zurich (Switzerland)	A	W	3-1	Neal 2 (1 pen), Heighway
			20. 4.77		H	W	3-0	Case 2, Keegan
		F	25. 5.77	Borussia Moenchenglad-bach (West Germany)	N	W	3-1	McDermott, Smith, Neal (pen)
1977-78	European Cup	1		bye				
		2	19.10.77	Dynamo Dresden (East Germany)	H	W	5-1	Hansen, Case 2, Neal (pen), Kennedy
			2.11.77		A	L	1-2	Heighway
		QF	1. 3.78	Benfica (Portugal)	A	W	2-1	Case, Hughes
			15. 3.78		H	W	4-1	Callaghan, Dalglish, McDermott, Neal
		SF	29. 3.78	Borussia Moenchenglad-bach (West Germany)	A	L	1-2	Johnson
			12. 4.78		H	W	3-0	Kennedy, Dalglish, Case
		F	10. 5.78	FC Bruges (Belgium)	N	W	1-0	Dalglish
1978-79	European Cup	1	13. 9.78	Nottingham Forest (England)	A	L	0-2	
			27. 9.78		H	D	0-0	
1979-80	European Cup	1	19. 9.79	Dynamo Tbilisi (USSR)	H	W	2-1	Johnson, Case
			3.10.79		A	L	0-3	

Season	Competition	Round	Date	Opponents (Country)	Venue	Result		Scorers
1980–81	European Cup	1	17. 9.80	Oulun Palloseura	A	D	1–1	McDermott
			1.10.80	(Finland)	H	W	10–1	Souness 3, (1 pen), Fairclough 2, McDermott 2, Dalglish, Lee, Kennedy (R)
		2	22.10.80	Aberdeen (Scotland)	A	W	1–0	McDermott
			5.11.80		H	W	4–0	Neal, Dalglish, Hansen, own goal
		QF	4. 3.81	CSKA Sofia	H	W	5–1	Souness 3, Lee, McDermott
			18. 3.81	(Bulgaria)	A	W	1–0	Johnson
		SF	8. 4.81	Bayern Munich	H	D	0–0	
			22. 4.81	(West Germany)	A	D	1–1*	Kennedy (R)
		F	27. 5.81	Real Madrid (Spain)	N	W	1–0	Kennedy (A)
1981–82	European Cup	1	16. 9.81	Oulun Palloseura	A	W	1–0	Dalglish
			30. 9.81	(Finland)	H	W	7–0	Dalglish, McDermott 2, Kennedy (R), Johnson, Rush, Lawrenson
		2	21.10.81	AZ 67 Holland)	A	D	2–2	Johnson, Lee
			4.11.81		H	W	3–2	McDermott (pen) Rush, Hansen
		QF	3. 3.82	CSKA Sofia	H	W	1–0	Whelan
			17. 3.82	(Bulgaria)	A	L	0–2	
1982–83	European Cup	1	14. 9.82	Dundalk (Eire)	A	W	4–1	Whelan 2, Rush, Hodgson
			28. 9.82		H	W	1–0	Whelan
		2	19.10.82	HJK Helsinki	A	L	0–1	
			2.11.82	(Finland)	H	W	5–0	Dalglish, Johnston Neal, Kennedy (A) 2
		QF	2. 3.83	Widzew Lodz	A	L	0–2	
			16. 3.83	(Poland)	H	W	3–2	Neal (pen), Rush, Hodgson
1965–66	Cup-Winners' Cup	1	29. 9.65	Juventus (Italy)	A	L	0–1	
			13.10.65		H	W	2–0	Lawler, Strong
		2	1.12.65	Standard Liege (Belgium)	H	W	3–1	Lawler 2, Thompson (P)
			15.12.65		A	W	2–1	Hunt, St John
		QF	1. 3.66	Honved (Hungary)	A	D	0–0	
			8. 3.66		H	W	2–0	Lawler, St John
		SF	14. 4.66	Celtic (Scotland)	A	L	0–1	
			19. 4.66		H	W	2–0	Smith, Strong
		F	5. 5.66	Borussia Dortmund (West Germany)	N	L	1–2	Hunt
1971–72	Cup-Winners' Cup	1	15. 9.71	Servette (Switzerland)	A	L	1–2	Lawler
			29. 9.71		H	W	2–0	Hughes, Heighway
		2	20.10.71	Bayern Munich	H	D	0–0	
			3.11.71	(West Germany)	A	L	1–3	Evans
1974–75	Cup-Winners' Cup	1	17. 9.74	Stromsgodset (Norway)	H	W	11–0	Lindsay (pen), Boersma 2, Heighway, Thompson (P B) 2, Smith, Cormack, Hughes, Callaghan, Kennedy
			1.10.74	Barcelona (Spain)	A	W	1–0	Kennedy
		2	23.10.74	Ferencvaros (Hungary)*	H	D	1–1	Keegan
			5.11.74		A	D	0–0	
1967–68	Fairs Cup	1	19. 9.67	Malmo FF (Sweden)	A	W	2–0	Hateley 2
			4.10.67		H	W	2–1	Yeats, Hunt
		2	7.11.67	Munich 1860 (West Germany)	H	W	8–0	St John, Hateley, Thompson (P), Smith (pen), Hunt 2, Callaghan 2
			14.11.67		A	L	1–2	Callaghan
		3	28.11.67	Ferencvaros (Hungary)	A	L	0–1	
			9. 1.68		H	L	0–1	
1968–69	Fairs Cup	1	18. 9.68	Atletico Bilbao (Spain)‡	A	L	1–2	Hunt
			2.10.68		H	W	2–1	Lawler, Hughes
1969–70	Fairs Cup	1	16. 9.69	Dundalk (Eire)	H	W	10–0	Evans, Smith 2, Graham 2, Lawler, Lindsay, Thompson (P), Callaghan
			30. 9.69		A	W	4–0	Thompson (P) 2, Graham, Callaghan
		3	11.11.69	Setubal (Portugal)*	A	L	0–1	
			26.11.69		H	W	3–2	Smith (pen), Evans, Hunt
1970–71	Fairs Cup	1	15. 9.70	Ferencvaros (Hungary)	H	W	1–0	Graham
			29. 9.70		A	D	1–1	Hughes
		2	21.10.70	Dynamo Bucharest	H	W	3–0	Lindsay, Lawler, Hughes
			4.11.70	(Rumania)	A	D	1–1	Boersma

Season	Competition	Round	Date	Opponents (Country)	Venue	Result		Scorers
		3	9.12.70	Hibernian (Scotland)	A	W	1–0	Toshack
			22.12.70		H	W	2–0	Heighway, Boersma
		QF	10. 3.71	Bayern Munich	H	W	3–0	Evans 3
			24. 3.71	(West Germany)	A	D	1–1	Ross
		SF	14. 4.71	Leeds United (England)	H	L	0–1	
			28. 4.71		A	D	0–0	
1972–73	UEFA Cup	1	12. 9.72	Eintracht Frankfurt	H	W	2–0	Keegan, Hughes
			26. 9.72	(West Germany)	A	D	0–0	
		2	24.10.72	AEK Athens (Greece)	H	W	3–0	Boersma, Cormack, Smith (pen)
			7.11.72		A	W	3–1	Hughes 2, Boersma
		3	29.11.72	Dynamo Berlin (East	A	D	0–0	
			12.12.72	(Germany)	H	W	3–1	Boersma, Heighway, Toshack
		QF	7. 3.73	Dynamo Dresden	H	W	2–0	Hall, Boersma
			21. 3.73	(East Germany)	A	W	1–0	Keegan
		SF	10. 4.73	Tottenham Hotspur	H	W	1–0	Lindsay
			25. 4.73	(England)	A	L	1–2*	Heighway
		F	10. 5.73	Borussia Moenchenglad-	H	W	3–0	Keegan 2, Lloyd
			23. 5.73	bach (West Germany)	A	L	0–2	
1975–76	UEFA Cup	1	17. 9.75	Hibernian (Scotland)	A	L	0–1	
			30. 9.75		H	W	3–1	Toshack 3
		2	22.10.75	Real Sociedad (Spain)	A	W	3–1	Heighway, Callaghan, Thompson (P B)
			4.11.75		H	W	6–0	Toshack, Kennedy 2, Fairclough, Heighway, Neal
		3	26.11.75	Slask Wroclaw (Poland)	A	W	2–1	Kennedy, Toshack
			10.12.75		H	W	3–0	Case 3
		QF	3. 3.76	Dynamo Dresden	A	D	0–0	
			17. 3.76	(East Germany)	H	W	2–1	Case, Keegan
		SF	30. 3.76	Barcelona (Spain)	A	W	1–0	Toshack
			14. 4.76		H	D	1–1	Thompson (P B)
		F	28. 4.76	FC Bruges (Belgium)	H	W	3–2	Kennedy, Case, Keegan (pen)
			19. 5.76		A	D	1–1	Keegan
1977–78	Super Cup	F	22.11.77	SV Hamburg (West	A	D	1–1	Fairclough
			6.12.77	Germany)	H	W	6–0	Thompson, McDermott 3, Fairclough, Dalglish
1978–79	Super Cup	F	4.12.78	Anderlecht (Belgium)	A	L	1–3	Case
			19.12.78		H	W	2–1	Hughes, Fairclough

MANCHESTER CITY

Season	Competition	Round	Date	Opponents (Country)	Venue	Result		Scorers
1968–69	European Cup	1	18. 9.68	Fenerbahce (Turkey)	H	D	0–0	
			2.10.68		A	L	1–2	Coleman
1969–70	Cup-Winners' Cup	1	17. 9.69	Atletico Bilbao (Spain)	A	D	3–3	Young, Booth, own goal
			1.10.69		H	W	3–0	Oakes, Bell, Bowyer
		2	12.11.69	Lierse (Belgium)	A	W	3–0	Lee 2, Bell
			26.11.69		H	W	5–0	Bell 2, Lee 2, Summerbee
		QF	4. 3.70	Academica Coimbra	A	D	0–0	
			18. 3.70	(Portugal)	H	W	1–0	Towers
		SF	1. 4.70	Schalke 04 (West	A	L	0–1	
			15. 4.70	Germany)	H	W	5–1	Young 2, Doyle, Lee, Bell
		F	29. 4.70	Gornik Zabrze (Poland)	N	W	2–1	Young, Lee (pen)
1970–71	Cup-Winners' Cup	1	16. 9.70	Linfield (Northern	H	W	1–0	Bell
			30. 9.70	Ireland)	A	L	1–2*	Lee
		2	21.10.70	Honved (Hungary)	A	W	1–0	Lee
			4.11.70		H	W	2–0	Bell, Lee
		QF	10. 3.71	Gornik Zabrze (Poland)	A	L	0–2	
			24. 3.71		H	W	2–0	Mellor, Doyle
			31. 3.71		N	W	3–1	Young, Booth, Lee
		SF	14. 4.71	Chelsea (England)	A	L	0–1	
			28. 4.71		H	L	0–1	
1972–73	UEFA Cup	1	13. 9.72	Valencia (Spain)	H	D	2–2	Mellor, Marsh
			27. 9.72		A	L	1–2	Marsh

Season	Competition	Round	Date	Opponents (Country)	Venue	Result		Scorers
1976–77	UEFA Cup	1	15. 9.76	Juventus (Italy)	H	W	1–0	Kidd
			29. 9.76		A	L	0–2	
1977–78	UEFA Cup	1	14. 9.77	Widzew Lodz (Poland)*	H	D	2–2	Barnes, Channon
			28. 9.77		A	D	0–0	
1978–79	UEFA Cup	1	13. 9.78	Twente Enschede	A	D	1–1	Watson
			27. 9.78	(Holland)	H	W	3–2	Kidd, Bell, own goal
		2	18.10.78	Standard Liege (Belgium)	H	W	4–0	Hartford, Kidd 2 (1 pen), Palmer
			1.11.78		A	L	0–2	
		3	23.11.78	AC Milan (Italy)	A	D	2–2	Kidd, Power
			6.12.78		H	W	3–0	Booth, Hartford, Kidd
		QF	7. 3.79	Borussia Moenchenglad-	H	D	1–1	Channon
			21. 3.79	bach (West Germany)	A	L	1–3	Deyna

MANCHESTER UNITED

Season	Competition	Round	Date	Opponents (Country)	Venue	Result		Scorers
1956–57	European Cup	Pr	12. 9.56	Anderlecht (Belgium)	A	W	2–0	Viollet, Taylor (T)
			26. 9.56		H	W	10–0	Viollet 4, Taylor (T) 3, Whelan 2, Berry
		1	17.10.56	Borussia Dortmund	H	W	3–2	Viollet 2, Pegg
			21.11.56	(West Germany)	A	D	0–0	
		QF	16. 1.57	Atletico Bilbao (Spain)	A	L	3–5	Taylor (T), Viollet, Whelan
			6. 2.57		H	W	3–0	Viollet, Taylor (T), Berry
		SF	11. 4.57	Real Madrid (Spain)	A	L	1–3	Taylor (T)
			24. 4.57		H	D	2–2	Taylor (T), Charlton
1957–58	European Cup	Pr	25. 9.57	Shamrock Rovers (Eire)	A	W	6–0	Whelan 2, Taylor (T) 2, Berry, Pegg
			2.10.57		H	W	3–2	Viollet 2, Pegg
		1	20.11.57	Dukla Prague	H	W	3–0	Webster, Taylor (T), Pegg
			4.12.57	(Czechoslovakia)	A	L	0–1	
		QF	14. 1.58	Red Star Belgrade	H	W	2–1	Charlton, Colman
			5. 2.58	(Yugoslavia)	A	D	3–3	Viollet, Charlton 2
		SF	8. 5.58	AC Milan (Italy)	H	W	2–1	Viollet, Taylor (E) (pen)
			14. 5.58		A	L	0–4	
1965–66	European Cup	Pr	22. 9.65	HJK Helsinki (Finland)	A	W	3–2	Herd, Connelly, Law
			6.10.65		H	W	6–0	Connelly 3, Best 2, Charlton
		1	17.11.65	Vorwaerts Berlin	A	W	2–0	Law, Connelly
			1.12.65	(East Germany)	H	W	3–1	Herd 3
		QF	2. 2.66	Benfica (Portugal)	H	W	3–2	Herd, Law, Foulkes
			9. 3.66		A	W	5–1	Best 2, Connelly, Crerand, Charlton
		SF	13. 4.66	Partizan Belgrade	A	L	0–2	
			20. 4.66	(Yugoslavia)	H	W	1–0	own goal
1967–68	European Cup	1	20. 9.67	Hibernians (Malta)	H	W	4–0	Sadler 2, Law 2
			27. 9.67		A	D	0–0	
		2	15.11.67	Sarajevo (Yugoslavia)	A	D	0–0	
			29.11.67		H	W	2–1	Aston, Best
		QF	28. 2.68	Gornik Zabrze (Poland)	H	W	2–0	Kidd, own goal
			13. 3.68		A	L	0–1	
		SF	24. 4.68	Real Madrid (Spain)	H	W	1–0	Best
			15. 5.68		A	D	3–3	Sadler, Kidd, Foulkes
		F	29. 5.68	Benfica (Portugal)	N	W	4–1	Charlton 2, Best, Kidd
1968–69	European Cup	1	18. 9.68	Waterford (Eire)	A	W	3–1	Law 3
			2.10.68		H	W	7–1	Stiles, Law 4, Burns, Charlton
		2	13.11.68	Anderlecht (Belgium)	H	W	3–0	Kidd, Law 2
			27.11.68		A	L	1–3	Sartori
		QF	26. 2.69	Rapid Vienna (Austria)	H	W	3–0	Best 2, Morgan
			5. 3.69		A	D	0–0	
		SF	23. 4.69	AC Milan (Italy)	A	L	0–2	
			15. 5.69		H	W	1–0	Charlton
1963–64	Cup Winners' Cup	1	25. 9.63	Tilburg Willem II (Holland)	A	D	1–1	Herd
			15.10.63		H	W	6–1	Setters, Law 3, Charlton, Chisnall
		2	3.12.63	Tottenham Hotspur	A	L	0–2	
			10.12.63	(England)	H	W	4–1	Herd 2, Charlton 2
		QF	26. 2.64	Sporting Lisbon	H	W	4–1	Law 3 (2 pens), Charlton
			18. 3.64	(Portugal)	A	L	0–5	

Season	Competition	Round	Date	Opponents (Country)	Venue	Result		Scorers
1977–78	Cup-Winners' Cup	1	14. 9.77	St Etienne (France)	A	D	1–1	Hill
			5.10.77		H	W	2–0	Pearson, Coppell
		2	19.10.77	Porto (Portugal)	A	L	0–4	
			2.11.77		H	W	5–2	Coppell 2, own goals 2, Nicholl
1964–65	Fairs Cup	1	23. 9.64	Djurgaarden (Sweden)	A	D	1–1	Herd
			27.10.64		H	W	6–1	Law 3 (1 pen), Charlton 2, Best
		2	11.11.64	Borussia Dortmund	A	W	6–1	Herd, Charlton 3, Best, Law
			2.12.64	(West Germany)	H	W	4–0	Charlton 2, Law, Connelly
		3	20. 1.65	Everton (England)	H	D	1–1	Connelly
			9. 2.65		A	W	2–1	Connelly, Herd
		QF	12. 5.65	Strasbourg (France)	A	W	5–0	Connelly, Herd, Law 2, Charlton
			19. 5.65		H	D	0–0	
		SF	31. 5.65	Ferencvaros (Hungary)	H	W	3–2	Law (pen), Herd 2
			6. 6.65		A	L	0–1	
			16. 6.65		A	L	1–2	Connelly
1976–77	UEFA Cup	1	15. 9.76	Ajax (Holland)	A	L	0–1	
			29. 9.76		H	W	2–0	Macari, McIlroy
		2	20.10.76	Juventus (Italy)	H	W	1–0	Hill
			3.11.76		A	L	0–3	
1980–81	UEFA Cup	1	17. 9.80	Widzew Lodz*	H	D	1–1	McIlroy
			1.10.80	(Poland)	A	D	0–0	
1982–83	UEFA Cup	1	15. 9.82	Valencia (Spain)	H	D	0–0	
			29. 9.82		A	L	1–2	Robson

NEWCASTLE UNITED

Season	Competition	Round	Date	Opponents (Country)	Venue	Result		Scorers
1968–69	Fairs Cup	1	11. 9.68	Feyenoord (Holland)	H	W	4–0	Scott, Robson (B), Gibb, Davies
			17. 9.68		A	L	0–2	
		2	30.10.68	Sporting Lisbon	A	D	1–1	Scott
			20.11.68	(Portugal)	H	W	1–0	Robson (B)
		3	1. 1.69	Real Zaragoza (Spain)	A	L	2–3	Robson (B), Davies
			15. 1.69		H	W	2–1*	Robson (B), Gibb
		QF	12. 3.69	Setubal (Portugal)	H	W	5–1	Robson (B 2, Gibb, Davies, Foggon
			26. 3.69		A	L	1–3	Davies
		SF	14. 5.69	Rangers (Scotland)	A	D	0–0	
			22. 5.69		H	W	2–0	Scott, Sinclair
		F	29. 5.69	Ujpest Dozsa (Hungary)	H	W	3–0	Moncur 2, Scott
			11. 6.69		A	W	3–2	Moncur, Arentoft, Foggon
1969–70	Fairs Cup	1	15. 9.69	Dundee United (Scotland)	A	W	2–1	Davies 2
			1.10.69		H	W	1–0	Dyson
		2	19.11.69	Porto (Portugal)	A	D	0–0	
			26.11.69		H	W	1–0	Scott
		3	17.12.69	Southampton (England)	H	D	0–0	
			13. 1.70		A	D	1–1*	Robson (B)
		QF	11. 3.70	Anderlecht (Belgium)*	A	L	0–2	
			18. 3.70		H	W	3–1	Robson (B) 2, Dyson
1970–71	Fairs Cup	1	23. 9.70	Inter-Milan (Italy)	A	D	1–1	Davies
			30. 9.70		H	W	2–0	Moncur, Davies
		2	21.10.70	Pecs Dozsa (Hungary)†	H	W	2–0	Davies 2
			4.11.70		A	L	0–2	
1977–78	UEFA Cup	1	14. 9.77	Bohemians (Eire)	A	D	0–0	
			28. 9.77		H	W	4–0	Gowling 2, Craig 2
		2	19.10.77	Bastia (France)	A	L	1–2	Cannell
			2.11.77		H	L	1–3	Gowling

NEWPORT COUNTY

Season	Competition	Round	Date	Opponents (Country)	Venue	Result		Scorers
1980–81	Cup-Winners' Cup	1	16. 9.80	Crusaders (Northern Ireland)	H	W	4–0	Gwyther, Moore, Aldridge, Bruton
			1.10.80		A	D	0–0	
		2	22.10.80	Haugar (Norway)	A	D	0–0	
			4.11.80		H	W	6–0	Gwyther, Lowndes, Aldridge, Tynan 2, Moore
		QF	4. 3.81	Carl Zeiss Jena	A	D	2–2	Tynan 2
			18. 3.81	(East Germany)	H	L	0–1	

Season	Competition	Round	Date	Opponents (Country)	Venue	Result		Scorers

NOTTINGHAM FOREST

Season	Competition	Round	Date	Opponents (Country)	Venue	Result		Scorers
1961–62	Fairs Cup	1	13. 9.61	Valencia (Spain)	A	L	0–2	
			4.10.61		H	L	1–5	Cobb
1967–68	Fairs Cup	1	20. 9.67	Eintracht Frankfurt	A	W	1–0	Baker
			17.10.67	(West Germany)	H	W	4–0	Baker 2, Chapman, Lyons
		2	31.10.67	Zurich (Switzerland)*	H	W	2–1	Newton, Moore (pen)
			14.11.67		A	L	0–1	
1978–79	European Cup	1	13. 9.78	Liverpool (England)	H	W	2–0	Birtles, Barrett
			27. 9.78		A	D	0–0	
		2	18.10.78	AEK Athens (Greece)	A	W	2–1	McGovern, Birtles
			1.11.78		H	W	5–1	Needham, Woodcock, Anderson, Birtles 2
		QF	7. 3.79	Grasshoppers · (Switzerland)	H	W	4–1	Birtles, Robertson (pen), Gemmill, Lloyd
			21. 3.79		A	D	1–1	O'Neill
		SF	11. 4.79	IFC Cologne (West	H	D	3–3	Birtles, Bowyer, Robertson
			25. 4.79	Germany)	A	W	1–0	Bowyer
		F	30. 5.79	Malmo FF (Sweden)	N	W	1–0	Francis
1979–80	European Cup	1	19. 9.79	Oster (Sweden)	H	W	2–0	Bowyer, own goal
			3.10.79		A	D	1–1	Woodcock
		2	24.10.79	Arges Pitesti (Rumania)	H	W	2–0	Woodcock, Birtles
			7.11.79		A	W	2–1	Bowyer, Birtles
		QF	5. 3.80	Dynamo Berlin (East	H	L	0–1	
			19. 3.80	Germany)	A	W	3–1	Francis 2, Robertson (pen)
		SF	9. 4.80	Ajax (Holland)	H	W	2–0	Francis, Robertson (pen)
			23. 4.80		A	L	0–1	
		F	28. 5.80	SV Hamburg (West Germany)	N	W	1–0	Robertson
1980–81	European Cup	1	17. 9.80	CSKA Sofia	A	L	0–1	
			1.10.80	(Bulgaria)	H	L	0–1	
1979–80	Super Cup		30. 1.80	Barcelona (Spain)	H	W	1–0	George
			5. 2.80		A	D	1–1	Burns
1980–81	Super Cup	F	25.11.80	Valencia*	H	W	2–1	Bowyer 2
			17.12.80	(Spain)	A	L	0–1	

QUEEN'S PARK RANGERS

Season	Competition	Round	Date	Opponents (Country)	Venue	Result		Scorers
1976–77	UEFA Cup	1	15. 9.76	Brann Bergen (Norway)	H	W	4–0	Bowles 3, Masson
			29. 9.76		A	W	7–0	Bowles 3, Givens 2, Thomas, Webb
		2	20.10.76	Slovan Bratislava	A	D	3–3	Bowles 2, Givens
			3.11.76	(Czechoslovakia)	H	W	5–2	Givens 3, Bowles, Clement
		3	24.11.76	IFC Cologne (West	H	W	3–0	Givens, Webb, Bowles
			7.12.76	Germany)	A	L	1–4*	Masson
		QF	2. 3.76	AEK Athens (Greece)	H	W	3–0	Francis 2 (2 pens), Bowles
			16. 3.77		A	L	0–3†	

SHEFFIELD WEDNESDAY

Season	Competition	Round	Date	Opponents (Country)	Venue	Result		Scorers
1961–62	Fairs Cup	1	12. 9.61	Lyon (France)	A	L	2–4	Ellis, Young
			4.10.61		H	W	5–2	Fantham 2, Griffin, McAnearney (pen), Dobson
		2	29.11.61	AS Roma (Italy)	H	W	4–0	Fantham, Young 3
			13.12.61		A	L	0–1	
		QF	28. 2.62	Barcelona (Spain)	H	W	3–2	Fantham 2, Finney
			28. 3.62		A	L	0–2	
1963–64	Fairs Cup	1	25. 9.63	DOS Utrecht (Holland)	A	W	4–1	Holliday, Layne, Quinn, own goal
			15.10.63		H	W	4–1	Layne 3 (1 pen), Dobson
		2	6.11.63	IFC Cologne (West	A	L	2–3	Pearson 2
			27.11.63	Germany)	H	L	1–2	Layne

Season	Competition	Round	Date	Opponents (Country)	Venue	Result		Scorers

SOUTHAMPTON

Season	Competition	Round	Date	Opponents (Country)	Venue	Result		Scorers
1976–77	Cup-Winners' Cup	1	15. 9.76	Marseille (France)	H	W	4–0	Waldron, Channon 2 (1 pen), Osgood
			29. 9.76		A	L	1–2	Peach
		2	20.10.76	Carrick Rangers (Northern Ireland)	A	W	5–2	Stokes, Channon 2, McCalliog, Osgood
			3.11.76		H	W	4–1	Williams, Hayes 2, Stokes
		QF	2. 3.77	Anderlecht (Belgium)	A	L	0–2	
			16. 3.77		H	W	2–1	Peach (pen), MacDougall
1969–70	Fairs Cup	1	17. 9.69	Rosenborg (Norway)	A	L	0–1	
			1.10.69		H	W	2–0	Davies, Paine
		2	4.11.69	Vitoria Guimaraes	A	D	3–3	Channon, Davies, Paine
			12.11.69	(Portugal)	H	W	5–1	Gabriel, Davies 2 (1 pen), Channon, own goal
		3	17.12.69	Newcastle United	A	D	0–0	
			13. 1.70	(England)*	H	D	1–1	Channon
1971–72	UEFA Cup	1	15. 9.71	Atletico Bilbao (Spain)	H	W	2–1	Jenkins, Channon (pen)
			29. 9.71		A	L	0–2	
1981–82	UEFA Cup	1	16. 9.81	Limerick (Eire)	A	W	3–0	Moran 2, Armstrong
			29. 9.81		H	D	1–1	Keegan
		2	21.10.81	Sporting Lisbon	H	L	2–4	Keegan (pen), Channon
			4.11.81	(Portugal)	A	D	0–0	
1982–83	UEFA Cup	1	15. 9.82	Norrkoping	H	D	2–2	Williams, Wright
			29. 9.82	(Sweden)	A	D	0–0	

STOKE CITY

Season	Competition	Round	Date	Opponents (Country)	Venue	Result		Scorers
1972–73	UEFA Cup	1	13. 9.72	Kaiserslautern (West Germany)	H	W	3–1	Conroy, Hurst, Ritchie
			27. 9.72		A	L	0–4	
1974–75	UEFA Cup	1	18. 9.74	Ajax (Holland)*	H	D	1–1	Smith
			2.10.74		A	D	0–0	

SUNDERLAND

Season	Competition	Round	Date	Opponents (Country)	Venue	Result		Scorers
1973–74	Cup-Winners' Cup	1	19. 9.73	Vasas-Budapest	A	W	2–0	Hughes, Tueart
			3.10.73	(Hungary)	H	W	1–0	Tueart (pen)
		2	24.10.73	Sporting Lisbon	H	W	2–1	Kerr, Horswill
			7.11.73	(Portugal)	A	L	0–2	

SWANSEA CITY

Season	Competition	Round	Date	Opponents (Country)	Venue	Result		Scorers
1961–62	Cup-Winners' Cup	1	16. 9.61	Motor Jena	H	D	2–2	Reynolds, Nurse (pen)
			18.10.61	(East Germany) (in Linz, Austria)	A	L	1–5	Reynolds
1966–67	Cup-Winners' Cup	1	21. 9.66	Slavia Sofia (Bulgaria)	H	D	1–1	Todd
			5.10.66		A	L	0–4	
1981–82	Cup-Winners' Cup	1	16. 9.81	Lokomotive Leipzig	H	L	0–1	
			30. 9.81	(East Germany)	A	L	1–2	Charles
1982–83	Cup-Winners' Cup	Pr	17. 8.82	Braga	H	W	3–0	Charles 2, own goal
			25. 8.82	(Portugal)	A	L	0–1	
		1	15. 9.82	Sliema Wanderers (Malta)	H	W	12–0	Charles 2, Loveridge 2, Irwin, Latchford, Hadziabdic, Walsh 3, Rajkovic, Stevenson
			29. 9.82		A	W	5–0	Curtis, 2, Gale 2, Toshack
		2	20.10.82	Paris St Germain	H	L	0–1	
			3.11.82	(France)	A	L	0–2	

Season	Competition	Round	Date	Opponents (Country)	Venue	Result		Scorers

TOTTENHAM HOTSPUR

Season	Competition	Round	Date	Opponents (Country)	Venue	Result		Scorers
1961–62	European Cup	Pr	13. 9.61	Gornik Zabrze (Poland)	A	L	2–4	Jones, Dyson
			20. 9.61		H	W	8–1	Blanchflower (pen), Jones 3, Smith 2, Dyson, White
		1	1.11.61	Feyenoord (Holland)	A	W	3–1	Dyson, Saul 2
			15.11.61		H	D	1–1	Dyson
		QF	14. 2.62	Dukla Prague	A	L	0–1	
			26. 2.62	(Czechoslovakia)	H	W	4–1	Smith 2, Mackay 2
		SF	21. 3.62	Benfica (Portugal)	A	L	1–3	Smith
			5. 4.62		H	W	2–1	Smith, Blanchflower (pen)
1962–63	Cup-Winners' Cup	1	bye					
		2	31.10.62	Rangers (Scotland)	H	W	5–2	White, Greaves, Allen, Norman, own goal
			11.12.62		A	W	3–2	Greaves, Smith 2
		QF	5. 3.63	Slovan Bratislava	A	L	0–2	
			14. 3.63	(Czechoslovakia)	H	W	6–0	Mackay, Smith, Greaves 2, Jones, White
		SF	24. 4.63	OFK Belgrade	A	W	2–1	White, Dyson
			1. 5.63	(Yugoslavia)	H	W	3–1	Mackay, Jones, Smith
		F	15. 5.63	Atletico Madrid (Spain)	N	W	5–1	Greaves 2, White, Dyson 2
1963–64	Cup-Winners' Cup	1	exempt					
		2	3.12.63	Manchester United	H	W	2–0	Mackay, Dyson
			10.12.63	(England)	A	L	1–4	Greaves
1967–68	Cup-Winners' Cup	1	20. 9.67	Hajduk Split (Yugoslavia)	A	W	2–0	Robertson, Greaves
			27. 9.67		H	W	4–3	Robertson 2, Gilzean, Venables
		2	29.11.67	Lyon (France)*	A	L	0–1	
			13.12.67		H	W	4–3	Greaves 2 (1 pen), Jones, Gilzean
1981–82	Cup-Winners' Cup	1	16. 9.81	Ajax (Holland)	A	W	3–1	Falco 2, Villa
			29. 9.81		H	W	3–0	Galvin, Falco, Ardiles
		2	21.10.81	Dundalk (Eire)	A	D	1–1	Crooks
			4.11.81		H	W	1–0	Crooks
		QF	3. 3.82	Eintracht Frankfurt	H	W	2–0	Miller, Hazard
			17. 3.82	(West Germany)	A	L	1–2	Hoddle
		SF	7. 4.82	Barcelona (Spain)	H	D	1–1	Roberts
			21. 4.82		A	L	0–1	
1982–83	Cup-Winners' Cup	1	15. 9.82	Coleraine	A	W	3–0	Crooks 2, Archibald
			28. 9.82	(Northern Ireland)	H	W	4–0	Crooks, Mabbutt, Brooke, Gibson
		2	20.10.82	Bayern Munich	H	D	1–1	Archibald
			3.11.82	(West Germany)	A	L	1–4	Hughton
1971–72	UEFA Cup	1	14. 9.71	Keflavik (Iceland)	A	W	6–1	Gilzean 3, Coates, Mullery 2
			28. 9.71		H	W	9–1	Chivers 3, Gilzean 2, Perryman, Coates, Knowles, Holder
		2	20.10.71	Nantes (France)	A	D	0–0	
			2.11.71		H	W	1–0	Peters
		3	8.12.71	Rapid Bucharest	H	W	3–0	Peters, Chivers 2
			15.12.71	(Rumania)	A	W	2–0	Pearce, Chivers
		QF	7. 3.72	UT Arad (Rumania)	A	W	2–0	Morgan, England
			21. 3.72		H	D	1–1	Gilzean
		SF	5. 4.72	AC Milan (Italy)	H	W	2–1	Perryman 2
			19. 4.72		A	D	1–1	Mullery
		F	3. 5.72	Wolverhampton	A	W	2–1	Chivers 2
			17. 5.72	Wanderers (England)	H	D	1–1	Mullery
1972–73	UEFA Cup	1	13. 9.72	Lyn Oslo (Norway)	A	W	6–3	Peters, Pratt, Gilzean 2, Chivers 2
			27. 9.72		H	W	6–0	Chivers 3, Coates 2, Pearce
		2	25.10.72	Olympiakos Piraeus	H	W	4–0	Pearce 2, Chivers, Coates
			8.11.72	(Greece)	A	L	0–1	
		3	29.11.72	Red Star Belgrade	H	W	2–0	Chivers, Gilzean
			13.12.72	(Yugoslavia)	A	L	0–1	
		QF	7. 3.73	Setubal (Portugal)	H	W	1–0	Evans
			21. 3.73		A	L	1–2*	Chivers
		SF	10. 4.73	Liverpool (England)*	A	L	0–1	
			25. 4.73		H	W	2–1	Peters 2

Season	Competition	Round	Date	Opponents (Country)	Venue	Result		Scorers
1973–74	UEFA Cup	1	19. 9.73	Grasshoppers	A	W	5–1	Chivers 2, Evans, Gilzean 2
			3.10.73	(Switzerland)	H	W	4–1	Peters 2, England, own goal
		2	24.10.73	Aberdeen (Scotland)	A	D	1–1	Coates
			7.11.73		H	W	4–1	Peters, Neighbour, McGrath 2
		3	28.11.73	Dynamo Tbilisi (USSR)	A	D	1–1	Coates
			12.12.73		H	W	5–1	McGrath, Chivers 2, Peters 2
		QF	6. 3.74	IFC Cologne	A	W	2–1	McGrath, Peters
			20. 3.74	(West Germany)	H	W	3–0	Chivers, Coates, Peters
		SF	10. 4.74	Lokomotive Leipzig	A	W	2–1	Peters, McGrath
			24. 4.74	(East Germany)	H	W	2–0	McGrath, Chivers
		F	21. 5.74	Feyenoord (Holland)	H	D	2–2	England, own goal
			29. 5.74		A	L	0–2	

WEST BROMWICH ALBION

Season	Competition	Round	Date	Opponents (Country)	Venue	Result		Scorers
1968–69	Cup-Winners' Cup	1	18. 9.68	FC Bruges (Belgium)	A	L	1–3	Hartford
			2.10.68		H	W	2–0*	Brown (T), Hartford
		2	13.11.68	Dynamo Bucharest	A	D	1–1	Hartford
			27.11.68	(Rumania)	H	W	4–0	Lovett, Astle, Brown (T) 2 (1 pen)
		QF	15. 1.69	Dunfermline Athletic	A	D	0–0	
			19. 2.69	(Scotland)	H	L	0–1	
1966–67	Fairs Cup	1	bye					
		2	2.11.66	DOS Utrecht (Holland)	A	D	1–1	Hope
			9.11.66		H	W	5–2	Brown (T) 3 (1 pen), Clark, Kaye
		3	2. 2.67	Bologna (Italy)	A	L	0–3	
			8. 3.67		H	L	1–3	Fairfax
1978–79	UEFA Cup	1	13. 9.78	Galatasaray (Turkey)	A	W	3–1	Robson, Regis, Cunningham
			27. 9.78		H	W	3–1	Robson, Cunningham (pen), Trewick
		2	18.10.78	Sporting Braga	A	W	2–0	Regis 2
			1.11.78	(Portugal)	H	W	1–0	Brown (A)
		3	22.11.78	Valencia (Spain)	A	D	1–1	Cunningham
			6.12.78		H	W	2–0	Brown (T) 2, (1 pen)
		QF	7. 3.79	Red Star Belgrade	A	L	0–1	
			21. 3.79	(Yugoslavia)	H	D	1–1	Regis
1979–80	UEFA Cup	1	19. 9.79	Carl Zeiss Jena	A	L	0–2	
			3.10.79	(East Germany)	H	L	1–2	Wile
1981–82	UEFA Cup	1	16. 9.81	Grasshoppers	A	L	0–1	
			30. 9.81	(Switzerland)	H	L	1–3	Robertson

WEST HAM UNITED

Season	Competition	Round	Date	Opponents (Country)	Venue	Result		Scorers
1964–65	Cup-Winners' Cup	1	23. 9.64	La Gantoise (Belgium)	A	W	1–0	Boyce
			7.10.64		H	D	1–1	Byrne
		2	25.11.64	Sparta Prague	H	W	2–0	Bond, Sealey
			9.12.64	(Czechoslovakia)	A	L	1–2	Sissons
		QF	16. 3.65	Lausanne (Switzerland)	A	W	2–1	Dear, Byrne
			23. 3.65		H	W	4–3	Dear 2, Peters, own goal
		SF	7. 4.65	Real Zaragoza (Spain)	H	W	2–1	Dear, Byrne
			28. 4.65		A	D	1–1	Sissons
		F	19. 5.65	Munich 1860 (West Germany)	N	W	2–0	Sealey 2
1965–66	Cup-Winners' Cup	1	bye					
		2	24.11.65	Olympiakos Piraeus	H	W	4–0	Hurst 2, Byrne, Brabrook
			1.12.65	(Greece)	A	D	2–2	Peters 2
		QF	2. 3.66	Magdeburg (East Germany)	H	W	1–0	Byrne
			16. 3.66		A	D	1–1	Sissons
		SF	5. 4.66	Borussia Dortmund	H	L	1–2	Peters
			13. 4.66	(West Germany)	A	L	1–3	Byrne
1976–76	Cup-Winners' Cup	1	17. 9.75	Lahden Reipas (Finland)	A	D	2–2	Brooking, Bonds
			1.10.75		H	W	3–0	Robson (K), Holland, Jennings
		2	22.10.75	Ararat Erevan (USSR)	A	D	1–1	Taylor (A)
			5.11.75		H	W	3–1	Paddon, Robson (K), Taylor (A)
		QF	3. 3.76	Den Haag (Holland)	A	L	2–4	Jennings 2
			17. 3.76		H	W	3–1*	Taylor (A), Lampard, Bonds (pen)

Season	Competition	Round	Date	Opponents (Country)	Venue	Result		Scorers
		SF	31. 3.76	Eintracht Frankfurt	A	L	1–2	Paddon
			14. 4.76	(West Germany)	H	W	3–1	Brooking 2, Robson (K)
		F	5. 5.76	Anderlecht (Belgium)	N	L	2–4	Holland, Robson (K)
1980 81	Cup Winners' Cup	1	17. 9.80	Castilla	A	L	1–3	Cross
			1.10.80	(Spain)	H	W	5–1	Pike, Cross 3, Goddard
		2	22.10.80	Poli. Timisoara (Rumania)	H	W	4–0	Bonds, Goddard, Stewart (pen), Cross
			5.11.80		A	L	0–1	
		QF	4. 3.81	Dynamo Tbilisi	H	L	1–4	Cross
			18. 3.81	(USSR)	A	W	1–0	Pearson

WOLVERHAMPTON WANDERERS

Season	Competition	Round	Date	Opponents (Country)	Venue	Result		Scorers
1958–59	European Cup	Pr		bye				
		1	12.11.58	Schalke 04	H	D	2–2	Broadbent 2
			18.11.58	(West Germany)	A	L	1–2	Jackson
1959–60	European Cup	Pr	30. 9.59	Vorwaerts (East Germany)	A	L	1–2	Broadbent
			7.10.59		H	W	2–0	Broadbent, Mason
		1	11.11.59	Red Star Belgrade	A	D	1–1	Deeley
			24.11.59	(Yugoslavia)	H	W	3–0	Murray, Mason 2
		QF	10. 2.60	Barcelona (Spain)	A	L	0–4	
			2. 3.60		H	L	2–5	Murray, Mason
1960–61	Cup-Winners' Cup	Pr		bye				
		QF	12.10.60	FK Austria (Austria)	A	L	0–2	
			30.11.60		H	W	5–0	Kirkham 2, Mason, Broadbent 2
		SF	29. 3.61	Rangers (Scotland)	A	L	0–2	
			19. 4.61		H	D	1–1	Broadbent
1971–72	UEFA Cup	1	15. 9.71	Academica Coimbra	H	W	3–0	McAlle, Richards, Dougan
			29. 9.71	(Portugal)	A	W	4–1	Dougan 3, McAlle
		2	20.10.71	Den Haag (Holland)	A	W	3–1	Dougan, McCalliog, Hibbitt
			3.11.71		H	W	4–0	Dougan, own goals 3
		3	24.11.71	Carl Zeiss Jena	A	W	1–0	Richards
			8.12.71	(East Germany)	H	W	3–0	Hibbitt, Dougan 2
		QF	7. 3.72	Juventus (Italy)	A	D	1–1	McCalliog
			21. 3.72		H	W	2–1	Hegan, Dougan
		SF	5. 4.72	Ferencvaros (Hungary)	A	D	2–2	Richards, Munro
			19. 4.72		H	W	2–1	Bailey, Munro
		F	3. 5.72	Tottenham Hotspur	H	L	1–2	McCalliog
			17. 5.72	(England)	A	D	1–1	Wagstaffe
1973–74	UEFA Cup	1	26. 9.73	Belenenses (Portugal)	A	W	2–0	Richards, Dougan
			3.10.73		H	W	2–1	Eastoe, McCalliog
		2	24.10.73	Lokomotive Leipzig	A	L	0–3	
			7.11.73	(East Germany)	H	W	4–1	Kindon, Munro, Dougan, Hibbitt
1974–75	UEFA Cup	1	18. 9.74	Porto (Portugal)	A	L	1–4	Bailey
			2.10.74		H	W	3–1	Bailey, Daley, Dougan
1980–81	UEFA Cup	1	17. 9.80	PSV Eindhoven	A	L	1–3	Gray
			1.10.80.	(Holland)	H	W	1–0	Eves

WREXHAM

Season	Competition	Round	Date	Opponents (Country)	Venue	Result		Scorers
1972–73	Cup Winners' Cup	1	13. 9.72	Zurich (Switzerland)	A	D	1–1	Kinsey
			27. 9.72		H	W	2–1	Ashcroft, Sutton
		2	25.10.72	Hajduk Split	H	W	3–1	Tinnion, Smallman, own goal
			8.11.72	(Yugoslavia)*	A	L	0–2	
1975–76	Cup-Winners' Cup	1	17. 9.75	Djurgaarden (Sweden)	H	W	2–1	Griffiths, Davis
			1.10.75		A	D	1–1	Whittle
		2	22.10.75	Stal Rzeszow (Poland)	H	W	2–0	Ashcroft 2
			5.11.75		A	D	1–1	Sutton
		QF	3. 3.76	Anderlecht (Belgium)	A	L	0–1	
			17. 3.76		H	D	1–1	Lee
1978–79	Cup-Winners' Cup	1	13. 9.78	Rijeka (Yugoslavia)	A	L	0–3	
			27. 9.78		H	W	2–0	McNeil, Cartwright
1979–80	Cup-Winners' Cup	1	19. 9.79	Magdeburg (East Germany)	H	W	3–2	McNeil, Fox, Buxton
			3.10.79		A	L	2–5	Vinter, Hill

SCOTTISH LEAGUE CLUBS

Season	Competition	Round	Date	Opponents (Country)	Venue	Result		Scorers

ABERDEEN

Season	Competition	Round	Date	Opponents (Country)	Venue	Result		Scorers
1980–81	European Cup	1	17. 9.80	Austria Vienna	H	W	1–0	McGhee
			1.10.80	(Austria)	A	D	0–0	
		2	22.10.80	Liverpool	H	L	0–1	
			5.11.80	(England)	A	L	0–4	
1967–68	Cup-Winners' Cup	1	6. 9.67	KR Reykjavik (Iceland)	H	W	10–1	Munro 3, Storrie 2, Smith 2, McMillan, Petersen, Taylor
			13. 9.67		A	W	4–1	Storrie 2, Buchan, Munro
		2	29.11.67	Standard Liege (Belgium)	A	L	0–3	
			6.12.67		H	W	2–0	Munro, Melrose
1970–71	Cup-Winners' Cup	1	16. 9.70	Honved (Hungary)†	H	W	3–1	Graham, Harper, Murray (S)
			30. 9.70		A	L	1–3	Murray (S)
1978–79	Cup-Winners' Cup	1	13. 9.78	Marek Stanke (Bulgaria)	A	L	2–3	Jarvie, Harper
			27. 9.78		H	W	3–0	Strachan, Jarvie, Harper
		2	18.10.78	Fortuna Dusseldorf	A	L	0–3	
			1.11.78	(West Germany)	H	W	2–0	McLelland, Jarvie
1982–83	Cup-Winners' Cup	Pr	18. 8.82	Sion (Switzerland)	H	W	7–0	Black 2, Strachan, Hewitt, Simpson, McGhee, Kennedy
			1. 9.82		A	W	4–1	Hewitt, Miller, McGhee 2
		1	15. 9.82	Dynamo Tirana	H	W	1–0	Hewitt
			29. 9.82	(Albania)	A	D	0–0	
		2	20.10.82	Lech Poznan	H	W	2–0	McGhee, Weir
			3.11.82	(Poland)	A	W	1–0	Bell
		QF	2. 3.83	Bayern Munich	A	D	0–0	
			16. 3.83	(West Germany)	H	W	3–2	Simpson, McLeish, Hewitt
		SF	6. 4.83	Waterschei (Belgium)	H	W	5–1	Black, Simpson, McGhee 2, Weir
			19. 4.83		A	L	0–1	
		F	11. 5.83	Real Madrid	N	W	2–1	Black, Hewitt
1968–69	Fairs Cup	1	17. 9.68	Slavia Sofia (Bulgaria)	A	D	0–0	
			2.10.68		H	W	2–0	Robb, Taylor
		2	23.10.68	Real Zaragoza (Spain)	H	W	2–1	Forrest, Smith
			30.10.68		A	L	0–3	
1971–72	UEFA Cup	1	15. 9.71	Celta Vigo (Spain)	A	W	2–0	Harper, own goal
			29. 9.71		H	W	1–0	Harper
		2	27.10.71	Juventus (Italy)	A	L	0–2	
			17.11.71		H	D	1–1	Harper
1972–73	UEFA Cup	1	13. 9.72	Borussia Moenchenglad-	H	L	2–3	Harper, Jarvie
			27. 9.72	bach (West Germany)	A	L	3–6	Harper 2, Jarvie
1973–74	UEFA Cup	1	19. 9.73	Finn Harps (Eire)	H	W	4–1	Miller (R), Jarvie 2, Graham
			3.10.73		A	W	3–1	Robb, Graham, Miller (R)
		2	24.10.73	Tottenham Hotspur	H	D	1–1	Hermiston (pen)
			7.11.73	(England)	A	L	1–4	Jarvie
1977–78	UEFA Cup	1	14. 9.77	RWD Molenbeek	A	D	0–0	
			28. 9.77	(Belgium)	H	L	1–2	Jarvie
1979–80	UEFA Cup	1	19. 9.79	Eintracht Frankfurt (West	H	D	1–1	Harper
			3.10.79	Germany)	A	L	0–1	
1981–82	UEFA Cup	1	16. 9.81	Ipswich Town	A	D	1–1	Hewitt
			30. 9.81	(England)	H	W	3–1	Strachan (pen), Weir 2
		2	21.10.81	Arges Pitesti	H	W	3–0	Strachan, Weir, Hewitt
			4.11.81	(Rumania)	A	D	2–2	Strachan (pen), Hewitt
		3	25.11.81	SV Hamburg	H	W	3–2	Black, Watson, Hewitt
			9.12.81	(West Germany)	A	L	1–3	McGhee

Season	Competition	Round	Date	Opponents (Country)	Venue	Result		Scorers

CELTIC

Season	Competition	Round	Date	Opponents (Country)	Venue	Result		Scorers
1966–67	European Cup	1	28. 9.66	Zurich (Switzerland)	H	W	2–0	Gemmell, McBride
			5.10.66		A	W	3–0	Gemmell 2 (1 pen), Chalmers
		2	30.11.66	Nantes (France)	A	W	3–1	McBride, Lennox, Chalmers
			7.12.66		H	W	3–1	Johnstone, Lennox, Chalmers
		QF	1. 3.66	Vojvodina (Yugoslavia)	A	L	0–1	
			8. 3.66		H	W	2–0	Chalmers, McNeill
		SF	12. 4.67	Dukla Prague	H	W	3–1	Johnstone, Wallace 2
			25. 4.67	(Czechoslovakia)	A	D	0–0	
		F	25. 5.67	Inter-Milan (Italy)	N	W	2–1	Gemmell, Chalmers
1967–68	European Cup	1	20. 9.67	Dynamo Kiev (USSR)	H	L	1–2	Lennox
			4.10.67		A	D	1–1	Lennox
1968–69	European Cup	1	18. 8.68	St Etienne (France)	A	L	0–2	
			2.10.68		H	W	4–0	Gemmell (pen), Craig, Chalmers, McBride
		2	13.11.68	Red Star Belgrade (Yugoslavia)	H	W	5–1	Murdoch, Johnstone 2, Lennox, Wallace
			27.11.68		A	D	1–1	Wallace
		QF	19. 2.69	AC Milan (Italy)	A	D	0–0	
			12. 3.69		H	L	0–1	
1969–70	European Cup	1	17. 9.69	Basle (Switzerland)	A	D	0–0	
			1.10.69		H	W	2–0	Hood, Gemmell
		2	12.11.69	Benfica (Portugal)	H	W	3–0	Gemmell, Wallace, Hood
			26.11.69		A	L	0–3‡	
		QF	4. 3.70	Fiorentina (Italy)	H	W	3–0	Auld, Wallace, own goal
			18. 3.70		A	L	0–1	
		SF	1. 4.70	Leeds United (England)	A	W	1–0	Connolly
			15. 4.70		H	W	2–1	Hughes, Murdoch
		F	6. 5.70	Feyenoord (Holland)	N	L	1–2	Gemmell
1970–71	European Cup	1	16. 9.70	KPV Kokkola (Finland)	H	W	9–0	Hood 3, Wilson 2, Hughes, McNeill, Johnstone, Davidson
			30. 9.70		A	W	5–0	Wallace 2, Callaghan, Davidson, Lennox
		2	21.10.70	Waterford (Eire)	A	W	7–0	Wallace 3, Murdoch 2, Macari 2
			4.11.70		H	W	3–2	Hughes, Johnstone 2
		QF	10. 3.70	Ajax (Holland)	A	L	0–3	
			24. 3.71		H	W	1–0	Johnstone
1971–72	European Cup	1	15. 9.71	BK 1903 Copenhagen	A	L	1–2	Macari
			29. 9.71	(Denmark)	H	W	3–0	Wallace 2, Callaghan
		2	20.10.71	Sliema Wanderers (Malta)	H	W	5–0	Gemmell, Macari 2, Hood, Brogan
			3.11.71		A	W	2–1	Hood, Lennox
		QF	8. 3.72	Ujpest Dozsa (Hungary)	A	W	2–1	Macari, own goal
			22. 3.72		H	D	1–1	Macari
		SF	5. 4.72	Inter-Milan (Italy)†	A	D	0–0	
			19. 4.72		H	D	0–0	
1972–73	European Cup	1	13. 9.72	Rosenborg (Norway)	H	W	2–1	Macari, Deans
			27. 9.72		A	W	3–1	Macari, Hood, Dalglish
		2	25.10.72	Ujpest Dozsa (Hungary)	H	W	2–1	Dalglish 2
			8.11.72		A	L	0–3	
1973–74	European Cup	1	19. 9.73	Turun (Finland)	A	W	6–1	Callaghan 2, Hood, Johnstone, Connelly (pen), Deans
			3.10.73		H	W	3–0	Deans, Johnstone 2
		2	24.10.73	Vejle (Denmark)	H	D	0–0	
			6.11.73		A	W	1–0	Lennox
		QF	27. 2.74	Basle (Switzerland)	A	L	2–3	Wilson, Dalglish
			20. 3.74		H	W	4–2	Dalglish, Deans, Callaghan, Murray
		SF	10. 4.74	Atletico Madrid (Spain)	H	D	0–0	
			24. 4.74		A	L	0–2	
1974–75	European Cup	1	18. 9.74	Olympiakos Piraeus	H	D	1–1	Wilson
			2.10.74	(Greece)	A	L	0–2	
1977–78	European Cup	1	14. 9.77	Jeunesse D'Esch (Luxembourg)	H	W	5–0	McDonald, Wilson, Craig 2, McLaughlin
			28. 9.77		A	W	6–1	Lennox 2, Edvaldsson 2, Glavin, Craig
		2	19.10.77	SW Innsbruck (Austria)	H	W	2–1	Craig, Burns
			2.11.77		A	L	0–3	

Season	Competition	Round	Date	Opponents (Country)	Venue	Result		Scorers
1979–80	European Cup	1	19. 9.79	Partizan Tirana (Albania)	A	L	0–1	
			3.10.79		H	W	4–1	McDonald, Aitken 2, Davidson
		2	24.10.79	Dundalk (Eire)	H	W	3–2	McDonald, McCluskey, Burns
			7.11.79		A	D	0–0	
		QF	5. 3.80	Real Madrid	H	W	2–0	McCluskey, Doyle
			19. 3.80	(Spain)	A	L	0–3	
1981–82	European Cup	1	16. 9.81	Juventus (Italy)	H	W	1–0	MacLeod
			30. 9.81		A	L	0–2	
1982–83	European Cup	1	15. 9.82	Ajax (Holland)	H	D	2–2	Nicholas, McGarvey
			29. 9.82		A	W	2–1	Nicholas, McCluskey
		2	20.10.82	Real Sociedad (Spain)	A	L	0–2	
			3.11.82		H	W	2–1	MacLeod 2
1963–64	Cup-Winners' Cup	1	17. 9.63	Basle (Switzerland)	A	W	5–1	Divers, Hughes 3, Lennox
			9.10.63		H	W	5–0	Johnstone, Divers 2, Murdoch, Chalmers
		2	4.12.63	Dynamo Zagreb	H	W	3–0	Chalmers 2, Hughes
			11.12.63	(Yugoslavia)	A	L	1–2	Murdoch
		QF	26. 2.64	Slovan Bratislava	H	W	1–0	Murdoch (pen)
			4. 3.64	(Czechoslovakia)	A	W	1–0	Hughes
		SF	15. 4.64	MTK Budapest	H	W	3–0	Johnstone, Chalmers 2
			29. 4.64	(Hungary)	A	L	0–4	
1965–66	Cup-Winners' Cup	1	29. 9.65	Go Ahead Deventer (Holland)	A	W	6–0	Gallagher 2, Hughes, Johnstone 2 Lennox
			7.10.65		H	W	1–0	McBride
		2	3.11.65	Aarhus (Denmark)	A	W	1–0	McBride
			17.11.65		H	W	2–0	McNeill, Johnstone
		QF	12. 1.66	Dynamo Kiev (USSR)	H	W	3–0	Gemmell, Murdoch 2
			26. 1.66		A	D	1–1	Gemmell
		SF	14. 4.66	Liverpool (England)	H	W	1–0	Lennox
			19. 4.66		A	L	0–2	
1975–76	Cup-Winners' Cup	1	16. 9.75	Valur Reykjavik (Iceland)	A	W	2–0	Wilson, McDonald
			1.10.75		H	W	7–0	Edvaldsson, Dalglish, McCluskey (P) (pen), Hood 2, Deans, Callaghan
		2	22.10.75	Boavista (Portugal)	A	D	0–0	
			5.11.75		H	W	3–1	Dalglish, Edvaldsson, Deans
		QF	3. 3.76	Sachsenring Zwickau	H	D	1–1	Dalglish
			17. 3.76	(West Germany)	A	L	0–1	
1980–81	Cup-Winners' Cup	Pr	20. 8.80	Diosgyor (Hungary)	H	W	6–0	McGarvey 2, McCluskey 2, Sullivan, own goal
			3. 9.80		A	L	1–2	Nicholas
		1	17. 9.80	Poli. Timisoara*	H	W	2–1	Nicholas 2
			1.10.80	(Rumania)	A	L	0–1	
1962–63	Fairs Cup	1	26. 9.62	Valencia (Spain)	A	L	2–4	Carrol 2
			24.10.62		H	D	2–2	Crerand, own goal
1964–65	Fairs Cup	1	23. 9.64	Leixoes (Portugal)	A	D	1–1	Murdoch
			7.10.64		H	W	3–0	Murdoch (pen), Chalmers 2
		2	18.11.64	Barcelona (Spain)	A	L	1–3	Hughes
			2.12.64		H	D	0–0	
1976–77	UEFA Cup	1	15. 9.76	Wisla Krakow (Poland)	H	D	2–2	McDonald, Dalglish
			29. 9.76		A	L	0–2	

DUNDEE

Season	Competition	Round	Date	Opponents (Country)	Venue	Result		Scorers
1962–63	European Cup	Pr	5. 9.62	IFC Cologne (West Germany)	H	W	8–1	Gilzean 3, own goal, Wishart, Robertson, Smith, Penman
			26. 9.62		A	L	0–4	
		1	24.10.62	Sporting Lisbon	A	L	0–1	
			31.10.62	(Portugal)	H	W	4–1	Gilzean 3, Cousin
		QF	6. 3.63	Anderlecht (Belgium)	A	W	4–1	Gilzean 2, Cousin, Smith
			13. 3.63		H	W	2–1	Cousin, Smith
		SF	24. 4.63	AC Milan (Italy)	A	L	1–5	Cousin
			1. 5.63		H	W	1–0	Gilzean
1964–65	Cup-Winners' Cup	1		bye				
		2	18.11.64	Real Zaragoza (Spain)	H	D	2–2	Murray, Houston
			8.12.64		A	L	1–2	Robertson

Season	Competition	Round	Date	Opponents (Country)	Venue	Result		Scorers
1967–68	Fairs Cup	1	27. 9.67	DWS Amsterdam	A	L	1–2	McLean (G)
			4.10.67	(Holland)	H	W	3–0	Wilson (S), McLean 2 (1 pen)
		2	1.11.67	Liege (Belgium)	H	W	3–1	Stuart 2, Wilson (S)
			14.11.67		A	W	4–1	McLean (G) 4
		3		hye				
		QF	27. 3.68	Zurich (Switzerland)	H	W	1–0	Easton
			3. 4.68		A	W	1–0	Wilson (S)
		SF	1. 5.68	Leeds United (England)	H	D	1–1	Wilson (R)
			15. 5.68		A	L	0–2	
1971–72	UEFA Cup	1	15. 9.71	Akademisk Copenhagen	H	W	4–2	Bryce 2, Wallace, Lambie
			29. 9.71	(Denmark)	A	W	1–0	Duncan
		2	19.10.71	IFC Cologne (West	A	L	1–2	Kinninmonth
			3.11.71	Germany)	H	W	4–2	Duncan 3, Wilson (R)
		3	24.11.71	AC Milan (Italy)	A	L	0–3	
			8.12.71		H	W	2–0	Wallace, Duncan
1973–74	UEFA Cup	1	19. 9.73	Twente Enschede	H	L	1–3	Stewart
			3.10.73	(Holland)	A	L	2–4	Johnston, Scott (J)
1974–75	UEFA Cup	1	18. 9.74	RWD Molenbeek	A	L	0–1	
			2.10.74	(Belgium)	H	L	2–4	Duncan, Scott (J)

DUNDEE UNITED

Season	Competition	Round	Date	Opponents (Country)	Venue	Result		Scorers
1974–75	Cup-Winners' Cup	1	18. 9.74	Jiul Petrosani (Rumania)	H	W	3–0	Narey, Copland, Gardner
			2.10.74		A	L	0–2	
		2	23.10.74	Bursaspor (Turkey)	H	D	0–0	
			6.10.74		A	L	0–1	
1966–67	Fairs Cup	1		bye				
		2	25.10.66	Barcelona (Spain)	A	W	2–1	Hainey, Seeman
			16.11.66		H	W	2–0	Mitchell, Hainey
		3	8. 2.67	Juventus (Italy)	A	L	0–3	
			8. 3.67		H	W	1–0	Dossing
1969–70	Fairs Cup	1	15. 9.69	Newcastle United	H	L	1–2	Scott
			1.10.69	(England)	A	L	0–1	
1970–71	Fairs Cup	1	15. 9.70	Grasshoppers	H	W	3–2	Reid (I), Markland, Reid (A)
			30. 9.70	(Switzerland)	A	D	0–0	
		2	21.10.70	Sparta Prague	A	L	1–3	Traynor
			4.11.70	(Czechoslovakia)	H	W	1–0	Gordon
1975–76	UEFA Cup	1	23. 9.75	Keflavik (Iceland)	A	W	2–0	Narey 2
			30. 9.75		H	W	4–0	Hall 2, Hegarty (pen), Sturrock
		2	22.10.75	Porto (Portugal)	H	L	1–2	Rennie
			5.11.75		A	D	1–1	Hegarty
1977–78	UEFA Cup	1	14. 9.77	KB Copenhagen	H	W	1–0	Sturrock
			27. 9.77	(Denmark)	A	L	0–3	
1978–79	UEFA Cup	1	12. 9.78	Standard Liege	A	L	0–1	
			27. 9.78	(Belgium)	H	D	0–0	
1979–80	UEFA Cup	1	19. 9.79	Anderlecht (Belgium)	H	D	0–0	
			2.10.79		A	D	1–1*	Kopel
		2	24.10.79	Diosgyor (Hungary)	H	L	0–1	
			7.11.79		A	L	1–3	Kopel
1980–81	UEFA Cup	1	17. 9.80	Slask Wroclaw	A	D	0–0	
			1.10.80	(Poland)	H	W	7–2	Dodds 2, Pettigrew 2, Stark, Hegarty, Payne (pen)
		2	22.10.80	Lokeren*	H	D	1–1	Pettigrew
			5.11.80	(Belgium)	A	D	0–0	
1981–82	UEFA Cup	1	16. 9.81	Monaco (France)	A	W	5–2	Bannon 2 (1 pen) Dodds 2, Kirkwood
			30. 9.81		H	L	1–2	Milne
		2	20.10.81	Borussia Moenchenglad-	A	L	0–2	
			3.11.81	bach (West Germany)	H	W	5–0	Milne, Kirkwood, Sturrock, Hegarty, Bannon
		3	1.12.81	Winterslag (Belgium)	A	D	0–0	
			9.12.81		H	W	5–0	Bannon, Narey, Hegarty, Milne 2
		QF	3. 3.82	Radnicki Nis	H	W	2–0	Narey, Dodds
			17. 3.82	(Yugoslavia)	A	L	0–3	

Season	Competition	Round	Date	Opponents (Country)	Venue	Result		Scorers
1982–83	UEFA Cup	1	15. 9.82	PSV Eindhoven	H	D	1–1	Dodds
			29. 9.82	(Holland)	A	W	2–0	Kirkwood, Hegarty
		2	20.10.82	Viking Stavanger	A	W	3–1	Milne 2, Sturrock
			3.11.82	(Norway)	H	D	0–0	
		3	24.11.82	Werder Bremen	H	W	2–1	Milne, Narey
			8.12.82	(West Germany)	A	D	1–1	Hegarty
		QF	2. 3.83	Bohemians	A	L	0–1	
			16. 3.83	(Czechoslovakia)	H	D	0–0	

DUNFERMLINE ATHLETIC

Season	Competition	Round	Date	Opponents (Country)	Venue	Result		Scorers
1961–62	Cup-Winners' Cup	1	12. 9.61	St Patrick's Athletic (Eire)	H	W	4–1	Melrose, Peebles, Dickson, Macdonald
			27. 9.61		A	W	4–0	Peebles 2, Dickson 2
		2	25.10.61	Vardar Skoplje (Yugoslavia)	H	W	5–0	Smith, Dickson 2, Melrose, Peebles
			8.11.61		A	L	0–2	
		QF	13. 2.62	Ujpest Dozsa (Hungary)	A	L	3–4	Smith, Macdonald 2
			20. 2.62		H	L	0–1	
1967–68	Cup-Winners' Cup	1	18. 9.68	Apoel (Cyprus)	H	W	10–1	Robertson 2, Renton 2, Barry, Callaghan (W) 2, Gardner, Edwards, Callaghan (T)
			2.10.68		A	W	2–0	Gardner, Callaghan (W)
		2	13.11.68	Olympiakos Piraeus	H	W	4–0	Edwards 2, Fraser, Mitchell
			27.11.68	(Greece)	A	L	0–3	
		QF	15. 1.69	West Bromwich Albion	H	D	0–0	
			19. 2.69	(England)	A	W	1–0	Gardner
		SF	9. 4.69	Slovan Bratislava	H	D	1–1	Fraser
			23. 4.69	(Czechoslovakia)	A	L	0–1	
1962–63	Fairs Cup	1	24.10.62	Everton (England)	A	L	0–1	
			31.10.62		H	W	2–0	Miller, Melrose
		2	12.12.62	Valencia (Spain)	A	L	0–4	
			19.12.62		H	W	6–2	Melrose, Sinclair 2, McLean, Peebles, Smith
			6. 2.63		N	L	0–1	
1964–65	Fairs Cup	1	13.10.64	Oergryte (Sweden)	H	W	4–2	McLaughlin 2, Sinclair 2
			20.10.64		A	D	0–0	
		2	17.11.64	Stuttgart (West Germany)	H	W	1–0	Callaghan (T)
			1.12.64		A	D	0–0	
		3	27. 1.65	Atletico Bilbao (Spain)	A	L	0–1	
			3. 3.65		H	W	1–0	Smith
			16. 3.65		A	L	1–2	Smith
1965–66	Fairs Cup	1		bye				
		2	3.11.65	KB Copenhagen (Denmark)	H	W	5–0	Fleming, Paton 2, Robertson, Callaghan (T)
			17.11.65		A	W	4–2	Edwards, Paton, Fleming, Ferguson
		3	26. 1.66	Spartak Brno	H	W	2–0	Paton, Ferguson (pen)
			16. 2.66	(Czechoslovakia)	A	D	0–0	
		QF	16. 3.66	Real Zaragoza (Spain)	H	W	1–0	Paton
			20. 3.66		A	L	2–4	Ferguson 2
1966–67	Fairs Cup	1	24. 8.66	Frigg Oslo (Norway)	A	W	3–1	Fleming 2, Callaghan (T)
			28. 9.66		H	W	3–1	Delaney 2, Callaghan (T)
		2	26.10.66	Dynamo Zagreb*	H	W	4–2	Delaney, Edwards, Ferguson 2
			11.11.66	(Yugoslavia)	A	L	0–2	
1969–70	Fairs Cup	1	16. 9.69	Bordeaux (France)	H	W	4–0	Paton 2, Mitchell, Gardner
			30. 9.69		A	L	0–2	
		2	5.11.69	Gwardia Warsaw	H	W	2–1	McLean, Gardner
			18.11.69	(Poland)	A	W	1–0	Renton
		3	17.12.69	Anderlecht (Belgium)*	A	L	0–1	
			14. 1.70		H	W	3–2	McLean 2, Mitchell

Season	Competition	Round	Date	Opponents (Country)	Venue	Result		Scorers

HEARTS

Season	Competition	Round	Date	Opponents (Country)	Venue	Result		Scorers
1958–59	European Cup	Pr	3. 9.58	Standard Liege	A	L	1–5	Crawford
			9. 9.58	(Belgium)	H	W	2–1	Bauld 2
1960–61	European Cup	Pr	29. 9.60	Benfica (Portugal)	H	L	1–2	Young
			5.10.60		A	L	0 3	
1976–77	Cup-Winners'	1	15. 9.76	Lokomotive Leipzig	A	L	0–2	
	Cup		29. 9.76	(East Germany)	H	W	5–1	Kay, Gibson 2, Brown, Busby
		2	20.10.76	SV Hamburg (West	A	L	2–4	Park, Busby
			3.11.76	Germany)	H	L	1–4	Gibson
1961–62	Fairs Cup	1	27. 9.61	Union St Gilloise	A	W	3–1	Blackwood, Davidson 2
			4.10.61	(Belgium)	H	W	2–0	Wallace, Stenhouse
		2	6.11.61	Inter-Milan (Italy)	H	L	0–1	
			22.11.61		A	L	0–4	
1963–64	Fairs Cup	1	25. 9.63	Lausanne (Switzerland)	A	D	2–2	Traynor, Ferguson
			9.10.63		H	D	2–2	Cumming, Hamilton (J)
			15.10.63		A	L	2–3	Wallace, Ferguson
1965–66	Fairs Cup	1		bye				
		2	18.10.65	Valerengen (Norway)	H	W	1–0	Wallace
			27.10.65		A	W	3–1	Kerrigan 2, Traynor
		3	12. 1.66	Real Zaragoza (Spain)	H	D	3–3	Anderson, Wallace, Kerrigan
			26. 1.66		A	D	2–2	Anderson, Wallace
			2. 3.66		A	L	0–1	

HIBERNIAN

Season	Competition	Round	Date	Opponents (Country)	Venue	Result		Scorers
1955–56	European Cup	1	14. 9.55	Rot-Weiss Essen	A	W	4–0	Turnbull 2, Reilly, Ormond
			12.10.55	(West Germany)	H	D	1–1	Buchanan (J)
		QF	23.11.55	Djurgaarden (Sweden)	H	W	3–1	Combe, Mulkerrin, own goal
			28.11.55		A	W	1–0	Turnbull (pen)
		SF	4. 4.56	Reims (France)*	A	L	0–2	
			18. 4.56		H	L	0–1	
1972–73	Cup Winners'	1	13. 9.72	Sporting Lisbon	A	L	1–2	Duncan
	Cup		27. 9.72	(Portugal)	H	W	6–1	Gordon 2, O'Rourke 3, own goal
		2	25.10.72	Besa (Albania)	H	W	7–1	Cropley, O'Rourke 3, Duncan 2, Brownlie
			8.11.72		A	D	1–1	Gordon
		QF	7. 3.73	Hajduk Split (Yugoslavia)	H	W	4–2	Gordon 3, Duncan
			21. 3.73		A	L	0–3	
1960–61	Fairs Cup	1		Lausanne (Switzerland) Lausanne withdrew				
		QF	27.12.60	Barcelona (Spain)	A	D	4–4	McLeod, Preston, Baker 2
			22. 2.61		H	W	3–2	Kinloch 2 (1 pen), Baker
		SF	19. 4.61	AS Roma (Italy)	H	D	2–2	Baker, McLeod
			26. 4.61		A	D	3–3	Baker 2, Kinloch
			27. 5.61		A	L	0–6	
1961–62	Fairs Cup	1	4. 9.61	Belenenses (Portugal)	H	D	3–3	Fraser 2, Baird (pen)
			27. 9.61		A	W	3–1	Baxter 2, Stevenson
		2	1.11.61	Red Star Belgrade	A	L	0–4	
			15.11.61	(Yugoslavia)	H	L	0–1	
1962–63	Fairs Cup	1	3.10.62	Stavenet (Denmark)	H	W	4–0	Byrne 2, Baker, own goal
			23.10.62		A	W	3–2	Stevenson 2, Byrne
		2	27.11.62	DOS Utrecht (Holland)	A	W	1–0	Falconer
			12.12.62		H	W	2–1	Baker, Stevenson
		QF	13. 3.63	Valencia (Spain)	A	L	0–5	
			3. 4.63		H	W	2–1	Preston, Baker
1965–66	Fairs Cup	1	8. 9.65	Valencia (Spain)	H	W	2–0	Scott, McNamee
			12.10.65		A	L	0–2	
			3.11.65		A	L	0–3	
1967–68	Fairs Cup	1	20. 9.67	Porto (Portugal)	H	W	3–0	Cormack 2, Stevenson
			4.10.67		A	L	1–3	Stanton (pen)
		2	22.11.67	Napoli (Italy)	A	L	1–4	Stein
			29.11.67		H	W	5–0	Duncan, Quinn, Cormack, Stanton, Stein
		3	20.12.67	Leeds United (England)	A	L	0–1	
			10. 1.68		H	D	1–1	Stein

Season	Competition	Round	Date	Opponents (Country)	Venue	Result		Scorers
1968–69	Fairs Cup	1	18. 9.68	Ljubljana (Yugoslavia)	A	W	3–0	Stevenson, Stein, Marinello
			2.10.68		H	W	2–1	Davis 2 (2 pens)
		2	13.11.68	Lokomotive Leipzig	H	W	3–1	McBride 3
			20.11.68	(East Germany)	A	W	1–0	Grant
		3	18.12.68	SV Hamburg (West	A	L	0–1	
			15. 1.69	Germany)*	H	W	2–1	McBride 2
1970–71	Fairs Cup	1	16. 9.70	Malmo FF (Sweden)	H	W	6–0	McBride 3, Duncan 2, Blair
			30. 9.70		A	W	3–2	Duncan, McEwan, Stanton
		2	14.10.70	Vitoria Guimaraes	H	W	2–0	Duncan, Stanton
			28.10.70	(Portugal)	A	L	1–2	Graham
		3	9.12.70	Liverpool (England)	H	L	0–1	
			22.12.70		A	L	0–2	
1973–74	UEFA Cup	1	19. 9.73	Keflavik (Iceland)	H	W	2–0	Black, Higgins
			3.10.73		A	D	1–1	Stanton
		2	24.10.73	Leeds United (England)†	A	D	0–0	
			2.10.74		H	D	0–0	
1974–75	UEFA Cup	1	18. 9.74	Rosenborg (Norway)	A	W	3–2	Stanton, Gordon, Cropley
			2.10.74		H	W	9–1	Harper 2, Munro 2, Stanton 2, Cropley 2 (2 pens), Gordon
		2	23.10.74	Juventus (Italy)	H	L	2–4	Stanton, Cropley
			6.11.74		A	L	0–4	
1975–76	UEFA Cup	1	17. 9.75	Liverpool (England)	H	W	1–0	Harper
			30. 9.75		A	L	1–3	Edwards
1976–77	UEFA Cup	1	15. 9.76	Sochaux (France)	H	W	1–0	Brownlie
			29. 9.76		A	D	0–0	
		2	20.10.76	Osters Vaxjo (Sweden)	H	W	2–0	Blackley, Brownlie (pen)
			3.11.76		A	L	1–4	Smith
1978–79	UEFA Cup	1	13. 9.78	Norrkoping (Sweden)	H	W	3–2	Higgins 2, Temperley
			27. 9.78		A	D	0–0	
		2	18.10.78	Strasbourg (France)	A	L	0–2	
			1.11.78		H	W	1–0	McLeod (pen)

KILMARNOCK

1965–66	European Cup	Pr	8. 9.65	Nendori Tirana (Albania)	A	D	0–0	
			29. 6.65		H	W	1–0	Black
		1	17.11.65	Real Madrid (Spain)	H	D	2–2	McLean (pen), McInally
			1.12.65		A	L	1–5	McIlroy
1964–65	Fairs Cup	1	2. 9.64	Eintracht Frankfurt	A	L	0–3	
			22. 9.64	(West Germany)	H	W	5–1	Hamilton, McIlroy, McFadzean, McInally, Sneddon
		2	11.11.64	Everton (England)	H	L	0–2	
			23.11.64		A	L	1–4	McIlroy
1966–67	Fairs Cup	1		bye				
		2	25.10.66	Antwerp (Belgium)	A	W	1–0	McInally
			2.11.66		H	W	7–2	McInally 2, Queen 2, McLean 2, Watson
		3	14.12.66	La Gantoise (Belgium)	H	W	1–0	Murray
			21.12.66		A	W	2–1	McInally, McLean
		QF	19. 4.67	Lokomotive Leipzig	A	L	0–1	
			26. 4.67	(East Germany)	H	W	2–0	McFadzean, McIlroy
		SF	19. 5.67	Leeds United (England)	A	L	2–4	McIlroy 2
			24. 5.67		H	D	0–0	
1969–70	Fairs Cup	1	16. 9.69	Zurich (Switzerland)	A	L	2–3	McLean (J), Mathie
			30. 9.69		H	W	3–1	McGrory, Morrison, McLean (T)
		2	19.11.69	Slavia Sofia (Bulgaria)	H	W	4–1	Mathie 2, Cook, Gilmour
			26.11.69		A	L	0–2	
		3	17.12.69	Dynamo Bacau	H	D	1–1	Mathie
			13. 1.70	(Yugoslavia)	A	L	0–2	
1970–1	Fairs Cup	1	15. 9.70	Coleraine (Northern	A	D	1–1	Mathie
			29. 9.70	Ireland)	H	L	2–3	McLean (T), Morrison

MORTON

1968–69	Fairs Cup	1	18. 9.68	Chelsea (England)	A	L	0–5	
			30. 9.68		H	L	3–4	Thorop, Mason, Taylor

Season	Competition	Round	Date	Opponents (Country)	Venue	Result	Scorers
PARTICK THISTLE							
1963–64	Fairs Cup	1	16. 9.63	Glentoran (Northern	A	W 4–1	Hainey, Yard 2, Wright
			30. 9.63	Ireland)	H	W 3–0	Smith 2, Harvey (pen)
		2	18.11.63	Spartak Brno	H	W 3–2	Yard, Harvey (pen), Ferguson
			27.11.63	(Czechoslovakia)	A	L 0–4	
1972–73	UEFA Cup	1	13. 9.72	Honved (Hungary)	A	L 0–1	
			27. 9.72		H	L 0–3	
RANGERS							
1956–57	European Cup	Pr		bye			
		1	24.10.56	Nice (France)	H	W 2–1	Murray, Simpson
			14.11.56		A	L 1–2	Hubbard (pen)
			28.11.56		N	L 1–3	own goal
1957–58	European Cup	Pr	4. 9.57	St Etienne (France)	H	W 3–1	Kichenbrand, Scott, Simpson
			25. 9.57		A	L 1–2	Wilson
		1	27.11.57	AC Milan (Italy)	H	L 1–4	Murray
			11.12.57		A	L 0–2	
1959–60	European Cup	Pr	16. 9.59	Anderlecht (Belgium)	H	W 5–2	Millar, Scott, Matthew, Baird 2
			24. 9.59		A	W 2–0	Matthew, McMillan
		1	11.11.59	Red Star Belgrade	H	W 4–3	McMillan, Scott, Wilson, Millar
			18.11.59	(Czechoslovakia)	A	D 1–1	Scott
		QF	9. 3.60	Sparta Rotterdam	A	W 3–2	Wilson, Baird, Murray
			16. 3.60	(Holland)	H	L 0–1	
			30. 3.60		N	W 3–2	Baird 2, own goal
		SF	13. 4.60	Eintracht Frankfurt	A	L 1–6	Caldow (pen)
			5. 5.60	(West Germany)	H	L 3–6	McMillan 2, Wilson
1961–62	European Cup	Pr	5. 9.61	Monaco (France)	A	W 3–2	Baxter, Scott 2
			12. 9.61		H	W 3–2	Christie 2, Scott
		1	15.11.61	Vorwaerts (East Germany)	A	W 2–1	Caldow (pen), Brand
			23.11.61		H	W 4–1	McMillan 2, Henderson, own goal
		QF	7. 2.62	Standard Liege (Belgium)	A	L 1–4	Wilson
			14. 2.62		H	W 2–0	Brand, Caldow (pen)
1963–64	European Cup	Pr	25. 9.63	Real Madrid (Spain)	H	L 0–1	
			9.10.63		A	L 0–6	
1964–65	European Cup	Pr	2. 9.64	Red Star Belgrade	H	W 3–1	Brand 2, Forrest
			9. 9.64	(Yugoslavia)	A	L 2–4	Greig, McKinnon
			4.11.64		N	W 3–1	Forrest 2, Brand
		1	18.11.64	Rapid Vienna (Austria)	H	W 1–0	Wilson
			8.12.64		A	W 2–0	Forrest, Wilson
		QF	17. 2.65	Inter-Milan (Italy)	A	L 1–3	Forrest
			3. 3.65		H	W 1–0	Forrest
1975–76	European Cup	1	17. 9.75	Bohemians (Eire)	H	W 4–1	Fyfe, Johnstone, O'Hara, own goal
			1.10.75		A	D 1–1	Johnstone
		2	22.10.75	St Etienne (France)	H	L 0–2	
			5.11.75		A	L 1–2	MacDonald
1976–77	European Cup	1	15. 9.76	Zurich (Switzerland)	H	D 1–1	Parlane
			29. 9.76		A	L 0–1	
1978–79	European Cup	1	13. 9.78	Juventus (Italy)	A	L 0–1	
			27. 9.78		H	W 2–0	MacDonald, Smith
		2	18.10.78	PSV Eindhoven (Holland)	H	D 0–0	
			1.11.78		A	W 3–2	MacDonald, Johnstone, Russell
		QF	6. 3.79	IFC Cologne (West	A	L 0–1	
			22. 3.79	Germany)	H	D 1–1	McLean
1960–61	Cup-Winners' Cup	Pr	28. 9.60	Ferencvaros (Hungary)	H	W 4–2	Davis, Millar 2, Brand
			12.10.60		A	L 1–2	Wilson
		QF	15.11.60	Borussia Moenchenglad-	A	W 3–0	Millar, Scott, McMillan
			30.11.60	bach (West Germany)	H	W 8–0	Baxter, Brand 3, Millar 2, Davis. own goal
		SF	29. 3.61	Wolverhampton	H	W 2–0	Scott, Brand
			19. 4.61	Wanderers (England)	A	D 1–1	Scott
		F	17. 5.61	Fiorentina (Italy)	H	L 0–2	
			27. 5.61		A	L 1–2	Scott
1962–63	Cup-Winners' Cup	1	5. 9.62	Seville (Spain)	H	W 4–0	Millar 3, Brand
			26. 9.62		A	L 0–2	

Season	Competition	Round	Date	Opponents (Country)	Venue	Result		Scorers
		2	31.10.62	Tottenham Hotspur	A	L	2–5	Brand, Millar
			11.12.62	(England)	H	L	2–3	Brand, Wilson
1966–67	Cup-Winners' Cup	1	27. 9.66	Glentoran (Northern	A	D	1–1	McLean
			5.10.66	Ireland)	H	W	4–0	Johnston, Smith (D), Setterington, McLean
		2	23.11.66	Borussia Dortmund	H	W	2–1	Johansen, Smith (A)
			6.12.66	(West Germany)	A	D	0–0	
		QF	1. 3.67	Real Zaragoza (Spain)‡	H	W	2–0	Smith, Willoughby
			22. 3.67		A	L	0–2	
		SF	19. 4.67	Slavia Sofia (Bulgaria)	A	W	1–0	Wilson
			3. 5.67		H	W	1–0	Henderson
		F	31. 5.67	Bayern Munich (West Germany)	N	L	0–1	
1969–70	Cup-Winners' Cup	1	17. 9.69	Steaua Bucharest	H	W	2–0	Johnston 2
			1.10.69	(Rumania)	A	D	0–0	
		2	12.11.69	Gornik Zabrze (Poland)	A	L	1–3	Persson
			26.11.69		H	L	1–3	Baxter
1971–72	Cup-Winners' Cup	1	15. 9.71	Rennes (France)	A	D	1–1	Johnston
			28. 9.71		H	W	1–0	MacDonald
		2	20.10.71	Sporting Lisbon	H	W	3–2	Stein 2, Henderson
			3.11.71	(Portugal)	A	L	3–4*	Stein 2, Henderson
		QF	8. 3.72	Torino (Italy)	A	D	1–1	Johnston
			22. 3.72		H	W	1–0	MacDonald
		SF	5. 4.72	Bayern Munich	A	D	1–1	own goal
			19. 4.72	(West Germany)	H	W	2–0	Jardine, Parlane
		F	24. 5.72	Dynamo Moscow (USSR)	N	W	3–2	Johnstone 2, Stein
1973–74	Cup Winners' Cup	1	19. 9.73	Ankaragucu (Turkey)	A	W	2–0	Conn, McLean
			3.10.73		H	W	4–0	Greig 2, O'Hara, Johnstone
		2	24.10.73	Borussia Moenchenglad-	A	L	0–3	
			7.11.73	bach (West Germany)	H	W	3–2	Conn, Jackson, MacDonald
1977–78	Cup-Winners' Cup	Pr	17. 8.77	Young Boys (Switzerland)	H	W	1–0	Greig
			31. 8.77		A	D	2–2	Johnstone, Smith
		1	14. 9.77	Twente Enschede	H	D	0–0	
			28. 9.77	(Holland)	A	L	0–3	
1979–80	Cup-Winners' Cup	Pr	21. 8.79	Lillestrom (Norway)	H	W	1–0	Smith
			5. 9.79		A	W	2–0	MacDonald (A), Johnstone
		1	19. 9.79	Fortuna Dusseldorf (West	H	W	2–1	Macdonald (A), McLean
			3.10.79	Germany)	A	D	0–0	
		2	24.10.79	Valencia (Spain)	A	D	1–1	McLean
			7.11.79		H	L	1–3	Johnstone
1981–82	Cup-Winners' Cup	1	16. 9.81	Dukla Prague	A	L	0–3	
			30. 9.81	(Czechoslovakia)	H	W	2–1	Bett, MacDonald (J)
1967–68	Fairs Cup	1	21. 9.67	Dynamo Dresden	A	D	1–1	Ferguson
			4.10.67	(East Germany)	H	W	2–1	Penman, Greig
		2	8.11.67	IFC Cologne (West	H	W	3–0	Ferguson 2, Henderson
			28.11.67	Germany)	A	L	1–3	Henderson
		3		bye				
		QF	26. 3.68	Leeds United (England)	H	D	0–0	
			9. 4.68		A	L	0–2	
1968–69	Fairs Cup	1	18. 9.68	Vojvodina (Yugoslavia)	H	W	2–0	Greig (pen), Jardine
			2.10.68		A	L	0–1	
		2	30.10.68	Dundalk (Eire)	H	W	6–1	Henderson 2, Ferguson 2, Greig, own goal
			13.11.68		A	W	3–0	Mathieson, Stein 2
		3	11. 1.69	DWS Amsterdam	A	W	2–0	Johnstone, Henderson
			22. 1.69	(Holland)	H	W	2–1	Smith, Stein
		QF	19. 3.69	Atletico Bilbao (Spain)	H	W	4–1	Ferguson, Penman, Persson Stein
			2. 4.69		A	L	0–2	
		SF	14. 5.69	Newcastle United	H	D	0–0	
			22. 5.69	(England)	A	L	0–2	
1970–71	Fairs Cup	1	16. 9.70	Bayern Munich	A	L	0–1	
			30. 9.70	(West Germany)	H	D	1–1	Stein
1982–83	UEFA Cup	1	15. 9.82	Borussia Dortmund	A	D	0–0	
			29. 9.82	(West Germany)	H	W	2–0	Cooper, Johnstone
		2	20.10.82	IFC Cologne	H	W	2–1	Johnstone, McClelland
			3.11.82	(West Germany)	A	L	0–5	
1972–73	Super Cup	F	16. 1.73	Ajax (Holland)	H	L	1–3	MacDonald
			24. 1.73		A	L	2–3	MacDonald, Young

Season	Competition	Round	Date	Opponents (Country)	Venue	Result		Scorers

ST JOHNSTONE

Season	Competition	Round	Date	Opponents (Country)	Venue	Result		Scorers
1971–72	UEFA Cup	1	15. 9.71	SV Hamburg	A	L	1–2	Pearson
			29. 9.71	(West Germany)	H	W	3–0	Hall, Pearson, Whitelaw
		2	20.10.71	Vasas Budapest (Hungary)	H	W	2–0	Connolly (pen), Pearson
			2.11.71		A	L	0–1	
		3	24.11.71	Zeljeznicar (Yugoslavia)	H	W	1–0	Connolly
			8.12.71		A	L	1–5	Rooney

ST MIRREN

Season	Competition	Round	Date	Opponents (Country)	Venue	Result		Scorers
1980–81	UEFA Cup	1	17. 9.80	Elfsborg (Sweden)	A	W	2–1	Somner, Abercromby
			1.10.80		H	D	0–0	
		2	22.10.80	St Etienne	H	D	0–0	
			5.11.80	(France)	A	L	0–2	

IRISH LEAGUE CLUBS

ARDS

Season	Competition	Round	Date	Opponents (Country)	Venue	Result		Scorers
1958–59	European Cup	Pr	17. 9.58	Reims (France)	H	L	1–4	Lowry
			8.10.58		A	L	2–6	Lawther, Quee
1969–70	Cup-Winners' Cup	1	17. 9.69	AS Roma (Italy)	H	D	0–0	
			1.10.69		A	L	1–3	Crothers
1974–75	Cup-Winners' Cup	1	18. 9.74	PSV Eindhoven (Holland)	A	L	0–10	
			2.10.74		H	L	1–4	Guy
1973–74	UEFA Cup	1	12. 9.73	Standard Liege (Belgium)	H	W	3–2	Cathcart, McAvoy (pen), McAteer (pen)
			19. 9.73		A	L	1–6	Guy

BALLYMENA UNITED

Season	Competition	Round	Date	Opponents (Country)	Venue	Result		Scorers
1978–79	Cup-Winners' Cup	1	13. 9.78	Beveren (Belgium)	A	L	0–3	
			27. 9.78		H	L	0–3	
1981–82	Cup-Winners' Cup	1	16. 9.81	AS Roma (Italy)	H	L	0–2	
			30. 9.81		A	L	0–4	
1980–81	UEFA Cup	1	17. 9.80	Vorwaerts (East	H	W	2–1	McQviston, Sloan
			1.10.80	Germany)	A	L	0–3	

CARRICK RANGERS

Season	Competition	Round	Date	Opponents (Country)	Venue	Result		Scorers
1976–77	Cup-Winners' Cup	1	15. 9.76	Aris Bonnevoie	H	W	3–1	Prenter 2, Connor
			6.10.76	(Luxemburg)	A	L	1–2	Irwin
		2	20.10.76	Southampton (England)	H	L	2–5	Irwin, Prenter
			3.11.76		A	L	1–4	Reid

CLIFTONVILLE

Season	Competition	Round	Date	Opponents (Country)	Venue	Result		Scorers
1979–80	Cup-Winners' Cup	1	20. 9.79	Nantes (France)	H	L	0–1	
			3.10.79		A	L	0–7	

COLERAINE

Season	Competition	Round	Date	Opponents (Country)	Venue	Result		Scorers
1974–75	European Cup	1	18.11.74	Feyenoord (Holland)	A	L	0–7	
			2.10.74		H	L	1–4	Simpson
1965–66	Cup-Winners' Cup	1	2. 9.65	Dynamo Kiev (USSR)	H	L	1–6	Curley
			8. 9.65		A	L	0–4	
1975–76	Cup-Winners' Cup	1	16. 9.75	Eintracht Frankfurt	A	L	1–5	Cochrane
			30. 9.75	(West Germany)	H	L	2–6	McCurdy, Cochrane

Season	Competition	Round	Date	Opponents (Country)	Venue	Result		Scorers
1969–70	Fairs Cup	1	17. 9.69	Jeunesse D'Esch	A	L	2–3	Hunter, Murray
			1.10.69	(Luxembourg)	H	W	4–0	Dickson 2, Wilson, Jennings
		2	11.11.69	Anderlecht (Belgium)	A	L	1–6	Murray
			20.11.69		H	L	3–7	Dickson 2, Irwin
1970–71	Fairs Cup	1	15. 9.70	Kilmarnock (Scotland)	H	D	1–1	Mullan
			29. 9.70		A	W	3–2	Dickson 3
		2	20.10.70	Sparta Rotterdam	A	L	0–2	
			4.11.70	(Holland)	H	L	1–2	Jennings
1977–78	Cup-Winners' Cup	1	14. 9.77	Lokomotive Leipzig	H	L	1–4	Tweed
			28. 9.77	(East Germany)	A	D	2–2	Guy 2
1982–83	Cup-Winners' Cup	1	15. 9.82	Tottenham Hotspur	H	L	0–3	
			28. 9.82	(England)	A	L	0–4	

CRUSADERS

Season	Competition	Round	Date	Opponents (Country)	Venue	Result		Scorers
1973–74	European Cup	1	19. 9.73	Dynamo Bucharest	H	L	0–1	
			3.10.73	(Rumania)	A	L	0–11	
1976–77	European Cup	1	14. 9.76	Liverpool (England)	A	L	0–2	
			28. 9.76		H	L	0–5	
1967–68	Cup-Winners' Cup	1	20. 9.67	Valencia (Spain)	A	L	0–4	
			11.10.67		H	L	2–4	Trainor, Magill
1968–69	Cup-Winners' Cup	1	18. 9.68	Norrkoping (Sweden)	H	D	2–2	Jameson, Parke
			2.10.68		A	L	1–4	McPolin
1980–81	Cup-Winners' Cup	1	16. 9.80	Newport County	A	L	0–4	
			1.10.80	(Wales)	H	D	0–0	

DERRY CITY

Season	Competition	Round	Date	Opponents (Country)	Venue	Result		Scorers
1965–66	European Cup	Pr	31. 8.65	Lyn Oslo (Norway)	A	L	3–5	Wood (R), Gilbert 2
			9. 9.65		H	W	5–1	Wilson 2, Crossan, Wood (R), McGeough
		1	23.11.65	Anderlecht (Belgium)	A	L	0–9	
				Derry City	withdrew			
1964–65	Cup-Winners' Cup	1	9. 9.64	Steaua Bucharest	A	L	0–3	
			16. 9.64	(Rumania)	H	L	0–2	

DISTILLERY

Season	Competition	Round	Date	Opponents (Country)	Venue	Result		Scorers
1963–64	European Cup	Pr	25. 9.63	Benfica (Portugal)	H	D	3–3	John Kennedy, Hamilton, Ellison
			2.10.63		A	L	0–5	
1971–72	Cup-Winners' Cup	1	15. 9.71	Barcelona (Spain)	H	L	1–3	O'Neill
			29. 9.71		A	L	0–4	

GLENAVON

Season	Competition	Round	Date	Opponents (Country)	Venue	Result		Scorers
1957–58	European Cup	Pr	11. 9.57	Aarhus (Denmark)	A	D	0–0	
			25. 9.57		H	L	0–3	
1960–61	European Cup	Pr		withdrew				
1961–62	Cup-Winners' Cup	1	13. 9.61	Leicester City (England)	H	L	1–4	Jones
			27. 9.61		A	L	1–3	Wilson
1977–78	UEFA Cup	1	14. 9.77	PSV Eindhoven	H	L	2–6	Malone (pen), McDonald
			28. 9.77	(Holland)	A	L	0–5	
1979–80	UEFA Cup	1	18. 9.79	Standard Liege (Belgium)	H	L	0–1	
			3.10.79		A	L	0–1	

GLENTORAN

Season	Competition	Round	Date	Opponents (Country)	Venue	Result		Scorers
1964–65	European Cup	Pr	16. 9.64	Panathinaikos (Greece)	H	D	2–2	Turner, Thompson
			30. 9.64		A	L	2–3	Turner, Pavis
1967–68	European Cup	1	13. 9.67	Benfica (Portugal)*	H	D	1–1	Colrain (pen)
			4.10.67		A	D	0–0	
1968–69	European Cup	1	18. 9.68	Anderlecht (Belgium)	A	L	0–3	
			2.10.68		H	D	2–2	Morrow, Johnston

Season	Competition	Round	Date	Opponents (Country)	Venue	Result		Scorers
1970–71	European Cup	1	16. 9.70	Waterford (Eire)	H	L	1–3	Hall
			30. 9.70		A	L	0–1	
1977–78	European Cup	1	15. 9.77	Valur (Iceland)	A	L	0–1	
			29. 9.77		H	W	2–0	Robson, Jamison
		2	19.10.77	Juventus (Italy)	H	L	0–1	
			2.11.77		A	L	0–5	
1981–82	European Cup	1	16. 9.81	Progres Niedercorn	A	D	1–1	Cleary
			30. 9.81	(Luxembourg)	H	W	4–0	Blackledge 2, Jameson, Manley
		2	21.10.81	CSKA Sofia	A	L	0–2	
			4.11.81	(Bulgaria)	H	W	2–1	Cleary, Manley
1966–67	Cup-Winners' Cup	1	27. 9.66	Rangers (Scotland)	H	D	1–1	Sinclair
			5.10.66		A	L	0–4	
1973–74	Cup-Winners' Cup	1	19. 9.73	Chimia Ramnicu	A	D	2–2	Jamison, McCreary
			3.10.73	(Rumania)	H	W	2–0	Jamison, Craig
		2	24.10.73	Brann Bergen (Norway)	A	D	1–1	Feeney
			7.11.73		H	W	3–1	Feeney, Jamison 2
		QF	5. 3.74	Borussia Moenchenglad-	H	L	0–2	
			20. 3.74	bach (West Germany)	A	L	0–5	
1962–63	Fairs Cup	1	26. 9.62	Real Zaragoza (Spain)	H	L	0–2	
			10.10.62		A	L	2–6	Doherty 2
1963–64	Fairs Cup	1	16. 9.63	Partick Thistle (Scotland)	H	L	1–4	Thompson
			30. 9.63		A	L	0–3	
1965–66	Fairs Cup	1	28. 9.65	Antwerp (Belgium)	A	L	0–1	
			6.10.65		H	D	3–3	Hamilton, Thompson 2
1969–70	Fairs Cup	1	9. 9.69	Arsenal (England)	A	L	0–3	
			29. 9.69.		H	W	1–0	Henderson
1971–72	UEFA Cup	1	14. 9.71	Eintracht Brunswick	H	L	0–1	
			28. 9.71	(West Germany)	A	L	1–6	McCaffrey
1975–76	UEFA Cup	1	16. 9.75	Ajax (Holland)	H	L	1–6	Jamison
			1.10.75		A	L	0–8	
1976–77	UEFA Cup	1	14. 9.76	Basle (Switzerland)	H	W	3–2	Feeney 2, Dickenson
			29. 9.76		A	L	0–3	
1978–79	UEFA Cup	1	5. 9.78	IBV Westmann (Iceland)	A	D	0–0	
			14. 9.78		H	D	1–1	Caskey (W)
1982–83	UEFA Cup	1	15. 9.82	Banik Ostrava	H	L	1–3	Bowers
			29. 9.82	(Czechoslovakia)	A	L	0–1	

LINFIELD

Season	Competition	Round	Date	Opponents (Country)	Venue	Result		Scorers
1959–60	European Cup	Pr	9. 9.59	Gothenburg (Sweden)	H	W	2–1	Milburn 2
			23. 9.59		A	L	1–6	Dickson
1961–62	European Cup	Pr	30. 8.61	Vorwaerts (East Germany)	A	L	0–3	
					withdrew			
1962–63	European Cup	Pr	5. 9.62	Esbjerg (Denmark)	H	L	1–2	Dickson
			19. 9.62		A	D	0–0	
1966–67	European Cup	1	7. 9.66	Aris Bonnevoie	A	D	3–3	Hamilton, Pavis, Scott
			16. 9.66	(Luxembourg)	A	W	6–1	Thomas 3, Scott 2, Pavis
		2	26.10.66	Valerengen (Norway)	A	W	4–1	Scott, Pavis, Thomas, Shields
			8.11.66		H	D	1–1	Thomas
		QF	1. 3.67	CSKA Sofia (Bulgaria)	H	D	2–2	Hamilton, Shields
			15. 3.67		A	L	0–1	
1969–70	European Cup	1	17. 9.69	Red Star Belgrade	A	L	0–8	
			1.10.69	(Yugoslavia)	H	L	2–4	McGraw 2
1971–72	European Cup	1	15. 9.71	Standard Liege (Belgium)	A	L	0–2	
			29. 9.71		H	L	2–3	Magee, Larmour
1975–76	European Cup	1	17. 9.75	PSV Eindhoven (Holland)	H	L	1–2	Malone (P)
			1.10.75		A	L	0–8	
1978–79	European Cup	1	13. 9.78	Lillestrom (Norway)	H	D	0–0	
			27. 9.78		A	L	0–1	
1979–80	European Cup	Pr	29. 8.79	Dundalk (Eire)	A	D	1–1	Feeney
			5. 9.79	(in Haarlem, Holland)	H	L	0–2	
1980–81	European Cup	1	16. 9.80	Nantes (France)	H	L	0–1	
			30. 9.80		A	L	0–2	
1982–83	European Cup	1	15. 9.82	17 Nendori (Albania)	A	L	0–1	
			29. 9.82		H	W	2–1	Gibson, Anderson

Season	Competition	Round	Date	Opponents (Country)	Venue	Result		Scorers
1963–64	Cup-Winners'	1		bye				
	Cup	2	13.11.63	Fenerbahce (Turkey)	A	L	1–4	Dickson
			11.12.63		H	W	2–0	Craig, Ferguson
1970–71	Cup-Winners'	1	16. 9.70	Manchester City	A	L	0–1	
	Cup		30. 9.70	(England)*	H	W	2–1	Millen 2
1967–68	Fairs Cup	1	19. 9.67	Lokomotive Leipzig	A	L	1–5	Pavis
			4.10.67	(East Germany)	H	W	1–0	Hamilton
1968–69	Fairs Cup	1	18. 9.68	Setubal (Portugal)	A	L	0–3	
			9.10.68		H	L	1–3	Scott
1981–82	UEFA Cup	1	16. 9.81	Beveren (Belgium)	A	L	0–3	
			29. 9.81		H	L	0–5	

PORTADOWN

Season	Competition	Round	Date	Opponents (Country)	Venue	Result		Scorers
1962–63	Cup-Winners'	1		bye				
	Cup	2	7.11.62	OFK Belgrade	A	L	1–5	Clements
			22.11.62	(Yugoslavia)	H	W	3–2	Burke, Jones, Cush
1974–75	UEFA Cup	1	18. 9.74	Valur (Iceland)	A	D	0–0	
			1.10.74		H	W	2–1	MacFaul, Morrison (pen)
		2	23.10.74	Partizan Belgrade	A	L	0–5	
			6.11.74	(Yugoslavia)	H	D	1–1	Malcolmson

LEAGUE OF IRELAND CLUBS

ATHLONE TOWN

Season	Competition	Round	Date	Opponents (Country)	Venue	Result		Scorers
1981–82	European Cup	1	16. 9.81	KB Copenhagen	A	D	1–1	O'Connor (M)
			30. 9.81	(Denmark)	H	D	2–2	Davis 2
1975–76	UEFA Cup	1	18. 9.75	Valerengen (Norway)	H	W	3–0	Martin, Davis 2
			1.10.75		A	D	1–1	Martin
		2	22.10.75	AC Milan (Italy)	H	D	0–0	
			5.11.75		A	L	0–3	

BOHEMIANS

Season	Competition	Round	Date	Opponents (Country)	Venue	Result		Scorers
1975–76	European Cup	1	17. 9.75	Rangers (Scotland)	A	L	1–4	Flanagan
			1.10.75		H	D	1–1	O'Connor (T)
1978–79	European Cup	1	13. 9.78	Omonia Nicosia (Cyprus)	A	L	1–2	O'Connor (P)
			27. 9.78		H	W	1–0	Joyce
		2	18.10.78	Dynamo Dresden	H	D	0–0	
			1.11.78	(East Germany)	A	L	0–6	
1970–71	Cup-Winners'	Pr	26. 8.70	Gottwaldov	H	L	1–2	Swan (pen)
	Cup		2. 9.70	(Czechoslovakia)	A	D	2–2	O'Connell, Dunne
1976–77	Cup-Winners'	1	15. 9.76	Esbjerg (Denmark)	H	W	2–1	Ryan (B), own goal
	Cup		29. 9.76		A	W	1–0	Mitten
		2	20.10.76	Slask Wroclaw (Poland)	A	L	0–3	
			3.11.76		H	L	0–1	
1972–73	UEFA Cup	1	13. 9.72	IFC Cologne (West	A	L	1–2	Daly
			27. 9.72	Germany)	H	L	0–3	
1974–75	UEFA Cup	1	18. 9.74	SV Hamburg (West	A	L	0–3	
			2.10.74	Germany)	H	L	0–1	
1979–80	UEFA Cup	1	19. 9.79	Sporting Lisbon	A	L	0–2	
			3.10.79	(Portugal)	H	D	0–0	

CORK CELTIC

Season	Competition	Round	Date	Opponents (Country)	Venue	Result		Scorers
1974–75	European Cup	1		walkover				
		2	23.10.74	Ararat Erevan (USSR)	H	L	1–2	Tambling
			6.11.74		A	L	0–5	
1964–65	Cup-Winners'	1	30. 9.64	Slavia Sofia (Bulgaria)	A	D	1–1	Leahy
	Cup		7.10.64		H	L	0–2	

Season	Competition	Round	Date	Opponents (Country)	Venue	Result		Scorers

CORK HIBS

Season	Competition	Round	Date	Opponents (Country)	Venue	Result		Scorers
1971–72	European Cup	1	15. 9.71	Borussia Moenchenglad-	H	L	0–5	
			29. 9.71	bach (West Germany)	A	L	1–2	Dennehy
1972–73	Cup-Winners'	1	10. 9.72	Pezoporikos (Cyprus)	A	W	2–1	Lawson (pen), Sheehan
	Cup		13. 9.72		H	W	4–1	Wallace, Lawson 2, Dennehy
		2	25.10.72	Schalke 04 (West	H	D	0–0	
			8.11.72	Germany)	A	L	0–3	
1973–74	Cup-Winners'	1	19. 9.73	Banik Ostrava	A	L	0–1	
	Cup		3.10.73	(Czechoslovakia)	H	L	1–2	Humphries
1970–71	Fairs Cup	1	16. 9.70	Valencia (Spain)	H	L	0–3	
			26. 9.70		A	L	1–3	Wigginton

DRUMCONDRA

Season	Competition	Round	Date	Opponents (Country)	Venue	Result		Scorers
1958–59	European Cup	Pr	17. 9.58	Atletico Madrid (Spain)	A	L	0–8	
			1.10.58		H	L	1–5	Fullam (pen)
1961–62	European Cup	Pr	23. 8.61	IFC Nuremberg (West	A	L	0–5	
			13. 9.61	Germany)	H	L	1–4	Fullam
1965–66	European Cup	Pr	15. 9.65	Vorwaerts (East Germany)	H	W	1–0	Morrissey
			22. 9.65		A	L	0–3	
1962–63	Fairs Cup	1	3.10.62	Odense BK 09 (Denmark)	H	W	4–1	Dixon 2, Morrissey, McCann
			17.10.62		A	L	2–4	Rice, Morrissey
		2	4.12.62	Bayern Munich (West	A	L	0–6	
			12.12.62	Germany)	H	W	1–0	Dixon
1966–67	Fairs Cup	1	21. 9.66	Eintracht Frankfurt	H	L	0–2	
			5.10.66	(West Germany)	A	L	1–6	Whelan

DUNDALK

Season	Competition	Round	Date	Opponents (Country)	Venue	Result		Scorers
1963–64	European Cup	Pr	11. 9.63	Zurich (Switzerland)	H	L	0–3	
			25. 9.63		A	W	2–1	Cross, Hasty
1967–68	European Cup	1	20. 9.67	Vasas Budapest (Hungary)	H	L	0–1	
			11.10.67		A	L	1–8	Hale
1976–77	European Cup	1	15. 9.76	PSV Eindhoven (Holland)	H	D	1–1	McDowell
			29. 9.76		A	L	0–6	
1979–80	European Cup	Pr	29. 8.79	Linfield (Northern Ireland)	H	D	1–1	Devine
			5. 9.79	(in Haarlem, Holland)	A	W	2–0	Muckian 2
		1	19. 9.79	Hibernians (Malta)	H	W	2–0	Carlyle, Devine
			26. 9.79		A	L	0–1	
		2	24.10.79	Celtic (Scotland)	A	L	2–3	Muckian, Lawlor
			7.11.79		H	D	0–0	
1982–83	European Cup	1	14. 9.82	Liverpool (England)	H	L	1–4	Flanagan
			28. 9.82		A	L	0–1	
1977–78	Cup-Winners'	1	14. 9.77	Hajduk Split	H	W	1–0	Flanagan
	Cup		28. 9.77	(Yugoslavia)	A	L	0–4	
1981–82	Cup Winners'	1	16. 9.81	Fram (Iceland)	A	L	1–2	Fairclough
	Cup		30. 9.81		H	W	4–0	Flanagan (pen), Fairclough, Lawlor, Duff
		2	21.10.81	Tottenham Hotspur	H	D	1–1	Fairclough
			4.11.81	(England)	A	L	0–1	
1968–69	Fairs Cup	1	11. 9.68	DOS Utrecht (Holland)	A	D	1–1	Stokes
			1.10.68		H	W	2–1	Stokes, Morrissey
		2	30.10.68	Rangers (Scotland)	A	L	1–6	Murray (pen)
			13.11.68		H	L	0–3	
1969–70	Fairs Cup	1	16. 9.69	Liverpool (England)	A	L	0–10	
			30. 9.69		H	L	0–4	
1980–81	UEFA Cup	1	16. 9.80	Porto (Portugal)	A	L	0–1	
			1.10.80		H	D	0–0	

FINN HARPS

Season	Competition	Round	Date	Opponents (Country)	Venue	Result		Scorers
1974–75	Cup-Winners'	1	18.11.74	Bursaspor (Turkey)	A	L	2–4	Ferry, Bradley
	Cup				H	D	0–0	
1973–74	UEFA Cup	1	19. 9.73	Aberdeen (Scotland)	A	L	1–4	Harkin
			3.10.73		H	L	1–3	Harkin
1976–77	UEFA Cup	1	15. 9.76	Derby County (England)	A	L	0–12	
			29. 9.76		H	L	1–4	own goal
1978–79	UEFA Cup	1	12. 9.78	Everton (England)	H	L	0–5	
			26. 9.78		A	L	0–5	

Season	Competition	Round	Date	Opponents (Country)	Venue	Result		Scorers

HOME FARM

Season	Competition	Round	Date	Opponents (Country)	Venue	Result		Scorers
1975–76	Cup-Winners' Cup	1	17. 8.75	Lens (France)	H	D	1–1	Brophy
			1.10.75		A	L	0–6	

LIMERICK

Season	Competition	Round	Date	Opponents (Country)	Venue	Result		Scorers
1960–61	European Cup	Pr	31. 8.60	Young Boys (Switzerland)	H	L	0–5	
			5.10.60		A	L	2–4	Lynam, O'Reilly
1980–81	European Cup	1	17. 9.80	Real Madrid	H	L	1–2	Kennedy
			1.10.80	(Spain)	A	L	1–5	Kennedy
1965–66	Cup-Winners' Cup	1	7.10.65	CSKA Sofia (Bulgaria)	H	L	1–2	O'Connor
			13.10.65		A	L	0–2	
1971–72	Cup Winners' Cup	1	15. 9.71	Torino (Italy)	H	L	0–1	
			29. 9.71		A	L	0–4	
1982–83	Cup-Winners' Cup	1	15. 9.82	AZ 67 (Holland)	H	D	1–1	Nolan
			30. 9.82		A	L	0–1	
1981–82	UEFA Cup	1	16. 9.81	Southampton	H	L	0–3	
			29. 9.81	(England)	A	D	1–1	Morris

SHAMROCK ROVERS

Season	Competition	Round	Date	Opponents (Country)	Venue	Result		Scorers
1957–58	European Cup	Pr	25. 9.57	Manchester United	H	L	0–6	
			2.10.57	(England)	A	L	2–3	McCann, Hamilton
1959–60	European Cup	Pr	26. 8.59	Nice (France)	A	L	2–3	Hamilton, Tuohy
			23. 9.59		H	D	1–1	Hennessy
1964–65	European Cup	Pr	16. 9.64	Rapid Vienna (Austria)	A	L	0–3	
			30. 9.64		H	L	0–2	
1962–63	Cup-Winners' Cup	1		bye				
		2	24.10.62	Botev Plovdiv (Bulgaria)	H	L	0–4	
			14.11.62		A	L	0–1	
1966–67	Cup-Winners' Cup	1	28. 9.66	Spora (Luxembourg)	H	W	4–1	Fullam, Dixon, Kearin, O'Neill (pen)
			5.10.66		A	W	4–1	Kearin, Dixon 2, O'Neill
		2	9 11.66	Bayern Munich (West	H	D	1–1	Dixon
			2⌣.11.66	Germany)	A	L	2–3	Gilbert, O'Neill
1967–68	Cup-Winners' Cup	1	20. 9.67	Cardiff City (Wales)	H	D	1–1	Gilbert
			4.10.67		A	L	0–2	
1968–69	Cup-Winners' Cup	1	18. 9.68	Randers Freja (Denmark)	A	L	0–1	
			2.10.68		H	L	1–2	Fullam
1969–70	Cup-Winners' Cup	1	17. 9.69	Schalke 04 (West	H	W	2–1	Barber 2
			1.10.69	Germany)	A	L	0–3	
1978–79	Cup-Winners' Cup	1	13. 9.78	Apoel Nicosia (Cyprus)	H	W	2–0	Giles, Lynex
			27. 9.78		A	W	1–0	Lynex
		2	18.10.78	Banik Ostrava	A	L	0–3	
			1.11.78	(Czechoslovakia)	H	L	1–3	Giles
1963–64	Fairs Cup	1	18. 9.63	Valencia (Spain)	H	L	0–1	
			10.10.63		A	D	2–2	O'Neill, Mooney
1965–66	Fairs Cup	1		bye				
		2	17.11.65	Real Zaragoza (Spain)	H	D	1–1	Tuohy
			24.11.65		A	L	1–2	Fullam
1982–83	UEFA Cup	1	15. 9.82	Fram (Iceland)	A	W	3–0	Murphy, Campbell, Gaynor
			30. 9.82		H	W	4–0	O'Carroll, Buckley, Beglin, Gaynor
		2	21.10.82	Uni Craiova	H	L	0–2	
			3.11.82	(Rumania)	A	L	0–3	

SHELBOURNE

Season	Competition	Round	Date	Opponents (Country)	Venue	Result		Scorers
1962–63	European Cup	Pr	19. 9.62	Sporting Lisbon	H	L	0–2	
			27. 9.62	(Portugal)	A	L	1–5	Hennessy
1963–64	Cup-Winners' Cup	1	24. 9.63	Barcelona (Spain)	H	L	0–2	
			15.10.63		A	L	1–3	Bohnam (pen)
1964–65	Fairs Cup	1	16. 9.64	Belenenses (Portugal)	A	D	1–1	Barber
			14.10.64		H	D	0–0	
			28.10.64		N	W	2–1	Hannigan, Conroy (M)

Season	Competition	Round	Date	Opponents (Country)	Venue	Result		Scorers
		2	25.11.64	Atletico Madrid (Spain)	H	L	0–1	
			2.12.64		A	L	0–1	
1971–72	UEFA Cup	1	15. 9.71	Vasas Budapest	A	L	0–1	
			29. 9.71	(Hungary)	H	D	1–1	Murray

ST PATRICK'S ATHLETIC

Season	Competition	Round	Date	Opponents (Country)	Venue	Result		Scorers
1961–62	Cup-Winners' Cup	Pr	12. 9.61	Dunfermline Athletic	A	L	1–4	O'Rourke
			27. 9.61	(Scotland)	H	L	0–4	
1967–68	Fairs Cup	1	13. 9.67	Bordeaux (France)	H	L	1–3	Hennessy
			11.10.67		A	L	3–6	Campbell 2, Ryan

WATERFORD

Season	Competition	Round	Date	Opponents (Country)	Venue	Result		Scorers
1966–67	European Cup	Pr	31. 8.66	Vorwaerts Berlin (East	H	L	1–5	Lynch
			9. 9.66	Germany)	A	L	0–6	
1968–69	European Cup	1	18. 9.68	Manchester United	H	L	1–3	Matthews
			2.10.68	(England)	A	L	1–7	Casey
1969–70	European Cup	1	17. 9.69	Galatasaray (Turkey)	A	L	0–2	
			1.10.69		H	L	2–3	Buck, Morley
1970–71	European Cup	1	16. 9.70	Glentoran (Northern	A	W	3–1	O'Neill, McGeough, Casey
			30. 9.70	Ireland)	H	W	1–0	Casey
		2	21.10.70	Celtic (Scotland)	H	L	0–7	
			4.11.70		A	L	2–3	Matthews, own goal
1972–73	European Cup	1	13. 9.72	Omonia Nicosia (Cyprus)	H	W	2–1	Hale 2
			27. 9.72		A	L	0–2	
1973–74	European Cup	1	19. 9.73	Ujpest Dozsa (Hungary)	H	L	2–3	Kirby, O'Neill
			3.10.73		A	L	0–3	
1979–80	Cup-Winners' Cup	1	19. 9.79	Gothenburg (Sweden)	A	L	0–1	
			3.10.79		H	D	1–1	Keane
1980–81	Cup-Winners' Cup	1	17. 9.80	Hibernians	A	L	0–1	
			1.10.80	(Malta)	H	W	4–0	Kirk 2, Finucane, Fitzpatrick
		2	22.10.80	Dynamo Tbilisi	H	L	0–1	
			5.11.80	(USSR)	A	L	0–4	

WELSH NON-LEAGUE CLUBS

BANGOR CITY

Season	Competition	Round	Date	Opponents (Country)	Venue	Result		Scorers
1962–63	Cup-Winners' Cup	1	5. 9.62	Napoli (Italy)	H	W	2–0	Matthews, Birch (pen)
			26. 9.62		A	L	1–3	McAlister
			10.10.62		N	L	1–2	McAlister

BOROUGH UNITED

Season	Competition	Round	Date	Opponents (Country)	Venue	Result		Scorers
1963–64	Cup-Winners' Cup	1	15. 9.63	Sliema Wanderers	A	D	0–0	
			3.10.63	(Malta)	H	W	2–0	Duffy, Pritchard (M)
		2	11.12.63	Slovan Bratislava	H	L	0–1	
			15.12.63	(Czechoslovakia)	A	L	0–3	

REPRESENTATIVE TEAM

LONDON

Season	Competition	Round	Date	Opponents (Country)	Venue	Result		Scorers
1955–58	Fairs Cup	Gp. C	4. 6.55	Basle (Switzerland)	A	W	5–0	Firmani 2, Holton 3
			4. 5.56		H	W	1–0	Robb
			26.10.56	Frankfurt	H	W	3–2	Jezzard 2, Robson
			27. 3.57	(West Germany)	A	L	0–1	
		SF	16. 9.57	Lausanne	A	L	1–2	Haverty
			23.10.57	(Switzerland)	H	W	2–0	Greaves, Holton
		F	5. 3.58	Barcelona (Spain)	H	D	2–2	Greaves, Langley (pen)
			1. 5.58		A	L	0–6	

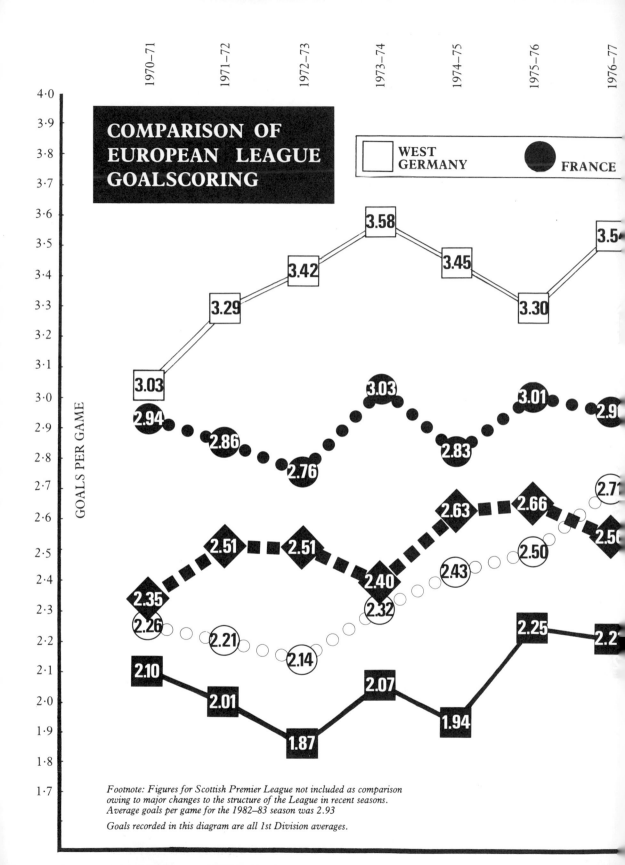

COMPARISON OF EUROPEAN LEAGUE GOALSCORING

WEST GERMANY

FRANCE

GOALS PER GAME

1970–71 1971–72 1972–73 1973–74 1974–75 1975–76 1976–77

3.03 3.29 3.42 3.58 3.45 3.30 3.5

2.94 2.86 2.76 3.03 2.83 3.01 2.9

2.35 2.51 2.51 2.40 2.63 2.66 2.5

2.26 2.21 2.14 2.32 2.43 2.50 2.7

2.10 2.01 1.87 2.07 1.94 2.25 2.2

Footnote: Figures for Scottish Premier League not included as comparison owing to major changes to the structure of the League in recent seasons. Average goals per game for the 1982–83 season was 2.93

Goals recorded in this diagram are all 1st Division averages.

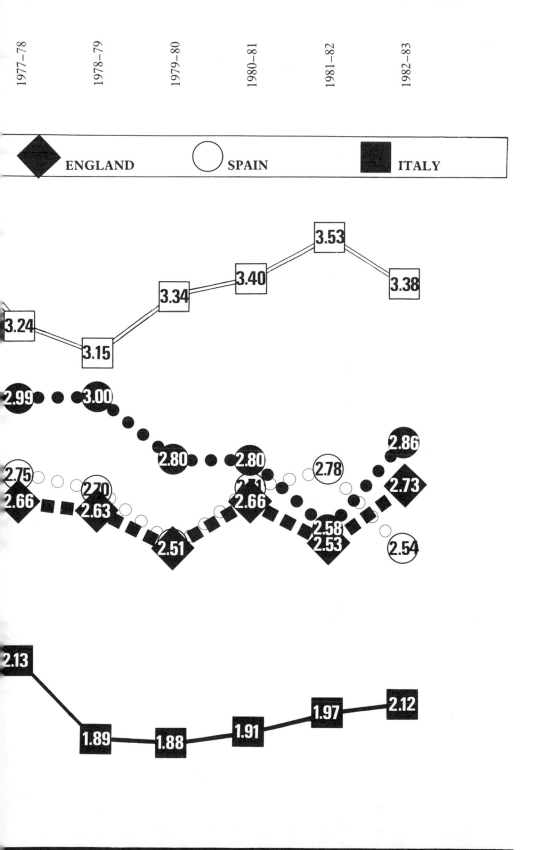

1977–78 1978–79 1979–80 1980–81 1981–82 1982–83

◆ ENGLAND ◯ SPAIN ■ ITALY

3.53
3.40
3.34
3.38
3.24
3.15

2.99 3.00
2.86
2.80 2.80 2.78 2.73
2.75
2.70
2.66 2.66
2.63
2.58
2.51 2.53 2.54

2.13
2.12
1.97
1.91
1.89 1.88

European Survey 1981/82

	Champions / Matches	Points	Clubs in Division	Most Wins	Fewest Defeats	Most Goals	Fewest Conceded	Most Drawn	Average g/s per game	Top Scorer	Cup Final Result
ALBANIA	17 Nendori / 26	37	14	17 Nendori 15	17 Nendori 4	17 Nendori 42	Flamurtari 12	Naftetari 13	1.90	Ruci (Flamurtari) 12	Dinamo Tirana beat 17 Nendori 1–0, 3–4
AUSTRIA	Rapid Vienna / 36	47	10	Rapid, Austria Vienna 18	Rapid 7	Rapid 69	Austria Vienna 32	Rapid 11	2.77	Bakota (Sturm Graz) 24	Austria Vienna beat SW Innsbruck 3–1, 1–0
BELGIUM	Standard Liege / 34	48	18	Standard, Anderlecht 19	Standard, La Gantoise 5	Standard 59	La Gantoise 21	La Gantoise 13	2.50	Van Den Bergh (Lierse) 25	Waterschei 2 Waregem 0
BULGARIA	CSKA Sofia / 30	47	16	CSKA 22	Levski 4	CSKA 73	CSKA 27	Etar 10	2.70	Valtjev (Levski) 24	Lokomotiv Sofia 1 Lokomotiv Plovdiv 0 (a.e.t)
CYPRUS	Omonia / 26	44	14	Omonia 20	Omonia, Apoel 2	Omonia 61	Omonia 9	Apoel 14	2.27	Kaiafas (Omonia) 19	Omonia beat Apollon 2–2, 4–1
CZECHOSLOVAKIA	Dukla Prague / 30	42	16	Dukla 18	Dukla 6	Dukla 54	Dukla 20	Slavia 10	2.45	Vizek (Dukla) 15	Slovan Bratislava beat Bohemians 4–2 on pens. after 0–0 draw
DENMARK	Hvidovre / 30	40	16	Lyngby 16	Hvidovre, Naestved 5	Lyngby 54	Hvidovre 25	Vejle 15	2.93	Hansen (Odense) 28	Vejle 2 Frem 1
ENGLAND	Liverpool[2] / 42	87	22	Liverpool, Ipswich 26	Liverpool 7	Liverpool 80	Manchester Utd 29	West Ham 16	2.54	Keegan (Southampton) 26	Tottenham Hotspur beat QPR 1–0 after 1–1 draw
FINLAND	HJK Helsinki* / 29		12	HJK 17	KPT 4	Ilves 59	TPS 27	KPT 12	3.12	Himanka (Oulu) 21	HJK 4 Kuusysi 0
FRANCE	Monaco / 38	55	20	Monaco 24	St. Etienne 6	St. Etienne 74	Monaco 29	Metz 16	2.58	Onnis (Tours) 29	Paris St Germain beat St Etienne 6–5 on pens after 2–2 draw
EAST GERMANY	Dynamo Berlin / 26	41	14	Dynamo Berlin 18	Dynamo Berlin 3	Dynamo Berlin 73	Dynamo Dresden 24	Erfurt 8	3.30	Schnuphase (Carl Zeiss Jena) 19	Dynamo Dresden beat Dynamo Berlin 5–4 on pens after 1–1 draw
WEST GERMANY	Hamburg / 34	48	18	Bayern Munich 20	Bayern Munich, Hamburg 4	Hamburg 95	Cologne 38	Dusseldorf 13	3.50	Hrubesch (Hamburg) 27	Bayern Munich 4 Nuremberg 2
GREECE	Olympiakos / 34	50	18	Olympiakos 19	Panathinaikos 2	Olympiakos 58	Panathinaikos 21	Panathinaikos 14	2.31	Charalambidis (Panathinaikos) 21	Panathinaikos 1 Larissa 0
HUNGARY	Raba Gyor / 34	49	18	Raba 21	Raba, Tatabanya 6	Raba 102	Csepel 34	Zalaegerszeg, Csepel 14	2.95	Hannich (Raba) 22	Ujpest Dozsa 2 Videoton 0
ICELAND	Vikingur / 18	25	10	Vikingur 11	Fram 2	Vikingur, Valur 30	Fram, Akranes 17	Fram 9	2.69	Gudmundsson (Vikingur), Thorleifsson (Vikingur)	IBV 3 Fram 2

Final league tables, leading scorers and cup finals — European countries.

Country	Champions	Pts	Leading goalscorer (club) goals	Goal avg.	Cup final
N. IRELAND	Linfield	37	Dickson, Healy (Coleraine) 18	3.27	Linfield 2 Coleraine 1
ITALY	Juventus	46	Pruzzo (Roma) 15	1.98	Internazionale beat Torino 1–0, 1–1
LIECHTENSTEIN	No national league; teams play in Swiss regional leagues				Balzers 5 Eschen 0
LUXEMBOURG	Avenir Beggen	36	Krings (Avenir) 25	3.14	Red Boys 2 Rumelange 1
MALTA	Hibernians	25	Spiteri-Gonzi (Hibernians) 13	2.80	Hibernians 1 Sliema 0
NETHERLANDS	Ajax	56	Kieft (Ajax) 32	3.31	AZ'67 Alkmaar beat Utrecht 5–1, 0–1
NORWAY	Valerengen	29	Jacobsen (Valerengen) 16	2.78	Lillestrom 3 Moss 1
POLAND	Widzew Lodz	39	Kapica (Bytom) 15	2.22	Lech Poznan 1 Pogon 0
PORTUGAL	Sporting	46	Pereira (Porto) 27	2.35	Sporting Lisbon 4 Braga 0
RUMANIA	Dynamo Bucharest	47	Iordanescu (Steaua) 20	2.45	Dynamo 3 Baia Mare 2
SCOTLAND	Celtic	55	McCluskey (Celtic) 21	2.77	Aberdeen 4 Rangers 1 a.e.t.
SPAIN	Real Sociedad	47	Quini (Barcelona) 26	2.79	Real Madrid 2 Gijon 1
SWEDEN	Oster Vaxjo	40	Nilsson (Gothenburg) 20	2.93	Kalmar 4 Elfsborg 0
SWITZERLAND	Grasshoppers	49	Sulser (Grasshoppers) 22	3.22	Sion 1 Basle 0
TURKEY	Besiktas	44	Selcuk (Fenerbahce) 16	1.80	Galatasaray beat Ankaragucu 3–0, 1–2
USSR	Dynamo Kiev	53	Shengelia (Tbilisi) 23	2.55	SKV Rostov 1 Spartak Moscow 0
YUGOSLAVIA	Dynamo Zagreb	49	Cerin (Dynamo) 19	2.62	Red Star Belgrade beat Dynamo Zagreb 4–2, 2–2
WALES	(No national league competition)				Swansea City beat Cardiff City 0–0, 2–1

* Play-offs producing 7 games added to 22 in Championship qualifying competition

† Teams level on points at top of table play-off for title: Olympiakos beat Panathinaikos 2–1

1 Four points for away win; three home; two points for away draw, one at home

2 Three points for win

European Survey 1982/83

	Champions Matches	Points	Clubs in Division	Most Wins	Fewest Defeats	Most Goals	Fewest Conceded	Most Drawn	Average gls per game	Top Scorer	Cup Final Result
ALBANIA	Vllaznia 26	34	14	Partizani 13	Vllaznia 4	Vllaznia 39	Partizani 17	Vllaznia, Labinoti, Tomori 10	2.01	Bajaziti (Besa) 16	17 Nendori 1 Flamurtari 0
AUSTRIA	Rapid 30	48	16	Austria Vienna 22	Rapid 2	Austria Vienna 76	Rapid 18	Eisenstadt 13	2.92	Krankl (Rapid) 23	Rapid beat SW Innsbruck 3–0, 5–0
BELGIUM	Standard Liege 34	50	18	Standard 22	Anderlecht 5	Standard 78	Antwerp 30	CS Bruges 15	2.81	Van Den Bergh (Anderlecht) 21	Beveren 3 FC Bruges 1
BULGARIA	CSKA Sofia 30	45	16	CSKA, Levski 18	CSKA 3	Trakia 59	CSKA 20	Tschernomore 9	2.62	Petrivanov (Trakia) 22	CSKA 4 Spartak Varna 0
CYPRUS	Omonia 26	38	14	Omonia 16	Omonia, Anortosi 4	Omonia 52	Omonia 17	Paralimni 13	2.43	Chatzilosu (Aris) 17	Omonia 2 Paralimni 1
CZECHOSLOVAKIA	Bohemians 30	42	16	Bohemians 18	Bohemians, Ostrava 6	Bohemians 69	Inter 24	Inter, Cheb 11	2.87	Herda (Slavia) 15	Dukla Prague 2 Slovan Bratislava 1
DENMARK	Odense 30	41	16	Odense 18	Aarhus 6	Aarhus 61	Odense 28	Kolding 14	2.83	Jacquet (Vejle) 20	B 93 beat B 1903 3–3, 1–0
ENGLAND	Liverpool 42	82	22	Liverpool 24	Liverpool 8	Liverpool 87	Liverpool 37	Sunderland, Birmingham 14	2.73	Blissett (Watford) 27	Manchester Utd beat Brighton 4–0 after 2–2 draw
FINLAND	Kuusysi* 29		12	Kuusysi 16	Haka 5	TPS 64	Kuusysi, KPT 30	Haka 12	3.28	Ismail (HJK) 19	Haka 3 KPV 2
FRANCE	Nantes 38	58	20	Nantes 24	Nantes 4	Nantes 77	Nantes 29	Sochaux 17	2.86	Halilhodzic (Nantes) 27	Paris St Germain 3 Nantes 2
EAST GERMANY	Dynamo Berlin 26	46	14	Dynamo Berlin 20	Dynamo Berlin Nil	Dynamo Berlin 72	Dynamo Berlin 22	Erfurt, Magdeburg 9	3.24	Streich (Magdeburg) 19	Magdeburg 4 Karl-Marx-Stadt 0
WEST GERMANY	Hamburg 34	52	18	Werder Bremen 23	Hamburg 2	Stuttgart 80	Hamburg, Bayern 33	Kaiserslautern 13	3.38	Voller (Bremen) 23	Cologne 1 Fortuna Cologne 0
GREECE	Olympiakos 34	48	18	Olympiakos 20	Olympiakos 4	Larissa, AEK, Ofi, Heraklis 54	Olympiakos 22	Iannina 13	2.40	Anastopoulos (Olympiakos) 29	AEK Athens 2 PAOK 0
HUNGARY	Raba Gyor 30	44	16	Gyor, Ferencvaros 19	Gyor, Honved 5	Gyor 82	Honved 33	Csepel, Tatabanya, Diosgyor 11	3.12	Dobany (Haladas, Pecs) 23	Ujpest Dozsa 3 Honved 2
ICELAND	Vikingur 18	23	10	IBV 9	Vikingur, KR 2	IBI 27	KR 12	KR 11	2.18	Karlsson (Vikingur), Thorleifsson	IB Akranes 2 IB Keflavikur 1

European football — national league and cup results

Country	Champions / placings	Leading scorer (avg)	Cup competition result
N. IRELAND	Linfield 22 ...... 35 ...... 12 ...... Linfield 15 ...... 2 ...... Linfield 13 ...... 17; Portadown, 9; Coleraine 6; (Athlone) 18; (Ards) 18	Campbell (Ards) 18, 3.03	Bohemians 1; Glentoran beat Linfield 2–1 after 1–1 draw
ITALY	Roma 30 ...... 43 ...... 16 ...... Roma 16 ...... Roma 3; Juventus 20; Udinese 24; 52	Platini (Juventus) 18, 2.12	Juventus beat Verona 0–2, 3–0
LIECHTENSTEIN	No national league; teams play in Swiss regional leagues		Not played at press time
LUXEMBOURG	Jeunesse Esch 34 ...... 22 ...... 12 ...... 16; Jeunesse, Aris, Progres; Avenir, Jeunesse, Hamrun 69; Avenir 23	Simon (Jeunesse) 23, 3.25	Avenir Beggen 4; Union 2
MALTA	Hamrun 14 ...... 24 ...... 8 ...... Hamrun 10 ...... Nil; Hibernians, Floriana 7; Hamrun 24; 4	Refalo (Hamrun) 7, 1.96	Hamrun 2; Valletta 0
NETHERLANDS	Ajax 34 ...... 58 ...... 18 ...... Ajax 26 ...... Ajax; PSV Eindhoven 34; Feyenoord 2; Groningen 15	Houtman (Feyenoord) 30, 3.15	Ajax beat NEC Breda 3–1, 3–1
NORWAY	Viking 22 ...... 29 ...... 12 ...... Viking ...... Lillestrom; Hamark 11; Viking 4; Valerengen 21; Rosenborg 9	Granerud (Hamark), Johannesen (Viking) 11, 2.69	Brann 3 Molde 2
POLAND	Lech Poznan 30 ...... 39 ...... 16 ...... Lech 17 ...... Widzew 5; Ruch 22; Cracovia 15	Okonski (Slask) 15, 2.27	Lech Danzig 2; Piast Gliwice 1
PORTUGAL	Benfica 30 ...... 51 ...... 16 ...... Benfica 22 ...... Benfica 16; Porto 73; Guimaraes, Varzim 10; Benfica 13	Gomes (Porto) 36, 2.35	Not played at press time
RUMANIA	Dynamo Bucharest 34 ...... 49 ...... 18 ...... Dynamo 1 ...... Craiova 2; Craiova 66; Dynamo	Grosu (Bihor) 20, 2.58	Craiova 2; Timisoara 1
SCOTLAND	Dundee Utd 36 ...... 56 ...... 10 ...... Celtic ...... Dundee Utd 4; Aberdeen 25, 24; Celtic 90; Hibs 15	Nicholas (Celtic) 29, 2.93	Aberdeen 1; Rangers 0
SPAIN	Athletic Bilbao 34 ...... 50 ...... 18 ...... Bilbao ...... Real Madrid 5; Real Madrid 71; Gijon 15	Rincon (Betis) 20, 2.54	Barcelona 2; Real Madrid 1
SWEDEN	Gothenburg† 22 ...... 29 ...... 12 ...... Hammarby ...... Gothenburg, Malmo 4; Gothenburg, Malmo 11	Corneliusson (Gothenburg) 12, 2.62	Gothenburg 3; Oster 2
SWITZERLAND	Grasshoppers 30 ...... 49 ...... 16 ...... Grasshoppers ...... Servette 4; Servette 86; Sion 11	Brigger (Servette) 23, 3.23	Grasshoppers beat Servette 3–0 after 2–2 draw
TURKEY	Fenerbahce 34 ...... 49 ...... 18 ...... Fenerbahce 3; Galatasaray 50; Trabzonspor 19; Ankaragucu 18	Selcuk (Fenerbahce) 17, 2.07	Fenerbahce 2; Mersin 1
USSR	Dynamo Minsk 34 ...... 47 ...... 18 ...... Dynamo Minsk, Dynamo Minsk, Dynamo Kiev 6; Torpedo Moscow, 25; Dynamo Kiev 63; Dnjepr 12	Jakubik (Pachtakor) 23, 2.54	Dynamo Kiev 1; Torpedo Moscow 0
YUGOSLAVIA	Partizan 34 ...... 45 ...... 18 ...... Partizan 17 ...... Dynamo Zagreb 5; Olimpija 31; Hajdik; Partizan 58; Dynamo Zagreb 15; 18	Halilovic (Vinkovice) 18, 2.69	Dynamo Zagreb 3; Sarajevo 2
WALES	(No national league competition)		Swansea beat Wrexham 2–1, 2–0

* Play-offs producing 7 games added to 22 in championship qualifying competition
† Top finishing eight clubs then played knock-out competition final of which Gothenburg won by beating Hammarby 1–2, 3–1
England, Republic of Ireland 3 pts for win

European Club Directory

(up to and including 1981–82)

Country	Championship wins	Cup wins	European and other honours
ALBANIA	(1945) Dinamo Tirana 15; Partizan Tirana 12; 17 Nendori 6; Vlaznia 4	(1948) Dinamo Tirana 13; Partizan Tirana 9; 17 Nendori 4; Vlaznia 3; Besa 1; Labinoti 1	None
AUSTRIA	(1912) Rapid Vienna 26; Austria Vienna (previously FK Austria and WAC) 16; Admira-Energie-Wacker (previously Sportklub Admira and Admira-Energie) 8; First Vienna 6; Tirol-Svarowski-Innsbruck (previously Wacker-Innsbruck) 5; Wiener Sportklub 3; FAC 1; Hakoah 1; Linz ASK 1; Wacker Vienna 1; WAF 1; Voest Linz 1	(1919) Austria Vienna 21; Rapid Vienna 9; Admira-Energie-Wacker 5; Tirol-Svarowski-Innsbruck 5; First Vienna 3; Linz ASK 1; Wacker Vienna 1; WAF 1; Wiener Sportklub 1; Graz AK 1	European Cup-Winners' Cup (runners-up) Austria/WAC 1978
BELGIUM	(1896) Anderlect 17; Union St Gilloise 11; Beerschot 7; Standard Liege 7; FC Bruges 6; RC Brussels 6; FC Liege 5; Daring Brussels 5; Antwerp 4; Lierse SK 3; Malines 3; CS Bruges 3; RWD Molenbeek 1; Beveren 1	(1954) Anderlecht 5; Standard Liege 4; FC Bruges 3; Beerschot 2; Waterschei 2; Antwerp 1; La Gantoise 1; Lierse SK 1; Tournai 1; Waregem 1; Beveren 1	European Cup (runners-up) FC Bruges 1978. European Cup-Winners' Cup (winners) Anderlecht 1976, 1978; (runners-up) Anderlecht 1977, Standard Liege 1982. European Fairs Cup (runners-up) Anderlecht 1970. UEFA Cup (runners-up) FC Bruges 1976
BULGARIA	(1925) CSKA Sofia (previously CDNA) 22; Levski Spartak (previously Levski Sofia) 13; Slavia Sofia 6; Vladislav Varna 3; Lokomotiv Sofia 3; AS23 Sofia 1; Botev Plovdiv 1; SC Sofia 1; Sokol Varna 1; Spartak Plovdiv 1; Tichka Varna 1; Trakia Plovdiv 1; ZSK Sofia 1	(1946) Levski Spartak 13; CSKA Sofia 10; Slavia Sofia 6; Lokomotiv Sofia 3; Botev Plovdiv 1; Sparktak Plovdiv 1; Sparktak Sofia 1; Marek Stanke 1; Trakia Plovdiv 1	None
CYPRUS	(1935) Apoel 12; Omonia 11; Anorthosis 6; AEL 5; EPA 3; Olympiakos 3; Chetin Kayal 1; Pezoporikos 1; Trast 1	(1935) Apoel 10; EPA 5; Omonia 5; AEL 3; Trast 3; Chetin Kayal 2; Apollon 2; Pezoporikos 2; Anorthosis 2; Paralimni 1; Olympiakos 1	None
CZECHOSLOVAKIA	(1926)* Sparta Prague 13; Slavia Prague 12; Dukla Prague (previously UDA) 11; Slovan Bratislava 6; Spartak Trnava 5; Banik Ostrava 3; Inter-Bratislava 1; Spartak Hradec Kralove 1; Viktoria Zizkov 1; Zbrojovka Brno 1	(1961) Dukla Prague 5; Slovan Bratislava 5; Sparta Prague 4; Spartak Trnava 3; Banik Ostrava 2; Lokomotiv Kosice 2; TJ Gottwaldov 1	European Cup-Winners' Cup (winners) Slovan Bratislava 1969
DENMARK	(1913) KB Copenhagen 15; B93 Copenhagen 9; AB (Akademisk) 9; B 1903 Copenhagen 7; Frem 6; Esbjerg BK 5; AGF Aarhus 4; Vejle BK 4; Hvidovre 3; B 1909 Odense 2; Koge BK 2; Odense BK 1	(1955) Vejle BK 6; AGF Aarhus 5; B 1909 Odense 3; Randers Freja 3; Aalborg BK 2; Frem 2; KB Copenhagen 1; Vanlose 1; B 1903 Copenhagen 1; Hvidovre 1; B 93 Copenhagen 1	None

Country	Championship wins	Cup wins	European and other honours
FINLAND	(1949)* Turun Palloseura 5; Kuopion Palloseura 5; Valkeakosken Haka 4; Helsinki JK 4; Lahden Reipas 3; IF Kamraterna 2; Kotkan TP 2; Oulu Palloseura 2; Turun Pyrkiva 1; IF Kronohagens 1; Helsinki PS 1; Ilves-Kissat 1; Kokkolan PV 1; IF Kamraterna 1; Vasa 1	(1955) Lahden Reipas 7; Valkeakosken Haka 6; Kotkan TP 4; Mikkelin 2; Helsinki JK 2; IFK Abo 1; Drott 1; Helsinki PS 1; Kuopion Palloseura 1; Pallo-Peikot 1; Ilves Tampere 1	None
FRANCE	(1933) Saint Etienne 10; Stade de Reims 6; Nantes 5; OGC Nice 4; Olympique Marseille 4; AS Monaco 4; Lille OSC 3; FC Sete 2; Sochaux 2; Racing Club Paris 1; Roubaix-Tour-coing 1; Girondins Bordeaux 1; Strasbourg 1	(1918) Olympique Marseille 9; Saint Etienne 6; Lille OSC 5; Racing Club Paris 5; Red Star 5; Olympique Lyon 3; AS Monaco 3; CAS Generaux 2; OGC Nice 2; Racing Club Strasbourg 2; Sedan 2; FC Sete 2; Stade de Reims 2; Stade Rennes 2; Nancy-Lorraine 2; AS Cannes 1; Club Francais 1; Excelsior Roubaix 1; Girondins Bordeaux 1; Le Havre 1; SO Montpelier 1; Olympique de Pantin 1; CA Paris 1; Sochaux 1; Toulouse 1; Nantes 1; Bastiali Paris St Germain 1	European Champions' Cup (runners-up) Stade de Reims 1956, 1959; Saint Etienne 1976. UEFA Cup (runners-up) Bastia 1978
EAST GERMANY (GDR)	(1950) ASK Vorwaerts 6; Dynamo Dresden 5; Wismut Karl-Marx-Stadt 4; FC Magdeburg 4; Dynamo Berlin 4; Carl Zeiss Jena (previously Motor Jena) 3; Chemie Leipzig 2; Turbine Erfurt 2; Turbine Halle 1; Zwickau Horch 1; Empor Rostock 1	(1949) Carl Zeiss Jena 5; Dynamo Dresden 4; FC Magdeburg 3; Lokomotiv Leipzig 3; Chemie Leipzig 2; Magdeburg Aufbau 2; Motor Zwickau 2; ASK Vorwaerts 2; Dresden Einheit SC 1; Dresden PV 1; Dynamo Berlin 1; Halle Chemie SC1; North Dessau Waggonworks 1; Thale EHW 1; Union East Berlin 1; Wismut Karl-Marx-Stadt 1; Sachsenring Zwickau 1	European Cup-Winners' Cup (winners) FC Magdeburg 1974; (runners-up) Carl Zeiss Jena 1981
WEST GERMANY	(1903) 1 FC Nuremberg 9; Schalke 7; Bayern Munich 7; Borussia Moenchengladbach 5; SV Hamburg 5; VfB Leipzig 3; SpV Furth 3; Borussia Dortmund 3; IFC Cologne 3; Viktoria Berlin 2; Hertha Berlin 2; Hanover 96 2; Dresden SC 2; VfB Stuttgart 2; 1FC Kaiserslautern 2; Munich 1860 1; SV Werder Bremen 1; Union Berlin 1; FC Freibourg 1; Phoenix Karlsruhe 1; Karlsruher FV 1; Holstein Kiel 1; Fortuna Dusseldorf 1; Rapid Vienna 1; VfR Mannheim 1; Rot-Weiss Essen 1; Eintracht Frankfurt 1; Eintracht Brunswick 1	(1935) Bayern Munich 6; 1FC Nuremberg 3; IFC Cologne 3; Eintracht Frankfurt 3; Dresden SC 2; Fortuna Dusseldorf 2; Karlsruher SC 2; Munich 1860 2; Schalke 2; VfB Stuttgart 2; Borussia Moenchengladbach 2; SV Hamburg 2; Borussia Dortmund 1; First Vienna 1; VfB Leipzig 1; Kickers Offenbach 1; Rapid Vienna 1; Rot-Weiss Essen 1; SW Essen 1; Werder Bremen 1	World Club Championship (winners) Bayern Munich 1976. European Champions' Cup (winners) Bayern Munich 1974, 1975, 1976; (runners-up) Eintracht Frankfurt 1960, Borussia Moenchengladbach 1977, SV Hamburg 1980, Bayern Munich 1982. European Cup-Winners' Cup (winners) Borussia Dortmund 1966, Bayern Munich 1967, SV Hamburg 1977; (runners-up) Munich (1860) 1965, SV Hamburg 1968, Fortuna Dusseldorf 1979. UEFA Cup (winners) Borussia Moenchengladbach 1975, 1979, Eintracht Frankfurt 1980; (runners-up) Borussia Moenchengladbach 1973, 1980, SV Hamburg 1982
GREECE	(1928) Olympiakos 23; Panathinaikos 12; AEK Athens 7; Aris Salonika 3; PAOK Salonika 1	(1932) Olympiakos 18; AEK Athens 8; Panthinaikos 7; PAOK Salonika 2; Aris Salonika 1; Ethnikos 1; Iraklis 1; Panionios 1; Kastoria 1	European Champions' Cup (runners-up) Panathinaikos 1971

Country	Championship wins	Cup wins	European and other honours
HUNGARY	(1901) Ferencvaros (previously FTC) 23; MTK-VM Budapest (previously Hungaria, Bastya, and Voros Lobogo) 18; Ujpest Dozsa 18; Vasas Budapest 6; Honved 6; Csepel 4; BTC 2; Raba Gyor (previously Vasas Gyor) 2; Nagyvarad 1	(1901) Ferencvaros 14; MTK-VM Budapest 9; Ujpest Dozsa 5; Raba (Vasas) Gyor 4; Diosgyor 2; Vasas Budapest 2; Bocksal 1; Honved 1; Ill Ker 1; Kispesti AC 1; Soroksar 1; Szolnoki MAV	European Cup-Winners' Cup (runner-up) MTK Budapest 1964, Ferencvaros 1975. European Fairs Cup (winners) Ferencvaros 1965; (runners-up) Ferencvaros 1968, Ujpest Dozsa 1969
ICELAND	(1912) KR Reykjavik 20; Valur 17; Fram 15; 1A Akranes 10; IBK Keflavik 3; Vikingur 3; IBV Vestmann 2	(1960) KR Reykjavik 7; Valur 4; Fram 4; IBV Vestmann 3; IBA Akureyri 1; Vikingur 1; IBK Keflavik 1; IA Akranes 1	None
IRELAND (Republic)	(1922) Shamrock Rovers 10; Shelbourne 7; Bohemians 7; Waterford 6; Dundalk 6; Cork United 5; Drumcondra 5; St Patrick's Athletic 3; St James's Gate 2; Cork Athletic 2; Sligo Rovers 2; Limerick 2; Dolphin 1; Cork Hibernians 1; Cork Celtic 1; Athlone Town 1	(1922) Shamrock Rovers 21; Dundalk 7; Drumcondra 5; Bohemians 4; Shelbourne 3; Cork Athletic 2; Cork United 2; St James's Gate 2; St Patrick's Athletic 2; Cork Hibernians 2; Limerick 2; Waterford 2; Alton United 1; Athlone Town 1; Cork 1; Fordsons 1; Transport 1; Finn Harps 1; Home Farm 1	None
ITALY	(1898) Juventus 20; Inter-Milan 12; AC Milan 10; Genoa 9; Torino 8; Pro Vercelli 7; Bologna 7; Fiorentina 2; Casale 1; Novese 1; AS Roma 1; Cagliari 1; Lazio 1	(1922) Juventus 6; Torino 4; Fiorentina 4; AC Milan 4; AS Roma 4; Inter-Milan 3; Napoli 2; Bologna 2; Atalanta 1; Genoa 1; Lazio 1; Vado 1; Venezia 1	World Club Championship (winners) Inter-Milan 1964, 1965, AC Milan 1969. European Champions' Cup (winners) AC Milan 1963, 1969, Inter-Milan 1964, 1965; (runners-up) Fiorentina 1957, AC Milan 1958, Inter-Milan 1967, 1972, Juventus 1973. European Cup-Winners' Cup (winners) Fiorentina 1961, AC Milan 1968, 1973; (runners-up) Fiorentina 1962, AC Milan 1974. European Fairs Cup (winners) AS Roma 1961; (runners-up) Juventus 1965, 1971. UEFA Cup (winners) Juventus 1977

LIECHTENSTEIN has no National League. Teams compete in Swiss Regional Leagues.

Country	Championship wins	Cup wins	European and other honours
LUXEMBOURG	(1910) Jeunesse Esch 17; Spora Luxembourg 10; Stade Dudelange 10; Red Boys Differdange 6; US Hollerich-Bonnevoie 5; Fola Esch 5; US Luxembourg 3; Aris Bonnevoie 3; Progres Niedercorn 3; Sporting Luxembourg 2; Avenir Beggen 2; Racing Luxembourg 1; National Schifflge 1	(1922) Red Boys Differdange 15; Spora Luxembourg 8; Jeunesse Esch 8; US Luxembourg 6; Stade Dudelange 4; Progres Niedercorn 4; Fola Esch 3; Alliance Dudelange 2; US Rumelange 2; Aris Bonnevoie 1; US Dudelange 1; Jeunesse Hautcharage 1; National Schifflge 1; Racing Luxembourg 1; SC Tetange 1	None
MALTA	(1910) Floriana 24; Sliema Wanderers 21; Valletta 11; Hibernians 6; Hamrun Spartans 3; St George's 1; KOMR 1	(1935) Sliema Wanderers 16; Floriana 15; Valletta 5; Hibernians 5; Gzira United 1; Melita 1	None

Country	Championship wins	Cup wins	European and other honours
NETHERLANDS	(1898) Ajax Amsterdam 20; Feyenoord 12; HVV The Hague 8; PSV Eindhoven 7; Sparta Rotterdam 6; Go Ahead Deventer 4; HBS The Hague 3; Willem II Tilburg 3; RCH Haarlem 2; RAP 2; Heracles 2; ADO The Hague 2; Quick the Hague 1; BVV Scheidam 1; NAC Breda 1; Eindhoven 1; Enschede 1; Volewijckers Amsterdam 1; Limburgia 1; Rapid JC Haarlem 1; DOS Utrecht 1; DWS Amsterdam 1; Haarlem 1; Be Quick Groningen 1; SVV Scheidam 1; AZ67 Alkmaar 1	(1899) Ajax Amsterdam 8; Feyenoord 5; Quick The Hague 4; PSV Eindhoven 4; HEC 3; Sparta Rotterdam 3; AZ67 Alkmaar 3; DFC 2; Fortuna Geleen 2; Haarlem 2; HBS The Hague 2; RCH 2; VOC 2; Wageningen 2; Willem II Tilburg 2; FC Den Haag 2; Concordia Rotterdam 1; CVV 1; Eindhoven 1; HVV The Hague 1; Longa 1; Quick Njimegen 1; RAP 1; Roermond 1; Schoten 1; Velocitas Breda 1; Velocitas Groningen 1; VSV 1; VUC 1; VVV1; ZFC 1; NAC Breda 1; Twente Enschede 1	World Club Championship (winners) Feyenoord 1970, Ajax 1972. European Champions' Cup (winners) Feyenoord 1970, Ajax 1971, 1972, 1973; (runners-up) Ajax 1969. UEFA Cup (winners) Feyenoord 1974; PSV Eindhoven 1978; (runners-up) Twente Enschede 1975; AZ67 Alkmaar 1981
NORWAY	(1938) Fredrikstad 9; Viking Stavanger 6; Lillestrom 3; Rosenborg Trondheim 3; Larvik Turn 3; Brann Bergen 2; Lyn Oslo 2; Valerengen 2; IK Start 2; Friedig 1; Fram 1; Skeid Oslo 1; Stromsgodset Drammen 1	(1902) Odds BK Skein 11; Fredrikstad 9; Lyn Oslo 8; Skeid Oslo 8; Sarpsborgs Fk 6; Orn Fk Horten 4; Brann Bergen 4; Mjondalens IF 3; Rosenborgs BK Trondheim 3; Stromsgodset Drammen 3; Viking Stavanger 3; Lillestrom 3; Mercantile 2; Grane Nordstrand 1; Kvik Haldn 1; Sparta 1; Gjovik 1; Bodo-Glimt 1; Valerengen 1	None
POLAND	(1921) Ruch Chorzow 12; Gornik Zabrze 10; Wisla Krakow 6; Cracovia 5; Pogon Lwow 4; Legia Warsaw 4; Warta Poznan 2; Polonia Bytom 2; Stal Mielec 2; Widzew Lodz 2; Garbarnia Krakow 1; Polonia Warsaw 1; LKS Lodz 1; Slask Wroclaw 1; Szombierki Bytom 1	(1951) Legia Warsaw 7; Gornik Zabrze 6; Zaglebie Sosnowiec 2; Ruch Chorzow 2; Gwardia Warsaw 1; LKS Lodz 1; Polonia Warsaw 1; Wisla Krakow 1; Stal Rzeszow 1; Slask Wroclaw 1; Arka Gydnia1; Lech Poznan 1	European Cup-Winners' Cup (runners-up) Gornik Zabrze 1970
PORTUGAL	(1935)* Benfica 24; Sporting Lisbon 16; FC Porto 7; Belenenses 1	(1939) Benfica 17; Sporting Lisbon 10; FC Porto 4; Boavista 3; Belenenses 2; Vitoria Setubal 2; Academica Coimbra 1; Leixoes Porto 1; Sporting Braga 1	European Champions' Cup (winners) Benfica 1961, 1962; (runners-up) Benfica 1963, 1965, 1968. European Cup-Winners' Cup (winners) Sporting Lisbon 1964
RUMANIA	(1910) Dynamo Bucharest 10; Steaua Bucharest (previously CCA) 9; Venus Bucharest 7; CSC Temesvar 6; UT Arad 6; Rapid Bucharest 4; Ripensia Temesvar 3; Petrolul Ploesti 3; Uni Craiova 3; Olimpia Bucharest 2; CAC Bucharest 2; Arges 2; Soc RA Bucharest 1; Prahova Ploesti 1; CSC Brasov 1; Juventus Bucharest 1; SSUD Resita 1; Craiova Bucharest 1; Progresul 1; Ploesti United 1	(1934) Steaua Bucharest 13; Rapid Bucharest 7; Dynamo Bucharest 4; Uni Craiova 3; UT Arad 2; CFR Bucharest 2; Progresul 2; RIP Timisoara 2; ICO Oradeo 1; Metal Ochimia Resita 1; Petrolul Ploesti 1; Stinta Cluj 1; Stinta Timisoara 1; Turnu Severin 1; Chimia Ramnicu 1; Jiul Petroseni 1; Poli-Timisoara 1	None
SPAIN	(1929) Real Madrid 20; Barcelona 9; Atletico Madrid 8; Athletic Bilbao 6; Valencia 4; Real Sociedad 2; Betis 1; Seville 1	(1902) Athletic Bilbao 22; Barcelona 19; Real Madrid 15; Atletico Madrid 5; Valencia 5; Real Union de Irun 3; Seville 3; Espanol 2; Real Zaragoza 2; Arenas 1; Ciclista Sebastian 1; Racing de Irun 1; Vizcaya Bilbao 1; Real Betis 1	European Champions' Cup (winners) Real Madrid 1956, 1957, 1958, 1959, 1960, 1966; (runners-up) Real Madrid 1962, 1964, 1981, Barcelona 1961, Atletico Madrid 1974. World Club Championship (winners) Real Madrid 1960, Atletico Madrid 1974.

SPAIN continued

European Cup-Winners' Cup (winners) Atletico Madrid 1962, Barcelona 1979, 1982, Valencia 1980; (runners-up) Atletico Madrid 1963, Barcelona 1969, Real Madrid 1971. European Fairs Cup (winners) Barcelona 1958, 1960, 1966; Valencia 1962, 1963, Zaragoza 1964; (runners-up) Barcelona 1962, Valencia 1964, Zaragoza 1966. UEFA Cup (runners-up) Athletic Bilbao 1977

SWEDEN	(1896)	(1941)	European Champions'
	Oergryte IS Gothenburg 13; Malmo FF 12; IFK Norrkoping 11; Djurgaarden 8; AIK Stockholm 8; IFK Gothenburg 7; GAIS Gothenburg 6; IF Halsingborg 5; Boras IF Elfsborg 4; Oster Vaxjo 4; Atvidaberg 2; Halmstad 2; IFK Ekilstund 1; IF Gavie Brynas 1; IF Gothenburg 1; Fassbergs 1; Norrkoping IK Slepner 1	Malmo FF 11; IFK Norrkoping 3; AIK Stockholm 3; Atvidaberg 2; IFK Gothenburg 2; GAIS Gothenburg 1; IFK Halsingborg 1; Raa 1; Landskrona 1; Oster Vaxjo 1	Cup (runners-up) Malmo FF 1979

SWITZERLAND	(1898)	(1926)	None
	Grasshoppers 18; Servette 14; Young Boys Berne 10; FC Zurich 9; FC Basle 8; Lausanne 7; La Chaux-de-Fonds 3; FC Lugano 3; Winterthur 3; FC Aarau 2; FC Anglo-Americans 1; St Gallen 1; FC Bruhl 1; Cantonal-Neuchatel 1; Biel 1; Bellinzona 1; FC Etoile la Chaux de Fonds 1	Grasshoppers 13; Lausanne 7; La Chaux-de-Fonds 6; FC Basle 5; FC Zurich 5; Young Boys Berne 5; Servette 5; FC Sion 4; FC Lugano 2; FC Granges 1; Lucerne 1; St Gallen 1; Urania Geneva 1; Young Fellows Zurich 1	

TURKEY	(1960)	(1963)	None
	Fenerbahce 8; Galatasaray 5; Trabzonspor 5; Besiktas 4	Galatasaray 7; Fenerbahce 3; Goztepe Izmir 2; Trabzonspor 2; Altay Izmir 2; Ankaragucu 2; Eskisehirspor 1; Besiktas 1	

USSR	(1936)	(1936)	European Cup-Winners'
	Dynamo Moscow 11; Spartak Moscow 10; Dynamo Kiev 10; CSKA Moscow 6; Torpedo Moscow 3; Dynamo Tbilisi 2; Saria Voroshilovgrad 1; Ararat Erevan 1	Spartak Moscow 9; Torpedo Moscow 5; Dynamo Moscow 5; Dynamo Kiev 5; CSKA Moscow 4; Donets Shaktyor 3; Lokomotiv Moscow 2; Ararat Erevan 2; Dynamo Tbilisi 2; Karpaty Lvov 1; Zenit Leningrad 1; Ska Rostov 1	Cup (winners) Dynamo Kiev 1975, Dynamo Tbilisi 1981; (runners-up) Dynamo Moscow 1972

YUGOSLAVIA	(1923)	(1947)	European Champions'
	Red Star Belgrade 14; Hajduk Split 9; Partizan Belgrade 8; Gradjanski Zagreb 5; BSK Belgrade 5; Dynamo Zagreb 4; Jugoslovija Belgrade 2; Concordia Zagreb 2; HASK Zagreb 1; Vojvodina Novi Sad 1; FC Sarajevo 1; Zeljeznicar 1	Red Star Belgrade 10; Dynamo Zagreb 7; Hajduk Split 6; Partizan 4; BSK Belgrade 2; OFK Belgrade 2; Rijeka 2; Vardar Skopije 1; Velez Mostar 1	Cup (runners-up) Partizan Belgrade 1966. European Fairs Cup (winners) Dynamo Zagreb 1967; (runners-up) Dynamo Zagreb 1963. UEFA Cup (runners-up) Red Star Belgrade 1979

* Championships began earlier in these countries

WORLD SOCCER

Around The World Stories

Albania's coach of their 1982–84 European Championship squad was Shyqyri Rreli, trainer for the Dinamo Tirana club and a former volley-ball player.

Artificial footsteps
Of Algeria's eight largest grounds apart from the national stadium (capacity 80 000), six had Astroturf surfaces according to FIFA's 1982 survey.

All goalkeepers are mad
Argentine goalkeeper Hugo Gatti, known as 'El Loco' because of an unorthodox approach to his duties on the field, was the longest-serving player in Division One football in the country during 1981. Recalled by Boca Juniors after an absence of 27 matches he almost conceded an early goal after one of his injudicious sorties. He had to be rescued by a defender clearing off the line in his come-back game against Estudiantes.

But after 37 minutes he moved to the edge of his penalty area, beat one opponent with the ball before moving upfield to the rooted amazement of other Estudiantes players. Deep in his opponents half he passed to an unmarked colleague who scored the only goal of the game.

Gatti had made his Division One debut for Atlanta on 8 August 1962.

Upside down under
In September 1981 Australian clubs in the Philips League voted to switch from winter to summer in an attempt to attract larger crowds.

Worth the wait
The first Bulgarian to play in Austrian football was Petko Petkov who joined Austria Memphis Vienna from Beroe Stara Zagora in 1981.

The Austrians had been trying to sign him on for eight years ever since he scored seven out of the ten goals by which Beroe defeated them in in the first round of the 1972–73 UEFA Cup (first leg 7–0, second leg 3–1).

Repair Man
In 1982 the Belgian club Lierse axed their coach Hans Croon and replaced him temporarily with their youth team manager Gust Baeten. It was not the first time Baeten had taken on a caretaker role with the club. It happened originally in 1971 when he took over from Frans De Munck, again after Robert Willems in 1974 and once more from Staf Vandenbergh in 1977.

Bully for Bolivar
Bolivar the Bolivian club, was named after Simon Bolivar, soldier, statesman and leader of the revolutions which resulted in the independence from Spain of six South American countries in the 19th century. They won the 1982 championship delayed because of strikes which paralysed the country for a time.

No, No, No, Nino!
In October 1982 defender Jorge Nino scored three of Atletico Mineiro's goals in a 5–1 win over Democrata, eliminating the latter team from the Minas Gerais State championship. Un-

fortunately, Nino was a member of the Democrata club and his hat-trick came from a trio of own goals.

Military Muscle
CSKA Sofia, the Bulgarian Army club and the most successful championship team in post-war Europe having reached 22 titles with their 1981–82 success, caters for 28 different sports and achieved five gold medals at the 1980 Moscow Olympics.

All done in threes
The Cameroon who succeeded in competing in the World Cup finals for the first time in 1982 and remained unbeaten, despite being eliminated in the opening phase, had three different coaches in four months before the tournament in Spain.

Yugoslav Branko Zutic who was in charge during their successful qualifying attempts, had a disagreement with Cameroon officials over playing in the African Cup and was replaced by the West German Rudi Gutendorf who had been in charge of Australia at the time of their qualification for the 1974 World Cup.

But the Cameroon played without distinction in the African Cup, drawing all three games and scoring just one goal. Gutendorf was axed after a few weeks and the man who led them in Spain was Jean Vincent, a former French international forward who had played with credit in the 1958 World Cup when France finished third.

In 1982 Cameroon drew all three matches in the World Cup finals including 1–1 against Italy, the eventual winners.

Digging for victory
The Chilean club Cobreloa were formed in 1976. Their name is derived from *cobre* (Spanish for copper) and the river Loa. In 1977 they were promoted as runners-up in the Second Division. The team is organised by the Chiquimata Copper Mine and financed by deductions from the miners' pay packets. They have since won the Chilean championship twice and reached the final of the South American Cup on two occasions as well.

Away day specials
Bohemians, the Prague club who had never won either the League or Cup in Czechoslovakia, reached the semi-final of the UEFA Cup in 1982–83, the first club side from the country to go as far in the competition.

Clinical success
Coach to the 1982 Colombia champions America was Gabriel Ochoa Uribe a Doctor by profession. He had been in charge when America won the title previously in 1979. In 1982 America played 62 championship matches winning 33, drawing 18 and losing eleven. Their goal difference was 96–51.

Scent of success
In 1981–82 Omonia Nicosia completed 1270 minutes (14 games, ten minutes) without conceding a goal between 30 October and 13 February, in winning the championship of Cyprus.

East goes west
The People's Republic of China undertook their first tour of Europe in 1982, opening their fixtures with a match at Hereford on 9 August which they won 2–1 against United.

Pulling power
On 31 March 1983 Allan Simonsen played his first domestic game in Denmark for eleven years. Playing for his former club Vejle after spells in West Germany with Borussia Moenchengladbach, Spain with Barcelona and Charlton Athletic in England, he attracted a crowd of 6000 away to Koege, ten times that club's average attendance. But when Simonsen had to go off in the second half with an ankle injury, the crowd also started to leave the ground.

Safety in numbers
Ecuador had five different coaches before their opening match in the 1982 World Cup qualifying competition. Local coach Hector Morales was the first to quit and was followed by the resignation of Argentine Miguel Ignominielo. The Brazilian Otto Vieira took over but complained of fixture congestion and Ecuadorian Juan Araujo the national youth coach replaced him. Three weeks before the opening game Eduardo Hohberg, an Argentine-born former Uruguayan international forward, assumed control.

At sixes and sevens
On 15 August 1981 Fijian goalkeeper Akuila Nataro Rovono conceded seven first half goals to New Zealand in a World Cup qualifying match. He was replaced during the interval by Semi Bai who let in six. Two days earlier Fiji had lost 10–0 to Australia.

Buying British
In 1981 there were nineteen foreigners in

Finland's Division One and Two clubs: 16 from Britain, two from Poland and one Hungarian.

Uniform regulations
In the 1981–82 season all Division One clubs in East Germany had adapted a 1–3–3–3 system with two wingers to help national team selection.

Bumper Bavarians
Bayern Munich have provided more international players to the West German team than any other club in the country. Up to the beginning of the 1982–83 season they had had 37 different players capped for a total of 649 international appearances.

Not all Greek
In 1982 a two-year wrangle over the nationality of Panathinaikos forward Juan Ramon Rocha who was playing in Greece under the name of Boublis was resolved when the Interior Ministry's Nationality Council ruled that he was an Argentine. Panathinaikos then had to loan out one of their two other foreign players to another club to remain within their quota.

No watching brief
On 26 September 1981 angry supporters threw missiles and lit bonfires on the terraces when Charlie George failed for the second time to make his debut for Bulova in the Hong Kong League. A back injury had prevented his original baptism after a £90 000 move from England. Bulova beat Caroline Hill 4–2 but George did not watch the game.

Century set-back
Hungary's 100th goal in World Cup qualifying and final tournament games came in their 3–1 home defeat in Budapest against England on 6 June 1981.

Cold comfort
The Icelandic Football Association were hard hit by direct coverage on television of the 1982 World Cup during their own mid-season. It resulted in a 40% fall in attendances at League matches. Subsequent European Championship games against Holland and East Germany were watched respectively by crowds of only 2800 and 2200.

Indian summit
The first major football tournament played in India culminated in the Nehru Cup Final played in Calcutta on 4 March 1982 and won by Uruguay who beat China 2–0.

Over a million spectators watched the 16-day tournament in which Uruguay sent a professional team, Italy and Yugoslavia their amateurs and South Korea, China and India full national sides.

House power
The national team players who helped Iraq to beat São Paulo (Brazil) in the Merdeka Festival Tournament in September 1981 each received a car and a house from President Saddam Hussain.

Finger-lickin' incentives
In 1981–82 the League of Ireland introduced a new points system awarding four for an away win, three at home, two for an away draw and one at home. The League was sponsored by Kentucky Fried Chicken.

Treble-shooter
Benny Tabak scored a hat-trick in 30 minutes for Israel against Portugal in a World Cup qualifying match on 28 October 1981. His goals came in the sixth, 18th and 30th minutes. Israel won 4–1, though both sides missed penalties.

Lire lure
In the 1982–83 season there were 29 foreigners playing in the Italian Division One. Argentina and Brazil provided four each, Holland three, Austria, Denmark, Poland, Peru and Uruguay two each while the others came from the Ivory Coast, Rumania, Belgium, West Germany, France, the Republic of Ireland, England and Yugoslavia.

Eighteen of the players had appeared in the 1982 World Cup finals.

Boots of gold
When Kuwait qualified for the 1982 World Cup finals in Spain, Crown Prince Sheik Saad Abdullah Al Sabah showered gifts on the players. The 24-man squad each received a Cadillac car, luxury villa, plot of land, gold watch and a speedboat.

Long way to debut
Liechtenstein's first international fixture against another national side was played in Seoul, South Korea, against Malta in June 1981 and ended in a 1–1 draw.

One over the eight
When Luxembourg were beaten 9–0 by England at Wembley on 15 December 1982, it was the heaviest defeat suffered by a team in the

history of the European Championship.

One team's loss . . .
North Korea were suspended from international competition for two years following an incident in the Asian Games match against Kuwait in New Delhi on 30 November 1982.

A controversial penalty decision enabled Kuwait to beat them 3–2 after extra time but North Korean players and reserves attacked Thai referee Vijit who was knocked to the ground, then kicked and punched until rescued by police.

. . . another's fortune
In December 1982 South Korea replaced North Korea in the Asian Youth Championship in Bangkok and eventually won the tournament by beating China 2–0 with goals from Kim Pan Ken.

Away day experiences
A ban imposed on Malta by UEFA, following crowd disturbances during a World Cup qualifying match against Poland, forced them to play their first two home games in the European Championship 1982–84 on neutral territory. They went to Messina, Italy to beat Iceland 2–1, only their second success in the tournament and then lost 6–0 to Holland in Aachen, West Germany.

Spectator sees more
Universidad de Nuevo Leon won the 1981–82 Mexican Division One title, beating Atlante 3–1 on penalty kicks after the two-legged play-off had finished all square. But the club's Uruguayan coach Carlos Miloc had to watch the final stages in the dressing room on television as he had been sent off from the touchline for protesting to the referee.

Putting them on the spot
During the 1982–83 Dutch Division One campaign Johan Cruyff took a penalty kick for Ajax against Helmond Sport. Instead of attempting a shot he tapped the ball to Jesper Olsen who in turn pushed it forward for Cruyff to score. Ajax, already a goal ahead, won 5–0.

Keep it in the family
In 1982 the Paraguayan club Olimpia again appointed Uruguayan coach Luis Cubillas as team manager. He brought with him his two sons who had been playing in Uruguay.

In 1979 he had been in charge of Olimpia when they won the South American Cup and then both the World Cup Championship and Inter-American Cup. When he then left to take up an appointment with Argentina's Newell's Old Boys, Olimpia gave his brother Pedro the position.

Few goals or fans
When Atletico Chalaco entertained Leon de Huanuco in a Division One match in Peru during 1981 there were only 58 paying spectators. At the time Chalaco had played ten games with a goal difference of just seven goals for and four against.

Long lasting Lato
Polish winger Grzegorz Lato became the most capped international in his country during the 1982 World Cup finals in Spain when he completed his 103rd appearance. Lato who began his career with Stal Mielec had joined Lokeren in Belgium before the World Cup and afterwards moved to Mexico to play for Atlante.

Not sporting at all
Benfica the Portuguese team established a club record when they completed 28 matches undefeated from the start of the 1982–83 season. Their run included League games, cup matches and friendlies and ended with a 1–0 defeat in the League championship against Sporting Lisbon who beat them with a penalty kick.

Seven-year stretch
Rumanian footballer Florea Dumitrache was banned from all UEFA matches for seven years until 31 December 1989 for assaulting the referee and a linesman in the UEFA Cup game for Corvinul Hunedoara against Sarajevo.

Barcelona the best
Barcelona's average League attendance during the 1981–82 season was 102 039, an increase of 14 981 on average over the previous term. They finished runners-up in the Spanish championship.

A change for the Swedes
In 1982 the Swedish championship was changed with a reduced Division One of 12 clubs competing in it. The first eight teams to finish were involved in play-offs while the last four finishing took part in test matches for relegation and promotion with the top four from Division Two.

Max the life
The Swiss club Neuchâtel Xamax derives its second name from Max, one of three famous

Abbeglen brothers whose name is used both ways in the club's title.

Chickened out

When Turkey beat Albania 1–0 in a European Championship match in October 1982, it was their first win for three years and only the second goal they had scored in that time. The previous effort had been from a penalty kick.

Morena Milestone

When Uruguayan club Penarol brought back centre-forward Fernando Morena from Spain in 1982 he achieved his 603rd goal in competitive football in a 1–0 win over local rivals, Nacional.

Third World War?

On 8 January 1983 the United States defeated the Soviet Union 'B' beam 2–1 in the third International Granatkin Junior Soccer tournament in Leningrad. Lane Kenworfie and Jorge Jelnovac scored for the USA, Sergei Savchenko for the USSR. But the Americans finished bottom of the tournament.

Dynamic scorer

Oleg Blokhin of Dynamo Kiev became the highest scoring player in the history of League football in the USSR when he scored in a 2–0 win over Moscow Spartak in 1981 to record his 153rd goal.

Better late . . .

Venezuela recorded the first World Cup win in their history when they beat Bolivia 1–0 at Caracas on 15 March 1981 with a goal from Pedro Acosta after 24 minutes.

Ban the bribes

Eight referees, and two officials were given suspended prison sentences in Yugoslavia during April 1983 for their part in a slush fund involving Yugoslavia Division Two club Maribor. Bojan Ban, he former club secretary, received the stiffest penalty, a two-year sentence for handing out bribes totalling approximately £7300 to 13 referees between 1979 and 1981.

Odd calls it quits

Norwegian international centre-forward Odd Iversen retired in 1982 at the age of 37, having scored 307 goals including 158 in 244 Division One matches for Rosenborg Trondheim.

Kiwis on trial

During the 1981–82 season the Football Combi-
nation had two New Zealand World Cup players appearing in it. Wynton Rufer along with his brother Shane made their debuts for Norwich City Reserves against Reading Reserves on 26 September 1981. Wynton Rufer scored twice in a 7–0 win.

Later in the season, defender Ricky Herbert had a two-month trial with Southampton playing in five reserve games and a first team friendly against Gothenburg.

Wynton Rufer (below) and his brother Shane who played for Norwich City Reserves in 1981–82, joined FC Zurich in 1982–83. *Eastern Counties Newspapers*

World Club Championship

On 12 December 1982 Penarol (Uruguay) won the World Club Championship beating Aston Villa 2–0 in Tokyo. It was the third time the match had been staged in Japan and was sponsored again by Toyota. It also meant a trio of disappointments for English clubs. In 1980 Nacional (Uruguay) had beaten Nottingham Forest 1–0 while in 1981 Flamengo (Brazil) defeated Liverpool 3–0. All three finals were watched by capacity crowds of 62 000.

Year
1960 Real Madrid (Spain) beat Penarol (Uruguay) 0–0, 5–1
1961 Penarol (Uruguay) beat Benfica (Portugal) 0–1, 5–0, 2–1
1962 Santos (Brazil) beat Benfica (Portugal) 3–2, 5–2
1963 Santos (Brazil) beat AC Milan (Italy) 2–4, 4–2, 1–0
1964 Inter-Milan (Italy) beat Independiente (Argentina) 0–1, 2–0, 1–0
1965 Inter-Milan (Italy) beat Independiente (Argentina) 3–0, 0–0
1966 Penarol (Uruguay) beat Real Madrid (Spain) 2–0, 2–0
1967 Racing Club (Argentina) beat Celtic (Scotland) 0–1, 2–1, 1–0
1968 Estudiantes (Argentina) beat Manchester United (England) 1–0, 1–1
1969 AC Milan (Italy) beat Estudiantes (Argentina) 3–0, 1–2
1970 Feyenoord (Holland) beat Estudiantes (Argentina) 2–2, 1–0
1971 Nacional (Uruguay) beat Panathinaikos (Greece) 1–1, 2–1
1972 Ajax (Holland) beat Independiente (Argentina) 1–1, 3–0
1973 Independiente (Argentina) beat Juventus (Italy) 1–0
1974 Atletico Madrid (Spain) beat Independiente (Argentina) 0–1, 2–0
1975 Independiente (Argentina) and Bayern Munich (West Germany) could not agree on dates; the matches were not played.
1976 Bayern Munich (West Germany) beat Cruzeiro (Brazil) 2–0, 0–0

1977 Boca Juniors (Argentina) beat Borussia Moenchengladbach (West Germany) 2–2, 3–0
1978 Not contested
1979 Olimpia (Paraguay) beat Malmo (Sweden) 1–0, 2–1
1980 Nacional (Uruguay) beat Nottingham Forest (England) 1–0
1981 Flamengo (Brazil) beat Liverpool (England) 3–0
1982 Penarol (Uruguay) beat Aston Villa (England) 2–0

Summary of leading winners: **Penarol 3 wins, Independiente 2, Inter-Milan 2, Santos 2.**

Super Cup

Aston Villa won the 1982 Super Cup beating Barcelona (Spain) 3–1 on aggregate. Barcelona won the first leg on 19 January 1983 but Villa beat Barcelona 3–0 after extra time in the return game at Villa Park on 26 January.

Year
1973 Ajax (Holland) beat Rangers (Scotland) 3–1, 3–2
1974 Ajax (Holland) beat AC Milan (Italy) 0–1, 6–0
1975 Dynamo Kiev (USSR) beat Bayern Munich (West Germany) 1–0, 2–0
1976 Anderlecht (Belgium) beat Bayern Munich (West Germany) 4–1, 1–2
1977 Liverpool (England) beat Hamburg SV (West Germany) 1–1, 6–0
1978 Anderlecht (Belgium) beat Liverpool (England) 3–1, 1–2
1979 Nottingham Forest (England) beat Barcelona (Spain) 1–0, 1–1
1980 Valencia (Spain) beat Nottingham Forest (England) 1–2, 1–0 (on away goals rule)
1981 not contested
1982 Aston Villa (England) beat Barcelona (Spain) 0–1, 3–0

Summary of leading winners: **Ajax 2, Anderlecht 2.**

Penarol's Brazilian forward Jair puts them ahead in the World Club Championship against Aston Villa in December 1982. Jair won a Toyota car after the match—but his colleagues, who had apparently agreed to share any prizes, were none too happy about him keeping it alone. *Sports Projects*

Above: Bryan Robson who had put England ahead against France in the opening World Cup game of their group after only 27 seconds, a record in the competition, heads his second goal. Left: Paul Mariner seeks diplomatic immunity among seven Spanish defenders but the outcome is failure to reach the final stages.
ASP

L'HOME DEL PARTIT ES :
EL HOMBRE DEL PARTIDO ES
L'HOMME DU MATCH EST :
PAOLO ROSSI
(ITALIA)

Above: Referee Coelho (Brazil), accompanied by his linesmen Klein and Christov in the World Cup Final. Left and inset: The crowd salutes Paolo Rossi, the Italian hero of the World Cup winners, suitably described by the electronic scoreboard as the Man of the Match. *ASP*

Right: Among the crowd for the final the former Mr Tennis himself, Bjorn Borg. *Tommy Hindley*

Below: Blue-shirted Italian defender Claudio Gentile bowls over West German winger Pierre Littbarski in the World Cup Final. *ASP*

Bryan Robson further enhanced his reputation in the 1982 World Cup Finals in Spain as one of the most consistent players produced in recent years. *ASP*

Billy Bingham was Northern Ireland's popular team manager in Spain and deservedly considered to be the best of the home-grown coaches out there. *ASP*

Above: Diego Maradona, the Argentine midfield player, went into the World Cup in 1982 with a high reputation but had a difficult tournament. Top, right: Brazil's captain Socrates and (above, right:) Michel Platini the French midfield player. *ASP*

Left: Arsenal supporters contrast with a splash of colour while flying the flag on the Continent. *All Sport*

Above: The weather in Moscow requires the almost universal use of umbrellas for the Olympic clash in 1980 between the USSR and Zambia. *All Sport*

Managers so rarely seem to be looking at anything in the same way that the direction this quartet is taking seems to be a refreshing change. Left: Lawrie McMenemy (Southampton), Bobby Robson (then Ipswich Town). Below: West Germany's Jupp Derwall and John Toshack (Swansea City). *All Sport*

World Soccer Competitions

Inter-American Cup

1969	Estudiantes de la Plata (Argentina)
1972	Nacional (Uruguay)
1973	Independiente (Argentina)
1974	Independiente (Argentina)
1976	Independiente (Argentina)
1978	America (Mexico)
1979	FAS (El Salvador)
1980	Olimpia (Paraguay)
1981	UNAM (Mexico)

Concacaf Champions Cup

1967	Alianza (El Salvador)
1968	Toluca (Mexico)
1969	Cruz Azul (Mexico)
1970	Zone winners: Cruz Azul (Mexico), in North; Saprissa (Costa Rica) in Centre; Transvaal (Surinam) in Caribbean.
1971	Cruz Azul (Mexico)
1972	Olimpia (Honduras)
1973	Transvaal (Surinam)
1974–75	Municipal (Guatemala)
1975–76	Atletico Espanol (Mexico)
1976–77	America (Mexico)
1977–78	FAS (El Salvador)
1978–79	FAS (El Salvador)
1979–80	UNAM (Mexico)
1980–81	UNAM (Mexico)
1981–82	UNAM (Mexico)

African Cup

1957	Egypt	1972	Congo
1959	Egypt	1974	Zaire
1961	Ethiopia	1976	Morocco
1963	Ghana	1978	Ghana
1965	Ghana	1980	Nigeria
1968	Zaire	1982	Ghana
1970	Sudan		

World Youth Cup

1977	USSR (in Tunisia)
1979	Argentina (in Japan)
1981	West Germany (in Australia)
1983	Brazil (in Mexico)

European Under-21 Championship

1970–72	Czechoslovakia*		
1972–74	Hungary*	1978–80	USSR
1974–76	USSR*	1980–82	England
1976–78	Yugoslavia	*Under-23 championship	

South American Cup (Copa Libertadores)

1960	Penarol (Uruguay)
1961	Penarol
1962	Santos (Brazil)
1963	Santos
1964	Independiente (Argentina)
1965	Independiante
1966	Penarol
1967	Racing (Argentina)
1968	Estudiantes de la Plata (Argentina)
1969	Estudiantes de la Plata
1970	Estudiantes de la Plata
1971	Nacional (Uruguay)
1972	Independiente
1973	Independiente
1974	Independiente
1975	Independiente
1976	Cruzeiro (Brazil)
1977	Boca Juniors (Argentina)
1978	Boca Juniors
1979	Olimpia (Paraguay)
1980	Nacional
1981	Flamengo (Brazil)
1982	Penarol

Balkan Club Cup

1968	Beroe Stara Zagora (Bulgaria)
1969	Beroe Stara Zagora
1972	Trakia Plovdiv (Bulgaria)
1973	Lokomotiv Sofia (Bulgaria)
1974	Akademik Sofia (Bulgaria)
1982	Beroe Stara Zagora

East and Central African Club Championships

1974	Simba (Tanzania)
1975	Young Africans (Tanzania)
1976	Luo Union (Kenya)
1977	Luo Union
1978	Kampala CC (Uganda)
1979	Leopards (Kenya)
1980	Gor (Kenya)
1981	Gor
1982	Leopards
1983	Leopards

South America

SOUTH AMERICAN DIRECTORY
up to and including 1982

Championship wins
Argentina (1893–)
Boca Juniors 18; River Plate 17; Racing Club 15; Alumni 9; Independiente 9; San Lorenzo 8; Huracan 5; Lomas 5; Belgrano 3; Estudiantes de la Plata 3; Porteno 2; Estudiantil Porteno 2; Quilmes 2; Dock Sud 1; Chacarita Juniors 1; Lomas Academicals 1; English High School 1; Gimnasia y Esgrima la Plata 1; Sportivo Barracas 1; Newell's Old Boys 1.

(National League 1967–)
Boca Juniors 3; Independiente 3; River Plate 3; Rosario Central 3; San Lorenzo 2; Velez Sarsfield 1; Oeste 1.

Bolivia (1914–)
The Strongest 19; Bolivar 11; Jorge Wilsterman 7; Deportivo Municipal 4; Litoral 3; Universitario 3; Always Ready 2; Chaco Petrolero 2; Oriente Petrolero 2; Colegio Militar 1; Nimbles Sport 1; Deportivo Militar 1; Nimbles Rail 1; Ayacucho 1; Ferroviario 1; Guabira 1.

Brazil
(Rio League 1906–)
Fluminense 22; Flamengo 22; Vasco da Gama 15; Botafogo 12; America 7; Bangu 2; San Christavao 1; Paysandu 1.

(Sao Paulo League 1902–)
Corinthians 19; SE Palmeiras (formerly Palestra Italia) 18; Santos 13; Sao Paulo 13; Paulistano 12; SP Athletic 4; AA des Palmeiras 3; Portuguesa 3; Sao Bento 2; Germania 2; Americano 2; Internacional 1.

(National Championship 1971–)
Internacional Porto Alegre 3; Flamengo 2; Palmeiras 2; Atletico Mineiro 1; Vasco da Gama 1; Sao Paulo 1; Guarani 1; Gremio Porto Alegre 1.

Chile (1933–)
Colo Colo 13; Universidad de Chile 7; Union Espanola 5; Magallanes 4; Audax Italiano 4; Universidad Catolica 4; Everton 3; Wanderers (Valpariso) 2; Palestino 2; Cobreloa 2; Santiago Morning 1; Green Cross 1; Hauchipato 1; Union San Felipe 1.

Colombia (1948–)
Millionarios 11; Independiente Santa Fe 6; Deportivo Cali 5; Independiente Medellin 2; Nacional Medellin 2; Atletico Nacional 2; America 2; Deportes Caldas 1; Atletico Quindio 1; Union Magdalena 1; Junior Barranquilla 1; Atletico Junior 1.

Ecuador (1957–)
Nacional 6; Barcelona 6; Emelec 5; Liga Deportiva Universitaria 3; Everest 2; Deportivo Quito 2.

Paraguay (1906–)★
Olimpia 29; Cerro Porteno 19; Libertad 8; Guarani 7; Nacional 6; Sporting Luqueno 2; Presidente Hayes 1.

Peru (1928–)
Alianza 16; Universitario 15; Sporting Cristal 7; Sport Boys 5; Deportivo Municipal 4; Atletico Chalaco 2; Mariscal Sucre 2; Union Huaral 1; Defensor Lima 1; Melgar 1.

Uruguay (1900–)
Penarol 37; Nacional 33; River Plate 4; Montevideo Wanderers 3; Defensor 1; Rampla Juniors 1

Venezuela (1956–)
Deportivo Italia 5; Portuguesa 5; Deportivo Portugues 3; Deportivo Galicia 3; Valencia 2; Deportivo Tachira 2; Lasalle 1; Tiquire Aragua 1; Celta Deportivo 1; Lara 1; Union Deportiva Canarias 1; Estudiantes 1; San Cristobal 1.

★Leagues began earlier in these countries

ARGENTINA

Argentina celebrated 50 years of professional soccer in 1981. The most successful club during this period were River Plate with 16 First Division titles and two National honours. They had played and won more matches than any other team.

Record: *Played* 1928 *Won* 1025 *Drawn* 429 *Lost* 374 *Goals for* 3783 *Goals against* 2213

BRAZIL

The Brazilian national championship is now reduced to 40 clubs, divided into eight groups in which teams play each other twice. The top three to finish in each group proceed to the second round. These 24 teams are joined by the four top teams in a secondary championship and another four from the best of the non-qualifiers of the first round, decided after a series of play-offs.

These 32 teams are split into eight groups of four with the top two in each progressing. The 16 survivors are placed in four groups of four, the top two in each moving into the fourth round.

The eight remaining teams are split into four two-leg quarter-finals followed by knock out semi-finals and a two-legged final.

In May 1983 Flamengo beat Santos 4–2 on aggregate in the two-legged final.

URUGUAY

Fernando Morena reached his 600th goal in all matches during 1982.

Years	Club	Goals
1969–72	River Plate (Montevideo)	51
1972–79	Penarol	347
1979–80	Rayo Vallecano (Spain)	20
1980–81	Valencia	39
1981–82	Penarol	56
other goals:		
1972–79	Uruguay national team	79
1979–82	other representative games	8
	Total	600

His 600th was scored in a South American Cup game against Defensor (Uruguay) for Penarol in a 3–0 win. Before the World Club Championship against Aston Villa he had reached 627 goals.

Sold to Rayo Vallecano in 1979 for £300 000 he was transferred from Valencia back to Penarol for £507 500 the player's share being £60 000. But Penarol paid only £145 500 down and completed the deal in instalments.

North America

A further erosion of member clubs in the North American Soccer League saw the 24 teams in 1980 dwindle to 21 in 1981 and only 14 in 1982. Before the play-offs even began three of these 14 announced that their franchises were up for sale. Twelve teams competed in 1983.

Average attendances 1982:
New York Cosmos 28 747
Montreal 21 320

Tampa Bay 18 507
Vancouver 18 248
Tulsa 14 502
Seattle 12 539
Fort Lauderdale 12 345
San Jose 11 011
Chicago 9 337
Portland...8 786
San Diego..8 527
Toronto 8 152
Jacksonville 7 160
Edmonton 4 921

Only Toronto Blizzard showed an increase over the 1981 season.

Giorgio Chinaglia (New York Cosmos) was the leading scorer in the regular schedule of 32 matches, scoring 20 goals and obtaining 15 assists for a total of 55 points. He had achieved his 300th goal for Cosmos against Los Angeles Aztecs the previous season on 21 June 1981, their third goal in a 3–0 win and his second in the game. His total was then made up from 116 in international exhibition matches, 38 in NASL play-offs and the rest in regular League games.

The Soccer Bowl '82 was held in the Jack Murphy Stadium in San Diego, California on a baseball field which was part grass and part dirt. Cosmos beat Seattle Sounders 1–0 with a goal from Chinaglia before a crowd of 22 000.

SOCCER BOWL

Previous winners:
1967 Oakland Clippers★
1968 Atlanta Chiefs
1969 Kansas City Spurs
1970 Rochester Lancers
1971 Dallas Tornado
1972 New York Cosmos
1973 Philadelphia Atoms
1974 Los Angeles Aztecs
1975 Tampa Bay Rowdies
1976 Toronto Metro-Croatia
1977 New York Cosmos
1978 New York Cosmos
1979 Vancouver Whitecaps
1980 New York Cosmos
1981 Chicago Sting
1982 New York Cosmos
*National Professional Soccer League

Awards

European Footballer of the Year
The magazine *France Football* organises this annual award each December. A panel of journalists from various European countries cast votes.

1956 Stanley Matthews (England)
1957 Alfredo di Stefano (Argentina, Spain)
1958 Raymond Kopa (France)
1959 Alfredo di Stefano (Argentina, Spain)
1960 Luis Suarez (Spain)
1961 Omar Sivori (Argentina)
1962 Joseph Masopust (Czechoslovakia)
1963 Lev Yashin (USSR)
1964 Denis Law (Scotland)
1965 Eusebio (Portugal)
1966 Bobby Charlton (England)
1967 Florian Albert (Hungary)
1968 George Best (Northern Ireland)
1969 Gianni Rivera (Italy)
1970 Gerd Muller (West Germany)
1971 Johan Cruyff (Holland)
1972 Franz Beckenbauer (West Germany)
1973 Johan Cruyff (Holland)
1974 Johan Cruyff (Holland)
1975 Oleg Blokhin (USSR)
1976 Franz Beckenbauer (West Germany)
1977 Allan Simonsen (Denmark)
1978 Kevin Keegan (England)
1979 Kevin Keegan (England)
1980 Karl-Heinz Rummenigge (West Germany)
1981 Karl-Heinz Rummenigge (West Germany)
1982 Paolo Rossi (Italy)

South American Footballer of the Year
This is organised along similar lines to the European Footballer of the Year.

1971 Tostao (Brazil)
1972 Teofilo Cubillas (Peru)
1973 Pele (Brazil)
1974 Elias Figueroa (Chile)
1975 Elias Figueroa (Chile)
1976 Elias Figueroa (Chile)
1977 Zico (Brazil)
1978 Mario Kempes (Argentina)
1979 Diego Maradona (Argentina)
1980 Diego Maradona (Argentina)
1981 Zico (Brazil)
1982 Zico (Brazil

African Footballer of the Year
This is also organised by *France Football* along the lines of the European award.

1971 Ibrahim Sunday (Ghana)
1972 Cherif Souleymane (Guinea)
1973 Bwanga Tschimen (Zaire)
1974 Paul Moukila (Congo)
1975 Ahmed Faras (Morocco)
1976 Roger Milla (Cameroun)
1977 Tarak Dhiab (Tunisia)
1978 Abdoul Razak (Ghana)
1979 Thomas N'Kono (Cameroun)
1980 Jean Manga Onguene (Cameroun)
1981 Lakhdar Belloumi (Algeria)
1982 Thomas N'Kono (Comeroun)

Bravo award
This is organised by the Italian magazine *Guerin Sportivo* and given to the best under-24-year-old player in Europe.

1978 Jimmy Case (Liverpool)
1979 Garry Birtles (Nottingham Forest)
1980 Hansi Muller (Stuttgart)
1981 John Wark (Ipswich Town)
1982 Gary Shaw (Aston Villa)

World Cup

The World Cup trophy itself is now the second in the lifetime of the competition. The first was named after Jules Rimet, the late Honorary President of FIFA from 1921 to 1954. Brazil won this cup outright in 1970.

A new trophy of solid gold 36 cm high known as the FIFA World Cup and designed by an Italian from an entry of some 53 submitted for selection was used in 1974 for the first time.

World Cup 1930–1982 Final series

	P	W	D	L	F	A
Brazil	57	37	10	10	134	62
West Germany*	54	31	11	12	122	78
Italy	43	24	9	10	74	46
Argentina	34	16	5	13	63	50
England	29	13	8	8	40	29

*Including Germany 1934–1938

	P	W	D	L	F	A
Uruguay	29	14	5	10	57	39
Hungary	29	14	3	12	85	48
USSR	24	12	5	7	37	25
Poland	21	12	4	5	38	22
Yugoslavia	28	12	4	12	47	36
Sweden	28	11	6	11	48	46
France	27	11	3	13	59	50
Austria	23	11	2	10	38	40
Spain	23	8	5	10	26	30
Czechoslovakia	25	8	5	12	34	40
Holland	16	8	3	5	32	19
Chile	21	7	3	11	26	32
Switzerland	18	5	2	11	28	44
Scotland	14	3	5	6	20	29
Peru	15	4	3	8	19	31
Portugal	6	5	0	1	17	8
Norway	10	3	4	3	11	17
Mexico	24	3	4	17	21	62
Belgium	14	3	2	9	15	30
East Germany	6	2	2	2	5	5
Paraguay	7	2	2	3	12	19
USA	7	3	0	4	12	21
Wales	5	1	3	1	4	4
Rumania	8	2	1	5	12	17

Bryan Robson's goal for England in the World Cup after 27 seconds against France. *ASP*

	P	W	D	L	F	A
Algeria	3	2	0	1	5	5
Bulgaria	12	0	4	8	9	29
Tunisia	3	1	1	1	3	2
Cameroon	3	0	3	0	1	1
Cuba	3	1	1	1	5	12
North Korea	4	1	1	2	5	9
Turkey	3	1	0	2	10	11
Honduras	3	0	2	1	2	3
Israel	3	1	0	2	1	3
Kuwait	3	0	1	2	2	6
Morocco	3	0	1	2	2	6
Australia	3	0	1	2	0	5
Colombia	3	0	1	2	5	11
Iran	3	0	1	2	2	8
Norway	1	0	0	1	1	2
Egypt	1	0	0	1	2	4
Dutch East Indies	1	0	0	1	0	6
South Korea	2	0	0	2	0	16
New Zealand	3	0	0	3	2	12

	P	W	D	L	F	A
Haiti	3	0	0	3	2	14
Zaire	3	0	0	3	0	14
Bolivia	3	0	0	3	0	16
El Salvador	6	0	0	6	1	22

The 1982 World Cup final tournament produced a number of records: the first hat-trick by a substitute, Laszlo Kiss (Hungary) v El Salvador; the fastest goal in 27 seconds by Bryan Robson (England) v France; the first penalty miss in the final by Antonio Cabrini (Italy) v West Germany; record score by one team: Hungary 10 El Salvador 1; first match decided by penalty kicks: France v West Germany.

World Cup appearances and goalscorers 1982 tournament

Details of all matches played plus appearances which include those as substitute with goals in brackets:

Algeria
P3 W2 D0 L1 F5 A5
Three: Cerbah, Guendouz, Kourichi, Merzakane, Mansouri, Dhaleb, Fergani, Madjer (1), Bensaoula (1), Assad (2). **Two:** Belloumi (1), Larbes, Zidane. **One:** Tiemcani, Bourebbou, Yahi.

Argentina
P5 W2 D0 L3 F8 A7
Five: Fillol, Olguin, Galvan, Passarella (2), Tarantini, Ardiles (1), Maradona (2), Bertoni (2), Kempes. **Four:** Gallego, Diaz (1), Calderon. **Two:** Valdano, Santamaria, Barbas. **One:** Valencia.

Austria
P5 W2 D1 L2 F5 A4
Five: Koncilia, Krauss, Obermayer, Pezzey (1), Hintermaier (1), Prohaska, Schachner (2). **Four:** Degeorgi, Baumeister, Hattenberger, Krankl (1). **Three:** Weber, Welzl. **Two:** Jurtin. **One:** Jara, Pichler, Hagmayr, Pregesbauer.

Belgium
P5 W2 D1 L2 F3 L5
Five: Luc Millecamps, Coeck (1), Vercauteren, Czerniatynski (1), Van den Bergh (1), Ceulemans. **Four:** Baecke, Vandermissen, Meeuws. **Three:** Pfaff, Gerets, Van Moer, **Two:** de Schrijver, Van der Elst, Plessers, Renquin. **One:** Custers, Munaron, Marc Millecamps, Verheyen.

Brazil
P5 W4 D0 L1 F15 A6
Five: Valdir Peres, Leandro, Oscar (1), Luizinho, Junior (1), Socrates (2), Serginho (2), Zico (4), Eder (2), Falcao (3). **Four:** Paulo Isidoro, Cerezo. **One:** Dirceu, Edinho, Edevaldo, Batista.

Cameroon
P3 W0 D3 L0 F1 A1
Three: N'Kono, M'Bom, Aoudou, Onana, Kaham, Abega, M'Bida (1), Kunda, Milla, Tokoto, N'Djeya. **Two:** N'Gusta. **One:** Bahoken.

Chile
P3 W0 D0 L3 F3 A8
Three: Osben, Figueroa, Valenzuela, Bigorra, Bonvallet, Dubo, Neira (1), Moscoso (1), Yanez. **Two:** Garrido, Gamboa, Caszely, Soto, Letelier (1). **One:** Manuel Rojas, Galindo

Czechoslovakia
P3 W0 D2 L1 F2 A4
Three: Barmos, Jurkemik, Fiala, Janecka, Nehoda, Vizek. **Two:** Panenka (2), Berger, Kriz, Bicovsky, Stromsik, Vojacek, Masny. **One:** Hruska, Kukucka, Petrzela, Seman, Radimec, Chaloupka, Stambacher

El Salvador
P3 W0 D0 L3 F1 A13
Three: Mora, Jovel, Rodriguez, Zapata (1), Ventura, Huezo, Gonzalez, Rivas. **Two:** Recinos, Osorto, Fagoaga. **One:** Castillo, Rugamas, Hernandez F, Diaz, Arevalo, Alfaro, Ortiz

England
P5 W3 D2 L0 F6 A1
Five: Shilton, Mills, Thompson, Wilkins, Mariner (2), Francis (2), Rix. **Four:** Sansom, Butcher, Robson (2), Coppell. **Two:** Neal, Hoddle, Woodcock. **One:** Brooking, Foster, Keegan.
N.B. An own goal by Barmos (Czechoslovakia) was credited to Mariner.

France
P7 W4 D2 L1 F16 A12
(France v West Germany listed as a draw)
Seven: Tresor (1), Six (2). **Six:** Ettori, Bossis (1), Giresse (3), Soler (1), Janvion. **Five:** Tigana, Girard (1), Platini (2), Amoros, Genghini (2). **Four:** Rocheteau (2), **Three:** Battiston, Lopez, Lacombe, Couriol (1). **Two:** Larios. **One:** Castaneda, Mahut, Bellone.

Honduras
P3 W0 D2 L1 F2 A3
Three: Arzu, Costly, Villegas, Zelaya (1), Gilberto, Maradiaga, Betancourt, Figueroa. **Two:** Gutierrez, Bulnes, Norales, Laing (1). **One:** Droumond, Caballero, Cruz, Murillo

Hungary
P3 W1 D1 L1 F12 A6
Three: Meszaros, Martos, Garaba, Nyilasi (2), Sallai, Fazekas (2), Kiss (3), Poloskei (2), **Two:** Balint, Toth (1), Muller, Torocsik, Szentes (1), Varga (1). **One:** Rab, Kerekes, Csongradi.

Italy
P7 W4 D3 L0 F12 A6
Seven: Zoff, Cabrini (1), Collovati, Scirea, Tardelli (2), Conti (1); Graziani (1), Rossi (6). **Six:** Gentile, Antognoni, **Five:** Oriali, Marini. **Three:** Bergomi, Altobelli (1). **Two:** Causio.

Kuwait
P3 W0 D1 L2 F2 A6
Three: Al Tarabulsi, Neem Saed, Mayoof, Mahboub, Waleed Jasem, Al Buloushi (1), Al Houti, Fathi Kameel, Al Dakheel (1), Al Anbari. **Two:** Karam, Jasem Yacoub, Al Shemmari. **One:** Al Suwayed.

New Zealand
P3 W0 D0 L3 F2 A12
Three: Van Hattum, Elrick, Cole, Herbert, Sumner (1), Mackay, Cresswell, Boath, Rufer, Wooddin (1). **Two:** Almond, Dods. **One:** Hill, Malcolmson, Brian Turner.

Northern Ireland
P5 W1 D3 L1 F5 A7
Five: Jimmy Nicholl, Chris Nicholl, McClelland, McIlroy, Martin O'Neill, McCreery, Armstrong (1), Hamilton (2), Whiteside. **Four:** Jennings, Donaghy. **Two:** Brotherston, Nelson. **One:** Healy, Cassidy, John O'Neill, Platt.

Peru
P3 W0 D2 L1 F2 A6
Three: Quiroga, Duarte, Diaz (1), Uribe, Cueto, Olaechea, Velasquez, Leguia, La Rosa (1), Cubillas, Barbadillo, Oblitas. **Two:** Salguero. **One:** Gonzales.

Poland
P7 W3 D3 L1 F11 A5
Seven: Mlynarczyk, Majewski (1), Zmuda, Janas, Buncol (1), Lato (1). **Six:** Boniek (4), Matysik, Smolarek (1). **Five:** Kupcewicz (1). **Four:** Ciolek (1), Dziuba. **Three:** Kusto, Jalocha. **Two:** Iwan, Palasz, Szarmach (1). **One:** Wojcicki.

Scotland
P3 W1 D1 L1 F8 A8
Three: Rough, Frank Gray, Hansen, Souness (1), Strachan, Narey (1), Wark (2), Archibald (1), Robertson (1). **Two:** McGrain, Dalglish (1), Brazil, Miller. **One:** Evans, Hartford, McLeish, Jordan (1)

Spain
P5 W1 D2 L2 F4 A5
Five: Arconada, Gordillo, Camacho, Alonso, Alesanco, Tendillo. **Four:** Juanito (1), Saura (1), Sanchez, Satrustegui, Zamora (1), Lopez Ufarte (1). **Three:** Quini. **Two:** Urquiaga, Santillana. **One:** Joaquim, Uralde, Macedo, Gallego.

Soviet Union
P5 W2 D2 L1 F7 A4
Five: Dasayev, Chivadze (1), Baltacha (1), Demyanenko, Shengelia (1), Bessonov, Gavrilov (1), Blokhin (1). **Four:** Sulakvelidze, Bal (1), Daraselia. **Three:** Andreyev, Oganesian (1), Borovsky **Two:** Rodionov **One:** Susloparov.

West Germany
P7 W3 D2 L2 F12 A10
Seven: Schumacher, Kaltz, Stielike, Karl-Heinz Forster, Briegel, Dremmler, Breitner (1), Rummenigge (5), Littbarski (2). **Six:** Fischer (2). **Five:** Hrubesch (1), **Four:** Magath, Bernd Forster. **Three:** Reinders (1). **Two:** Matthaus, Muller.

Yugoslavia
P3 W1 D1 L1 F2 A2
Three: Pantelic, Gudelj (1), Zafec, Stojkovic, Petrovic (1), Slijvo, Zlatko Vujovic, Susic, Jovanovic, Surjak. **Two:** Krmpotic, Halilhodzic, Sestic. **One:** Hrstic.

1930–1982 World Cup Attendances and Goals

Year	Venue	Attendances	Average	Matches	Goals	Average
1930	Uruguay	434 500	24 139	18	70	3·88
1934	Italy	395 000	23 235	17	70	4·11
1938	France	483 000	26 833	18	84	4·66
1950	Brazil	1 337 000	60 772	22	88	4·00
1954	Switzerland	943 000	36 270	26	140	5·38
1958	Sweden	868 000	24 800	35	126	3·60
1962	Chile	776 000	24 250	32	89	2·78
1966	England	1 614 677	50 458	32	89	2·78
1970	Mexico	1 673 975	52 312	32	95	2·96
1974	West Germany	1 774 022	46 685	38	97	2·55
1978	Argentina	1 610 215	42 374	38	102	2·68
1982	Spain	1 766 277	33 967	52	146	2·81

WORLD CUP WINNERS ANALYSIS (Final tournaments)

Uruguay (1930), Italy (1938) and Brazil (1970) have been the only winners with 100% records in one final series. They are also three of the four countries who have won the competition more than once, along with West Germany who have been the highest scorers in one tournament. They scored 25 in six matches (1954) which produced the highest average of 4·16 goals per game. England had the best defensive record in 1966 with only three goals conceded in six matches.

Year	Winners	Matches						Goals	Players used	Appearances (goals)
			P	W	D	L	F	A			
1930	Uruguay		4	4	0	0	15	3		15	Ballesteros, Nasazzi, Cea (5), Andrade (J), Fernandez, Gestido, Iriarte (2) 4 each; Dorado (2), Mascheroni, Scarone (1) 3 each; Castro (2), Anselmo (3) 2 each; Tejera, Urdinaran, Petrone 1 each.

Final: **Uruguay 4 Argentina 2**, 90 000 Montevideo

| 1934 | Italy | | 5 | 4 | 1 | 0 | 12 | 3 | | 17 | Combi, Allmandi, Monti, Meazza (2), Orsi (3) 5 each; Monzeglio, Bertolini, Schiavio (4), Ferrari (2), Guaita (1) 4 each; Ferraris IV 3; Pizziolo 2; Rosetta, Guarisi, Castellazzi, Borel, Demaria 1 each. |

Final: **Italy 2 Czechoslovakia 1**, 50 000 Rome (after extra time)

Year	Winners	Matches				Goals		Players used	Appearances (goals)
		P	W	D	L	F	A		
1938	**Italy**	4	4	0	0	11	5	14	Olivieri, Rava, Serantoni, Andreolo, Locatelli, Meazza (1), Piolo (5), Ferrari (1) 4 each; Foni, Biavati, Colaussi (4) 3 each; Monzeglio, Pasinati, Ferraris II 1 each.
Final: **Italy 4 Hungary 2,** 45 000 Paris									
1950	**Uruguay**	4	3	1	0	15	5	14	Gonzales (M), Tejera, Valera (1), Andrade (R), Ghiggia (4), Perez, Miguez (4), Schiaffino (5) 4 each; Maspoli, Vidal (1) 3 each; Gonzales (W), Gambetta 2 each; Paz, Moran 1 each.
Deciding match: **Uruguay 2 Brazil 1,** 199 850 Rio de Janeiro									
1954	**West Germany**	6	5	0	1	25	14	18	Eckel, Walter (F) (3) 6 each; Turek, Kohlmeyer, Posipal, Mai, Morlock (6), Walter (O) (4), Schafer (4) 5 each; Liebrich, Rahn (4) 4 each; Laband 3; Klodt (1), Bauer 2 each; Herrmann (1), Mebus, Kwaitowski, Pfaff (1) 1 each. (own goal 1).
Final: **West Germany 3 Hungary 2,** 60 000 Berne									
1958	**Brazil**	6	5	1	0	16	4	16	Gilmar, Nilton Santos (1), Bellini, Orlando, Didi (1), Zagalo (1), 6 each; De Sordi 5; Vava (5), Zito, Garrincha, Pele (6), 4 each; Mazzola (2) 3; Dino, Joel 2 each; Djalma Santos, Dida 1 each.
Final: **Brazil 5 Sweden 2,** 49 737 Stockholm									
1962	**Brazil**	6	5	1	0	14	5	12	Gilmar, Djalma Santos, Mauro, Zizimo, Nilton Santos, Zito (1), Didi, Garrincha (4), Vara (4), Zagalo (1), 6 each; Amarildo (3) 4; Pele (1) 2.
Final: **Brazil 3 Czechoslovakia 1,** 68 679 Santiago									
1966	**England**	6	5	1	0	11	3	15	Banks, Cohen, Wilson, Stiles, Charlton (J), Moore, Charlton (R) (3), Hunt (3), 6 each; Peters (1) 5; Ball 4; Greaves, Hurst (4) 3; Paine, Callaghan, Connelly 1 each.
Final: **England 4 West Germany 2,** 93 802 Wembley (after extra time)									
1970	**Brazil**	6	6	0	0	19	7	15	Felix, Carlos Alberto (1), Piazza, Brito, Clodoaldo (1), Jairzinho (7), Tostao (2), Pele (4), 6 each; Everaldo, Rivelino (3) 5; Gerson (1) 4; Paulo Cesar 2 + 2 subs; Marco Antonio 1 + 1 sub; Roberto 2 subs; Fontana 1; Edu 1 sub.
Final: **Brazil 4 Italy 1,** 107 412 Mexico City									
1974	**West Germany**	7	6	0	1	13	4	18	Maier, Vogts, Breitner (3), Schwarzenbeck, Beckenbauer, Muller (4), Overath (2), 7 each; Hoeness (1) 6 + 1 sub; Grabowski (1) 5 + 1 sub; Holzenbein 4 + 2 subs; Bonhof (1) 4; Cullmann (1) 3; Flohe 1 + 2 subs; Heynckes, Herzog 2 each; Wimmer 1 + 1 sub; Netzer, Hottges 1 sub each.
Final: **West Germany 2 Holland 1,** 77 833 Munich									
1978	**Argentina**	7	5	1	1	15	4	17	Fillol, Luis Galvan, Olguin, Passarella (1) Tarantini (1), Gallego, Kempes (6) 7 each; Ardiles 6; Bertoni 5 + 1 sub; Ortiz 4 + 2 subs; (2) Luque (4) 5; Houseman (1) 3 + 3 subs; Valencia 4; Larrosa 1 + 1 sub; Alonso 3 subs; Villa 2 subs; Oviedo 1 sub.
Final: **Argentina 3 Holland 1,** 77 000 Buenos Aires (after extra time)									
1982	**Italy**	7	4	3	0	12	6	15	Zoff, Scirea, Collovati, Cabrini (1), Tardelli (2), Rossi (6), Conti, Graziani (1) 7 each; Gentile, Antognoni 6 each; Oriali 5; Marini 2 + 3 subs; Bergomi 2 + 1 sub; Altobelli 3 subs (1); Causio 2 subs.
Final: **Italy 3 West Germany 1,** 90 089 Madrid									

World Cup Appearances

Antonio Carbajal (Mexico) is the only player to have appeared in five World Cup final tournaments. He kept goal for Mexico in 1950, 1954, 1958, 1962 and 1966, with eleven appearances in all.

Uwe Seeler (West Germany) established a record in World Cup final tournaments by making a total of 21 appearances in 1958, 1962, 1966 and 1970 as a centre-forward.

Pele (Brazil) is the only player to have been with three World Cup winning teams, though he missed the final of the 1962 competition because of injury. He made four appearances in the 1958 final tournament, two in 1962 before injury and six in 1970. He also appeared in two matches in 1966 for a total of 14 appearances in all.

Mario Zagalo is the only man who has won a World Cup winners medal and managed a World Cup winning team. He played in the 1958 and 1962 World Cup winning teams of Brazil and was manager when they achieved their third success in 1970.

Dino Zoff (Italy) became the oldest player at the age of 40 to win a World Cup winners medal when he captained his country to their 1982 success.

Apart from Zoff only one other goalkeeper had captained a World Cup winning side. He was Gianpiero Combi the Italian goalkeeper in 1934.

Norman Whiteside at 17 became the youngest to appear in the World Cup finals when he played for Northern Ireland in 1982. His first team experience for Manchester United had consisted of just two appearances in their Division One side, one of them as a substitute.

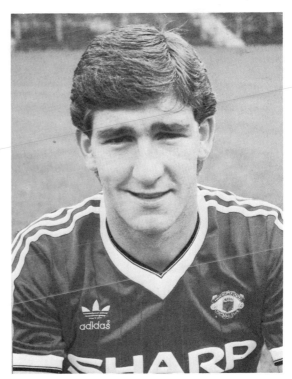

Norman Whiteside, the Manchester United and Northern Ireland international centre-forward.
Manchester Evening News

World Cup Goalscoring

The record margin of victory in a World Cup final is nine goals: in 1982: Hungary 10 El Salvador 1; in 1954: Hungary 9 South Korea 0 and in 1974: Yugoslavia 9 Zaire 0. The record scoreline in any World Cup match is New Zealand 13 Fiji 0 in a qualifying match on 15 August 1981.

Just Fontaine (France) scored a record 13 goals in six matches of the 1958 World Cup final tournament. **Gerd Muller** (West Germany) scored 10 goals in 1970 and four in 1974 for the highest aggregate of 14 goals. Fontaine and Jairzinho (Brazil) are the only two players to have scored in every match in a final series, as **Jairzinho** scored seven goals in six matches in 1970.

Including World Cup qualifying matches in the 1970 series, **Muller** scored a total of 19 goals with nine coming from six preliminary games and ten in the final stages.

Pele is the third highest scorer in World Cup final tournaments, having registered 12 goals in his four competitions.

Geoff Hurst (England) is the only player to have scored a hat-trick in a final when he registered three of his side's goals in their 4–2 win over West Germany in 1966.

The first player to score as many as four goals in any World Cup match was **Paddy Moore** who registered all the Republic of Ireland's goals in the 4–4 draw with Belgium in Dublin during a World Cup qualifying match on 25 February 1934.

Robbie Rensenbrink (Holland) scored the 1000th goal in World Cup finals when he converted a penalty against Scotland in the 1978 tournament.

The first goal scored in the World Cup was credited to **Louis Laurent** for France against Mexico on 13 July 1930 in Montevideo. France won 4–1. With the time difference the news reached France on Bastille Day, 14 July.

The fastest goal scored in a World Cup final tournament, in 27 seconds, was credited to **Bryan Robson** of England against France on 16 June 1982 exactly 44 years to the day after Olle Nyberg of Sweden had scored in 30 seconds against Hungary in Paris. **Bernard Lacombe** scored for France against Italy in 31 seconds during the 1978 tournament.

Vava (real name **Edwaldo Izidio Neto**) of Brazil is the only player to have scored in successive World Cup finals. He did so against Sweden in 1958 (scoring twice) and against Czechoslovakia in 1962. Pele is the only other to score in two finals, twice in Sweden in 1958 and once against Italy in 1970.

Leading World Cup scorers (final tournament)

Year	Name	Country	Goals
1930	Guillermo Stabile	Argentina	8
1934	Angelo Schiavio	Italy	4
	Oldrich Nejedly	Czechoslovakia	4
	Edmund Cohen	Germany	4
1938	Leonidas da Silva	Brazil	8
1950	Ademir	Brazil	9
1954	Sandor Kocsis	Hungary	11
1958	Just Fontaine	France	13
1962	Drazen Jerkovic	Yugoslavia	5
1966	Eusebio	Portugal	9
1970	Gerd Muller	West Germany	10
1974	Grzegorz Lato	Poland	7
1978	Mario Kempes	Argentina	6
1982	Paolo Rossi	Italy	6

The record individual score in a World Cup final tournament is four goals, a feat which has been achieved on eight occasions:

Name		
Gustav Wetterstroem	Sweden v Cuba	1938
Leonidas da Silva	Brazil v Poland	1938
Ernest Willimowski	Poland v Brazil	1938
Ademir	Brazil v Sweden	1950
Juan Schiaffino	Uruguay v Bolivia	1950
Sandor Kocsis	Hungary v West Germany	1954
Just Fontaine	France v West Germany	1958
Eusebio	Portugal v North Korea	1966

World Cup endurance

Helmut Schoen who retired as West Germany's team manager after the 1978 World Cup finals was the most successful international coach. In 1966 his team finished runners-up in the World Cup, were third in 1970 and became European Championship winners in 1972. They won the World Cup in 1974 and were runners-up in the European Championship in 1976. Schoen had been in charge for 14 years.

Making his 100th international appearance for Poland, **Kazimierz Deyna** had a penalty kick saved by the Argentine goalkeeper Ubaldo Fillol in the 1978 tournament.

Italian goalkeeper **Dino Zoff** made his 100th international appearance against Poland in a goalless draw in the 1982 tournament.

The longest period that a goalkeeper has kept his charge intact during a World Cup final tournament is 475 minutes. **Josef 'Sepp' Maier** of West Germany conceded a penalty to Holland in the first minute of the 1974 World Cup Final itself and was not beaten again until Holland scored against him in the 1978 tournament.

Peter Shilton conceded a goal after 24 minutes of England's opening match in Bilbao against France in 1982 and then kept his charge intact against Czechoslovakia, Kuwait, West Germany and Spain, a total of seven hours six minutes (426 minutes).

New Zealand established a record in the 1982 qualifying competition by playing 15 matches. During this period goalkeeper **Richard Wilson** completed 15 hours 20 minutes without conceding a goal.

Not quite a walk in the Black Forest, but a training run there for the West Germans on the way to the 1982 World Cup finals.

Outstanding International Players

THE CENTURIANS

The following players have appeared in 100 or more matches for their countries:

Name	Country	From	To	Total
Dino Zoff	Italy	1968	1983	112
Franz Beckenbauer	West Germany	1965	1977	103
Jozsef Bozsik	Hungary	1947	1962	100
Bobby Charlton	England	1958	1970	106
Hector Chumpitaz	Peru	1963	1982	150
Gylmar	Brazil	1953	1969	100
Bobby Moore	England	1962	1973	108
Bjorn Nordqvist	Sweden	1963	1978	115
Pele	Brazil	1957	1971	111
Leonel Sanchez	Chile	1955	1967	104
Thorbjorn Svenssen	Norway	1947	1962	104
Djalma Santos	Brazil	1952	1968	107
Rivelino	Brazil	1968	1979	120
Billy Wright	England	1946	1959	105
Attouga	Tunisia	1963	1979	109
Kazimierz Deyna	Poland	1968	1978	102
Grzegorz Lato	Poland	1971	1982	103

DJALMA SANTOS (BRAZIL)
107 APPEARANCES 1952–1968
FULL-BACK
(Goals in brackets)

Date	Venue	Opponents	Result
1952			
10 Apr	Santiago	Peru	D 0–0
13 Apr	Santiago	Panama	W 5–0
16 Apr	Santiago	Uruguay	W 4–2
1953			
1 Mar	Lima	Bolivia	W 8–1
12 Mar	Lima	Ecuador	W 2–0
13 Mar	Lima	Uruguay	W 1–0
19 Mar	Lima	Peru	L 0–1
23 Mar	Lima	Chile	W 3–2
1 Apr	Lima	Paraguay	L 2–3
1954			
28 Feb	Santiago	Chile	W 2–1
7 Mar	Asuncion	Paraguay	W 1–0
14 Mar	Rio	Chile	W 1–0
21 Mar	Rio	Paraguay	W 4–1
2 May	Sao Paulo	Colombia	W 4–1
9 May	Rio	Colombia	W 2–0
19 Jun	Lausanne	Yugoslavia	D 1–1
27 Jun	Berne	Hungary (1)	L 2–4

1955			
17 Nov	Sao Paulo	Paraguay	D 2–2
1956			
10 Jan	Montevideo	Uruguay	D 0–0
21 Jan	Montevideo	Chile	L 1–4
29 Jan	Montevideo	Paraguay	D 0–0
1 Feb	Montevideo	Peru	W 2–1
5 Feb	Montevideo	Argentina	W 1–0
8 Apr	Lisbon	Portugal	W 1–0
11 Apr	Zurich	Switzerland	D 1–1
15 Apr	Vienna	Austria	W 3–2
21 Apr	Prague	Czechoslovakia	D 0–0
25 Apr	Milan	Italy	L 0–3
1 May	Istanbul	Turkey (1)	W 1–0
9 May	Wembley	England	L 2–4
12 Jun	Asuncion	Paraguay	W 2–0
17 Jun	Asuncion	Paraguay	W 5–2
24 Jun	Rio	Uruguay	W 2–0
1 Jul	Rio	Italy	W 2–0
8 Jul	Buenos Aires	Argentina	D 0–0
5 Aug	Rio	Czechoslovakia	L 0–1
8 Aug	Sao Paulo	Czechoslovakia	W 4–1
1957			
13 Mar	Lima	Chile	W 4–2
21 Mar	Lima	Ecuador	W 7–1
23 Mar	Lima	Colombia	W 9–0

Djalma Santos, the Brazilian centurian.

28 Mar	*Lima*	Uruguay	L	2–3
31 Mar	*Lima*	Peru	W	1–0
3 Apr	*Lima*	Argentina	L	0–3
13 Apr	*Lima*	Peru	D	1–1
21 Apr	*Rio*	Peru	W	1–0
10 Jul	*Sao Paulo*	Argentina	W	2–0
1958				
29 May	*Florence*	Fiorentina (sub)	W	4–0
1 Jun	*Milan*	Inter-Milan	W	4–0
29 Jun	*Stockholm*	Sweden	W	5–2
1959				
26 Mar	*Buenos Aires*	Uruguay	W	3–1
29 Mar	*Buenos Aires*	Paraguay	W	4–1
4 Apr	*Buenos Aires*	Argentina	D	1–1
13 May	*Rio*	England	W	2–0
17 Sep	*Rio*	Chile	W	7–0
20 Sep	*Sao Paulo*	Chile	W	1–0
1960				
29 Apr	*Cairo*	UAR	W	5–0
1 May	*Alexandria*	UAR	W	3–1
6 May	*Cairo*	UAR	W	3–0
8 May	*Malmo*	Malmo	W	7–1
10 May	*Copenhagen*	Denmark	W	4–3
12 May	*Milan*	Inter-Milan	D	2–2
16 May	*Lisbon*	Sporting Club	W	4–0
25 May	*Buenos Aires*	Argentina (1)	L	2–4
29 May	*Buenos Aires*	Argentina (1)	W	4–1
29 Jun	*Rio*	Chile	W	4–0
3 Jul	*Asuncion*	Paraguay	W	2–1
9 Jul	*Montevideo*	Uruguay	L	0–1
12 Jul	*Rio*	Argentina	W	5–1
1961				
29 Jun	*Rio*	Paraguay	W	3–2
1962				
21 Apr	*Rio*	Paraguay	W	6–0
24 Apr	*Sao Paulo*	Paraguay	W	4–0
6 May	*Sao Paulo*	Portugal	W	2–1
9 May	*Rio*	Portugal	W	1–0
12 May	*Rio*	Wales (sub)	W	3–1
16 May	*Sao Paulo*	Wales	W	3–1
30 May	*Vina Del Mar*	Mexico	W	2–0
2 Jun	*Vina Del Mar*	Czechoslovakia	D	0–0
6 Jun	*Vina Del Mar*	Spain	W	2–1
10 Jun	*Vina Del Mar*	England	W	3–1
13 Jun	*Santiago*	Chile	W	4–2
17 Jun	*Santiago*	Czechoslovakia	W	3–1
1963				
13 Apr	*Sao Paulo*	Argentina	L	2–3
16 Apr	*Rio*	Argentina	W	4–1
21 Apr	*Lisbon*	Portugal	L	0–1
24 Apr	*Brussels*	Belgium	L	1–5
26 Apr	*Paris*	Racing Club	L	0–2
28 Apr	*Paris*	France	W	3–2
3 May	*Eindhoven*	PSV	W	1–0
17 May	*Cairo*	UAR	W	1–0
19 May	*Tel Aviv*	Israel	W	5–0
22 May	*Berlin*	West Germany	W	3–0

1965				
2 Jun	*Rio*	Belgium	W	5–0
6 Jun	*Rio*	West Germany	W	2–0
9 Jun	*Rio*	Argentina	D	0–0
17 Jun	*Oran*	Algeria	W	3–0
24 Jun	*Oporto*	Portugal	D	0–0
30 Jun	*Solna*	Sweden	W	2–1
4 Jul	*Moscow*	USSR	W	3–0
21 Nov	*Rio*	USSR	D	2–2
1966				
15 May	*Sao Paulo*	Chile	D	1–1
8 Jun	*Rio*	Poland	W	2–1
27 Jun	*Atvidaberg*	Atvidaberg	W	8–2
4 Jul	*Stockholm*	AIK	W	4–2
6 Jul	*Malmo*	Malmo	W	3–1
12 Jul	*Liverpool*	Bulgaria	W	2–0
15 Jul	*Liverpool*	Hungary	L	1–3
1968				
9 Jun	*Sao Paulo*	Uruguay	W	2–0

DINO ZOFF (ITALY)
112 APPEARANCES 1968–1983
GOALKEEPER

Date	Venue	Opponents	Result	
1968				
20 Apr	*Naples*	Bulgaria	W	2–0
5 Jun	*Naples*	USSR	D	0–0
8 Jun	*Rome*	Yugoslavia	D	1–1
10 Jun	*Rome*	Yugoslavia	W	2–0
23 Oct	*Cardiff*	Wales	W	1–0
1969				
1 Jan	*Mexico City*	Mexico	W	3–2
29 Mar	*East Berlin*	East Germany	D	2–2
24 May	*Turin*	Bulgaria	D	0–0
22 Nov	*Naples*	East Germany	W	3–0
1970				
21 Feb	*Madrid*	Spain	D	2–2
17 Oct	*Berne*	Switzerland (sub)	D	1–1
1971				
20 Feb	*Cagliari*	Spain	L	1–2
10 May	*Dublin*	Eire	W	2–1
9 Jun	*Stockholm*	Sweden	D	0–0
25 Sep	*Genoa*	Mexico	W	2–0
9 Oct	*Milan*	Sweden	W	3–0
20 Nov	*Rome*	Austria	D	2–2
1972				
4 Mar	*Athens*	Greece	L	1–2
17 Jun	*Bucharest*	Rumania	D	3–3
20 Sep	*Turin*	Yugoslavia	W	3–1
7 Oct	*Luxembourg*	Luxembourg	W	4–0
21 Oct	*Berne*	Switzerland	D	0–0

Dino Zoff, the Italian centurian. *ASP*

1973

13 Jan	*Naples*	Turkey	D	0–0
25 Feb	*Istanbul*	Turkey	W	1–0
31 Mar	*Genoa*	Luxembourg	W	5–0
9 Jun	*Rome*	Brazil	W	2–0
14 Jun	*Milan*	England	W	2–0
29 Sep	*Milan*	Sweden	W	2–0
20 Oct	*Rome*	Switzerland	W	2–0
14 Nov	*Wembley*	England	W	1–0

1974

26 Feb	*Rome*	West Germany	D	0–0
8 Jun	*Vienna*	Austria	D	0–0
15 Jun	*Munich*	Haiti	W	3–1
19 Jun	*Stuttgart*	Argentina	D	1–1
23 Jun	*Stuttgart*	Poland	L	1–2
28 Sep	*Zagreb*	Yugoslavia	L	0–1
20 Nov	*Rotterdam*	Holland	L	1–3
29 Dec	*Genoa*	Bulgaria	D	0–0

1975

19 Apr	*Rome*	Poland	D	0–0
5 Jun	*Helsinki*	Finland	W	1–0
8 Jun	*Moscow*	USSR	L	0–1
27 Sep	*Rome*	Finland	D	0–0
26 Oct	*Warsaw*	Poland	D	0–0
22 Nov	*Rome*	Holland	W	1–0
30 Dec	*Florence*	Greece	W	3–2

1976

7 Apr	*Turin*	Portugal	W	3–1
23 May	*Washington*	Team America	W	4–0
28 May	*New York*	England	L	2–3
31 May	*New Haven*	Brazil	L	1–4
5 Jun	*Milan*	Rumania	W	4–2
22 Sep	*Copenhagen*	Denmark	W	1–0
25 Sep	*Rome*	Yugoslavia	W	3–0
16 Oct	*Luxembourg*	Luxembourg	W	4–1
17 Nov	*Rome*	England	W	2–0
22 Dec	*Lisbon*	Portugal	L	1–2

1977

26 Jan	*Rome*	Belgium	W	2–1
8 Jun	*Helsinki*	Finland	W	3–0
8 Oct	*Berlin*	West Germany	L	1–2
15 Oct	*Turin*	Finland	W	6–1
16 Nov	*Wembley*	England	L	0–2
3 Dec	*Rome*	Luxembourg	W	3–0

1978

8 Feb	*Naples*	France	D	2–2
8 May	*Rome*	Yugoslavia	D	0–0
2 Jun	*Mar Del Plata*	France	W	2–1
6 Jun	*Mar Del Plata*	Hungary	W	3–1
10 Jun	*Buenos Aires*	Argentina	W	1–0
14 Jun	*Buenos Aires*	West Germany	D	0–0
18 Jun	*Buenos Aires*	Austria	W	1–0
21 Jun	*Buenos Aires*	Holland	L	1–2
24 Jun	*Buenos Aires*	Brazil	L	1–2
20 Sep	*Turin*	Bulgaria	W	1–0
8 Nov	*Bratislava*	Czechoslovakia	L	0–3
21 Dec	*Rome*	Spain	W	1–0

1979

24 Feb	*Milan*	Holland	W	3–0
26 May	*Rome*	Argentina	D	2–2
26 Sep	*Florence*	Sweden	W	1–0
17 Nov	*Udinese*	Switzerland	W	2–0

1980

16 Feb	*Naples*	Rumania	W	2–1
15 Mar	*Milan*	Uruguay	W	1–0
19 Apr	*Turin*	Poland	D	2–2
12 Jun	*Milan*	Spain	D	0–0
15 Jun	*Turin*	England	W	1–0
18 Jun	*Rome*	Belgium	D	0–0
21 Jun	*Ndples*	Czechoslovakia	D	1–1
24 Sep	*Genoa*	Portugal	W	3–1
11 Oct	*Luxembourg*	Luxembourg	W	2–0
1 Nov	*Rome*	Denmark	W	2–0
15 Nov	*Turin*	Yugoslavia	W	2–0
6 Dec	*Athens*	Greece	W	2–0

1981

25 Feb	*Rome*	Europe XI	L	0–3
19 Apr	*Udinese*	East Germany	D	0–0
3 Jun	*Copenhagen*	Denmark	L	1–3
23 Sep	*Bologna*	Bulgaria	W	3–2
17 Oct	*Belgrade*	Yugoslavia	D	1–1
14 Nov	*Turin*	Greece	D	1–1
5 Dec	*Luxembourg*	Luxembourg	W	1–0

1982

23 Feb	*Paris*	France	L	0–2
14 Apr	*Leipzig*	East Germany	L	0–1
28 May	*Geneva*	Switzerland	D	1–1
14 Jun	*Vigo*	Poland	D	0–0
18 Jun	*Vigo*	Peru	D	1–1
23 Jun	*Vigo*	Cameroon	D	1–1
29 Jun	*Barcelona*	Argentina	W	2–1
5 Jul	*Barcelona*	Brazil	W	3–2
8 Jul	*Barcelona*	Poland	W	2–0
11 Jul	*Madrid*	West Germany	W	3–1
27 Oct	*Rome*	Switzerland	L	0–1
13 Nov	*Milan*	Czechoslovakia	D	2–2
4 Dec	*Florence*	Rumania	D	0–0

1983

12 Feb	*Limassol*	Cyprus	D	1–1
16 Apr	*Bucharest*	Rumania	L	0–1
26 May	*Stockholm*	Sweden	L	0–2

World Cup

FINAL SERIES 1930–1982 (PARTICIPATING COUNTRIES & RESULTS)

1930	1934	1938	1950	1954	1958
ALGERIA					
ARGENTINA France 1–0 Mexico 6–3 Chile 3–1 USA 6–1 Uruguay 2–4 (2nd)	Sweden 2–3				West Germany 1–3 Northern Ireland 3–1 Czechoslovakia 1–6
AUSTRALIA					
AUSTRIA	France 3–2 France 2–1 Italy 0–1 Germany 2–3 (4th)			Scotland 1–0 Czechoslavakia 5–0 Switzerland 7–5 West Germany 1–6 Uruguay 3–1 (3rd)	Brazil 0–3 USSR 0–2 England 2–2
BELGIUM USA 0–3 Paraguay 0–1	Germany 2–5	France 1–3		England 4–4 Italy 1–4	
BOLIVIA Yugoslavia 0–4 Brazil 0–4			Uruguay 0–8		
BRAZIL Yugoslavia 1–2 Bolivia 4–0	Spain 1–3	Poland 6–5 Czechoslovakia 1–1 Czechoslovakia (r) 2–1 Italy 1–2 Sweden 4–2 (3rd)	Mexico 4–0 Switzerland 2–2 Yugoslavia 2–0 Sweden 7–1 Spain 6–1 Uruguay 1–2 (2nd)	Mexico 5–0 Yugoslavia 1–1 Hungary 2–4	Austria 3–0 England 0–0 USSR 2–0 Wales 1–0 France 5–2 Sweden 5–2 (W)
BULGARIA					
CAMEROON					
CHILE Mexico 3–0 France 1–0 Argentina 1–3			England 0–2 Spain 0–2 USA 5–2		

Key: W=Winners; 2nd=Runners up; 3rd=Won match for third place;
4th=Lost match for third place; p-o=play-off; r=replay;
*=Won on penalties; †=Lost on penalties

1962	1966	1970	1974	1978	1982
					ALGERIA
					West Germany 2–1
					Austria 0–2
					Chile 3–2
					ARGENTINA
Bulgaria 1–0	Spain 2–1		Poland 2–3	Hungary 2–1	Belgium 0–1
England 1–3	West Germany 0–0		Italy 1–1	France 2–1	Hungary 4–1
Hungary 0–0	Switzerland 2–0		Haiti 4–1	Italy 0–1	El Salvador 2–0
	England 0–1		Netherlands 0–4	Poland 2–0	Italy 1–2
			Brazil 1–2	Brazil 0–0	Brazil 1–3
			East Germany 1–1	Peru 6–0	
				Netherlands 3–1 (W)	
					AUSTRALIA
			East Germany 0–2		
			West Germany 0–3		
			Chile 0–0		
					AUSTRIA
				Spain 2–1	Chile 1–0
				Sweden 1–0	Algeria 2–0
				Brazil 0–1	West Germany 0–1
				Netherlands 1–5	France 0–1
				Italy 0–1	Northern Ireland 2–2
				West Germany 3–2	
					BELGIUM
		El Salvador 3–0			Argentina 1–0
		USSR 1–4			El Salvador 1–0
		Mexico 0–1			Hungary 1–1
					Poland 0–3
					USSR 0–1
					BOLIVIA
					BRAZIL
Mexico 2–0	Bulgaria 2–0	Czechoslovakia 4–1	Yugoslavia 0–0	Sweden 1–1	USSR 2–1
Czechoslovakia 0–0	Hungary 1–3	England 1–0	Scotland 0–0	Spain 0–0	Scotland 4–1
Spain 2–1	Portugal 1–3	Rumania 3–2	Zaire 3–0	Austria 1–0	New Zealand 4–0
England 3–1		Peru 4–2	East Germany 1–0	Peru 3–0	Argentina 3–1
Chile 4–2		Uruguay 3–1	Argentina 2–1	Argentina 0–0	Italy 2–3
Czechoslovakia 3–1 (W)		Italy 4–1 (W)	Netherlands 0–2	Poland 3–1	
			Poland 0–1 (4th)	Italy 2–1 (3rd)	
					BULGARIA
Argentina 0–1	Brazil 0–2	Peru 2–3	Sweden 0–0		
Hungary 1–6	Portugal 0–3	West Germany 2–5	Uruguay 1–1		
England 0–0	Hungary 1–3	Morocco 1–1	Netherlands 1–4		
					CAMEROON
					Peru 0–0
					Poland 0–0
					Italy 1–1
					CHILE
Switzerland 3–1	Italy 0–2		West Germany 0–1		Austria 0–1
Italy 2–0	North Korea 1–1		East Germany 1–1		West Germany 1–4
West Germany 0–2	USSR 1–2		Australia 0–0		Algeria 2–3
USSR 2–1					
Brazil 2–4					
Yugoslavia 1–0 (3rd)					

1930	1934	1938	1950	1954	1958
COLOMBIA					
CUBA		Rumania 3–3 Rumania (r) 2–1 Sweden 0–8			
CZECHOSLOVAKIA	Rumania 2–1 Switzerland 3–2 Germany 3–1 Italy 1–2 (2nd)	Netherlands 3–0 Brazil 1–1 Brazil (r) 1–2		Uruguay 0–2 Austria 0–5	Northern Ireland 0–1 West Germany 2–2 Argentina 6–1 Northern Ireland 1–2 (p-o)
DUTCH EAST INDIES		Hungary 0–6			
EAST GERMANY (GDR)					
EGYPT	Hungary 2–4				
ENGLAND			Chile 2–0 USA 0–1 Spain 0–1	Belgium 4–4 Switzerland 2–0 Uruguay 2–4	USSR 2–2 Brazil 0–0 Austria 2–2 USSR 0–1 (p-o)
EL SALVADOR					
FRANCE	Mexico 4–1 Argentina 0–1 Chile 0–1	Austria 2–3	Belgium 3–1 Italy 1–3	Yugoslavia 0–1 Mexico 3–2	Paraguay 7–3 Yugoslavia 2–3 Scotland 2–1 Northern Ireland 4–0 Brazil 2–5 West Germany 6–3 (3rd)
GERMANY		Belgium 5–2 Sweden 2–1 Czechoslovakia 1–3 Austria 3–2 (3rd)	Switzerland 1–1 Switzerland (r) 2–4		
HAITI					

1962	1966	1970	1974	1978	1982

COLOMBIA

1962	1966	1970	1974	1978	1982
Uruguay 1–2					
USSR 4–4					
Yugoslavia 0–5					

CUBA

CZECHOSLOVAKIA

1962	1966	1970	1974	1978	1982
Spain 1–0		Brazil 1–4			Kuwait 1–1
Brazil 0–0		Rumania 1–2			England 0–2
Mexico 1–3		England 0–1			France 1–1
Hungary 1–0					
Yugoslavia 3–1					
Brazil 1–3 (2nd)					

DUTCH EAST INDIES

EAST GERMANY (GDR)

1962	1966	1970	1974	1978	1982
			Australia 2–0		
			Chile 1–1		
			West Germany 1–0		
			Brazil 0–1		
			Netherlands 0–2		
			Argentina 1–1		

EGYPT

ENGLAND

1962	1966	1970	1974	1978	1982
Hungary 1–2	Uruguay 0–0	Rumania 1–0			France 3–1
Argentina 3–1	Mexico 2–0	Brazil 0–1			Czechoslovakia 2–0
Bulgaria 0–0	France 2–0	Czechoslovakia 1–0			Kuwait 1–0
Brazil 1–3	Argentina 1–0	West Germany 2–3			West Germany 0–0
	Portugal 2–1				Spain 0–0
	West Germany 4–2 (W)				

EL SALVADOR

1962	1966	1970	1974	1978	1982
		Belgium 0–3			Hungary 1–10
		Mexico 0–4			Belgium 0–1
		USSR 0–2			Argentina 0–2

FRANCE

1962	1966	1970	1974	1978	1982
	Mexico 1–1			Italy 1–2	England 1–3
	Uruguay 1–2			Argentina 1–2	Kuwait 4–1
	England 0–2			Hungary 3–1	Czechoslovakia 1–1
					Austria 1–0
					Northern Ireland 4–1
					West Germany 3–3†
					Poland 2–3 (4th)

GERMANY

HAITI

1962	1966	1970	1974	1978	1982
			Italy 1–3		
			Poland 0–7		
			Argentina 1–4		

1930	1934	1938	1950	1954	1958

HONDURAS

HUNGARY

	Egypt 4–2	Dutch East Indies 6–0		South Korea 9–0	Wales 1–1
	Austria 1–2	Switzerland 2–0		West Germany 8–3	Sweden 1–2
		Sweden 5–1		Brazil 4–2	Mexico 4–0
		Italy 2–4 (2nd)		Uruguay 4–2	Wales 1–2 (p-o)
				West Germany 2–3	
				(2nd)	

IRAN

ISRAEL

ITALY

	USA 7–1	Norway 2–1	Sweden 2–3	Switzerland 1–2	
	Spain 1–1	France 3–1	Paraguay 2–0	Belgium 4–1	
	Spain (r) 1–0	Brazil 2–1		Switzerland 1–4 (p-o)	
	Austria 1–0	Hungary 4–2 (W)			
	Czechoslovakia 2–1				
	(W)				

SOUTH KOREA

| | | | | Hungary 0–9 | |
| | | | | Turkey 0–7 | |

KUWAIT

MEXICO

France 1–4			Brazil 0–4	Brazil 0–5	Sweden 0–3
Chile 0–3			Yugoslavia 1–4	France 2–3	Wales 1–1
Argentina 3–6			Switzerland 1–2		Hungary 0–4

MOROCCO

NETHERLANDS (HOLLAND)

| | Switzerland 2–3 | Czechoslovakia 0–3 | | | |

NEW ZEALAND

1962	1966	1970	1974	1978	1982
					HONDURAS
					Spain 1–1
					Northern Ireland 1–1
					Yugoslavia 0–1
					HUNGARY
England 2–1	Portugal 1–3			Argentina 1–2	El Salvador 10–1
Bulgaria 6–1	Brazil 3–1			Italy 1–3	Argentina 1–4
Argentina 0–0	Bulgaria 3–1			France 1–3	Belgium 1–1
Czechoslovakia 0–1	USSR 1–2				
					IRAN
				Netherlands 0–3	
				Scotland 1–1	
				Peru 1–4	
					ISRAEL
		Uruguay 0–2			
		Sweden 1–1			
		Italy 0–0			
					ITALY
West Germany 0–0	Chile 2–0	Sweden 1–0	Haiti 3–1	France 2–1	Poland 0–0
Chile 0–2	USSR 0–1	Uruguay 0–0	Argentina 1–1	Hungary 3–1	Peru 1–1
Switzerland 3–0	North Korea 0–1	Israel 0–0	Poland 1–2	Argentina 1–0	Cameroon 1–1
		Mexico 4–1		West Germany 0–0	Argentina 2–1
		West Germany 4–3		Austria 1–0	Brazil 3–2
		Brazil 1–4 (2nd)		Netherlands 1–2	Poland 2–0
				Brazil 1–2 (4th)	West Germany 3–1 (W)
					SOUTH KOREA
					KUWAIT
					Czechoslovakia 1–1
					France 1–4
					England 0–1
					MEXICO
Brazil 0–2	France 1–1	USSR 0–0		Tunisia 1–3	
Spain 0–1	England 0–2	El Salvador 4–0		West Germany 0–6	
Czechoslovakia 3–1	Uruguay 0–0	Belgium 1–0		Poland 1–3	
		Italy 1–4			
					MOROCCO
		West Germany 1–2			
		Peru 0–3			
		Bulgaria 1–1			
					NETHERLANDS (HOLLAND)
			Uruguay 2–0	Iran 3–0	
			Sweden 0–0	Peru 0–0	
			Bulgaria 4–1	Scotland 2–3	
			Argentina 4–0	Austria 5–1	
			East Germany 2–0	West Germany 2–2	
			Brazil 2–0	Italy 2–1	
			West Germany 1–2 (2nd)	Argentina 1–3 (2nd)	
					NEW ZEALAND
					Scotland 2–5
					USSR 0–3
					Brazil 0–4

1930	1934	1938	1950	1954	1958

NORTHERN IRELAND

1930	1934	1938	1950	1954	1958
					Czechoslovakia 1–0
					Argentina 1–3
					West Germany 2–2
					Czechoslovakia 2–1 (p-o)
					France 0–4

NORTH KOREA

NORWAY

1930	1934	1938	1950	1954	1958
		Italy 1–2			

PARAGUAY

1930	1934	1938	1950	1954	1958
USA 0–3			Sweden 2–2		France 3–7
Belgium 1–0			Italy 0–2		Scotland 3–2
					Yugoslavia 3–3

PERU

1930	1934	1938	1950	1954	1958
Rumania 1–3					
Uruguay 0–1					

POLAND

1930	1934	1938	1950	1954	1958
		Brazil 5–6			

PORTUGAL

RUMANIA

1930	1934	1938	1950	1954	1958
Peru 3–1	Czechoslovakia 1–2	Cuba 3–3			
Uruguay 0–4		Cuba (r) 1–2			

SCOTLAND

1930	1934	1938	1950	1954	1958
				Austria 0–1	Yugoslavia 1–1
				Uruguay 0–7	Paraguay 2–3
					France 1–2

SPAIN

1930	1934	1938	1950	1954	1958
	Brazil 3–1		USA 3–1		
	Italy 1–1		Chile 2–0		
	Italy (r) 0–1		England 1–0		
			Uruguay 2–2		
			Brazil 1–6		
			Sweden 1–3 (4th)		

	1962	1966	1970	1974	1978	1982
NORTHERN IRELAND						Yugoslavia 0–0 Honduras 1–1 Spain 1–0 Austria 2–2 France 1–4
NORTH KOREA		USSR 0–3 Chile 1–1 Italy 1–0 Portugal 3–5				
NORWAY						
PARAGUAY						
PERU			Bulgaria 3–2 Morocco 3–0 West Germany 1–3 Brazil 2–4		Scotland 3–1 Netherlands 0–0 Iran 4–1 Brazil 0–3 Poland 0–1 Argentina 0–6	Cameroon 0–0 Italy 1–1 Poland 1–5
POLAND				Argentina 3–2 Haiti 7–0 Italy 2–1 Sweden 1–0 Yugoslavia 2–1 West Germany 0–1 Brazil 1–0 (3rd)	West Germany 0–0 Tunisia 1–0 Mexico 3–1 Argentina 0–2 Peru 1–0 Brazil 1–3	Italy 0–0 Cameroon 0–0 Peru 5–1 Belgium 3–0 USSR 0–0 Italy 0–2 France 3–2 (3rd)
PORTUGAL		Hungary 3–1 Bulgaria 3–0 Brazil 3–1 North Korea 5–3 England 1–2 USSR 2–1 (3rd)				
RUMANIA			England 0–1 Czechoslovakia 2–1 Brazil 2–3			
SCOTLAND				Zaire 2–0 Brazil 0–0 Yugoslavia 1–1	Peru 1–3 Iran 1–1 Netherlands 3–2	New Zealand 5–2 Brazil 1–4 USSR 2–2
SPAIN	Czechoslovakia 0–1 Mexico 1–0 Brazil 1–2	Argentina 1–2 Switzerland 2–1 West Germany 1–2			Austria 1–2 Brazil 0–0 Sweden 1–0	Honduras 1–1 Yugoslavia 2–1 Northern Ireland 0–1 West Germany 1–2 England 0–0

1930	1934	1938	1950	1954	1958

SWEDEN

	Argentina 3–2	Cuba 8–0	Italy 3–2		Mexico 3–0
	Germany 1–2	Hungary 1–5	Paraguay 2–2		Hungary 2–1
		Brazil 2–4 (4th)	Brazil 1–7		Wales 0–0
			Uruguay 2–3		USSR 2–0
			Spain 3–1 (3rd)		West Germany 3–1
					Brazil 2–5 (2nd)

SWITZERLAND

	Netherlands 3–2	Germany 1–1	Yugoslavia 0–3	England 0–2	
	Czechoslovakia 2–3	Germany (r) 4–2	Brazil 2–2	Italy 2–1	
		Hungary 0–2	Mexico 2–1	Italy 4–1 (p-o)	
				Austria 5–7	

TUNISIA

TURKEY

				West Germany 1–4	
				South Korea 7–0	
				West Germany 2–7	
				(p-o)	

UNITED STATES of AMERICA

Belgium 3–0	Italy 1–7		Spain 1–3		
Paraguay 3–0			England 1–0		
Argentina 1–6			Chile 2–5		

URUGUAY

Peru 1–0			Bolivia 8–0	Czechoslovakia 2–0	
Rumania 4–0			Spain 2–2	Scotland 7–0	
Yugoslavia 6–1			Sweden 3–2	England 4–2	
Argentina 4–2 (W)			Brazil 2–1 (W)	Hungary 2–4	
				Austria 1–3 (4th)	

USSR

					England 2–2
					Austria 2–0
					Brazil 0–2
					England 1–0 (p-o)
					Sweden 0–2

WALES

					Hungary 1–1
					Mexico 1–1
					Sweden 0–0
					Hungary 2–1 (p-o)
					Brazil 0–1

WEST GERMANY

				Turkey 4–1	Argentina 3–1
				Hungary 3–8	Czechoslovakia 2–2
				Turkey 7–2 (p-o)	Northern Ireland 2–2
				Yugoslavia 2–0	Yugoslavia 1–0
				Austria 6–1	Sweden 1–3
				Hungary 3–2 (W)	France 3–6 (4th)

1962	1966	1970	1974	1978	1982

SWEDEN

		Italy 0–1	Bulgaria 0–0	Brazil 1–1	
		Israel 1–1	Netherlands 0–0	Austria 0–1	
		Uruguay 1–0	Uruguay 3–0	Spain 0–1	
			Poland 0–1		
			West Germany 2–4		
			Yugoslavia 2–1		

SWITZERLAND

Chile 1–3	West Germany 0–5				
West Germany 1–2	Spain 1–2				
Italy 0–3	Argentina 0–2				

TUNISIA

				Mexico 3–1	
				Poland 0–1	
				West Germany 0–0	

TURKEY

UNITED STATES OF AMERICA

URUGUAY

Colombia 2–1	England 0–0	Israel 2–0	Netherlands 0–2		
Yugoslavia 1–3	France 2–1	Italy 0–0	Bulgaria 1–1		
USSR 1–2	Mexico 0–0	Sweden 0–1	Sweden 0–3		
	West Germany 0–4	USSR 1–0			
		Brazil 1–3			
		West Germany 0–1			
		(4th)			

USSR

Yugoslavia 2–0	North Korea 3–0	Mexico 0–0			Brazil 1–2
Colombia 4–4	Italy 1–0	Belgium 4–1			New Zealand 3–0
Uruguay 2–1	Chile 2–1	El Salvador 2–0			Scotland 2–2
Chile 1–2	Hungary 2–1	Uruguay 0–1			Belgium 1–0
	West Germany 1–2				Poland 0–0
	Portugal 1–2 (4th)				

WALES

WEST GERMANY

Italy 0–0	Switzerland 5–0	Morocco 2–1	Chile 1–0	Poland 0–0	Algeria 1–2
Switzerland 2–1	Argentina 0–0	Bulgaria 5–2	Australia 3–0	Mexico 6–0	Chile 4–1
Chile 2–0	Spain 2–1	Peru 3–1	East Germany 0–1	Tunisia 0–0	Austria 1–0
Yugoslavia 0–1	Uruguay 4–0	England 3–2	Yugoslavia 2–0	Italy 0–0	England 0–0
	USSR 2–1	Italy 3–4	Sweden 4–2	Netherlands 2–2	Spain 2–1
	England 2–4 (2nd)	Uruguay 1–0 (3rd)	Poland 1–0	Austria 2–3	France 3–3*
			Netherlands 2–1 (W)		Italy 1–3 (2nd)

1930	1934	1938	1950	1954	1958

YUGOSLAVIA

Brazil 2–1			Switzerland 3–0	France 1–0	Scotland 1–1
Bolivia 4–0			Mexico 4–1	Brazil 1–1	France 3–2
Uruguay 1–6			Brazil 0–2	West Germany 0–2	Paraguay 3–3
					West Germany 0–1

ZAIRE

1962	1966	1970	1974	1978	1982

					YUGOSLAVIA
USSR 0–2			Brazil 0–0		Northern Ireland 0–0
Uruguay 3–1			Zaire 9–0		Spain 1–2
Colombia 5–0			Scotland 1–1		Honduras 1–0
West Germany 1–0			West Germany 0–2		
Czechoslovakia 1–3			Poland 1–2		
Chile 0–1 (4th)			Sweden 1–2		

					ZAIRE
			Scotland 0–2		
			Yugoslavia 0–9		
			Brazil 0–3		

French goalkeeper Jean-Luc Ettori saves from Norman Whiteside (left) with Marius Tresor in attendance, during the World Cup 1982 in Spain. *ASP*

EXTRA TIME

Facts and Feats

Tommy Walker established a record of League appearances for one season when he made 48 for two clubs in 1946–47: Chelsea (39) and Heart of Midlothian (9). An inside-forward he was born in Livingstone Station, Scotland and made his debut for Hearts in 1932. After two and a half years with the Stamford Bridge club he returned to Hearts later becoming their manager and then a director. He was capped on 21 occasions by Scotland.

Four into three
For a period of three months in 1968–69 Queen's Park Rangers had four different managers: Alec Stock, Bill Dodgin, Tommy Docherty and Les Allen.

First of the few
Former Chelsea manager David Calderhead was presented with the Football League long service medal in 1932, the first ex-professional to receive the award.

Roker nap
When Sunderland signed Welsh international Leighton James from Swansea City in January 1983, they completed a full hand of internationals, having already signed Frank Worthington (England), Iain Munro (Scotland) and Jimmy Nicholl (Northern Ireland) as well as having Eire youth international Graham Quinn on their books at the time.

Midweek fixture
The directors of The Wednesday FC expressed the wish on 23 June 1927 that the club should be known as Sheffield Wednesday. The legal title was The Wednesday. On 29 June 1929 the FA and Football League acknowledged the change to Sheffield Wednesday.

High and low
In the 1971–72 season Aston Villa attracted an average of 31 952 spectators to their Division Three matches. It was the thirteenth highest average that term in the Football League. Villa were champions of Division Three.

Unfitting outcome
The only occasion when a Football League club refused to complete a fixture occurred on 2 April 1974, when Exeter City had only nine fit players prior to their match at Scunthorpe United. Eight players were either ill or injured and another was under suspension. The League refused to postpone the game and awarded the points to Scunthorpe. Exeter were fined £5000 and with the compensation they had to pay it cost them £6026 altogether.

Wearside defiant
Sunderland goalkeeper Chris Turner was unbeaten for 573 minutes during the 1982–83 season, the sequence including seven matches without conceding a goal, a Sunderland club record. These began on 18 December in a 3–0 home win against Arsenal when Sunderland were bottom of Division One. The following games were: Manchester United (A) 0–0, Liverpool (H) 0–0, Nottingham Forest (A) 0–0, Notts County (A) 1–0 then two FA Cup matches, Manchester City (H) 0–0 and (A) 1–2 followed by two more League games, Aston Villa (H) 2–0 and Tottenham Hotspur (A) 1–1, where the run came to an end in the 19th minute. The overall run began in the 76th minute of Sunderland's 3–0 defeat at West Bromwich Albion on 11 December.

Few but too many

In the 1973–74 season Manchester United conceded only 48 goals in Division One matches, the best record of goals conceded by a relegated team from 42 matches. In 1901–02 Small Heath were relegated after conceding just 45 goals in 34 games.

Little in common

Two of England's smallest international goal-keepers were Teddy Davison (Sheffield Wednesday in 1922) and Alan Hodgkinson (Sheffield United in 1956–57). They were both 5 ft 7 in (1 m 70 cm) tall. Davison as Sheffield United's manager was the man who first signed Hodgkinson as a professional.

Neal takes a bow

Phil Neal completed his 400th consecutive appearance for Liverpool and also the 700th of his career against Manchester City in a Division One match on 4 April 1983. It was his 350th consecutive League game and he had missed only one of Liverpool's previous 498 senior games, a European Cup tie against Trabzonspor on 20 October 1976.

Neal, who was Bob Paisley's first signing as manager, began his run of matches on 14 December 1974 against Luton Town in Division One. His 400 was composed of 277 in the

Tommy Walker, the Chelsea and Hearts inside-forward, who achieved a unique record for League appearances.

Manchester United

Manchester United have averaged 43 000 spectators each season since the Second World War in Football League games to become the best supported club in England. They were the first British club to record a six-figure profit when they recorded a surplus of £100 000 in 1958.

In 1982–83 they finished with a higher average league gate than any other club for the eleventh season in succession.

In 1967–68 they had a League average attendance of 57 758, a record in the history of the competition. The following season the club sold 1 554 540 copies of the official programme 'United Review'—another record.

For the Manchester United v Arsenal game they disposed of 64 772 copies and averaged 51 818 sales for home matches. The same season they sold 74 680 copies of the World Club Championship match programme against Estudiantes de la Plata (Argentina) and in 1967–68, 60 462 copies of their European Cup match programme with Real Madrid.

League, 44 in the League Cup, 32 FA Cup, 38 European Cup, four Super Cup, four Charity Shield and one World Club Championship match. During this period he scored 50 goals, made up of 35 in the League, three in the League Cup, two FA Cup and 10 in Europe.

No luck for the Irish

Ballymena United qualified for the European Cup Winner's Cup in 1978–79 as Linfield's 3–1 victims in the Irish Cup Final. In the Irish League Ballymena had finished bottom, four points adrift of their nearest rivals and taking only ten points from 22 games. In the first round they lost both legs 3–0 to the Belgian club Beveren and were eliminated.

Simple fare

On 20 April 1901 Tottenham Hotspur met Sheffield United in the FA Cup Final at the Crystal Palace. Thomas Cook the travel agents offered a conducted drive, visiting principal places of interest in London in connection with Excursion trains being run to London by the Midland Railway. A meat breakfast was guaranteed on arrival, followed by the drive around London and dinner at the Crystal Palace. The inclusive charge of the day's outing was 6s. 6d. (32½p).

A magnificent seven

Seven of Sunderland's regular team, which was relegated from Division One for the first time in the club's history in 1958, subsequently became managers of Football League and non-league clubs: Stan Anderson, Billy Elliott, Billy Bingham, Don Revie, Alan O'Neill, Charlie Hurley, and Amby Fogarty. Bingham (Northern

Derby Match updates

Local derbies from previous editions up to date to end of the 1982–3 season:

Everton 44 Liverpool 45 drawn 39
Manchester City 31 Manchester United 38 drawn 37
Rangers 74 Celtic 58 drawn 56
Sheffield United 35 Sheffield Wednesday 30 drawn 27
Arsenal 36 Tottenham Hotspur 37 drawn 19
Hearts 61 Hibs 54 drawn 39
Newcastle United 38 Sunderland 38 drawn 30

Ireland) and Revie (England) also became national team managers.

Quartet in unison

During the 1981–82 season York City had four managers. Barry Lyons left in December, Kevin Randall in March and temporary manager Barry Swallow, a club director, vacated the position in May when Denis Smith became player-manager.

Lucky thirteen

Northampton Town did not win any of their opening 12 Division Four matches in 1981–82, during which they took only five points. On 24 October 1981 they beat Tranmere Rovers 3–2.

The waiting game

At the end of the 1982–83 season Tottenham Hotspur had not won at Liverpool since March 1912, Bolton Wanderers were reflecting on their last win at Bristol City in 1907 and Newcastle United were still seeking their first win at Cardiff City.

Uncanny opening

At the start of the 1950–51 season all the promoted teams lost on the first day, all the relegated sides won and the newly-elected clubs drew.

Two fives equal eight

On 5 December 1942 Jack Stone scored five goals in a row for Sheffield United against Mansfield Town in a wartime regional league game which ended in a 6–2 win for United. In December 1950 he hit five out of six goals for Boston United against York City reserves.

Beginners ill-luck

Norman Kirkham made his debut for Leicester City against Hull City on 29 August 1949 and suffered a broken nose. On 12 August 1950, on his debut for Southampton, he injured an eye.

Store and score keeper

Joe Lancaster was Manchester United's fourth choice goalkeeper when he was called upon for first team duty on 14 January 1950 against Chelsea.

Against Watford in an FA Cup tie on 28 January he became United's first amateur goalkeeper in the competition. A store keeper by trade he kept two clean sheets in these matches, as United beat both Chelsea and Watford 1–0.

Lancaster turned professional and made one other senior appearance in a 3–2 win over Burnley on 4 February 1950. The following season he joined Accrington Stanley but made only one League appearance for them.

The author at the Corinthian-Casuals Centenary Dinner at the Dorchester Hotel, flanked by former Cambridge Soccer Blues David Miller (left) of *The Times* and Chris Turnbull.

Identical records

David and Andrew Prentice were identical twins who played for Trowbridge in 1950. David worked in an Estate Agent's Office, Andrew in a solicitor's. They trained on the Trowbridge ground in the evenings and were both signed as part-time professionals by Bristol City in September 1950. In 1954 they were given free transfers, neither having played in the City first team.

Mac the Sassenach

Liverpool goalkeeper Bill McOwen was the odd man out in his team's first ever League game in 1893. The other ten were Scots leaving him the only Englishman in it.

Amateur milestone

Corinthian-Casuals celebrated their centenary in 1982–83 and as part of the year-long commemoration the Sheriff of London Shield was revived on 28 March 1983 with a match for them at Watford against the Division One side. Watford won 6–1. The previous occasion that the match had been staged Watford had won 7–1 in 1966–67.

Season to forget

Hull City full-back Bobby McNeil began the 1981–82 season by being struck in the eye by a ball during training. His left eye was damaged and he spent four days in hospital. The injury kept him out of action for six weeks.

Then, at Tranmere in February, he broke a bone in his left foot; only four comeback matches later he broke the same bone and at the end of the season he was given a free transfer.

Crowded days

Although the record official attendance for an FA Cup Final is 126 047 for the Bolton Wanderers v West Ham United game on 28 April 1923, this was the number of paid admissions only, as many thousands of other spectators obtained entry without paying. But in 1913 at the

Ron Greenwood in his days as England's manager.
Mick Alexander/Peter Robinson

Crystal Palace the crowd had been as high as 120 028 for the Aston Villa v Sunderland game.

Greenwood chopped down

Ron Greenwood, who joined Bradford Park Avenue in December 1945, was later dropped into the club's reserve side in the Midland League. In a game against Grantham that season he was on the losing side in a 9–6 defeat in which the opposing centre-forward, Jack Macartney, scored eight times.

Macartney joined Grantham in 1937–38 at 17

and in nearly 30 years scored over 400 goals for them until injury caused his retirement.

Phil's seventh heaven

Phil Thompson achieved his seventh Division One championship medal with Liverpool in 1982–83. He won six previously with the club in 1972–73, 1975–76, 1976–77, 1978–79, 1979–80 and 1981–82.

Turf Moor heads and tales

Burnley established a record 62 points in the 1972–73 season losing only four matches, their best since 1897–98 when they lost two in 12 fewer games. In 1972–73 they used 17 players, six of whom were ever present, another missed just one game and another was absent only twice. One player made three appearances, three others made just four substitute appearances between them. The club finished as Division Two champions one point ahead of Queen's Park Rangers.

Skating winger

Everton winger Jackie Coulter, who made eleven international appearances while with Belfast Celtic, Grimsby Town and Chelmsford City as well as the Goodison Park club in the 1930s, had also been roller skating champion of Ireland.

Recalled to glory

Alan Mullery was a Fulham player 24 hours before helping Tottenham Hotspur into the 1971–72 UEFA Cup Final. On loan to the Craven Cottage club he was recalled in time to play against AC Milan in the semi-final.

Forward famine

On 28 April 1923 only ten goals were scored in ten Division One matches. Thirteen teams failed to score.

Hunt for goals

In 1938–39 Walter Hunt scored four, four and three goals respectively in Division Three (Northern) matches against Lincoln City, Accrington Stanley and Rochdale for Carlisle United, the three clubs in question having been his former teams.

Day of feasting

On 1 February 1936, 209 goals were scored in the Football League: 46 in Division One, 46 in Division Two, 49 in Division Three (Southern) and 68 in Division Three (Northern).

Better late . . .

Billy Wardle, an outside-left, scored from the penalty spot for Grimsby Town on 5 October 1946. It was the first time he had registered a goal in ten years of professional service, having joined Southport originally in October 1936.

Official programme 2d   Saturday 17th August

Storm Stadium, Weatherley, kick-off 3.p.m.

Weatherley
United
v.

Trumpedup Travellers

CLUB NOTES

Well, here we are with another season—and one which cannot be worse than the last! After all completing our entire programme without a win, only five goals—two of which were penalties and the others by courtesy of the other side—and just six points from home games was not what we hoped for a year ago.

But how desparately unlucky we were in most of our fixtures, suffering from poor refereeing, inadequate support and opponents who continually provided far too strong tests for our boys.

This season, however, with a completely new line-up, we know things will improve and our visitors today, Trumpedup Travellers, will find Weatherley United a different proposition.

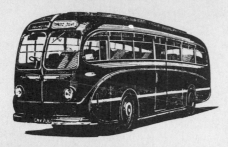
Weatherley United

				Tempest
				Outside left
		Snow	**Showers**	
		Left half	*Inside left*	
	Fogg			
	Left back	**Gale**	**Frost**	
Lightening		*Centre half*	*Centre forward*	
Goalkeeper	**Raine**			
	Right back	**Blizzard**	**Hails**	
		Right half	*Inside right*	
			Flood	
			Outside right	

Referee—C. N. TOFF

Trumpedup Travellers

Sunderland
Outside right

Bradford
Inside right

Bolton
Right half

Sheffield
Centre forward

Charlton
Centre half

Oldham
Right back

Oxford
Goalkeeper

Hull
Left back

Birmingham
Inside left

Watford
Left half

Mansfield
Outside left

Linesmen—B. LIND-PUGH (*Red Flag*) and P. DANTICK (*Yellow Flag*)

Pen Pictures of today's teams.

WEATHERLEY UNITED

Arthur Lightening South African-born goalkeeper previously with Nottingham Forest, Coventry City and Middlesbrough.

David Raine Right back, born in Darlington who was with Port Vale, Doncaster Rovers and Colchester United.

Dave Fogg Liverpool-born left-back who played for Wrexham and Oxford United.

Les Blizzard Right-half from Acton who was with Queen's Park Rangers, Bournemouth, Yeovil and Leyton Orient.

Tom Gale Centre-half who began as an amateur with Gateshead. Later with Sheffield Wednesday and York City.

George Snow Left-half who made his name with Wrexham and is the veteran member of the team.

John Flood Southampton-born right-winger who played for his local club and then Bournemouth.

Billy Hails Inside-right from Nettlesworth, formerly with Lincoln City, Peterborough United, Northampton Town and Luton Town.

Des Frost Centre-forward from Congleton. Previous clubs: Leeds United, Halifax Town, Rochdale, Crewe Alexandra.

Derek Showers Merthyr-born inside-left who has played for Cardiff City, Bournemouth, Portsmouth and Hereford United.

Dale Tempest Leeds-born outside-left who has played for Fulham.

TRUMPEDUP TRAVELLERS

Ken Oxford Manchester-born goalkeeper. Previous clubs: Manchester City Derby County (two spells), Chesterfield, Norwich City, Doncaster Rovers and Port Vale.

Eric Oldham Newcastle-born right-back previously with Bolton Wanderers, Gateshead and Hartlepool United.

Gary Hull Left-back born Sheffield and developed by Sheffield Wednesday.

Ron Bolton Golborne-born and formerly with Bournemouth (two spells) and Ipswich Town.

Jack Charlton Ashington-born centre-half who was previously with Leeds United.

Albert Watford Left-half, born in Chesterfield and played for the local club and later Lincoln City.

Alan Sunderland Outside-right. Mexborough-born and formerly with Wolverhampton Wanderers and Arsenal.

Geoff Bradford Inside-right who was Bristol-born and developed by Bristol Rovers.

Laurie Sheffield Centre-forward born in Swansea. Previously with Bristol Rovers, Newport County, Doncaster Rovers (two spells), Norwich City, Rotherham United, Oldham Athletic, Luton Town and Peterborough United.

Charlie Birmingham Inside-left who was born in Liverpool and began as an Everton amateur before joining Tranmere Rovers.

Ronnie Mansfield Romford-born outside-left and was with Ilford and Millwall before joining Southend United.

Printed by John Bull Printing Outfitters, Union St., Weatherley

Referees in Line Abreast

The diagonal system of refereeing with linesmen keeping mostly to one half of the touch-line instead of covering the whole line was first introduced by Stanley Rous in 1933. He used it when he refereed the FA Cup Final in 1934. When he subsequently submitted the idea to the FA Referees Committee, it was generally accepted and has since been included in the FA Referees' Chart and the FIFA Universal Guide for Referees.

But in Pickford's *Association Football*, 1905 it was stated that 'in practice the linesman is entrusted with the oversight of the touchline, the referee, the goal-line and goal positions. This is a useful division of the work, but it is not a peremptory one—the linesman should keep an active watch on the ball crossing the goal-line so that he can, if required, help the referee either by signal or by consultation. The linesman should act as far as he can as a goal judge. To achieve this, the suggestion is made that one linesman should work more along the touch-line on one half of the field of play and the other conversely.'

The book *Don Davies—an old international* by Jack Cox includes extracts from the writings of Don Davies of the *Manchester Guardian* who was killed in the 1958 Munich disaster. About famous referees the following is quoted on A E Fogg of Bolton:

'As a referee he was second only in renown to that fellow townsman of Bolton, J T Howcroft. Both were men of assertive character and progressive ideas and both left their mark on football. In the case of Howcroft it was largely a struggle for the purification of manners on the football field and for the submission to authority. By the time Fogg arrived (in 1923) that battle had been won. The burning question of his hour was how to control the game which, since the alteration of the offside law in 1925, had speeded up far beyond the powers of any mortal referee to attempt to keep up with the play. Fogg's contribution was to seize hold of the shadowy ideas of diagonal control (first mooted by the Secretary-Manager of the Burnley club in 1904 and later tried in Belgium), allocate separate and distinct duties to the linesmen in their respective halves of the field and so evolve a system which is now familiar, universally adopted and as effective as it is single.'

(N.B. The Secretary-Manager of Burnley in 1904 was Spen Whittaker who had previously had a long connection with the game in the Accrington district.)

Players and Places

Bryan Robson (West Bromwich Albion) broke his left leg three times in 1976–77 during a period of six months. His first break came on 2 October against Tottenham Hotspur. After eight weeks out he returned to play for the reserves but suffered a refracture against Stoke.

He regained his place in the League side but shortly after being selected for the England Under-21 team he broke his leg for a third time, playing against Manchester City on 16 April 1977; his leg was in plaster for 14 weeks.

Burning ambition
Albert Nightingale, an inside-forward, was with Sheffield United when Bramall Lane was blitzed during World War Two, at Huddersfield Town when the stand was burned out by fire in 1951 and with Leeds United when their stand went up in flames and smoke in September 1956.

Born at Thryburgh, he joined Sheffield United during the war and was transferred to Huddersfield in March 1948. He moved to Blackburn Rovers in October 1951 and Leeds United a year later. He made 346 League appearances and scored 87 goals.

Action replay
The first complete televised showing of a football match was in August 1936, when the BBC screened a film of the Arsenal v Everton game. The first live transmission came from Germany in November 1936.

Train of events
When Manchester United were still known as Newton Heath they arrived at Stoke on 7 January 1893 without goalkeeper Warner who had missed his train. Three different players Stewart, Fitzsimmons and Clements all had a turn in goal. United scored first but lost 7–1.

Insult to injury
Fred Corbett a full-back with Lincoln City, was playing at York in a Division Three (Northern) match on 4 December 1937 when he was injured badly enough to be carried to the dressing-room. After the match he was informed by the referee that he had been sent off. York won 3–1.

Born in Birmingham he had joined Torquay United from Worcester City in 1929. He was transferred to Manchester City with his full-back partner Sid Cann on 13 March 1930, although he made only 15 League appearances for them until moving to Lincoln City at the start of the 1936–

37 season when he became a regular choice for the Imps.

Early stardom

Joe Clennel scored more peacetime goals in the first of his 14 seasons in the Football League than in any others. He began his career with Silksworth United and then played for Seaham Harbour. He was on the books of Blackpool as an amateur before turning professional with them in 1910.

He was Blackpool's leading scorer with 20 goals from 32 appearances before being transferred to Blackburn Rovers in time to make three appearances, scoring two goals towards the end of the 1910–11 season.

He added a further 23 League appearances scoring ten goals at either centre- or inside-forward and was transferred to Everton for £1500 in January 1914.

During the First World War he became a more regular marksman for Everton. In 1915–16 he scored 31 in 33 appearances and worked at Liverpool docks during hostilities.

An injury in 1920 kept him out for a lengthy time and in October 1921 he was allowed to move to Cardiff City where he scored 37 goals in 118 League apparances before a further transfer to Stoke mid-way through 1924–25. He scored two goals in 22 matches for Stoke, five in 18 appearances for Bristol Rovers from 1926 and two goals in 14 matches for Rochdale from 1927.

Clennel then had some managerial experience with Distillery and became coach to Accrington Stanley in 1934. He had one of the finest collections of cartilages which he kept in bottles but had the misfortune to lose his football medals which were stolen by a burglar.

Dixon of the green

Kerry Dixon who scored four goals for Reading at Doncaster in a Division Three match in the 1982–83 season, yet still finished on the losing side, was the club's leading scorer during the season with 26 League goals.

He made his name with Dunstable, scoring 52 goals for them in one season having been released after a period with Tottenham Hotspur. In his first season with Reading during 1980–81 he combined part-time football with work as a tool-maker.

Goal formula

Brian McClair, a 19-year-old chemistry student at Glasgow University, scored all three goals for Motherwell in their 3–0 win over Rangers in a Scottish Premier Division game on 3 January 1983, then two including a penalty in a 2–1 win over Celtic on 15 January. He had joined Aston Villa at the age of 16 and spent one season at Villa Park.

No simple Symon

James Scot Symon played five times for Scotland at cricket in the period 1935–38 including a game against Australia, the only man to play for Scotland at both sports.

Scot Symon joined Dundee from the local club Violet in 1930 and was transferred to Portsmouth in 1935, having won schoolboy honours. He returned to Scotland with Rangers in 1938–39 and was capped that season against Hungary at left-half.

He played against the Aussies at cricket at Forthill in 1938, taking 6–33 in their first innings of 213.

Irish marksmen

On 26 October 1966 Linfield beat Valerengen 4–1 in Oslo in a first leg European Cup match, scoring all their goals in a spell of eight minutes in the first half.

Life with the Lyons

In 1939 Tommy Lyon, a Glasgow born Scottish inside-forward, was with Chesterfield while his brother Willie, born in Birkenhead was a centre-half with Celtic.

Willie Lyon was signed by Queen's Park from Kirkintilloch Rob Roy in the 1933–34 season as a centre-half. After two seasons he joined Celtic, making 38 League appearances and scoring six goals in 1935–36.

The following season Celtic met Queen's Park in the final of the Glasgow Charity Cup which Queen's Park had not won for 46 years. With the seconds ticking away towards the final whistle, the score at 3–3 and Queen's Park ahead on corner kicks which would have decided the issue in the event of a draw, Lyon scored the winning goal against his former club.

On 13 February 1937 Tommy Lyon lined up for Albion Rovers at inside-right in a Scottish Cup tie against a Celtic side in which his brother was playing centre-half. Celtic won 5–2.

On 16 March Tommy was transferred to Blackpool on the day of the transfer deadline. Albion finished bottom of the Scottish Division One and were relegated. Blackpool finished second in Division Two and were promoted to

Soccer Specials

The London and North-Eastern Railway introduced a batch of 23 locomotives for express passenger work in East Anglia during 1936–37 with Football League club names on them. The engines were scrapped between 1958–60.

Original Engine No.	Name	Panel Colours	BR No.
2848	Arsenal	Red	61648
2849	Sheffield United	Red and white	61649
2850	Grimsby Town	Black and white	61650
2851	Derby County	White	61651
2852	Darlington	Black and white	61652
2853	Huddersfield Town	Blue and white	61653
2854	Sunderland	Red and white	61654
2855	Middlesbrough	Red	61655
2856	Leeds United	Blue and old gold; white latterly	61656
2857	Doncaster Rovers	Red and white	61657
2858	Newcastle United*	Black and white	61658
2859 2839	Norwich City†	Dark green and yellow	61659
2860	Hull City	Blue; chrome yellow and black post-War	61660
2861	Sheffield Wednesday	Blue and white	61661
2862	Manchester United	Red	61662
2863	Everton	Blue	61663
2864	Liverpool	Red	61664
2865	Leicester City	Blue	61665
2866	Nottingham Forest	Red	61666
2867	Bradford	Black, yellow and red	61667
2868	Bradford City	Claret and amber	61668
2869	Barnsley	Red	61669
2870 2830	Tottenham Hotspur‡	White, with cockerel badges	61670
2871	Manchester City	Blue	—
2872	West Ham United	Claret and blue; red post-War	61672

*Name changed to *The Essex Regiment*.
†Originally named *Rendelsham Hall* but the nameplates were incorrectly spelled and in 1938 the Norwich City nameplates were put on it as 2859 had had a name change of its own to *East Anglian* in 1937.
‡Originally named *Manchester City* and later *City of London*.

Single-colour panels were usually edged with a $\frac{3}{16}$ in wide white surrounding lining, though *Nottingham Forest, Tottenham Hotspur, Manchester City* and *West Ham United* (post-War) had blue linings instead. Where two or three colours appeared on the panel they were arranged in stripes with a black edging (red in the case of *Grimsby Town*). The width and number of stripes varied considerably, whilst the stripes themselves could be vertical or horizontal. There were even variations over the years in the interpretation of any one arrangement— for example, *Doncaster Rovers* had horizontal stripes pre-War, vertical stripes post-War, all-red panels by 1958 and finally vertical stripes again when restored after withdrawal for presentation.

When No. 2854 *Sunderland* was needed for working a Cup Final special in 1937 (the year Sunderland won the Cup), it was under general repair at Gorton from 10 April to 15 May. So on 17 April No. 2851 went to Gorton to acquire 2854's number and nameplates. Its own number and nameplates were replaced during another short visit to Gorton from 9 to 13 May. It should perhaps be mentioned that there is in existence an official photograph taken at Darlington showing No. 2849 when new named *Darlington*. This was taken for Works photographic purposes only, and is doubly confusing in that this engine was originally allotted the name *Derby County*.

Division One. That season Willie Lyon won a Scottish Cup winners medal with Celtic whom he captained.

Tommy and Willie both played in wartime region football for several clubs and Tommy ended his career after it with New Brighton.

Madrid milestones
Real Madrid were unbeaten on their Santiago Bernabeu ground over eight years from February 1957 to March 1965, winning 114 matches and drawing eight.

Real's winger Francisco Gento played in 94 matches for the club in European competitions.

Alfredo di Stefano played his 400th game for Real Madrid against Real Sociedad in January 1961 and scored his 350th goal for them.

Ferenc Puskas joined Real on 11 May 1958 and scored two goals for them in a 6–1 friendly win against Manchester United on 1 October 1959 at Old Trafford. The other scorers were Di Stefano 2, Gento and Pipilli. Warren Bradley replied for United.

Real were involved in the first match to be played on a full size pitch completely under cover. It was staged in April 1967 at the Houston Astrodome in Texas. Real Madrid beat West Ham United 3–2 before a crowd of 33 351.

Togetherness
In 1963 two 15-year-olds from Scotland joined Leeds United from Glasgow schoolboy football. They were Jimmy Lumsden (Kinning Park) and Eddie Gray (Holy Rood). Lumsden spent seven years at Elland Road, moved to Southend United and subsequently became Celtic's youth team coach. Gray was appointed player-manager of the club in July 1982 and promptly appointed Lumsden as his assistant.

Penalty fiasco
On 23 February 1957 Jim Iley missed two penalty kicks in four minutes for Sheffield United against Notts County in a Division Two match. His first shot was saved, the second hit a post. The incidents came in the 73rd and 76th minutes of a 2–2 draw. On 13 October 1956 he had scored two penalties against Notts County in a 5–1 win at Bramall Lane.

Pre-Royal occasion
In February 1923 the Duke of York attended a second round Scottish Cup tie between Queen's Park and Bathgate at Hampden Park. The match ended in a 1–1 draw with Queen's Park winning the replay 2–0.

Foreign exiles
In the 1956–57 season Arthur Willis (Swansea Town) was often the only non-Welshman playing for the club's first team while Paddy Sowden (Accrington Stanley) had a similar experience as an Englishman among Scots.

Viewing time
Closed circuit televised screening of a Division One match at Highbury between Arsenal and Manchester United on 3 March 1967 attracted an attendance of 28 000 at Old Trafford.

Wood's day to forget
On 4 October 1913 in a Division Two match between Stockport County and Fulham, Norman Wood, the Stockport inside-left, headed through his own goal in the tenth minute in attempting to clear a corner kick to put Fulham in the lead. Five minutes later he accidentally knocked the ball down with his hand in the penalty area and Fred Mavin increased Fulham's lead from the resultant penalty kick.

Soon afterwards, at the other end, the Stockport inside-right Gault was brought down in the area by Fulham's left-back Houghton. Wood took the penalty kick but shot almost straight at the Fulham goalkeeper who saved easily. Fulham won 3–1.

Eagles in captivity
On 29 November 1920 the Crystal Palace directors decided to enclose the playing pitch of their ground, the Nest, with an unclimbable fence and ordered the work to be started immediately.

Sporting days
On 26 March 1921 in a Division One match between Arsenal and Sheffield United there was a tussle close to the United goal line between Dr Paterson (Arsenal) and Willie Cook the Sheffield full-back. The ball went over the line and the referee awarded a corner kick to Arsenal. However Dr Paterson walked across to the referee and protested that he had been last to play the ball, so the official changed his decision and awarded a goal kick.

Atlantic Fryer
In November 1920 the FA declared that William Fryer, a registered professional with Barnsley, having failed to observe the rules of the organisation, would be suspended *sine die* and would not be eligible to play for any other club.

Fryer a half-back and a native of Burradon, was with Hyker West End and had joined Barnsley during 1919–20. He made nine appearances that season in the League. He was retained for the 1920–21 season and received his summer wages. Fryer played for Barnsley at Oakwell against Notts County in their Division Two match on 6 September 1920, then disappeared leaving no trace.

It was not until Barnsley and the FA had letters from the New York FC in the USA asking for particulars of this player that it was discovered where he had gone. He had apparently played for New York in a National Cup tie and their opponents had lodged a protest against Fryer as a professional attached to an English club.

Kiwis revisited
Reg Boyne, a centre-forward, was invited by Aston Villa to come over from New Zealand in 1913. He arrived from Auckland and landed at Tilbury Docks on the morning of 6 December 1913.

Born in Leeds, he was 22 years old at the time of joining Villa and made four appearances for them in each of the 1913–14 and 1914–15 seasons. He later played for Brentford.

At the time of his arrival Villa had been trying

Molineux Floodlit Memories

Between 1953 and 1961 Wolverhampton Wanderers staged a number of successful floodlit friendly and competitive matches at Molineux.

It was their three games with Moscow Spartak, Honved and Moscow Dynamo which helped to fire the imagination of English followers towards European competition.

30.9.53: Wolves 3 South Africa 1 (33 681)
Scorers: Mullen, Broadbent, Swinbourne

14.10.53: Wolves 2 Celtic 0 (41 820)
Scorer: Wilshaw 2

10.3.54: Wolves 3 Racing (Buenos Aires) 1 (37 122)
Scorers: Taylor, Deeley, Mullen

29.9.54: (Charity Shield) Wolves 4 WBA 4 (40 800)
Scorers: Swinbourne 2, Deeley, Hancocks

13.10.54: Wolves 0 First Vienna 0 (39 969)

28.10.54: Wolves 10 Maccabi Tel Aviv 0 (26 901)
Scorers: Flowers, Swinbourne 3, Broadbent 2, Hancocks 2, Wilshaw, McDonald

16.11.54: Wolves 4 Moscow Spartak 0 (55 184)
Scorers: Wilshaw, Hancocks 2, Swinbourne

13.12.54: Wolves 3 Honved 2 (54 998)
Scorers: Hancocks (pen), Swinbourne 2

9.11.55: Wolves 2 Moscow Dynamo 1 (55 480)
Scorers: Slater, Mullen

29.10.56: Wolves 5 CCA Bucharest 0 (47 284)
Scorers: Murray 2, Hooper (pen), Broadbent, Booth

12.12.56: Wolves 1 Red Banner (Hungary) 1 (43 540)
Scorer: Neil
(£2312 3s. 4d—raised for the Hungarian Relief Fund)

27.3.57: Wolves 4 Borussia Dortmund 3 (26 900)
Scorers: Broadbent, Murray, Wilshaw, Hooper

10.4.57: Wolves 3 Valencia 0 (25 310)
Scorers: Thomson 2, Clamp

17.10.57: Wolves 3 Real Madrid 2 (55 169)
Scorers: Broadbent, Murray, Wilshaw

29.9.58: Wolves 1 South African International XI 0 (13 511)
Scorer: Horne

12.11.58: (European Cup) Wolves 2 Schalke 04 2 (45 767)
Scorer: Broadbent 2

7.10.59: (European Cup) Wolves 2 Vorwaerts Berlin 0 (55 747)
Scorers: Broadbent, Mason

24.11.59: (European Cup) Wolves 3 Red Star Belgrade 0 (55 519)
Scorers: Mason 2, Murray

2.3.60: (European Cup) Wolves 2 Barcelona 5 (55 535)
Scorers: Mason, Murray

10.11.60: Wolves 5 Dynamo Tbilisi 5 (34 006)
Scorers: Farmer 2, Durandt, Mason, Murray

30.11.60: (Cup Winners Cup) Wolves 5 FK Austria 0 (31 699)
Scorers: Broadbent 2, Kirkham 2, Mason

19.4.61: (Cup Winners Cup) Wolves 1 Rangers 1 (45 136)
Scorer: Broadbent

Record: Played 22; Won 15, Drawn 6, Lost 1. Goals for 68, against 28.

Appearances: Broadbent 19+1 sub, Slater 17, Stuart 17, Flowers 16, Wright 13, Deeley 12, Clamp 11, Murray 11, Wilshaw 11, Williams 10, Mason 10+1 sub, Hancocks 9+1 sub, Harris 9, Mullen 9, Showell 9, Shorthouse 8, Finlayson 7, Swinbourne 6, Hooper 4, Durandt 3+1 sub, Horne 3, Sidebottom 3, Lill 2+1 sub, Farmer 2, Guttridge 2, Short 2, Sims 2, Smith 2, Baxter 1, Booth 1, Jackson 1, Jones 1, Kirkham 1, Neil 1, Pritchard 1, Russell 1, McDonald 1, Stockin 1, Taylor 1, Tether 1, Thomson 1.

Goals: Broadbent 12, Swinbourne 9, Murray 7, Hancocks 6, Mason 6, Wilshaw 6, Mullen 3, Deeley 2, Farmer 2, Hooper 2, Kirkham 2, Thomson 2, Booth 1, Clamp 1, Durandt 1, Flowers 1, Horne 1, McDonald 1, Neil 1, Slater 1, Taylor 1.

Former Wolves stars left to right: Dennis Wilshaw, Peter Broadbent, Barry Stobart, Eddie Clamp, Malcolm Finlayson, Joe Gardiner, Johnny Hancocks and Roy Pritchard hoist latter day striker John Richards in his testimonial year.
Express and Star, Wolverhampton

to sign a player named Craig who was a member of the Australian Northern Union team touring England. Craig had been a useful soccer player in Australia before taking up Rugby. However, he was not a success, hence the club's interest in Boyne.

Brian Turner was born in West Ham but arrived at Chelsea in May 1968 as a midfield player from New Zealand where he had moved at the age of five.

He later played for Portsmouth where he made his Football League debut and ended his League career with Brentford, before returning to New Zealand where he became a member of the country's World Cup team for the 1982 finals in Spain.

Cheyne of events
Alec Cheyne who had scored direct from a corner for Scotland against England on 13 April 1929 later scored twice from corners in a cup-tie for Aberdeen. On 1 February 1930 he helped them beat Nithsdale Wanderers 5–1 in the second round of the Scottish Cup.

All round ability
Alan Hansen, the Liverpool and Scottsh inter-national defender in 1982–83 had played as a juvenile international at both volleyball and golf for his native country.

Foreign youth
Jacques Glassman was 16 years four months when he played in a UEFA Cup game for Strasbourg (France) against Duisburg (West Germany) in the 1978–79 season.

Worldly wise
Craig Johnston, the Johannesburg-born Australian-raised midfield player who joined Liverpool from Middlesbrough in April 1981 had suffered with a rare bone disease as a boy. An American specialist saved his leg from amputation.

Bond . . . 007th
Goalkeeper Len Bond started his career with Bristol City originally as an apprentice turning professional in September 1971. After making his League debut for them he was loaned out to five clubs at various periods: Exeter City, Cardiff City, Torquay United, Scunthorpe United, and Colchester United before joining Brentford, his seventh club in August 1977. Later he played for St Louis in the USA before linking up with Exeter City again in October 1980.

Thank you and good-bye
In 1978–79 Stuart Robertson, the Northampton

Town central defender, was voted Player of the Year by the club's supporters. A week later he was given a free transfer.

Port hit by a storm
On 13 April 1979 Wigan Athletic were losing their Division Four match at home to Port Vale by three goals when they scored five times in the last twenty-five minutes to win 5–3.

Six of one half a dozen . . .
On 28 April 1979 Peter Downsborough made his 650th League appearance in goal. Playing for Bradford City at home to Crewe Alexandra he had previously played for Halifax Town, Swindon Town and Brighton and Hove Albion (on loan). Bradford City beat Crewe 6–0 that day while Crewe reserves were reversing the score exactly against Bradford City.

Fatherland revisited
George Berry was born in Rostrup at an RAF base in West Germany. He was brought up in Blackpool the son of a Jamaican father and a Welsh mother who came from Mountain Ash in Glamorgan. Berry's grandfather was Scottish.

He made his League debut as a central defender with Wolverhampton Wanderers and later played for Stoke City. His first international appearance was as a substitute for Wales against West Germany on 17 October 1979 in Cologne.

Recovered from disaster
Jimmy O'Neill made his international debut in goal for the Republic of Ireland against Spain in Madrid on 1 June 1952. He found himself beaten twice before he touched the ball at all and once again before he had the opportunity of making any kind of save. Spain won 6–0. But he recovered to make 17 international appearances in his career spent mostly with Everton.

Certificate of a scorer
Nigerian centre-forward Tesi Balogun was born in Lagos and played for Peterborough United and Skegness after coming to this country in the 1950s. He was studying at the London School of Printing in the evenings and was paying 6d (2½p) a session for training facilities at Paddington Recreation Ground.

He wrote to Queen's Park Rangers for a trial and was signed in September 1956 making 13 appearances in the League and scoring three goals. Ten years later he wrote to Rangers from Nigeria, asking his former club to check his date of birth.

Heights of Hill
On 20 April 1975 Coventry City became the first

Football League club to appoint a Managing Director: Jimmy Hill. He resigned as Chairman on 3 April 1983.

The name's the same
In 1977 Manchester United signed 6 ft (1 m 83 cm) centre-forward Tony Whelan, a Salford-born local. In 1981 they signed a 6 ft Dublin-born defender Tony Whelan.

'King' Arthur
Arthur Rowley overtook Dixie Dean's record of 379 League goals on 29 April 1961 when he recorded his 380th League goal for Shrewsbury Town against Bradford City.

Double take
Mike Kearney had two separate spells with two different clubs. He joined Chester from Shrewsbury Town in March 1977 and moved to Reading in January 1978. In July 1980 he returned to Chester and came back to Reading in October the same year. Kearney, a Scottish-born striker he had originated with Peterhill.

Domestic complications
In May 1972 the father of the Leeds United and England defender or midfield player Paul Madeley married Paul's mother-in-law. Thus his father was his father-in-law, his wife his step-sister and his mother-in-law his step-mother.

No time to stagnate
Winger Dennis Woodhead was with Sheffield Wednesday when they were promoted to Division One in 1949–50, relegated in 1950–51, promoted in 1951–52, relegated in 1954–55 and with Derby County when they were promoted in 1956–57.

A family affair
On 17 February 1973 in a Division One match, Newcastle United drew 1–1 with Wolverhampton Wanderers, at Molineux. Kenny Hibbitt put Wolves ahead in the first half and his brother Terry equalised after the interval.

Mileage for Carr
In the 1980–81 season Graham Carr was manager of Nuneaton and could have claimed a varied career in the game. Born in Newcastle he won youth international honours for England and turned professional with Northampton Town in August 1962. He subsequently played as a half-back in all four divisions of the Football League, continuing his career with York City and Bradford Park Avenue. He later appeared in two FA Trophy finals at Wembley for Telford United and ended his career with Tonbridge, before managing Weymouth and Dartford.

The late Bob Hesford, an Army officer in the war and a schoolmaster who combined his work with professional football. Bob Hesford in his playing days with Huddersfield Town. *Huddersfield Examiner*

Unique among Scots
Jim Fallon, who was Clydebank's captain in the 1982–83 season, had been with the club for 16 years and was the only Scottish player to have played in Division Two, Division One and the Premier Division in successive seasons with the same club during his service with them. A part-time professional, he combined work as a physiotherapist with handicapped school children.

Injury Time
On 21 February 1948 in a Division One match between Sunderland and Huddersfield Town at Roker Park, the late Bob Hesford fractured his right ankle when he collided with Sunderland's Frank Bee who sustained a badly cut face and had to receive attention.

Jimmy Glazzard heads home for Huddersfield Town. He scored 139 League goals for them in 299 games before moving to Everton and finishing his League career with Mansfield Town. Mr Glazzard the grocer.

Huddersfield's inside-left Jimmy Glazzard went in goal and made one or two useful saves before being beaten in the second half by Len Shackleton and the recovered Bee who each scored their first goals for the club.

The kick-off had been due at 3.15 pm but the match had actually started at 3.10 pm and by the original kick-off time Hesford had already been injured and was in the dressing-room.

Historical trio
In 1981–82 three Football League clubs made administrative history. Cardiff City appointed Ron Jones as the first paid club director; Fulham

made Malcolm Macdonald the first manager to be given a seat on the board and Crystal Palace elected Ron Noades as the first paid chairman.

Ten year successes
In 1963 Colin Appleton was a member of the Leicester City team at left-half which was beaten 3–1 by Manchester United in the FA Cup Final. In 1973 he was manager of Scarborough when they won the FA Trophy at Wembley, beating Wigan Athletic 2–1; in 1983, as manager of Hull City, he guided them to promotion from Division Four.

Free child labour
The youngest FA Amateur Cup finalist was Leslie Smith who played outside-right for Wimbledon against Bishop Auckland at Stamford Bridge at the age of 16 in 1934–35. Bishops won 2–1 in a replay after a 0–0 draw which included extra time. He later turned professional with Aston Villa and Brentford.

Scoring donations
Cyril Done was leading scorer for two different Football League clubs during the 1954–55 season, playing 18 times for each of them. He began with Tranmere Rovers and scored 15 goals; he added another 13 after his transfer to Port Vale in December.

Full measure
When George Best signed for AFC Bournemouth in Division Three during the 1982–83 season it was his eleventh different club after leaving Manchester United: Jewish Guild (South Africa), Dunstable Town, Stockport County, Cork Celtic, Fulham, Los Angeles Aztecs, Fort Lauderdale Strikers, Hibernian and San Jose Earthquakes.

Young Brummies
On 7 October 1978 Birmingham City's full-backs against Manchester City in a Division One match were Pat Van Den Hauwe and Mark Dennis, both 17 years of age. They won 2–1.

Veteran Canaries
In the 1979–80 season Norwich City claimed the oldest active Football League player in 40 year old goalkeeper Kevin Keelan. In 1980–81 they included 39-year-old centre-half Duncan Forbes for a similar record.

Short Spriggs
Midfield player Stephen Spriggs, who captained Cambridge United in 1982–83, was probably the shortest Football League player since the last war when he was measured at only 5 ft (1 m 53 cm) on his 17th birthday while turning pro-

fessional for Huddersfield Town in February 1973.

Home and away
In 1980–81 the Scarborough centre-half Richard Dixey was living at Leicester and travelling 300 miles to home games in the Alliance Premier League. In 1946–47 the first season after the war, goalkeepers Matt Middleton and George Swindin were also involved in similar treks. Middleton lived at Sunderland and played for Plymouth Argyle; Swindin at Bradford and was turning out for Arsenal.

Dollar balance
When Steve Daley was transferred to Manchester City from Wolverhampton Wanderers for a reported fee of £1 437 500 in September 1979, his share of the move was said to have been over £60 000. In February 1981 he collected a reported £57 000 for a £300 000 move from City to Seattle Sounders in the USA.

Noble gesture
In February 1982 Chesterfield midfield player Geoff Salmons sacrificed three weeks wages voluntarily after being advised by a specialist to rest a hamstring injury.

Lighting-up goals
The first Scottish League game played under floodlights was on 7 March 1956 when Rangers beat Queen of the South 8–0 in Division One. Don Kichenbrand scored five goals.

Scottish cup draw
The highest aggregate of attendances in the Scottish Cup for one round occured in 1955 when the 16 third round matches were watched by 223 043 spectators.

Irish all rounder
Gerry McElhinney who made his debut for Bolton Wanderers in the 1981–82 season as a defender was signed from Distillery in Northern Ireland. He had been a double international at boxing and gaelic football and subsequently found himself chosen for a Northern Ireland soccer squad.

Custodians of old
John Jackson became the seventh goalkeeper since the war to play in the Football League after reaching the age of 40. The previous six had been Ted Sagar, Sam Bartram, Kevin Keelan, Alf Wood, Alex Ferguson and Neil McBain.

Jackson who started his career with Crystal Palace later played for Orient and Millwall, joining Ipswich Town at the start of the 1981–82 season. He was loaned to Hereford in 1982–83.

Dual sportsman
Viv Richards the Somerset and West Indies Test Cricketer played for Antigua in the qualifying competition for the 1978 World Cup.

Survivor at home
Martin Harris scored two goals for Workington when they were beaten 6–3 at Doncaster Rovers in a Division Four match on 19 April 1977. Doncaster-born Harris as substitute was the only survivor from Workington's team which met Doncaster Rovers in the FA Cup first round at Workington on 20 November 1982. Doncaster won 2–1.

Expensive trial
Kenny Dalglish spent a fortnight on trial with Liverpool in 1966 while on the books of Celtic. He played for Liverpool's 'B' team against Southport on 20 August 1966, wearing the No. 8 shirt in a match Southport won 1–0. He subsequently returned to Celtic and was loaned to Cumbernauld. Liverpool finally paid £440 000 for him in August 1977.

Milestones for two
On 15 January 1983 John Wile and Mick Mills each made their 600th League appearances, Wile for West Bromwich against Liverpool and Mills for Southampton against Coventry City. Centre-half Wile had previously made appearances for Peterborough United in the League and Mills as a midfield player or full-back for Ipswich Town.

Knee joint trouble
When Chris Robertson was a 16-year-old forward on the books of Rangers he had a cartilage operation on his right knee. Three years later a piece of bone was found lodged in the rear of the knee which necessitated a second operation.

A further three years, by which time he had moved to Heart of Midlothian, revealed more problems when it was discovered from an exploratory operation that the cartilage had grown back. Another operation followed from which he came back too quickly and spent nearly six months regaining fitness.

Towards the end of the 1980–81 season he returned to senior duty with Hearts.

Foreign fad
Jimmy Rooney, Dundee-born, became Australia's most experienced international when he played 99 times for them, including the 1974 World Cup finals in West Germany. He was dropped before he could complete his century because national team manager Rudi Gutendorf,

Steve Balcombe (Leeds United), only two senior matches but each of some weight. *Yorkshire Post Newspapers Ltd*

Ricky Villa, South American marksman in the 1981 FA Cup Final replay. *Syndication International*

Nigel Callaghan (centre) with two other overseas developments at Watford: John Barnes and Luther Blissett. *Echo and Post Ltd, Hemel Hempstead*

a German, thought it was wrong for a Scot to captain Australia.

A Villa abroad
The last hat-trick achieved in a Division One match by a foreign born player came from Tottenham Hotspur midfield player Ricky Villa, born in Argentina, against Wolverhampton Wanderers on 6 February 1982. Spurs won 6–1.

Overseas connections
During 1982–83, Watford's first season in Division One, they had three overseas forwards obtaining international honours for England. Luther Blissett born in Jamaica won full honours, John Barnes another Jamaican played for the Under-21's along with Singapore born Nigel Callaghan. Barnes was also fully capped.

Hectic season
Bangor born centre-forward Steve Balcombe scored on his League debut for Leeds United against Aston Villa on 3 October 1981 in a 1–1 draw in Division One. He also made one substitute appearance for the Welsh Under-21 side against France in Troyes on 24 February 1982 in a goalless draw. That was the total of his senior experience and he was given a free transfer at the end of the season when he tried to join clubs in West Germany (where his parents lived), Austria and Belgium.

Courageous equaliser
Goalkeeper Harry Dowd injured his finger after 55 minutes, playing for Manchester City against Bury in a Division Two match on 8 February 1964. Colin Bell had put Bury ahead after 25 minutes play. Dowd went into the forward line and equalised in the 83rd minute. Bell later played for Manchester City.

Reading revisited
Kevin Bremner joined Colchester United from the Highland League club Keith after a week's trial in 1980 signing on his 23rd birthday. On his 25th birthday he joined Birmingham City on a month's loan in October 1982. After being recalled by Colchester he went on loan to Wrexham, scoring for them against Reading on 1 January 1983. Loaned to Plymouth Argyle he scored against Reading again on 1 February and then on a transfer to Millwall he completed a hat-trick over Reading with another goal in Division Three at their expense on 30 April.

Ageing East Anglians
Tommy Lang made his debut for Ipswich Town on 9 November 1946 as a left-winger aged 40. He had been signed from Queen of the South and in pre-war days had played for Swansea Town, Manchester United, Huddersfield Town, Newcastle United and began with Larkhall Thistle.

A contemporary of Lang's at Ipswich was goalkeeper Mick Burns who had played pre-war for Chilton Colliery, Newcastle United and Preston North End. Burns was in his 44th year when he kept goal in a third round FA Cup tie against Gateshead in January 1952.

Ipswich's third post-war player over 40 was defender Ossie Parry, a former Wimbledon and Crystal Palace player.

Drinking his health
Ian Callaghan retired from the Football League after 954 senior games in a career with Liverpool, Swansea City and Crewe Alexandra. He also had a spell with Cork Hibs in the Republic of Ireland and later became a partner in a Merseyside public house, the historic Golden Lion hostelry in Rainford Village.

Ground for complaint
Goalkeeper Willie Fraser of Sunderland conceded 21 goals in three visits to Luton Town. Transferred to Nottingham Forest in December 1958 he let in seven goals on his debut and in his second game at Luton conceded five more.

Keeping company
Colin Court made only one appearance for Reading in goal during the 1981–82 season at home to Swindon Town on 20 February 1982 when he had the misfortune to put through his own goal. But in the same match drawn 1–1, Swindon's goalkeeper Jimmy Allan made the same error himself.

I'll drink to that—Geoff Strong and Ian Callaghan (right) outside their hostelry. *Liverpool Daily Post and Echo*

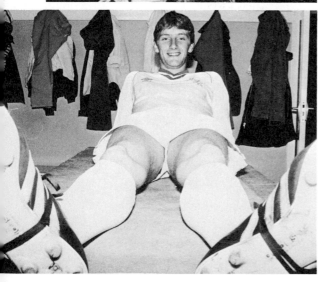

Left: **Soldier boy George Torrance is on target for Slough in the 1982–83 FA Cup.** *Bracknell News.*
Centre: **Phil Stant was a marksman for Reading in the 1982–83 season after service in the Falklands.** *Reading Chronicle* **and bottom: Montrose player John Craig with an outsize taste in feet.** *Chris Christie*

Busy vicar

The Rev. Kenneth Hunt was the first President of Pegasus in 1948, forty years after he scored for Wolverhampton Wanderers against Newcastle United in the FA Cup Final, which in itself was a week after playing for Oxford against Cambridge in the University Match. In 1903 he had played for Oxford City in the FA Amateur Cup Final.

Service calls

Private Phil Stant 20, of the 81 Ordnance Company at Aldershot made his debut for Reading against Newport County on 6 November 1982 in a 4–2 win, scoring Reading's second goal. Bolton-born Stant had served in the Falklands campaign earlier in the year. At Walsall on 13 November he scored Reading's goal in their 2–1 defeat in another Division Three match.

On 20 November neighbours Wokingham Town had the assistance of another soldier George Torrance in their FA Cup tie against Cardiff City. He scored in a 1–1 draw, after being flown in from his unit in West Germany.

Another Falklands connection concerned John Craig 21, a Montrose midfield player who had completed five and a half years in the Army and was serving in the Condor base in Arbroath when most of his unit was sent to the South Atlantic in April 1982.

However, the 6 ft 5 in (1 m 95 cm) player, one of the tallest playing in Scotland, had the misfortune to break a leg while playing against Stirling Albion at Annfield at the start of the following season.

Midland draught

Joe Laidlaw, who was Carlisle United's only ever present player in their 1973–74 promotion side in Division Two and scored the decisive goal against Aston Villa that ensured a place in Division One, has scored goals for five different League clubs. He began his career with Middlesbrough and joined Doncaster Rovers after leaving Carlisle. He subsequently played for Portsmouth and Hereford United. At the start of

Derek Dougan, the saviour of Wolverhampton Wanderers in their darkest hour.

the 1982–83 season he moved to Mansfield Town but did not succeed in scoring a League goal for them.

Misguided thanks

Edinburgh referee George Smith arrived in Belgrade to control a European Cup game between Red Star and Banik Ostrava (Czechoslovakia) in November 1981. On the morning of the match he contracted food poisoning and spent two and a half hours in a hospital bed on a glucose drip before being released to handle, rather shakily, the match which kicked-off at 4.30 pm.

Red Star won the game 3–0 and the tie 4–3 on aggregate but despite their disappointment, Banik officials wrote to Smith thanking him for his handling of the game. Unfortunately, they sent the letter to another Scottish referee Brian McGinlay who had been in charge of Real Madrid's match in East Germany against Carl Zeiss Jena on the same day.

Irish double

On 30 July 1982 a consortium headed by Derek Dougan completed a financial deal to save Wolverhampton Wanderers with just three minutes to spare before the club was forced into liquidation. Dougan, a former Wolves player and Northern Ireland international, had been the only Irish player to score a double century of Football League goals.

He began his career with Distillery, coming to England to play for Portsmouth.

Referee George Smith and his wife Pam. *Scotsman Publications Ltd*

He later played for Blackburn Rovers, Aston Villa, Peterborough United, Leicester City and Wolves, scoring 221 goals in 546 matches in the League. He also scored 12 goals in European games for Wolves, for whom he became Chairman and Chief Executive in August 1982.

Eventful season

Gordon Smith was playing for Brighton and Hove Albion Reserves at Swindon Town in a Football Combination game on 30 November 1982 when it was arranged for him to re-join his former club Rangers in time to play in the

Gordon Smith plucked out of Brighton reserves for a touch of Ibrox Revisited. *D O Thomson & Co Ltd*

Don Welsh, scoring goals by way of a Command Performance.

Scottish League Cup Final on 4 December.

Rangers lost 2–1 to Celtic and Smith later went back to Brighton where he helped the club reach the FA Cup Final against Manchester United.

Smith had started his career with Kilmarnock and had played in more than 250 Scottish League matches before joining Brighton as a forward.

Command performance

Don Welsh scored all five goals for the Western Command against London District on 17 March 1945, including three in the first 15 minutes. Welsh had originally been in the Royal Navy before leaving the services to play as an amateur, then professional for Torquay United. He was transferred to Charlton Athletic before the war, making his name as an inside-forward and being capped for England three times.

In November 1947 he was appointed manager of Brighton and later held a similar position with Liverpool.

Rowing honours

Keeping it on the island is a phrase which has gone out of usage in the game in recent years, but it has an added meaning at Gay Meadow, the home of Shrewsbury Town where, if the ball is kicked out on one side of the ground, it ends up in the river. Boatman Fred Davis has the task of retrieving the floating leather.

Argyle favourite

Bill Harper celebrated his 86th birthday in January 1983 and was still employed in an administrative capacity with Plymouth Argyle. A pre-war goalkeeper for the club, he later became trainer.

Quick promotion

David Burgess was recruited by Tranmere Rovers from local football and made his Football League debut in a Division Four game at home to York City on 29 August 1981. He completed a full programme of games for them that season and was the club's only ever present player.

Burgess had played for St Teresa's Youth Club with another Tranmere player, John Williams, and also for Liverpool County. He combined football with work as a forklift truck driver at a Speke factory and impressed Rovers manager Bryan Hamilton on the club's pre-season tour of Northern Ireland.

In pre-war days two other players who completed full League appearances in their first season after coming from junior circles were Ted

Far left: Fred Davis—a
ball buoy perhaps?
Shropshire Star

Left: David Burgess
who swapped a fork-lift
truck for a step up the
Football League ladder.
*Liverpool Daily Post and
Echo*

Longevity at Home
Park, Plymouth—left to
right: Maurice Tadman,
Bill Harper and George
Robertson. *Western
Morning News Co Ltd*

Harper of Blackburn Rovers and Wilf Copping of Leeds United. Harper was recruited by Rovers from Sheppey United in 1923 while Copping joined Leeds from Middlecliffe Rovers in 1930.

Unusual hat-trick

On 18 December 1948 in a Division Two match between Lincoln City and West Ham United, City centre-forward Jock Dodds scored the first goal against Hammers goalkeeper Ernie Gregory, who then had to go off the field with a fractured collar bone. Tom Moroney went in goal and Dodds scored his second against him.

George Dick became the third West Ham goalkeeper in the match and Dodds completed his hat-trick against him as Lincoln won 4–3.

Lucky mascot

Winger Ernie Shepherd played for three different clubs in the 1948–49 season: Fulham, West Bromwich Albion and Hull City and all three of them won promotion.

Busby babes

Manchester United have had more than their share of Under-18 debutants. Jeff Whitefoot was 16 years, 105 days when he appeared against

Portsmouth in 15 April 1950; Duncan Edwards 16 years 186 days against Cardiff City on 4 April 1953; George Best 17 years 115 days against West Bromwich Albion on 14 September 1963

Jack Wheeler the Notts County trainer and former Huddersfield Town and Birmingham City goalkeeper. *Nottingham Evening Post*

and Norman Whiteside 16 years 352 days against Brighton and Hove Albion on 24 April 1982.

Prodigal son

When Bobby Campbell was chosen to lead the Northern Ireland attack against Scotland on 28 April 1982 in a British International Championship match it ended an absence from international qualification which had lasted seven years.

In 1975 he had been banned for life after incidents off the field while playing for the Irish youth team in the South of France. The ban was lifted in 1982.

Campbell subsequently made a further full international appearance for Northern Ireland against Wales as substitute on 27 May 1982.

The 1981–82 season had been Campbell's best as he finished top scorer for Bradford City with 24 League goals in Division Four. He helped them to win promotion as runners-up.

Globetrotter

Scottish-born coach Danny McLennan took up a coaching appointment in Saudi Arabia in 1982, having previously been national coach of seven countries: Philippines, Mauritius, Rhodesia, Iran, Bahrain, Iraq and Jordan.

Sponge success

Notts County trainer Jack Wheeler completed 25 years with the club in June 1982, having officiated in the capacity in over 1100 consecutive games. A goalkeeper in his playing days he had served Cheltenham Town, making his debut v Ipswich Town, Birmingham City and Huddersfield Town and was a member of the Huddersfield defence which played unchanged throughout the 1952–53 season.

Scattering Rice

Merseyside referee George Rice was linesman at the UEFA Cup semi-final between Anderlecht and Bohemians on 20 April 1983. It was his second appointment in a spell of ten days which had started with him refereeing the Formby v Accrington Stanley game and continued with running the line at the Manchester United v Watford Division One match and ending with control of Burscough v Penrith.

Uplifting honour

When Bebington referee Derek Owen learned that he was to be linesman for the 1981–82 UEFA Cup Final between Hamburg and Gothenburg he was due to be linesman in the Eastham Junior League Under-14 Cup Final at Bromborough Pool.

Soccer in Show Business

In 1982 Tyne Tees Television screened a 90-minute film drama *The World Cup: A Captain's Tale* based on the true story of the amateur soccer team from the mining town of West Auckland, County Durham, that won the first ever World Cup tournament in 1910.

In the role of rugged miner Bob Jones, captain of West Auckland was Dennis Waterman while the cast also included Richard Griffiths as Sidney Barron, club secretary, Andrew Keir the Millionaire grocery king Sir Thomas Lipton, Nigel Hawthorne his right hand man Westwood, Derek Francis (President of the FA), Ken Hutchison, West Auckland's goalkeeper Jimmy Dickenson and Majorie Bland as Waterman's wife Edie.

Written by Neville Smith from an idea by Dennis Waterman, the film was made in association with Waterman/ Arlon Films and followed the adventures of the mining team

who succeeded in overcoming teams of the calibre of Red Star Zurich, Stuttgart and Juventus, the Italian side from Turin.

West Auckland returned to Italy the following year to beat Juventus in the final again and win the coveted trophy outright.

It had been Sir Thomas Lipton, Glasgow-born millionaire boss of a chain of grocery stores and well-known international yachtsman, who organised his own World Cup tournament in 1910 as a gesture of gratitude after being made a Knight of the Grand Order of Italy.

Sir Thomas, a renowned philanthropist with a flair for publicity, presented the trophy himself and laid down

the condition that if a club won the tournament two years in succession it automatically won the trophy outright.

The English soccer authorities were not particularly interested in the whims of the Knight so he invited West Auckland, third from bottom in the Northern Amateur League at the time, to represent England in Turin.

Dennis Waterman as Bob Jones, the captain of West Auckland.
Photos here and on page 244, courtesy of Tyne Tees TV

Their bid for success was not without its problems because with no more than a few pounds in the club coffers, it meant the miners losing wages at the pit and selling up furniture and personal treasures to finance the trip to Italy.

Filmed in the north-east of England and Italy, where the Juventus opposition was represented by footballers from the Italian semi-professional league, the climax came when the Italians lost 2–0 to West Auckland.

Television has produced several other stories concerning football though usually of a fictional nature. Granada's 'The Zoo' was featured in the 1970s but this was a one-off presentation compared to the serialisation on BBC of 'United' in the 1960s.

In the cinema there have been many films with soccer as a subject. Of British efforts alone one of the earliest was *The Winning Goal*, 1920. Then followed *The Ball of Fortune* in 1926, *The Great Game*, 1930 and then *The Arsenal Stadium Mystery* in 1939.

This was based on one of the most original detective stories written in the years preceding the last war by Leonard Gribble.

It was first serialised in the *Daily Express* and then filmed at Denham studios with Leslie Banks in the role of Antony Slade, the author's popular detective.

The story concerned a well-known footballer who dropped dead on the pitch during a match, having been injected with poison at half-time.

(Then) the heroes of West Auckland who beat Juventus in 1910. Top: and (Now) the team of actors who played the part of the West Auckland team.

The match in question was a friendly between Arsenal and The Trojans, an imaginary crack amateur side. For realism, actual film of Arsenal's last Division One match of the 1938–39 season on 6 May against Brentford was used extensively, as were the players themselves including Ted Drake. Arsenal's Manager George Allison had a supporting role in the film.

For close-ups in which the actors were seen, the Trojan players, who wore white shirts and black shorts, were drawn from Oxford University.

Another film entitled *The Great Game*, 1953 was followed by *Small Town Story* the same year. In 1979 Ian McShane starred in *Yesterday's Hero*; he was an appropriate choice for the lead as he was the son of

Harry McShane, a Scottish-born professional footballer of Football League class, who had joined Blackburn at 16 from Bellshill Athletic. During the war he toured Asia with Tommy Lawton's touring services team and made his League debut in September 1946, scoring against Derby County. He later broke a bone in his shoulder and was out for six weeks.

In 1981 *Gregory's Girl* told the story of a girl who succeeds in gaining a place in a boy's team on her ability as a player. The same year saw *Escape to Victory*, a World War Two adventure film in which Allied prisoners of war are forced to play in a life-and-death match against an enemy team. They plan to escape at half-time with the aid of the French Resistance but decide to stay and win the match instead.

Sylvester Stallone, Michael Caine and Max von Sydow starred in the film with players like Pele, Bobby Moore and Kevin Beattie who acted as Caine's actual stand-in for the action scenes on the pitch. The film was shot mainly on location in Hungary and the MTK ground in Budapest represented the Colombes Stadium in Paris.

Top: Not exactly waiting at the crossroads for something to happen—Ronald Allen (left) and John Breslin in a scene from 'United' a twice weekly serial from the 1960s, *BBC* and The Zoo—left to right: Nigel Collins, Jim Findley, Barry Lowe and Stephen Mallcoratt.

Left: Yesterday's Hero, in this case Ian McShane in the title role and Ian McShane's father Harry McShane in the Oldham Athletic line-up, during 1953–54.

The 1966 film *Goal*, which commemorated the World Cup finals in England, set a high standard for film documentaries on the game and later competitions produced their own versions.

As far as the theatre is concerned the stage has not had the right logistics for plays devoted to the game but the musical *Zigger Zagger* in the 1960s brought home the partisan feeling and violent commitment of football supporters.

Show business personalities have increasingly attached themselves to clubs for either their own publicity value or a genuine interest in the game or a particular club.

The Spanish singing star of the 1980s Julio Iglesias might well have developed as a goalkeeper in his own right with Real Madrid. While studying law at Madrid University he played for the Madrid club's youth team when a car accident not only ended his possible career but nearly left him crippled. He was paralysed for a time.

The rival sports programmes of the BBC and ITV have their share of former footballers as presenters. For the BBC Jimmy Hill had a playing career as an inside-forward for Reading, Brentford and Fulham before becoming Chairman of the PFA, while Bob Wilson kept goal for Arsenal and twice for Scotland.

For ITV, Ian St John was a more than useful marksman for Motherwell, Liverpool, Coventry City and Tranmere Rovers as well as the Scottish national team. St John's scoring feats included three

Escape to Victory and stars left to right: Sylvester Stallone, Max Von Sydow and sex symbol Michael Caine with a goalpost as a supporting role prepare to face a corner. *ITC Film Distributors Ltd*

Gregory's Girl—Dee Hepburn giving ample evidence of the need for integration in the game. *ITC Film Distributors Ltd*

Below: Ian St John, LWT football presenter, and a noted marksman in his playing days. *LWT*. Right: Zigger Zagger at the Shaw Theatre in December 1981. Richard Stone (left), Sarah Yorke and Joe Searby as Zigger. *Nobby Clark*

goals in 150 seconds against Hibs in 1959 and six goals against Flamengo, the Brazillian club, in 1960. Jimmy Greaves, a post-1982 World Cup addition to the presentation, was even more of a scoring legend for England with 44 goals in 57 appearances. Greaves hit 357 goals for three London clubs: Chelsea, Tottenham Hotspur and West Ham United and also had a brief spell in Italy with AC Milan.

In 1983 the respective early morning programmes saw the BBC's *Breakfast Time* with sports presenter David Icke a former Football League player who had to retire prematurely with an arthritic knee. Leicester-born he made 37 League appearances in goal for Hereford in 1972–73.

Frank Bough, a former front man for Grandstand, had played at Wembley for Oxford University in the 1950s.

Not to be outdone, ITV's *Good Morning Britain* had in their original Famous Five David Frost who had been on the books of Nottingham Forest in his youth.

Gary Bailey (right) tries to short left arm jab on Julio Iglesias at a Manchester United training session. *Manchester Evening News*.
Below: David Frost, the well known transatlantic jet-setter, gets down to solid ground for a change. *Robert Broeder*

Peter Desmond whose career was never short of variety. *Evening Gazette, Middlesbrough*

The other half
Claimed to be the world's highest paid referee at £500 a game is Arnaldo Coelho, the Brazilian who controlled the 1982 World Cup Final in Madrid. A stockbroker in Rio de Janeiro, he lives overlooking the Copacabana Beach where he trains every day.

No Xmas present
Albion Rovers moved to their present headquarters at Cliftonhill Park on Christmas Day 1919 and were beaten 2-0 by St Mirren.

Unbeaten runs
In 1946-47 East Fife won all six League Cup qualifying matches, scoring 22 goals without reply. In 1963-64 Motherwell scored 17 without reply, winning five and drawing one qualifying tie.

Penalty issue
On 9 December 1922 Willie McStay took three penalties for Celtic against Falkirk in a Division One match, missing two but scoring from a third in a 1-1 draw. Falkirk's goal also came from a spot kick.

The last encounter
Drew Busby who was appointed player-manager of Queen of the South in the 1982-83 season was born in Dumbarton and played in Third Lanark's last game in Scottish football when they lost 5-1 to Dumbarton in 1966-67. Busby scored for Third Lanark.

Unlucky for them
Stirling Albion failed to score in the last 13 matches of the 1980-81 season.

Ups and downs
On 21 September 1949 inside-left Peter Desmond played for the Republic of Ireland against England in their 2-0 win at Goodison Park. On 24 September he made his debut for Middlesbrough against Charlton Athletic in a Division One match. He had joined the club from Shelbourne in May 1949.

On 9 October 1949 he played in a World Cup qualifying game for the Republic against Finland in Helsinki which ended in a 1-1 draw; on the following Saturday, Desmond played at Hetton-le-Hole for Middlesbrough Reserves against Eppleton Colliery Welfare.

Down to earth
Brighton and Hove Albion beat Watford 6-0 on 30 April 1958 to achieve promotion to Division Two for the first time in their history. A crowd of 31 038 watched them. Adrian Thorne at inside-right and only aged 20 scored five of their goals. Their next League game on 23 August 1958 at Middlesbrough in Division Two resulted in a 9-0 loss, their heaviest defeat.

Fame and failure
In the 1938-39 season Doug Hunt scored 24 League goals for Sheffield Wednesday and Gilbert Alsop equalled this figure for Walsall. Hunt's best performance was scoring six of the seven goals by which Wednesday beat Norwich City on 19 November in a Division Two match. Alsop had a spell in which he scored 4 2 3 3 4 and then all four goals in an FA Cup replay against Notts County.

Wednesday missed promotion by one point but Walsall finished second from bottom in Division Three (Southern) and had to seek re-election.

Indestructible Ball
Allan Ball played his 800th first team game in goal for Queen of the South against Falkirk on 17 October 1981 and kept a clean sheet in a goalless draw. He made 819 appearances and was given a free transfer.

Quick off the mark
John Hewitt achieved the fastest goal in Scottish Cup history when he scored for Aberdeen against Motherwell in 9·6 seconds on 23 January 1982.

Long wait in the wilderness
In June 1982 Wolverhampton Wanderers cancelled the contract of Peter Knowles, 36 who left the club in 1969 to become a Jehovah's Witness.

They wanted Moore again
Bernard Moore was born in Brighton and made

his Football League debut for the local club in the 1947–48 season, scoring two goals in eight League appearances. He left the League the following season to play for Hastings United and in three seasons notched up 44, 57 and 44 goals before being persuaded to return to the League with Luton Town who had watched him score five goals against Headington United in January 1951. He scored 31 League goals in 73 matches for Luton before returning to Brighton and Hove Albion for whom he added a further ten goals in 29 appearances.

Oldham let it slip
Defeat in their last two home League games of the 1914–15 season cost Oldham Athletic the championship of Division One that term. They led the table for most of the season losing only twice in the first half of the campaign. On 20 April they were beaten 2–1 by Burnley and on 24 April they lost 2–0 to Liverpool. They finished runners-up to Everton one point behind.

Clarke in descending order
When Wolverhampton Wanderers were relegated at the end of the 1981–82 season from Division One it completed an unhappy sequence for the Clarke family. Wolves striker Wayne Clarke became the fifth brother to suffer a similar fate with different clubs. Allan Clarke was with Fulham when they went down in 1967–68, Frank with Carlisle in 1974–75, Derek with Oxford in 1975–76 and Kelvin with Walsall in 1978–79. Allan as manager of Leeds United in 1981–82 suffered a similar experience.

Substitute memories
John Ritchie was sent off 40 seconds after coming on as a substitute for Stoke City at Kaiserslautern in a UEFA Cup match on 27 September 1972. City lost 4–0 and the tie 5–3 on aggregate.

On 8 March 1978 Brendan O'Callaghan scored for Stoke on his debut after transfer from Doncaster Rovers, coming on as a substitute and scoring within ten seconds for the only goal of the game against Hull City.

Held no grudge
Reading-born striker Roger Smee was re-signed by his local club in 1973, three years after they had given him a free transfer. He had been on the books of Chelsea at one time. In 1983 he was the leader of a movement which made a takeover bid for Reading FC.

Nice four, Cyril
When Port Vale beat Liverpool 4–3 at Vale Park on 8 April 1955 centre-forward Cyril Done scored all Vale's goals. He was formerly with Liverpool.

Sporting behaviour
Receipts for the 1966 World Cup finals in England were £2 034 595. After deductions for expenses £1 427 830 was distributed to member countries of FIFA who praised the fair play of English soccer fans during the competition.

Sad departure
Peter Scarff had a short but distinguished career as a Celtic forward scoring exactly one goal every two matches for them. He made his debut in 1928–29 and remained a senior choice until 1931–32.

He had joined Celtic from Maryhill Hibs as an inside-forward and scored seven goals in 16 appearances in his first season. In 1929–30 he scored 18 times in 25 games and 18 again in 1930–31 when he also won a Scottish Cup winners medal. In 1931–32 he scored six times in 20 League games before he dropped out of the side because of illness and he died on 9 December 1933 aged 25. He made one full appearance for Scotland.

Early Exposure

Gresley Rovers won the Burton Junior Cup in 1892 even though they were beaten 7–2 in a replay against Tutbury.

Steve Bloomer was a member of the Tutbury team but Gresley protested that he and another player had both signed professional forms for Derby County between the original final and the replay. The protest was upheld and Gresley were presented with the trophy.

Bloomer played for Derby County reserves in 1891–92 in the Midland Alliance when they played under the name of Derby Town. That same season he was also playing and acting as captain for Derby Swifts. In 1892 Swifts amalgamated with County.

Bloomer made his first class debut as inside-left aged 18 years, seven months for Derby County in unusual circumstances at Stoke on 3 September 1892 where they won 3–1. He was one of three men brought into the Derby side when they discovered at the last moment that they had failed to register three of last year's players.

On the following Thursday, Bloomer helped Derby Town beat Heanor 4–2 in the Derbyshire Charity Cup and then played in the League side against Preston North End two days later.

Ian McParland coming down to earth in more ways than one for Notts. County 'A' team. *Notts Evening Post*

League of Nations

During the 1930s Celtic had a Swedish goalkeeper on their books called Julius Hjuliana, a Jewish player called Jerry Solis and an Egyptian called Abdul Salim who played several Alliance matches for the club with only bandages around his feet.

Young Toffeeman

Sandy Young was the first player to score as many as four goals in a Merseyside derby. He achieved this feat for Everton against Liverpool on 1 April 1904 in Division One at Goodison Park. Everton won 5–2.

Jobson for the boys

Watford paid £15 000 to Burton Albion for Richard Jobson, 19, a Nottingham University Civil Engineering student in October 1982. When he was named as substitute against Liverpool on 11 December they paid Burton a further £1000 with the promise of another £4000 once Jobson played in ten matches.

Miner's major success

George Richardson was working in the pit at Manton Colliery on the morning of Saturday, 8 April 1933. In the afternoon he played in the Colliery team and immediately afterwards was transferred to Huddersfield Town, playing in their Central League side on the Monday and the first team on the Wednesday.

Born at Worksop this was his only senior game for Huddersfield and he joined Sheffield United in 1934–35 and had made 34 League appearances for them as an inside-forward before moving to Hull City in 1938–39 where he made 20 appearances, finishing his career after the war in 1947–48 at the age of 35. His best season had been in 1937–38 with seven goals in 25 appearances for Sheffield United.

In at the deep end

Ian McParland joined Notts County from the Edinburgh team Ormiston Primrose during the 1980–81 season. Within three days he was standing in as substitute in a re-arranged side at centre-half in a Division Two match against Preston North End on 27 December. The following season he made three appearances against Aston Villa, Nottingham Forest and Liverpool in Division One, before playing on 30 January 1982 for the 'A' team against Aston Villa.

Merseyside's isolated memory

Harold McNaughton had the unusual distinction of appearing in a Merseyside derby for Liverpool against Everton, keeping a clean sheet as the unbeaten goalkeeper, yet never again playing for them in their League side.

On 23 October 1920 he was in goal for Liverpool in their 1–0 win against their rivals. He had been signed in the previous August from his Scottish junior club Edinburgh St Bernards.

At the Liverpool public trial that late summer he conceded seven goals, but he was named as Irish international goalkeeper Elisha Scott's understudy.

McNaughton's chance came when Scott was on international duty for Ireland against England at Sunderland. Scott returned to the Liverpool team on 30 October in the return match with Everton at Goodison Park, Liverpool again winning 3–0.

On 4 February 1921 Liverpool signed another goalkeeper Frank Mitchell. He had been born in Scotland and had joined Everton from Motherwell in 1913. Mitchell made his debut for Liverpool Reserves against Manchester United at Anfield the following day.

He had been signed because McNaughton was injured in a Central League game against Crewe on 15 January and spent most of the second half of that game off the field.

Mitchell made his League debut shortly afterwards, also against Manchester United, on 9 February 1921 in a 3–0 win and played in all but two of the season's remaining League fixtures. He played in 15 consecutive matches, losing only once in the first 13 of them, though Scott returned on 2 May after Liverpool had lost two in a row.

Liverpool were forced to use Connell, the son of their trainer, as reserve team goalkeeper after McNaughton's injury in January and later another custodian Fred Wood from 19 February.

First steps abroad

Although Noel Parkinson made his Football League debut on loan to Bristol Rovers during the 1979–80 season, he had already made two appearances as a substitute for Ipswich Town in the UEFA Cup that term. Parkinson played twice against Skeid Oslo as an 18-year-old before being loaned first to Rovers and then Brentford. He later joined Mansfield Town.

Wartime measures

The youngest players to have appeared for a Football League team and one from the Scottish League were prevented from entering the official record books because it was during the Second World War. Campbell Cameron Buchanan was 14 years, 57 days when he made his debut for Wolverhampton Wanderers against West Bromwich Albion on 26 September 1942 while Ronnie Simpson was 14 years, 304 days on his debut for Queen's Park in a Scottish Southern League Cup tie against Kilmarnock on 11 August 1945.

Twin experience

Brechin City signed twin brothers Dick and Ian Campbell in 1977. Dick, a full-back, came from Ross County, Ian a striker from Cowdenbeath. Dick combined his football with work as a planner in the Naval Dockyard at Rosyth while Ian was a P.E. teacher at Kirkcaldy High School.

Both had previous Scottish League experience: Dick with Dundee United, Cowdenbeath and Dunfermline Athletic, Ian with Dunfermline and Arbroath.

Berlin and back

Edwin Dutton was born in England in 1890 of English parents but was brought up in Berlin where his father had a sports business. He developed as a footballer playing outside-right for Prussen Berlin and was even given an international appearance for Germany against Hungary in Budapest on 4 April 1909, the match ending in a 3–3 draw.

When Newcastle United went on tour to Germany in 1910, Dutton impressed them and after a trial he was signed in October. In 1911–12 he won a Northumberland Senior Cup medal with the club. In 1912 he joined Newburn Steel, an amateur team playing in the Northern Alliance League, but the following year he returned to Germany as trainer to Prussen Berlin and was interned as a prisoner during the war years.

After hostilities he returned to the north-east of England becoming South Shields trainer, and

at the end of 1926–27 he became the first professional trainer employed by Ipswich Town.

In 1929–30 he was their trainer when they won the South Amateur League title and he returned to Newcastle in 1932.

Late Development

Tim Ward and Johnny Kelly were actively engaged as players in the 1982–83 season. Ward, a wing-half, had joined Derby County in April 1937 for £100 and made his League debut in January 1938 aged 19. In March 1951 he was transferred to Barnsley. Ward was capped twice by England.

Kelly joined Celtic as a winger from Arthurlie in 1939 and was transferred to Barnsley from Morton during the war. He was a contemporary of Ward's at Barnsley. Kelly returned to Scotland to play for Falkirk and then came south again with Halifax Town before ending his career in 1959 with Portadown.

In 1982–83 Ward was playing for Derby County's ex-Rams team in charity games while Kelly was turning out for the Old Crocks a team of ex-Rangers and Celtic players, at 62.

Vintage marksman

George Harrison scored more goals in the 19th season of his career than in any other. In 1928–29 he scored 16 League goals for Preston North End.

An outside-left he joined Leicester Fosse from Gresley Rovers in 1910. He moved to Everton in April 1913 and Preston in November 1923. Up to then he had scored 26 League goals in peacetime matches.

He became Preston's penalty taker and notched up 46 League goals for them in his first five seasons including 15 in 1927–28. After topping this achievement the following season he added a further seven goals in 1929–30 and six in 1930–31.

Harrison was transferred to Blackpool in November 1931 and scored twice during that season.

Farewell score

Bristol City's first goal in Division One for 65 years was scored by Paul Cheesley in August 1976 in a 1–0 win against Arsenal at Highbury. It was Cheesley's last League goal before a knee injury led to the end of his career.

After Extra Time

At 3 am on 15 March 1958 the respective managers of Darlington and Lincoln City had to scale an eight-foot wall at Darlington's Feethams Ground to obtain the boots of Ron Harbertson who was to make his debut for Lincoln against Liverpool later that day following his transfer from Darlington. Liverpool won 1–0.

Harbertson, a striker, began with North Shields and subsequently played for Newcastle United, Bradford City, Brighton and Hove Albion, Bradford City again, Grimsby Town, Ashington, Darlington, Lincoln City, Wrexham, Darlington again and Lincoln once more.

Hurrah for Hollywood
Manchester United fans in Hollywood in 1950

Neville Coleman: seven-up for Stoke City in his thirst for goals.

included Herbert Marshall, Nigel Bruce, Sarah Churchill and Angela Lansbury.

Affluent society
Blackburn Rovers full-back Bob Crompton, who played 41 times for England in his career, was said to have been the first professional footballer to drive to the ground in his own car, an event which took place in 1908.

Sequence of Sevens
On 4 January 1902 Stoke's pre-match meal at Liverpool was plaice but the players contracted food poisoning and were reduced to seven men in the second half through illness. They lost 7–0 and also lost their next seven games.

On 23 February 1957 outside-right Neville Coleman scored seven goals for Stoke City against Lincoln City in a Division Two match to establish a record in the League for a winger.

Treble shooter
During the 1937–38 season Jimmy Richardson played in all three divisions of the Football League. He started with Huddersfield Town in Division One, playing in ten League games and scoring two goals, was transferred to Newcastle United in Division Two scoring three times in 14 appearances and finishing in Division Three with Millwall scoring five goals in 12 Southern Section games.

Inflationary reminder
The ball used in Walsall's third round FA Cup success against Arsenal on 14 January 1933, when they won 2–0, is preserved in a glass case in the secretary's office. Receipts from this match had been £1487 from a 11 149 crowd after the club increased prices of admission.

Making a mountain...
On 20 February 1982 the amateur match in the Scottish village of Fintray between Jack Scott Vics and Westburn had to be postponed. Officials arrived at the ground to find it under a massive deluge of molehills.

Frozen assets
When Manchester United met Stoke City on 5 February 1947 in the severe winter that season the match was played at Maine Road on an ice covered pitch and ended in a 1–1 draw. The attendance was 7800.

Rae of sunshine?
On 7 November 1981 Robin Rae the Hibernians reserve goalkeeper dislocated a finger in the match at Dundee. He was taken to the local infirmary for treatment. On the evening of Friday the 13th he damaged a shoulder in a motor cycle

accident and missed the next game against Cowdenbeath.

Third time unlucky
Three years produced three breaks for Motherwell player Stuart Rafferty: a broken ankle, broken wrist and finally a dislocated collar bone in January 1982.

Time to forget
In January 1981 Stranraer midfield player Ian McGuigan found himself in hospital with a broken leg after stopping his lorry to help a lady motorist in a snowstorm, only to be hit by a passing car. A year later he was back in hospital awaiting an operation to have a disc removed in his back after an injury against Forfar just before Christmas, his only League appearance of the season.

Completing his set
A pre-season friendly for Walsall against Willenhall Town in August 1981 provided a milestone for Colin Harrison who established a record of League appearances for the club with 467 games between 1964 and 1982.

Against Willenhall he had to take over in goal for a ten-minute spell in the second half when the goalkeeper suffered concussion. That completed appearances for the Saddlers in every position on the field during which he wore all shirt numbers from 2 to 12 and also the goalkeeper's jersey.

Charlie saved the day
Len Shackleton has 13 letters in his name, played for England schoolboys at 13, made his first adult international appearance on 13 April 1946 and was transferred from Bradford Park Avenue to Newcastle United for £13 000. On his debut for United they won 13–0, Shackleton scoring six against Newport County in a Division Two match on 5 October 1946. But the sequence of 13 was almost ruined that day as Charlie Wayman missed a penalty for Newcastle.

Odd events repeated
Eric Westwood played for Manchester Boys against Southampton Boys in 1932–33 in the English Schools Shield Final, the matches being played at Maine Road and the Dell. His first two League games for Manchester City were against Tottenham Hotspur at Maine Road on 5 November 1938 in Division Two then at The Dell, Southampton the following week.

Clerical coverage
On 3 December 1910 the Division Two match between West Bromwich Albion and Blackpool was refereed by the Rev. J W Marsh while Rev. W F Strange was one of his linesmen.

Striking goalkeeper
On 29 August 1981 the referee of the Brazilian Cup game between Atletico Mineiro and Flamengo in Goiana abandoned the match after only 35 minutes with the score 0–0. Four Atletico players were sent off and then the goalkeeper lay down on the pitch and refused to continue the match which was subsequently awarded to Flamengo.

Dual international
Manfred Braschler of St Gallen, the Swiss Division One club, was born in Austria of Swiss parents. In 1978 he was playing for Innsbruck and was given his first full international appearance for Austria against Portugal. But he had been a Swiss citizen since his birth and an appeal was made by the Swiss FA to FIFA. Austria admitted their error and Braschler later won his first appearance for Switzerland against Italy in 1982.

Double stint
In 1981–82 Davie Whiteford was coaching two teams in Zambia, United in the National League on Saturdays and Rovers of Division Two on Sundays, two teams of the Roan Mining Company in Luanshya. Whiteford a former Motherwell, Falkirk and East Stirling full-back was formerly a PE teacher in Scotland. He trained United three nights a week, Rovers two.

These boots were made for . . .
David Mercer, Hull City's inside-right scored all his team's goals in a 6–1 win against Sheffield United on 4 January 1919. The Sheffield team arrived late and the start was delayed 30 minutes. They had no gear as their basket had not arrived at Sheffield station. Hull fixed them up as best they could but boots were an insoluble problem. Because of the light, only 40 minutes were played in the first half, 30 in the second.

The author, bottom of the page . . .

INDEX

* Includes Illustration

Index compiled by David Wilson